Danish Studies in Classical Archaeology
ACTA HYPERBOREA
3

© 1991 Collegium Hyperboreum and Museum Tusculanum Press

COLLEGIUM HYPERBOREUM
c/o Institute of Classical and Prehistoric Archaeology,
Vandkunsten 5, DK – 1467 Copenhagen K.

Published by
MUSEUM TUSCULANUM PRESS
Njalsgade 94, DK – 2300 Copenhagen S.

Printed in Denmark by
Special-Trykkeriet Viborg a-s
Reproductions of illustrations by F. Hendriksens Eftf.
Gl. Kongevej 3, 1610 Copenhagen V.

ISBN 87-7289-121-1
ISSN 0904-2067

Cover design: Thora Fisker.
Decorations on base of Protocorinthian clay box.
About 700 B.C.

Unless otherwise stated the English texts have been revised by
Peter Crabb.

The publication of this volume has been made possible by generous grants from the Carlsberg Foundation and the Ny Carlsberg Foundation.

Danish Studies in Classical Archaeology
ACTA HYPERBOREA

3

Recent Danish Research
in Classical Archaeology:
Tradition and Renewal

Edited
by
Tobias Fischer-Hansen, Pia Guldager, John Lund,
Marjatta Nielsen and Annette Rathje

MUSEUM TUSCULANUM PRESS
University of Copenhagen 1991

# CONTENTS

*Preface* .................................................. 9

*The Classical Archaeological Tradition in Denmark*

ANNETTE RATHJE & JOHN LUND: Danes Overseas – A Short History of Danish Classical Archaeological Fieldwork ... 11

*Danish Classical Archaeological Fieldwork Today*

BIRGITTE RAFN: Archaic and Classical Graves at Halieis: A Summary ............................................... 57

ERIK POULSGAARD MARKUSSEN: Out of Tarquinia. A Note on Another Painted Tomb at Blera ............. 73

LISE BENDER JØRGENSEN: Textiles from Mons Claudianus. A Preliminary Report ................................ 83

JANE FEJFER, NIELS HANNESTAD & HANS ERIK MATHIESEN: The Danish Archaeological Excavations at Ayios Kononas, Cyprus. A Preliminary Report of the First Season of Work (1989) ................................. 97

*Current Research Projects*

JAN STUBBE ØSTERGAARD: Terracotta Horses and Horsemen of Archaic Boeotia ........................... 111

LONE WRIEDT SØRENSEN: Three Corinthian Sherds from Rhodes – A Case Study .......................... 191

KELD GRINDER-HANSEN: Charon's Fee in Ancient Greece? – Some Remarks on a Well-known Death Rite ......... 207

HELLE W. HORSNÆS: The Ager Picentinus ............ 219

BIRTE POULSEN: A Relief from Croceae: Dioscuri in
Roman Laconia. With a Contribution by Jesper Carlsen .. 235

KAREN SLEJ: Hellenistic Black-glaze Ware from the
Temple of Castor and Pollux in the Forum
Romanum. The Stamps . . . . . . . . . . . . . . . . . . . . . . . . 249

JOHN LUND: Towards a Better Understanding of
the Production Pattern of Roman Lamps . . . . . . . . . . . . 269

LOTTE EMILIE HERTZ: Roma: aspetti della
fortificazione fluviale . . . . . . . . . . . . . . . . . . . . . . . . . . 297

MARGRETE HAHN: A Group of 15th/16th Century Jugs
from Western Crete . . . . . . . . . . . . . . . . . . . . . . . . . . . 311

*From the Danish Collections*

BODIL BUNDGAARD RASMUSSEN: Laconian Pottery in
the National Museum, Copenhagen . . . . . . . . . . . . . . . 321

HELLE SALSKOV ROBERTS: A New Bucchero Kantharos
with Incised Frieze Found at Vulci . . . . . . . . . . . . . . . 337

GUNHILD PLOUG: A Dated Palmyrene Bust in the
Danish National Museum. With a Contribution by
F. O. Hvidberg-Hansen . . . . . . . . . . . . . . . . . . . . . . . . 365

METTE MOLTESEN: A Doryphoros in Disguise. With
a Contribution by Ruth Tschäpe . . . . . . . . . . . . . . . . . 379

*Forum*

ALAN JOHNSTON: The Vase Trade: A Point of Order . . . . . 403

# PREFACE

The present volume – "Recent Danish Research in Classical Archaeology – tradition and renewal" – presents a number of articles on diverse subjects, a cross section of present day classical archaeological research in Denmark, spanning Greek, Etruscan and Roman archaeology, field research and museology.

The editors' decision to disregard the usual editorial policy of publishing only thematic issues stems from our wish to celebrate the centenary of the creation of an Institute of Classical Archaeology at the University of Copenhagen in 1890, the very first university institute of archaeology, although the discipline had been taught since the beginning of that century. An account of the history of Danish archaeological field work can be found in the first article of this volume, and it will be apparent that even today, miraculously, some archaeological field research in the Mediterranean has Danish parenthood.

However, it would be negligent to fail to mention the worrying situation of the subject in Denmark today, where, for instance, the existence of classical archaeology as an independently taught discipline at the University of Copenhagen is in jeopardy, and where the superb collections of the Department of Antiquities in the Danish National Museum so far survive, but under the cloud of an uncertain future.

The fact that Danish classical archaeological research can be undertaken today is mainly due to support from the Danish Research Council for the Humanities, different private foundations and not least to the generous support of the Carlsberg Foundation.

It is also a grant from this latter foundation that has made the publication of this volume of *Acta Hyperborea* possible. The Ny Carlsberg Foundation defrayed the costs of the illustrations and the editors wish to tender their warmest thanks to the two foundations for their generosity.

*Tobias Fischer-Hansen*   *Pia Guldager*   *John Lund*
*Marjatta Nielsen*   *Annette Rathje*

# DANES OVERSEAS – A SHORT HISTORY OF DANISH CLASSICAL ARCHAEOLOGICAL FIELDWORK[1]

## ANNETTE RATHJE & JOHN LUND

Archaeological fieldwork may for present purposes be defined as research carried out on the spot, in the form of excavation or survey. The history of Danish classical archaeological fieldwork in the Mediterranean and adjoining areas has been discussed before (DYGGVE 1943; JOHANSEN 1943; DYGGVE 1948; RIIS 1979; ZAHLE 1986; MOLTESEN 1989), but most of the relevant publications are written in Danish, and only *J. Zahle* and *M. Moltesen* dealt exclusively with the fieldwork aspect. The Danish contribution has, perhaps partly for this reason, not always received the recognition it deserves.

The aim of the present paper is not only to make a survey of the subject accessible to a non-Danish audience, but also to attempt a definition of the Danish classical archaeological scene of today. It is outside the scope of this article to present biographies of the scholars involved or an exhaustive history of research, all the more so because the situation in Denmark must be seen in a broader European perspective. Nonetheless, if we wish to understand the contemporary position of classical archaeology in Denmark, it is necessary to examine the background from which it grew.

Classical archaeology is in a sense an exotic field of research for a country only marginally touched by the classical civilizations, and the discipline has changed considerably since "the germ of an archaeological university organ was laid down at the University of Copenhagen in 1890" (RIIS 1979, 144). At the end of the last century the relevance of the history of the fine arts was hardly questioned, and this was a determining factor in the selection of research fields. Both art history and classical archaeology were still steeped in the German school of thought, embodied in the philosophy of *J.J. Winckelmann*, *I. Kant* and

*G. W. F. Hegel.* Classical art was studied for humanistic, ethical and even educational reasons with little regard to its contextual connotations (HIMMELMANN 1976, 18-20, 52-53; WHITLEY 1987). However, later generations of scholars have increasingly tended to dissociate themselves from this approach, pointing to the complex questions and different demands imposed by modern society.

In most other countries, students of classical archaeology have traditionally focused on Greece in the 5th and 4th centuries B.C., and to a lesser degree on the Hellenistic period and the Roman Empire – incidentally the periods best known from ancient literature. In Denmark, however, a broader geographical and chronological definition of the discipline was applied: "archaeological research based mainly on the material remains of the ancient cultures of Greece/the Hellenistic Kingdoms/Italy/the Roman Empire from the first appearance of man to and including Late Antiquity" (quoted from the study program at the University of Copenhagen). The archaeology of about 25 modern countries within the Graeco-Roman world is accordingly involved, and classical archaeology embraces the prehistoric as well as historic periods, thus incorporating a much-needed dialogue between the material and written sources that in other areas of world archaeology is about to begin.

The time when archaeology was an ancillary discipline to philology or history illustrating the ancient texts has passed, and classical archaeology has in the last century managed to remain an independent discipline at the Universities of Copenhagen and Aarhus; at the University of Odense it is taught at the Institute for Classical Studies established in 1976, which also comprises classical philology. One of the major challenges is the fact that the archaeological sources (including epigraphic material) continue to increase, whereas the number of known texts written by ancient authors is fairly stable. It is becoming clear, also to progressive historians, that ancient history cannot be written without incorporating archaeology – a situation comparable, for example, to the history-writing of Poland (BUCAILLE & PESEZ 1978, 278) or Black Africa.

The important work done by Danish architects on classical ground in the last two centuries is a subject which deserves a separate treatment elsewhere (cf. for example BENDTSEN 1990, FISCHER-HANSEN 1990, HAUGSTED 1990 and VILLADSEN 1990), and such contributions are re-

Fig. 1. Melchior Lorch: Drawing from Rome, dated to 1551 by E. Fischer (in a letter to the authors). British Museum Dept. of Prints & Darwings 1884-3-88-821, reproduced by kind permission of the Trustees of the British Museum.

ferred to in the following only when they clearly fall under the definition of fieldwork mentioned at the outset.

## Early travellers

Danes have visited the Mediterranean countries at least since the Age of the Vikings, and some early travellers have studied and recorded ancient monuments they met on the way. These activities seldomly qualify as archaeological fieldwork but cannot be ignored since they reflect a growing interest in the archaeology of the Mediterranean countries.

*Melchior Lorch* (1526/27-1583?), who was sponsored by the Danish King *Christian III* (1534-1559), thus visited Turkey and Greece as an artist attached to a diplomatic mission to Constantinople (FISCHER 1964; MÜLLER-HAAS 1989; MARTELS 1989). During the journey he drew various ancient monuments including the column of Arcadius in Istanbul, and in another period of his life he used the antiquities of Rome and Italy as a source of inspiration. Some of the drawings are faithful renderings of the ancient monuments (POULSEN 1933), but it is important to remember that Lorch was a Renaissance artist seeking inspiration in the works of the ancient masters, not an antiquarian.

*Fig. 1*

After the Reformation, a number of Danish noblemen travelled as pilgrims to Rome or beyond, to the Holy Land and Egypt, and some of them published accounts of their journeys with information about the monuments encountered on the way (HERMANSEN 1951; OTZEN 1978). Other scions of the upper classes travelled southward for educational purposes (HELK 1971), and a few acquired antiquities and brought them to Denmark. The same applies to the Danish officer *Moritz Hartmann* (1656?-1695), who purchased two marble heads in Athens in 1687. They were said to come from "the Temple of Diana in Ephesos", but it was later demonstrated that they originate from southern metope no. 4 of the Parthenon (BRØNDSTED 1830, 171-189; BOBÉ 1933; GUNDESTRUP 1990).[2]

*Ole Worm* (1588-1654) (SCHEPELERN 1971) deserves a special mention. It is uncertain if he visited *Ulisse Aldrovandi*'s museum at Bologna (DESITTERE 1984) which together with similar establishments is thought to have inspired him to found the Museum Wormianum, one of the roots of the present-day collection of classical antiquities at the Danish National Museum (GUNDESTRUP 1990). The connection established by Worm between archaeology and the University of Copenhagen was to prove important for future developments. In Denmark, classical archaeology developed as a discipline from the need for classification of material in the collections, and in this respect the situation differed from that of other European countries, where classical archaeology was usually an integrated part of university study (TILLEY 1989, 277).

The expedition to Egypt in 1737 led by the Frenchman *Pierre Joseph le Roux d'Esneval* and the young naval officer *F. L. Norden* (1708-1742) (KJØLSEN 1965; BUHL, & COLDING 1986) was supported by the Danish King *Christian VI* (1730-1746), the founder of the Danish Academy of Sciences, and had the purpose of exploring a new trade route to Ethiopia. However, Norden's drawings of the monuments of ancient Egypt can hardly be said to bear on the commercial aspects of the journey and surely reflect an interest in the archaeology of the Egypt of the Pharaohs. He also drew a number of monuments of Roman Egypt, for instance at Alexandria (BUHL 1990).

*Fig. 2*

Norden's work was in a sense continued by the expedition dispatched by King *Frederik V* (1746-1766) to *Arabia Felix* in 1760. This journey, of which *Carsten Niebuhr* (1733-1815) was the sole survivor, was planned on a much more scientific basis (RASMUSSEN 1986; RASMUSSEN 1990). The bulk of the work of the expedition was carried out far from the shores of the Mediterranean, but it should not be forgotten that Niebuhr also visited Rhodes, Alexandria, Jerusalem, Aleppo and Cyprus.

In the second half of the 18th century and at the beginning of the 19th century, artists such as the sculptor *J. Wiedewelt* (1731-1802) and scholars, such as *G. Zoëga* (1755-1809) (ANDREASEN ed. 1967; KRARUP 1976; BERGHAUS & SCHRECKENBERG 1983, 274) followed in the footsteps of earlier Danish travellers to Rome, where they became influenced by the ideas of J.J. Winckelmann. Zoëga retained a more critical and down-to-earth approach than the latter, always emphasizing the importance of a careful examination of the original monuments in order to make sure that one was not misled by post-Roman restorations (JOHANSEN 1935). Zoëga started as an egyptologist and numismatist, but later studied the Greek and Roman reliefs in Rome and wrote a major (and largely unpublished) work about the topography of Rome. He became convinced that all branches of the study of antiquity were interconnected, expressing his view on the subject in an often quoted letter from 1791: "I do not intend ... to lose sight of Egyptian antiquity

Fig. 2. The Column of Pompey in Alexandria drawn by F.L. Norden in 1737.

... It is indeed this which has caused me to investigate the Greek and Roman artefacts, when I found it impossible to make any progress with the latter without a detailed knowledge of the former ... and everywhere it seems to me that the entire study of antiquity is so complex that one cannot separate it into branches or gain a clear insight into one class so long as the others are left out. (The study of archaeology) can and should be treated just as seriously and systematically as the other disciplines are in our time. Antiquarians have hitherto not done this" (RIIS 1979, 133-134).

## Pioneers in the 19th century

Rome had been the centre of art and science for many centuries, but from the late 17th century on, Greece became more accessible to architects (ATHÈNES 1985, 47-60) and other students of the ancient world (TSIGAKOU 1981), and there was a growing awareness that Roman art, as reflected by the finds from Pompeii and Herculaneum, depended to a considerable degree on Greek precedents. The conception of ancient Greek art and civilization was in many cases idealized, but first-hand accounts by travellers and precise architectural depictions such as those of *J. Stuart* and *N. Revett* in their four volumes on the "Antiquities of Athens", published between 1762 and 1816, helped to produce a more accurate picture of ancient Greece and its monuments.

The philologist *P. O. Brøndsted* (1780-1842) (KRARUP 1976; BERGHAUS & SCHRECKENBERG 1983, 294; HAUGSTED 1990, 189) and his brother-in-law *G.H.C. Koës* (1782-1811) were among the first Danes to visit Greece in the early part of the 19th century. They travelled from Rome to Athens in the company of the Germans *C. Haller von Hallerstein* and *J. Linckh* and the Estonian *O. Magnus von Stackelberg*. Having reached their destination in the autumn of 1810, they formed a friendship with other students of antiquity: the Englishmen *Ch.R. Cockerell* and *J. Foster* (cf. for all of these BRACKEN 1975 106-158 and the biographical entries ibid., 185-204).

The Danes spent the following months studying the ancient monuments and enjoying the company of their friends. They also paid visits to the excavations which were being performed at the time in and around Athens, and the atmosphere during such a visit is conveyed by a passage in Brøndsted's diary (17.10 1810)[3]: "in the afternoon, with my friends and *Gropius* etc. to *Fauvel's* and *Lusieri's* excavations" (cf.

BRACKEN 1975, 191, 194 and 197). We found Mr. Fauvel with his Mr. *Pinko* there. Fatal Lusieri has today found a rather nice bas relief in marble: a young woman holding a small libation vessel or tear bottle in her hand. In Fauvel's excavation a grave had just been found and we were all curious to know what would come. But nothing special emerged: a few vase pieces. F. himself raked around among the pieces: "ca doit etre quelque-chose – non ce n'est rien –, c'est *moi* qui l'a découvert." While we were all standing there, 3 persons, some of them gold-braided, came galloping up from the town. It was *Lord Byron*, his little dragoman, and one of his janissaries. The young dragoman was very strangely decked out in a cap with gold brocade and a large ermine cape – he looked just like a woman. I was long in doubt as to which gender I should reckon this person, and Gropius later told me that he in fact belongs to both – he is a *polison* – and Lord Byron, etc. His lordship inspected the excavations, exchanged a couple of words with Fauvel, and galloped off again with his Antinous and his janissary." So much for the gossip at Athens (BRACKEN 1975, 110-111).

Brøndsted, Koës and Stackelberg embarked in April 1811 on an illfated excursion to Constantinople and Asia Minor; on his way back to Athens Koës tragically fell ill and died. The loss was a severe blow to

Fig. 3. View of Karthaia on the Island of Keos. From Brøndsted 1826 pl. 7.

Brøndsted, and the news was received with incredulity in Copenhagen, where the absurd story circulated that Koës was not dead but had been betrayed by his Greek servant to a slave trader from the Barbary and sold as a slave into Africa (BRØNDSTED 1844, 490-491) – a testimony to the fantastic misconceptions about the Greek world rampant in Denmark at the time.

In the autumn of 1811, a Scot named *Walsingham* arrived at Athens, where he made the acquaintance of Brøndsted and Linckh and gained their sympathy by explaining that he had come after hearing a rumor at Keos: that Cockerell, Foster and two English noblemen had been captured by a pirate who held them to ransom in a prison tower. Honest Walsingham (BRØNDSTED 1844, 496) now desired to buy his compatriots free. The rumor fortunately turned out to be false, and the Scotchman talked Brøndsted and Linckh into making a joint excursion to Keos in December 1811. Here they made topographical investigations and conducted excavations in a sanctuary of Apollo at Karthaia on the southeast coast of the island. Brøndsted thereby became the first Dane to excavate on Greek soil (DYGGVE 1943, 141), although the actual digging was presumably left to the twenty-four peasants hired for one and a quarter to one and half Levantine Piasters a day to do the job (BRØNDSTED 1826, 16 note 2). *Fig. 3*

A number of inscriptions and fragments of statues was unearthed during three to four weeks of digging, and Brøndsted bought the best pieces of sculpture from his two companions: "...two beautiful female torsos, another greater torso of Apollo and a quantity of smaller pieces, (such) as heads, legs, hands, etc., of the statues of which the bodies were not found...at least 15 or 16 pieces..." (P.O. Brøndsted in a letter to *J. Wilson* dated 19.6 1820). As luck would have it, Walsingham was acquainted with the captain of an English merchantman lying in the harbour of Keos at the time, and this fine fellow agreed to transport the sculptures to Malta on his ship and deposit them with an English firm. *Fig. 4*

However, when Brøndsted arrived in Malta eight years later to claim his property, he was told that only one or two pieces of damaged sculpture had reached their destination. A representative of the English company claimed that the person calling himself Walsingham[4] was "a notorious swindler ... an itinerant villain", who had cheated the firm of a large sum of money, and he added that he himself would dearly like to get hold of the captain of the ship on which the finds had been trans-

Fig. 4. Female torso from Karthaia, now apparently lost. Brøndsted 1826, pl. 9.

ported. But he, too, had vanished into thin air. – It is unlikely that we shall ever get to the bottom of this mystery: the fact is that most of the sculptural finds from the excavation at Karthaia were lost. Brøndsted recovered one of the torsos and perhaps a few more pieces at Keos, but it is not known what subsequently happened to these fragments. However, he later donated two Attic 5th century B.C. vases from Karthaia to the Danish king: an *oinochoe* by the Gela painter and a *chous* (I.N. CHR. VIII 342 AND 343; BREITENSTEIN 1951, 99 note 130 fig. 20).

In the summer of 1812 Brøndsted and his companions made the sensational discovery of the sculptured frieze at the Temple of Apollo at Bassai. He wrote a vivid account in Danish of the excavations, which was published after his death (BRØNDSTED 1861), but the enterprise is well documented from accounts by the other participants (cf. BRACKEN 1975, 139-158). 100-125 local workmen were occupied for six weeks in uncovering the sculptural remains, which were transported with considerable difficulty to Zante and later sold to the British Museum. Brøndsted, however, kept at least one find as a souvenir, which he gave to the Danish Crown Prince *Christian Frederik,* later King *Christian VIII* (1839-1848), as a Christmas present in 1820: a fragment comprising the left foot of one of the figures of the frieze (I.N. ABA 131b; BREITENSTEIN 1951, 92 note 114). Interestingly, on his first arrival in Athens, Brøndsted wrote indignantly in his diary (1.10.1810) about the spoliation of the Parthenon sculptures by "the villain" Lord ELGIN, quoting a dictum by G. Gropius: "quidquid liquerunt Gothi vastarunt Scoti". But, as we have seen, he later acted in much the same way himself.

The Crown Prince Christian Frederik had a vivid interest in archaeology, and he travelled from 1818 in Europe on a grand tour, in the course of which he acquired antiques in Italy. Furthermore, he visited the excavations at Pompeii and Nola (FABRITIUS, FRIIS & KORNERUP 1973, 229; 280-282), and a few ancient tombs at Cumae were opened in his presence. The contents of the graves at Cumae are kept at the

Fig. 5. Jug in African Red Slip ware from Thapsus in Tunisia; original drawing by C.T. Falbe, who presented the vase to the Danish Crown Prince Christian Frederik. The Danish National Museum, Department of Near Eastern and Classical Antiquities, i.n. Chr. VIII 376.

Danish National Museum; the material spans a period from the Iron Age to the Roman period (BREITENSTEIN 1951, 82-86). P.O. Brøndsted, who was by now Danish Court Agent at the Vatican in Rome also attended on this occasion, and he was later appointed Keeper of the Royal collection of Coins and Medals as well as Professor Ordinarius of Philology and Archaeology from 1832.

In the 1820es the Danish Consul-General in Tunisia, *C.T. Falbe* (1791-1849) (LIVENTHAL 1986), also cultivated the acquaintance of the future king by sending him antiques: vases, terracotta lamps and coins. Falbe was hardly a man of the world like Brøndsted, but a work-addict, who did not think highly of his more easy-going fellows. During Falbe's prolonged stay in Tunisia, he applied his restless energy to making a survey of the ancient remains in the territory of ancient Carthage, and he later published the first accurate plan of the area (FALBE 1833), which is still useful to archaeologists today. In connection with the topographical work, he made a number of soundings in the area of Carthage, and, what is more remarkable, drew conclusions based on observations of a stratigraphical nature in at least one instance (FALBE 1833, 46); the earliest stratigraphical excavations in Greece did not take place until 1834 (RIIS 1979, 141). After a spell as Danish Consul General in Athens, Falbe returned to Tunisia in 1837-1838 and took part in excavations in Carthage (LUND 1986). In the same year, he went on an excursion to the interior of the country, during which he investigated and identified a number of hitherto unknown ancient sites (LUND & SØRENSEN 1988; and forthcoming).

*Fig. 5*

## The background to the Rhodes Expedition

Brøndsted's travels in Greece were extensively publicized, i.a. in a series of lectures at the University of Copenhagen, and other Danes were inspired to follow in his footsteps, for instance the architects *J.H. Koch* (1787-1860), *Chr. Hansen* (1803-1883), *Th. Hansen* (1813-1891) and *M.G. Bindesbøll* (1800-1856), whose contribution (cf. PAPANICOLAOU-CHRISTENSEN 1985), as stated at the outset, is outside the scope of this paper. Others followed suit, and at the end of the nineteenth century it was even possible to enroll in an annual package tour of the major sites of ancient Greece arranged by the German Institute of Archaeology with *W. Dörpfeld* as guide (SØRENSEN 1986).

More adventurous travellers such as the scholar *J.L. Ussing* (1820-

1905) continued to go to Greece on individual trips. Ussing was a pupil of Brøndsted and succeeded him as Professor of philology and archaeology at the University of Copenhagen in 1842. He visited Greece and Italy as early as 1844-1846, and his most enduring contribution to the study of antiquity was in the field of epigraphy, which has continued to hold the interest of a number of later Danish archaeologists. More significantly, Ussing became a member of the board of directors of the Carlsberg Foundation, the Maecaenate of humanistic and scientific research in Denmark founded at a surprisingly early time (GLAMANN 1990, 220), and this enabled him to take the initiative to the first major Danish field archaeological project in the Mediterranean: the expedition to Lindos on Rhodes (project no. 1[5]).

Other possible targets for fieldwork had at first been deliberated:

Fig. 6. The Danish archaeologist K.F. Kinch on the acropolis of Lindos, Rhodes, painted by his wife H. Kinch, probably before 1905 (project no. 1). The Department of Near Eastern and Classical Archaeology at the Danish National Museum.

Nemea and Kleonai in Greece, as well as Cyrene in North Africa. The latter idea was abandoned only because the Ottoman Government would not allow foreigners to work in Libya (DIETZ & TROLLE 1974, 9). Ussing later published the arguments for deciding on Lindos: "The major excavations which have been carried out during the last half century in the cultural centres must appear not only more vividly and fully, but also in many ways in an entirely new light. Hereby archaeology must come to play a major role; it seemed that it must be that which laid the foundation stone of the new edifice which science is in the process of raising ... After careful weighing of the various possibilities which arose, we chose Lindos on the island of Rhodes, a town which in the 7th and 6th centuries BC was the island's most important city ... Lying on the east coast, as the most southeasterly outpost of Greece, it has played a major role in the ancient trade with the Orient." (USSING 1906, 228-229). It is especially interesting that the importance of the island for the trade routes between East and West is underlined.

*Fig. 6*   The Carlsberg foundation placed the practical execution of the Lindos project in the hands of *K.F. Kinch* (1853-1921) and *Chr. S. Blinkenberg* (1863-1948). The former was a pupil of Ussing's who had previously travelled extensively in Turkey and Northern Greece studying ancient sites and monuments on the Chalkidike peninsula, in Macedonia and at Thessaloniki (DYGGVE 1943, 149-150). Blinkenberg was keeper at the Danish National Museum, and later became the first Professor of archaeology at the University of Copenhagen. Kinch was the driving force in the fieldwork during the larger part of the campaigns from 1902 to 1908 and from 1913-1914, and the results fully lived up to the expectations.

With the expedition to Rhodes, Denmark joined the somewhat exclusive club of European nations conducting excavations in Greece (HAUSMANN 1969, 122-145). Germany (JANTZEN 1986), Britain (WATERHOUSE 1988), France and America had established schools of archeology in Athens before the turn of the century, and there was fierce competition between these countries as well as with Austria, Italy

*Fig. 7*   and others for the best sites. The German effort was at first shaped by *H. Schliemann's* obsession with the Heroic Age of Greece (TROJA, MYKENE 1990) and mainly directed at Bronze Age sites, known from the works of Homer, e.g. Troy, Mycenae and Tiryns. With time,

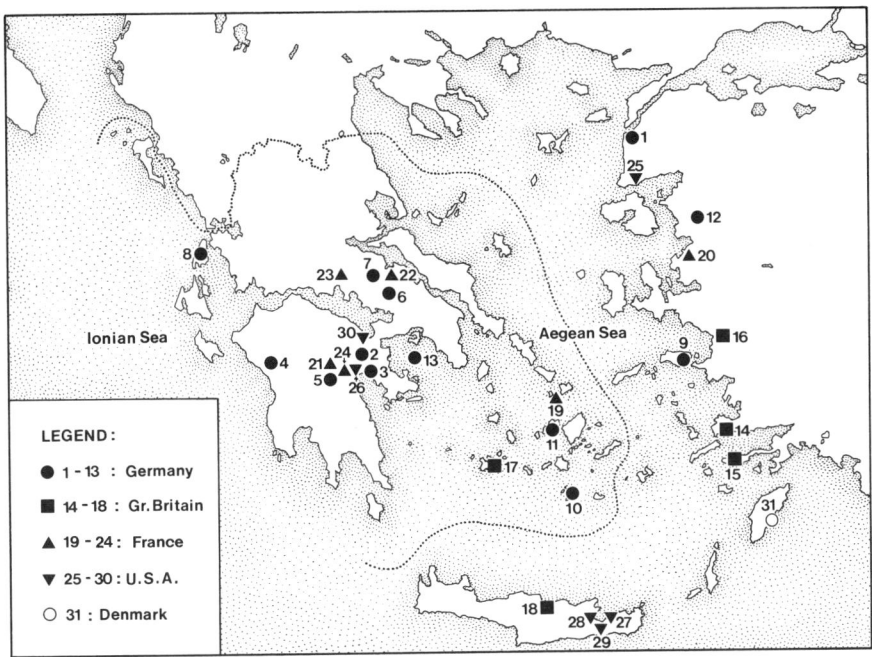

Fig. 7. The principal excavation sites of Greece up to the Lindos excavation. From the Baedecker of 1904.

no. 1) Troja
no. 2) Mycenae
no. 3) Tiryns
no. 4) Olympia
no. 5) Tegea
no. 6) Kabirion
no. 7) Orchomenos
no. 8) Ithaka
no. 9) Samos
no. 10) Thera
no. 11) Paros
no. 12) Pergamon
no. 13) Aigina, the temple of Aphaia
no. 14) Halikarnassos
no. 15) Knidos
no. 16) Ephesos
no. 17) Melos
no. 18) Knossos
no. 19) Delos
no. 20) Myrina
no. 21) Mantinea
no. 22) Orchomenos
no. 23) Delphi
no. 24) Argos
no. 25) Assos
no. 26) Argive Heraion
no. 27) Mochlos
no. 28) Gournia
no. 29) Vasiliki
no. 30) Corinth
no. 31) Lindos

however, the interest of German archaeologists seems to have shifted more and more toward temples and sanctuary sites, as evidenced by the excavations at Olympia, the Kabirion in Boeotia and the Temple of Athena Aphaia at Aegina; at the same time German archaeologists also evinced a growing interest in topographical studies. The French projects were right from the start mainly directed at sanctuaries, especially Delphi and Delos, but the French were also active in settlement excavations such as that at Myrina. At first, British archaeologists concentrated on Asia Minor with excavations at Ephesos and Halikarnassos, but they later shifted their interest to Bronze Age sites such as Phylakopi at Melos and, of course, Knossos on Crete.

It is easy to see why sanctuaries held a special attraction for archaeologists: they were almost certain to reward the excavator with a rich harvest of finds of votive gifts, i.e. art objects: statues, pottery, etc., and possibly also inscriptions. Furthermore, the location of many of the sanctuaries was well known, due to the presence of architectural remains. The Lindos project was a child of its time.

## Between the two World Wars

The First World War brought about a cessation of the archaeological activities in the Mediterranean countries, and when peace came, the map of Europe and the Near East had changed: the collapse of the Ottoman Empire brought Syria, Iraq and the Levantine coast under British and French jurisdiction. The Dodecanese islands came under Italian rule, and a continued Danish involvement at Rhodes was thereby rendered difficult.

The next Danish excavation in Greece proper took place at Kalydon (no. 2). The leading Danish figure was *F. Poulsen* (1876-1950), a colourful personality, who before the First World War had travelled extensively in Greece and taken part in the French excavations at Delos and Delphi. At Kalydon he worked with the Greek archaeologist *K. Rhomaios* – thereby starting a tradition for Danish collaboration with local archaeologists. Kalydon was, of course, an important place in Greek myth and legend, and once again the excavations centered on a sanctuary site. This was the first classical archaeological project funded by the Rask-Ørsted Foundation, which with the Carlsberg Foundation was to bear the largest financial burden of Danish projects before the Second World War.

At the same time, the geographical and chronological scope widened. A great-grandchild of P.O. Brøndsted, *J. Brøndsted* (1890-1965) of the Danish National Museum, and the architect *E. Dyggve* (1887-1961) were invited by the Yugoslav authorities to take part in the exploration of Salona (no. 6), and Dyggve subsequently functioned as technical conservator at the archaeological museum in Split over a three-year period (PIPLOVIC 1987). He was especially interested in the Late Ro-

Fig. 8. The Danish excavations at Hama 1933 (project no. 12). Daily life in the sector J 10-11; sketch by E. Fugmann, architect of the expedition.

man and Byzantine periods, which had hitherto received scant attention by Danish archaeologists, and this was also reflected in his excavations at Thessaloniki (no. 3), cut short by the Second World War.

The most important archaeological initiative at the time was the Hama expedition (no. 12), financed by the Carlsberg Foundation. Knowledge of the archaeology and history of the Near East had increased dramatically in the first third of the twentieth century, stimulated by many archaeological projects in the area conducted by Germany, Great Britain, France and the U.S.A. – with a rivalry for getting first to the promising sites, that was hardly less intense than in Greece (WINSTONE 1982 AND 1985). The excavations at Lindos and elsewhere in Greece had documented the importance of the Near East for the development of Greek art and culture in the first millennium B.C. (cf. *ActaHyp* 1 1988), and it was therefore natural for Danish archaeologists too to turn to the Near East.

*Harald Ingholt* (1896-1986) was appointed director of the Hama-expedition. His doctoral thesis had dealt with the sculpture of Palmyra, where he had excavated as early as the 1920es (no. 11). He adopted the methodology of the American excavations at Megiddo in the new project and was rewarded with the finding of important material from the

*Fig. 8*

Neolithic, Bronze Age and Iron Age. Most of this naturally fall under the heading of Near Eastern rather than classical archaeology, but it should not be forgotten that Cypriote and Mycenaean material as well as Greek Geometric pottery was found, and that the destruction of Hama by the Assyrians in 720 B.C. constitutes an excellent *terminus ante quem* for Greek Geometric pottery. The rich finds from the Hellenistic and Roman periods are also of significance, from a classical archaeological point of view.

An excavation on a much smaller scale reflecting a Danish interest in biblical archaeology was conducted at Shilo in Transjordan as it then was (no. 14); however, evidence of habitation from the Hellenistic through the Islamic period was also uncovered here.

## From World War II to 1990

The Second World War brought about a rupture in Danish archaeological projects in the Mediterranean, the consequences of which were felt for a surprisingly long time. When activities were resumed, they were at first an extension of work begun before the war. Dyggve returned to Thessaloniki in order to complete his research there (no. 3), the work at Shilo was briefly resumed (no. 14), and the Carlsberg Foundation sent an expedition to Tall Sukas on the northern coast of Syria (no. 13). *P.J. Riis*, then Professor of classical archaeology at the University of Copenhagen, directed this project, which was in a sense a logical follow-up to the excavations at Hama.

A new departure was when prehistorians from the Prehistoric Museum at Århus, accepted an invitation from Bahrein and launched an expedition which has acquired an almost legendary status in the Danish archaeological world, to the Persian Gulf (no. 18). Most of the results are of little relevance from a classical archaeological point of view, but important evidence from the Hellenistic period was also brought to

*Fig. 9* light by the expedition, especially at Failaka (no. 19).

From the second half of the 1960es on, the number of Danish archaeological expeditions increased, partly because small-scale investigations now became the rule rather than the exception. However, it is difficult to generalize, since the projects vary greatly not only in size, but also in aims and approach, and it is characteristic that many have provided work for Danish classical archaeologists without a secure position at the universities or museums.

Fig. 9. The cleaning of the inscription identifying the ancient name of the island of Failaka as Ikaros (project no. 19). Reproduced by kind permission of professor K. Jeppesen.

The focus of interest had by now shifted from Greece and the Balkans to other areas. True, Danes have been and still are excavating in Greece, but in the one case the project is a Greek-Swedish one (no. 5), and in the other it started as a Greek-Swedish project (no. 4), although it ended as a collaboration between Greece, Sweden and Denmark. The main objective was in both cases the Bronze Age civilizations of Greece, and all of this seems at first sight to constitute a break in the tradition from the pre-war research in Greece. However, this is not true if the excavations at the Mausoleum of Halikarnassos are taken into account (no. 7); they were directed by Professor *K. Jeppesen* of the University of Aarhus, where a chair of classical archaeology was established in 1949. Though for long under Persian rule, Halikarnassos was in ancient times to a large degree part of the Greek world.

29

Fig. 10. Survey in the area of the Roman Municipium of Segermes, Tunisia (project no. 24).

If Greece has receded somewhat into the background this is more than compensated for by the new areas explored by Danes. We have already referred to the work carried out in the Persian Gulf Area (nos. 18-21) and Turkey (nos. 7 and 8). To these areas can now be added Cyprus (nos. 9-10), Iran (no. 17), Egypt (no. 22), Tunisia (nos. 23-24), and Italy (nos. 25-35). The focus of interest has to a large degree shifted from sanctuary sites to settlements and landscape archaeology, and the problems of urbanization and the relationship between the settlements and the surrounding countryside are now in the foreground (nos. 28 and 35). This is also reflected by the growing importance of archaeological surveys (nos. 9; 17; 20; 24). A survey used to be a side-show of an excavation, but is now recognized as a valuable method of investigation in its own right.

Danish archaeologists have frequently collaborated with colleagues from the country involved (nos. 16; 24; 30 and 35), from Scandinavia (nos. 4; 5; 28; 33 and 34) or elsewhere (nos. 9; 21 and 22). One major difference between the situation before and after the Second World War is that the excavated finds are now rarely handed over to Denmark after the end of the work.

Fig. 11a. A visit by the Danish King *Christian IX* to the excavation of the temple of Castor and Pollux on the Forum Romanum in Rome. From *Illustreret Tidende* 5th of May 1872.

Fig. 11b. The recent Danish excavations at the temple of Castor and Pollux (project no. 34).

The emergence of Danish archaeological projects in Italy (nos. 25-35) is a consequence of the inauguration of the royally sponsored Danish Academy on the Via Omero in Rome in 1967 (LUNDBAK 1989). This institution is on the one hand capable of negotiating with the authorities and arranging excavations, and on the other provides facilities for the storage and study of archaeological finds. Some of the projects began as a consequence of the interest of the scholars starting them, but others were established through invitations from Italian archaeologists (nos. 28 and 29), the Soprintendenza Archeologica di Roma (no. 34) and the Soprintendenza Archeologica di Salerno (no. 35). Most of the sites explored by Danes are located in the vicinity of Rome and northern Lazio – within easy reach by car of the Danish Academy.

*Fig. 11a-b*

The Carlsberg Foundation and the Research Council for the Humanities (formed in 1972, and incorporating i.a. the Rask-Ørsted Foundation) continued to bear the greatest economic burdens, but other foundations and private individuals have also provided funds: the Foundation of Queen Margrethe and Prince Henrik (no. 22); Generalkonsul Gösta Enbom and the foundation which bears his name (nos. 4, 21, 23-24), Simon Spies (nos. 23-24), the Tuborg Foundation (no. 23), the Gad Foundation (no. 5), the Nordic Council (no. 28), the Hjerl Hansen Memorial Foundation (no. 15), the Universities of Copenhagen, Aarhus and Odense, the Danish National Museum, and others. Foreign financial support has also been given to Danish projects, either entirely (nos. 18-20; 30) or in part (25, 28 and 34).

It should not be forgotten that the expenses arising from field campaigns only constitute the tip of the iceberg. The work involved in the publication and printing of the results is extremely time-consuming and expensive, and the above-mentioned foundations, especially the Carlsberg Foundation and the Research Council for the Humanities, have financed this aspect of the work as well. Today, no excavation or survey deserves to receive financial support unless its director can produce a realistic plan for the publication at an early stage of the project. If the archaeologists taking part are occupied by a full time job elsewhere arrangements should be made to relieve them of this temporarily, so that they can complete their publications immediately after their return to Denmark.

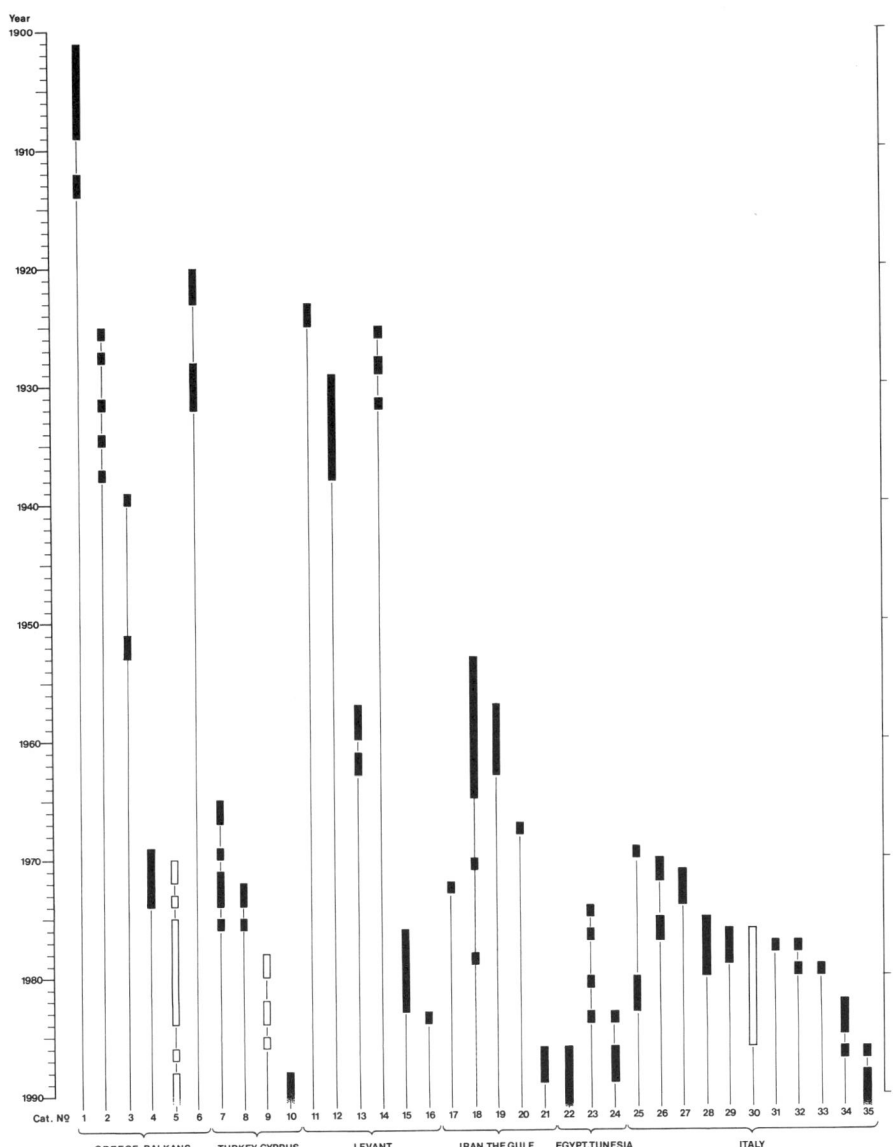

Fig. 12. Danish Classical Archaeological Fieldwork projects.

## Tradition and renewal

There is a clear tradition from P.O. Brøndsted's early investigations in Greece to the Lindos expedition and the excavations at Hama and Tall Sukas, which were in a sense a corollary to the latter. There is likewise a

*Fig. 12*

continuity between C.T. Falbe's pioneering work in Carthage in the early nineteenth century and the recent Danish projects in Tunisia. A link may also be established between the excavations carried out in the presence of the later King Christian VIII in Italy and the royal sponsorship of the Danish Academy in Rome, the establishment of which has inaugurated a new era of Danish classical archaeological fieldwork on the Appennine peninsula.

From the start there has been an openness towards collaboration with colleagues from the involved countries or other (mostly) European nations – perhaps arising from the fact that Denmark is a small nation without pretensions to be a great power. Projects begun in the first part of the twentieth century continue to have repercussions now, and surprisingly many Danish archaeologists of the younger generation are working on problems (e.g. the question of Near Eastern influence in early Greece and Etruria) put on the agenda in the first half of the twentieth century.

As for renewal, the clearest tendency is the widening geographical and chronological horizons. Furthermore, the importance of interdisciplinary collaboration[6] has come more and more to the fore, and it is almost universally realized that such efforts will be successful only if all the involved parties show respect for the other disciplines. We all work towards a common goal.

The historical approach in archaeology is becoming more and more popular. There is no longer a need to defend ourselves against the old "New Archaeology", as A.M. Snodgrass felt obliged to do in 1985 and 1987. What characterized New Archaeology more than anything was a disinterest in written sources and linguistics. This generated the widespread notion that classical archaeology did not count as archaeology at all. "The great divide" (RENFREW 1980) was the prehistorian's inclination to seek an explanation in the natural sciences and physical anthropology. Happily there is now a tendency to turn from sociology to history – in the broadest definition of the word, be it long term history or not.

It is deplorable that Near Eastern Archaeology was separated from the Institute of Near Eastern and Classical archaeology at the University of Copenhagen in 1982, and Boardman's statement about classical archaeology also applies to this discipline: each is a "most important testing ground for archaeological theory, ground on which even verification of hypothesis can be enjoyed" (BOARDMAN 1988, 797). Archaeology, a combination of a humanistic field of research with a technical/scientific skill, continues to be a rapidly changing discipline. But it should never be considered merely a technique for finding and collecting the broken pieces of the past, but rather a framework and theory for developing a faculty for reading the messages inherent in the material remains (movable objects, architectural remains and landscapes). In short a decoding, historical science.

## Conclusions

As members of a generation which grew up with Clarke's *Analytical Archaeology* (1968), the present authors are not inclined to reject the ongoing theoretical debate, although it may at times seem that it has been side-tracked by empty rhetoric (GALLAY 1989). We cannot speak of a Danish school of classical archaeology, although it could be argued that the Danish tradition has stood for a combination of German thoroughness and methodological approach with British pragmatism and common sense – sprinkled with occasional Gallic wit.

Classical archaeology is a fascinating chapter in the European history of learning, and it seems relevant to conclude by asking whether Danes have followed trends developed outside the borders of our nation, or sailed boldly against the stream of fashionable research topics. It would appear that the former was the case, although some characteristics may be more typical of the development in Denmark than elsewhere.

Philhellenism, which used to dominate (and to a certain degree still dominates) the situation in other nations, played a minor role in Denmark – perhaps as a result of the expeditions to the Near East. The study of Phoenicians and other Semitic cultures, which Frederik Poulsen brought into focus in his epoch-making work: *Der Orient und die frühgriechische Kunst* (1912), did not fall victim to anti-Semitism here as it did elsewhere (BERNAL 1987), perhaps because Danes have traditionally been less afflicted by this disease than others.

There was a growing interest in Etruscan studies in Denmark in the 1930'ies, but this was not reflected in the start of archaeological field projects at the time. The archaeology of ancient Etruria was outside "the great tradition", and the Danish scholars were probably drawn to this subject partly by the rich collections of Etruscan antiquities in the museums of Copenhagen and partly by the connection between the Near Eastern civilizations and Etruria of the Orientalizing period.

Could it be that the limited interest in Roman archaeology up to the 1960es is to be explained by the exploitation of Rome and Roman culture by the Fascists? In more recent times it may be symptomatic that the organizers of a large Danish exhibition on "The World of the Etruscans" in 1982 consciously or subconsciously equated the Roman Empire with the European Economic Community, implying that the fate of Denmark would resemble that of the Etruscan cities subjugated by Rome. The study of Roman archaeology in Denmark was until recently dominated by art (especially portraiture) and architecture, but with the emergence of archaeological field projects centering on the Roman provinces (nos. 9, 10 and 24) the first steps have been taken to creating an interdisciplinary collaboration also in this field.

Classical archaeology is alive and kicking in Denmark. Unrestricted research still survives, and if the future may be predicted from the past, funds will continue to be made available for such work in the years to come. A recent development is that the Research Council for the Humanities has launched a grandiose research-program centered on the Hellenistic period, which is praiseworthy in its interdisciplinary approach, although it will hardly be a vehicle for commencing new archaeological fieldwork in the Mediterranean world.

In the area reviewed here, Denmark has over the years made contributions surpassing those of many other European nations in quantity and quality. If this development is to continue, it is a prerequisite that the classical archaeological infrastructure be preserved at the universities as well as the Danish National Museum. The government cuts in the funds available to the humanities have already had grave consequences for the discipline, and will no doubt continue to hang over its head as a Damocles' sword for some years to come. However, it is a good omen that field campaigns are planned in 1990 for some of the "old" projects (nos. 5, 10, 22, 35), and *P. Pedersen* will resume his investigation in the area of the Hellenistic city of Halikarnassos, an offspring of the Danish excavations at the Mausoleum site (no. 7). *F.G. Andersen* and *J. Strange* will take part in a new Scandinavian excavation to Tell el Furkhar in Jordania supported by the Nordic Council for the Humanities and directed by *M. Ottosen* of the University of Uppsala. And, finally, the Danish Palestinian Exploration Fund has decided to

Fig. 13. Danish students from the University of Copenhagen took briefly part in the excavations at Panticapeion during an excursion to Crimea in August 1990.

launch a preliminary archaeological survey in the Larnaca area of Cyprus directed by *L. Wriedt Sørensen*.

The next chapter in the history of Danish classical archaeological fieldwork in the Mediterranean is thus already in the offing.

*Fig. 13*

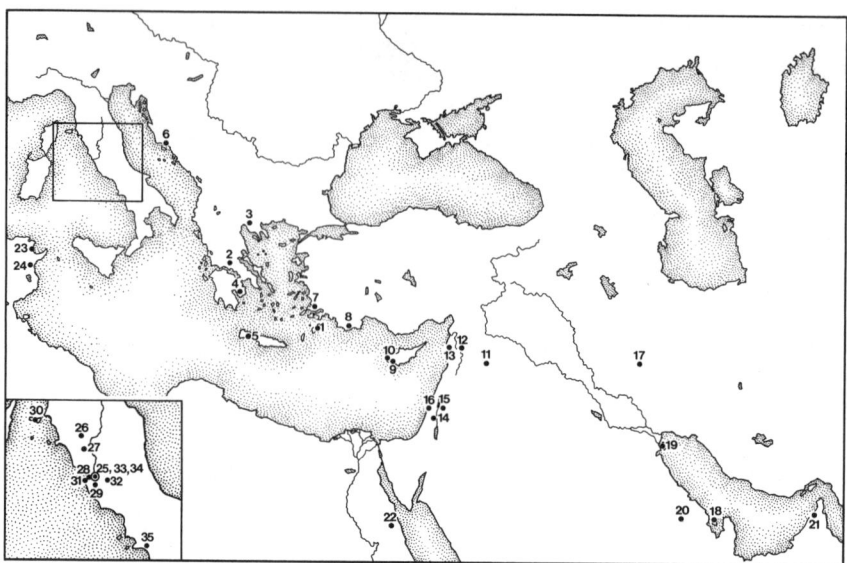

Fig. 14. A map showing the Danish project in the Mediterranean, Egypt and the Persian Gulf from 1900 onwards.

## APPENDIX. A CATALOGUE OF DANISH FIELDWORK IN THE MEDITERRANEAN, EGYPT AND THE PERSIAN GULF FROM 1900 ONWARDS

*Fig. 14* For reasons of space certain limitations have been imposed. Three non-Danish projects are included because Danes have taken part at the leadership level (nos. 5, 9 and 30), but participation in an excavation in the Mediterranean is obligatory for students of classical archaeology at the University of Copenhagen, and examples of such participation in foreign projects are too numerous to mention. The cases where Danish archaeologists have become involved in the publication of non-Danish projects are likewise not included. The years cited refer to field campaigns, not study seasons etc. The catalogue includes Danish Near Eastern archaeological projects which have produced classical archaeological material.

The summaries of the results of the excavations are only meant as a brief presentation of the main results; for the projects between 1973 and 1984 the text has to a certain extent been based on that of Jan Zahle (1986), which was in turn edited from information supplied by the excavators or others.

The bibliography is selective. Preliminary reports are not included if superseded by later works. Contributions written in Danish are usually included only if they have a summary in English, German or the like. Further references may be found in DYGGVE 1943, JOHANSEN 1943, DYGGVE 1948, RIIS 1979, ZAHLE 1986 and MOLTESEN 1989. For a comprehensive bibliography up to 1970, see HANSEN 1977.

### Greece and the Balkans

*1. Excavations and investigations at Lindos, Rhodes, Greece (1902-1909; 1913-1914).*
*Direction:* C. F. Kinch and Chr. Blinkenberg.
*Architects:* H. Koch, P. Baumann and H. Rasmussen.
*Financial support:* The Carlsberg Foundation.
*Goal:* To investigate one of the major sanctuaries and city-states of ancient Greece.
*Result:* Excavations were carried out on the acropolis of Lindos and in the surrounding areas in three major campaigns from 1902 to 1905. The earliest objects from here go back to the Protogeometric period, and the number of finds multiplies from the 8th century B.C. onwards. They correspond to those made in other Greek sanctuaries and comprise imported pieces from North Syria, Assyria, Cyprus, Phoenicia and Egypt. The earliest monumental structure is a staircase dated after 550 B.C. leading to a predecessor of the later temple. A large number of votive gifts, especially terracotta figurines, could be dated to the 6th and 5th centuries B.C. Inscriptions begin to appear from the 6th century B.C. on, the most important of which was a list of priests built into the new temple of Athena constructed about 350-340 B.C., and the so-called chronicle of the temple dated 99 B.C. A monumental propylon was added to the sanctuary about 300 B.C., and in the Hellenistic period the sanctuary was remodelled through the construction of a stoa and staircases.
*Associated fieldwork:* K.F. Kinch conducted a number of investigations and excavations in southern Rhodes exploring Mycenean chamber tombs at Apollakia (1903-4), Apsaktiras, Vati, Kalovriou and Passia (1904). In 1907 he began excavations at Vroulia on the southern tip of the island, a settlement with private houses, a sanctuary and a cemetery. The finds show that the settlement had a life span from ca. 600 to 550 B.C. More Mycenean rock-cut tombs were excavated at Granto near Kattavia (1908), and a cemetery from the Geometric period was excavated at Exochi (1914). In 1975 S. Dietz and S. Trolle from the Department of Classical and Near Eastern Antiquities at the Danish National Museum conducted a minor survey at the southern part of Rhodes supported by the Carlsberg Foundation. The purpose was to re-find and measure a number of sites discovered by K.F. Kinch at Kattavia, Sto Steno, Stous Mylous (today known as Trapezies Parailis), Passia and Apsaktiras.
*Bibliography:* M.P. Nilsson, *Timbres amphoriques de Lindos.* Copenhagen 1909; K. F. Kinch, *Fouilles de Vroulia (Rhodes).* Berlin 1914; Chr. Blinkenberg, *L'image d'Athana Lindia.* Copenhagen 1917; Chr. Blinkenberg, *Lindiaka II-IV.* Copenhagen 1926; Chr. Blinkenberg, *Fibules grecques et orientales (Lindiaka V).* Copenhagen 1926; Chr. Blinkenberg, *Lindos I, Les petits objets.* Berlin 1931; Chr. Blinkenberg, *Les prêtres de Poseidon Hippios, Études sur une inscription Lindienne (Lindiaka VI).* Copenhagen 1937; Chr. Blinkenberg, *Triemiolia, Étude sur un type de navire rhodien (Lindiaka VII).* Copenhagen 1938; Chr. Blinkenberg, *Deux documents chronologiques rhodiens (Lindiaka VIII).* Copenhagen 1938; Chr. Blinkenberg, *Lindos II, Inscriptions.* Berlin and Copenhagen 1941; K. Friis Johansen, *Exochi, Ein frührhodisches Gräberfeld.* Copenhagen 1958; E. Dyggve, *Lindos III. Le sanctuaire d'Athana Lindia et l'architecture lindienne avec un catalogue des sculptures trouvées sur l'acropole par V. Poulsen,* Berlin and Copenhagen 1960; S. Dietz, *Lindos IV, 1, Excavations and Surveys in Southern Rhodes: the Mycenaean Period.* Copenhagen 1984; M.-L. Buhl, Eleven Scarabs and One Fragment of a Faience Figurine Acquired at Lindos, *ActaArch* 56 1985, 197-200; L.W. Sørensen, Cypriote Terracottas from Lindos in the Light of New Discoveries, in: F. Vandenabeele & R. Laffineur

(eds.), *Cypriote Terracottas, Proceedings of the First International Confernce of Cypriote Studies*, Brussels-Liege-Amsterdam, 29 May-1 June, 1989, Brussels-Liege 1991, 224-240. L.W. Sørensen & P. Pentz, Lindos IV, 2, *Excavations and Surveys in Southern Rhodes: The Post-Mycenean and Medieval Periods*, forthcoming.

2. *Excavations at Kalydon, Greece (1926, 1928 and 1932, 1935, 1938).*
*Direction:* F. Poulsen & K. Rhomaios; from 1935 E. Dyggve.
*Architects:* M. Clemmensen and T. Christensen.
*Financial support:* The Rask-Ørsted Foundation.
*Goal:* To investigate the site of Kalydon known from Greek myths and legends.
*Result:* The expedition studied the ancient remains at the site of the ancient city of Kalydon, which was abandoned in 30 B.C. Excavations were conducted in the sanctuary of Artemis Laphria and a heroon – both located outside the city wall. Remains of two temples were found in the sanctuary: A) dedicated to Apollon (or Dionysos) and B) dedicated to Artemis. From the earliest structures (in both cases Doric temples in antis dated to the 7th century) come remains of terracotta decoration renewed in the first half of the 6th century B.C. A number of painted metopes of Corinthian origin from temple A) may be associated with this phase. A new temple of Artemis was constructed about 360: a Doric peripteral temple of poros but with marble roof. The Heroon (also known as the Leonteion after its owner, Leon of Kalydon) is a rectangular building with a peristyle courtyard at the centre and rooms on three sides. In a room with an apsis interpreted as the "Kultsaal", at least eleven portrait-medallions hung on the walls, depicting gods and heroes from the legendary past of Kalydon. The heroon is dated to the 2nd century B.C. on the basis of the ceramic finds.
*Bibliography:* E. Dyggve, F. Poulsen & K. Rhomaios, *Das Heroon von Kalydon*, Copenhagen 1934; E. Dyggve, *Das Laphrion, der Tempelbezirk von Kalydon mit einem religionsgeschichtlichen Beitrag von F. Poulsen*. Copenhagen 1948; E. Dyggve, A second Heroon at Kalydon, in: *Studies Presented to David Moore Robinson* I. St. Louis 1951, 360-364.

3. *Excavations at Thessaloniki, Greece (1939; 1952-1953).*
*Direction:* E. Dyggve.
*Architects:* A. Ludvigsen and E. Dyggve.
*Financial support:* The Carlsberg Foundation & the Rask-Ørsted Foundation.
*Goal:* To determine the location of a palace built by the emperor Galerius known from literary sources.
*Result:* The excavations were centered around the church Ag. Georgios and its surroundings. It was shown that no buildings had stood in this area of the city before the time of Galerius. The remains of a bath were encountered in a sounding ca. 70 m. west of the church, and more soundings were dug east of the church, which indicated that the church had originally stood inside a small temenos and that the palace should rather be sought to the south of the Arch of Galerius in the vicinity of the area where the location of the hippodrome had earlier been suspected. It was suggested that the circular church of Ag. Georgios had originally been built as a mausoleum for the emperor and was converted into a church about 400 A.D.
*Bibliography:* E. Dyggve, Kurzer vorläufiger Bericht über die Ausgrabungen im Palastviertel von Thessaloniki, Frühjahr 1939, *Dissertationes Pannonicae*, Series 2 no. 11, 1941, 63-71; E. Dyggve, Fouilles et recherches faites en 1939 et en 1952-53 à Thessaloniki. Recherches sur le palais impérial de Thessalonique: Architecture et mosaiques, in: *Università degli studi di Bologna. Corsi di cultura sull'arte ravennate e bizantina Ravenna, 31 marzo – 13 aprile 1957* 2. Ravenna 1957, 79-88.

4. *Excavations at Asine, Greece (1970-1974).*
*Direction:* C.G. Styrenius, Medelhavsmuseet, Stockholm and S. Dietz, the National Museum of Denmark.
*Financial support:* The Danish Research Council for the Humanities and G. Enbom.
*Goal:* Swedish archaeologists excavated in Asine between 1922 and 1930; the work was resumed as a sort of rescue-excavation in 1970 in an area east of Kastraki, which was to be used as a camping site.

*Result:* A sequence of layers was encountered spanning the period from the Middle Bronze Age to the Hellenistic Period. The early part of this period was represented by a burial ground dating from the Middle Helladic to the Late Helladic Period. The remaining part of the Mycenean period was represented by fill layers and architectural remains. There was an unbroken sequence from the Bronze Age to the Iron Age followed by three cist tombs from the 5th century B.C. and a Hellenistic burial ground.

*Bibliography:* B. Rafn, *Asine II, Results of the Excavations East of the Acropolis 1970-1974, fasc. 6, The Post-Geometric Periods Part 1: The Graves of the Early Fifth Century B.C.* Stockholm 1979; S. Dietz, *Asine II, Results of the Excavations East of the Acropolis 1970-1974, fasc. 2, The Middle Helladic Cemetery, The Middle Helladic and Early Mycenaean Deposits.* Stockholm 1980; S. Dietz, *Asine II, Results of the Excavations East of the Acropolis 1970-1974, fasc. 1, General Stratigraphical Analysis and Architectural Remains.* Stockholm 1982; S. Dietz, Kontinuität und Kulturwende in der Argolis von 2000 – 700 v. Chr. Ergebnisse der neuen schwedisch-dänischen Ausgrabungen in Asine in: *Kleine Schriften aus dem Vorgeschichtlichen Seminar Marburg* 17, 1984, 23-52; S. Dietz, *The Argolid at the Transition to the Mycenaean Age, Studies in the Chronology and Cultural Development in the Shaft Grave Period.* Copenhagen 1991.

*5. Excavations at Khania, Greece (1970-1974; 1976-1980; 1982-1984; 1987; 1989-).*
*Direction:* Y. Tzedakis, the Greek Ministry for Culture and Science and C.-G. Styrenius, Medelhavsmuseet in Stockholm. Since 1971 E. Hallager has functioned as daily leader of the Swedish part of the project.
*Architect:* G. Söderberg.
*Financial support:* The funding has mostly been supplied by the Swedish Research Council for the Humanities. The Danish Research Council for the Humanities and the Gad Foundation have also contributed to the work; the Carlsberg Foundation supported the study of the Byzantine and Post-Byzantine pottery.
*Goal:* To investigate a Minoan site in western Crete and provide a stratified basis for establishing the ceramic sequence.
*Results:* The excavations have documented a nearly unbroken settlement at the site from about 3000 B.C. to the present. Substantial architectural remains were unearthed, especially dating from the Early Minoan II period and from the Late Minoan I phase dated by the excavators to between ca. 1550 and 1450 B.C. However, the settlement was not abandoned and four rebuilding phases were in evidence until a short hiatus in the habitation about 1100 B.C. The finds, especially pottery, throw light on the interrelationship between Khania and the outside world, e.g. Greece, Cyprus and Southern Italy. A recent important development is the finding of Linear B tablets.
*Bibliography:* since 1982 reports by E. Hallager & Y. Tzedakis in *AAA*; E. Hallager, Two New Roundels with Linear A from Khania, *Kadmos* 23, 1984, 1-10; B.P. Hallager, A New Social Class in Late Bronze Age Crete: Foreign Traders in Khania, in O. Krzyszkowska & L. Nixon eds., *Minoan Society. Proceedings of the Cambridge Colloquium 1981.* Bristol 1983, 111-120; E. Hallager, The Master Impression. A Clay Sealing from the Greek-Swedish Excavations at Kastelli, Khania, *SIMA* 69, 1985; B.P. Hallager, Crete and Italy in the Late Bronze Age Period, *AJA* 89, 1985, 293-305; E. Hallager, The Greek-Swedish Excavations at Khania, in: *Proceedings of the Fifth International Cretological Congress at Ag. Nikolaos 1981.* Heraklion 1986, 139-154 (with bibliography up to 1981); B.P. Hallager, Mycenaean Pottery in the Late Minoan IIIA:1 Deposits in Khania, in: E.B. French & K.A. Wardle eds., *Papers presented at the centenary Conference of the British School at Athens, Manchester April 1986,* Bristol 1988, 173-183; E. Hallager, Khania and Late Minoan III Crete, *Cretan Studies* 1 1988, 115-124 pls. 62-71; E. Hallager, The Inscribed Stirrup Jars. Implications for Late Minoan III B Crete, *AJA* 91 1987, 171-190; M. Hahn, Byzantine and Postbyzantine Pottery from the Greek-Swedish Excavations at Khania, Crete, in: V. Déroche and J.-M. Speiser eds., Recherches sur la céramique byzantine, *BCH supplément* 18 1989, 227-232; E. Hallager, Roundels among Sealings in Minoan Administration: A Comprehensive Analysis of Function, in: Th. G. Palaima ed., Aegean Seals, Sealings and Administration, *Aegaeum* 5 1990, 121-142; E. Hallager & M. Vlasakis & B.P. Hallager, The First Linear B Tablet(s) from Khania, *Kadmos* 29 1990, forthcoming.

6. *Excavations at Salona, Yugoslavia (1921-1923; 1929-1932).*
*Direction:* J. Brøndsted, the Danish National Museum.
*Architect:* E. Dyggve.
*Financial support:* The Rask-Ørsted foundation.
*Goal:* To investigate ancient Salona.
*Result:* The excavations were centered around an early Christian cemetery basilica at Kapljuc with burials from the 1st to the 4th century A.D. Five Christian martyrs were buried here in the early 4th century A.D. Around this nucleus, a large basilica with three naves developed. Furthermore, a Roman temple and theatre at the site of Glavicine.
*Associated fieldwork:* In 1928 E. Dyggve excavated the Roman amphitheatre at Salona, and from 1929-1932 he functioned as technical conservator at the Archaeological Museum in Split, continued his research in several places at Salona and collaborated with Yugoslavian archaeologists in excavations at numerous other locations (the Medieval church of St. Mary at Nin, the Late Roman fortification of Cuker, a Medieval fortress at Keglavic, an early Christian church at Crkvina, at a monastery at Rizinice, an early Croatian church at Gornji Muc, an early Christian church at Glamoc, a monastery at the site of Suplja crkva, the early Croatian church of St. Peter at Priko.
*Bibliography:* E. Dyggve, *Recherches à Salone publié aux frais de la Fondation Rask-Ørsted* I. Copenhagen 1928; E. Dyggve, *Recherches à Salone publié aux frais de la Fondation Rask-Ørsted* II. Copenhagen 1933. For a comprehensive bibliography see A. Duplancic, The Dalmatica of Ejnar Dyggve, *Vjesnik za archeologiju i historiju Dalmatinsku* 80, 1987, 131-137.

## Turkey and Cyprus

7. *Excavations at the Mausoleum at Halikarnassos, Turkey (1966-1967; 1970; 1972-1973; 1974; 1976).*
*Direction:* Kr. Jeppesen, the University of Aarhus.
*Architect:* Kr. Jeppesen and K. Kjeldsen.
*Financial support:* The Carlsberg Foundation. The Research Foundation of Aarhus University and the Trustees of the British Museum supplied supplementary grants in 1972/73 and 1976 respectively.
*Goal:* To ascertain the full extent of the Mausoleum and its role in the ancient city and to find architectural remains and sculpture from the monument, one of the seven wonders of the ancient world, which had been missed in C.T. Newton's and A. Biliotti's excavation campaigns at the site in 1856/1858 and 1865.
*Result:* The dimensions of the terrace on which the Mausoleum was built were ascertained, and a large number of architectural fragments were unearthed, which have made it possible to attempt a more accurate reconstruction of the monument than previously possible. The burial chamber of the Mausoleum and remains of precious gifts was discovered, and a rich sacrifice consisting of slaughtered domestic animals was located in front of the entrance to the chamber.
*Associated fieldwork:* In 1978 a member of the expedition, Poul Pedersen, investigated the topography of the city of Halikarnassos.
*Bibliography:* K. Jeppesen, Explorations at Halicarnassus. Excavations at the Site of the Mausoleum, *ActaArch* 38, 1967, 29-58; K. Jeppesen & J. Zahle, Investigations on the Site of the Mausoleum, *AJA* 79, 1975, 67-79; K. Jeppesen & F. Højlund & K. Aaris-Sørensen, *The Maussolleion at Halikarnassos 1, The Sacrificial Deposit*. Copenhagen 1981 (with bibliography p. 20); P. Pedersen, Zwei ornamentierte Säulenhälse aus Halikarnassos, JdI 98, 1983, 87-121; K. Jeppesen & A. Luttrel, *The Maussolleion at Halikarnassos 2, The Written Sources and their Archaeological Background*. Aarhus 1986 (with bibliography p. 6). P. Pedersen, Town-planning in Halicarnassus and Rhodes, in: S. Dietz & I. Papachristodoulou eds., *Archaeology in the Dodecanese*. Copenhagen 1988, 98-103; P. Pedersen, Two Ionic buildings in Halicarnassus, *Arastirma Sonuclari Toplantisi* 1988, 359-368; P. Pedersen, *The Maussolleion at Halikarnassos 3, The Maussolleion Terrasse and Accessory Structures*, Aarhus 1991.

8. *Investigations and surveys in Lycia, Turkey (1973, 1974 and 1976).*
*Direction:* J. Zahle and Kj. Kjeldsen.

*Architect:* Kj. Kjeldsen.
*Financial support:* The Carlsberg Foundation and the New Carlsberg Foundation.
*Goal:* To record Lycian rock-cut tombs and reliefs, their distribution and architecture from the 6th to the 4th century B.C.
*Result:* A first gazetteer of about 1000 Lycian tombs and 85 reliefs was compiled. New sites, tombs and inscriptions were found. The different building constructions imitated in the tombs were illuminated and discussed in detail.
*Bibliography:* J. Zahle, Archaic Tumulus Tombs in Central Lycia (Phellos), Acta Arch 46, 1975, 77-94; K. Kjeldsen & J. Zahle, Lykische Graber, Ein vorlaufiger Bericht, AA 1975, 312-350; K. Kjeldsen & J. Zahle, A Dynastic Tomb in Central Lycia, Acta Arch 47, 1976, 29-46; J. Zahle, Lykische Felsgraber mit Reliefs aus dem 4. Jahrhundert v. Chr. Neue und alte Funde, *JdI* 94, 1979, 245-346; J. Zahle, Lycian Tombs and Lycian Cities, *Actes du colloque sur la Lycie antique, Bibliothèque de l'Institut français d'etudes anatoliennes d'Istanbul* 27, 1980, 37-49; J. Zahle, *Arkæologiske studier i lykiske klippegrave og deres relieffer. Sociale og religiøse aspekter.* Copenhagen 1983 (with a summary in German).

*9. Kouklia/Palaepaphos, Cyprus (1979-1980; 1983-1984; 1986).*
*Direction:* D. Rupp, Brock University and L.W. Sørensen.
*Financial support:* The project was financed by Canadian sources; the Carlsberg Foundation supplied funds for L.W. Sørensen in connection with her study of the Iron Age pottery, and the Danish Research Council for the Humanities has supported Danish students participating in the project.
*Goal:* To investigate the changing settlement patterns in the area surrounding Kouklia.
*Result:* the survey was centered on the areas surrounding the Ezousas, Dhiarizos and Xero rivers and the coastal plain between Paphos and Kouklia. The finds showed that Ezousas drainage was of major importance from the aceramic period onward, whereas the Xero river appears not to have been settled until the Late Geometric period. The documentation from the Classical period appeared to be scarce, but a dramatic growth in the number of sites can be evidenced in the Hellenistic and Early Roman periods.
*Bibliography:* D. W. Rupp, L. W. Sørensen, R. H. King & W. A. Fox, Canadian Palaipaphos (Cyprus) Survey Project: Second Preliminary Report, 1980-1982, *JFldA* 11, 1984, 134 (with bibliography); L. W. Sørensen, Canadian Palaepaphos Survey Project: Preliminary Report of the 1980 Ceramic Finds, *RDAC* 1983, 283 – 29; D. M. Rupp, L. W. Sørensen, J. Lund, R. H. King, W. A. Fox, T. E. Gregory & S. T. Stewart, The Canadian Palaipaphos (Cyprus) Survey Project, Third Preliminary Report,1983-1985, *ActaArch* 57 1986, 27-45; L. W. Sørensen, M. Korsholm, P. Guldager, J. Lund & T. Gregory, Canadian Palaepaphos Survey Project, Second preliminary report of the ceramic finds 1982-1983, *RDAC* 1987, 259-278.

*10. Agios Kononas (1989- ).*
*Direction:* L. and N. Hannestad, H.-E. Mathiesen and J. Fejfer, all from the Department of Classical Archaeology, University of Aarhus.
*Financial support:* The Carlsberg Foundation and the Research Foundation of Aarhus University; the Carlsberg breweries on Cyprus.
*Goal and result:* See the paper referred to below.
*Bibliography:* J. Fejfer, N. Hannestad & H. E. Mathiesen, The Danish Archaeological Excavations at Ayios Kononas, Cyprus. A Preliminary Report of the First Season of Work (1989), in this volume.

## The Levantine Coast and Adjacent Areas

*11. Excavations and investigations in Palmyra, Syria (1924 and 1925).*
*Direction:* H. Ingholt.
*Architects:* Ch. Christensen and J. Prip Møller.
*Financial support:* The Rask-Ørsted Foundation.
*Goal:* To conduct excavations of the subterranean tombs in the necropolis of Palmyra.

*Result:* The expedition discovered about fifty subterranean tombs, five of which were dated by inscriptions: The Tomb of 'Atenaten, built in 98 A.D. and with an exedra with painted Victories added in 229 A.D., the tomb of Julius Aurelius Malê from 109 A.D., the tomb of Malkû, built in 115 A.D., the tomb of Nasrallat from 141 A.D. and the tomb of Bar'â built in 186 A.D. These tombs constitute chronological fixed points for the associated sculptures, architectural details etc.
*Bibliography:* H. Ingholt, Five Dated Tombs from Palmyra, Berytus 2 1935, 57-120; H. Ingholt, Inscriptions and Sculptures from Palmyra, Berytus 3 1936, 83-128; H. Ingholt, Inscriptions and Sculptures from Palmyra, Berytus 5 1938, 93-140.

*12. Hama, Syria (1930-1938).*
*Direction:* H. Ingholt.
*Chief architect:* E. Fugmann.
*Financial support:* The Carlsberg Foundation.
*Goal:* To investigate the site, especially the town mound, of Hama, mentioned in the Old Testament, where inscriptions in so-called Hittite hieroglyphs had been found in 1812.
*Results:* The excavations documented the history of Hama from the Neolithic to the Islamic period. The most important evidence, from the Middle Bronze Age and Iron Age, pertains to Near Eastern rather than classical archaeology, but it should be mentioned that contacts with the Aegean Bronze Age civilizations are documented, for example by imported Mycenean and Cypriote pottery, and that such imports are also found in the Iron Age horizon (dated between ca. 1200 and 720 B.C.). Hama was devastated by the Assyrians in 720, providing a convenient terminus ante quem, and the site was more or less deserted until it was resettled in the 2nd century B.C. Substantial architectural remains were uncovered from the Hellenistic through the Roman periods, and the finds throw light on many aspects of daily life in a city in the Roman empire.
*Bibliography:* P. J. Riis, *Hama II 3, Les cimetières à crémation.* Copenhagen 1948; P. J. Riis, V. Poulsen & E. Hammerschaimb, *Hama IV 2, Les verreries et poteries médiévales.* Copenhagen 1957; E. Fugmann, *Hama II 1, L'architecture des périodes pré-hellénistiques.* Copenhagen 1958; P. J. Riis, *Temple, Church and Mosque.* Copenhagen 1965; G. Ploug, E. Oldenburg, E. Hammerschaimb, R. Thomsen & F. Løkkegaard, *Hama IV 3, Les petits objets médiévaux sauf les verreries et poteries.* Copenhagen 1967; A. Papanicolaou-Christensen, Ch. Friis Johansen, *Hama III 2, Les poteries hellénistiques et les terres sigillées orientales.* Copenhagen 1971; G. Ploug, *Hama III 1, The Graeco-Roman Town.* Copenhagen 1985; A. Papanicolaou-Christensen, R. Thomsen & G. Ploug, *Hama III 3, The Roman Pottery, the Hellenistic, Roman and Early Byzantine Lamps, Coins and Graves.* Copenhagen 1987; P.J. Riis, Ḥamā, Danske arkæologers udgravninger i Syrien 1930-38. Copenhagen 1987; P. Pentz, A medieval workshop for producing "Greek fire" grenades, Antiquity 62 1988, 89-93; P. J. Riis & M.-L. Buhl, *Hama II 2, Les objets de la période dite syro-hitite (Âge du Fer).* Copenhagen 1990; P. Pentz, *Hama IV 1, The Medieval Citadel and its Architecture,* forthcoming.

*13. Tall Sukas, Syria (1958-1960; 1962-1963).*
*Direction:* P. J. Riis.
*Chief architect:* E. Fugmann.
*Financial support:* The Carlsberg Foundation.
*Goal:* "a) To contribute towards a safer chronology of the Iron Age culture in Phoenicia, i.e. the period about 1200-500 B.C., b) To elucidate the relations between the Near East and Greece during the same period and thus checking the current Greek chronology, and c) To supplement the Danish archaeological collections ..." (Riis 1970, 10).
*Result:* Tall Sukas is situated on the coast of the Gabla plain, and the excavations revealed a sequence of habitation from the Neolithic period (the 7th or 6th millennium B.C.) to modern times. In the Late Bronze Age the town was in contact with Cyprus as well as Mycenean Greece, and in the following period H Greek pottery appeared, taken as a sign that Greeks had by now settled on the mound. This is followed by period G (Period of Greek Domination), which ended in a violent destruction at the beginning of the 5th century B.C. The site lay more or less depopulated until it was re-occupied about 380 B.C., in period F (Neo-Phoenician Period). New

building techniques indicate that the settlers were Phoenicians, which may have been dispatched from Arados. An earthquake, probably in 69 B.C., put an end to Sukas of period E (Hellenistic Period). The tell was uninhabited in the Roman Period (D), but revived briefly under the Crusaders.
*Associated fieldwork:* Minor excavations were carried out at Tall Daruk and 'Arab al-Milk and the Gabla plain was subjected to a topograpical investigation.
*Bibliography:* Riis 1970; G. Ploug, *Sūkās II. The Aegean, Corinthian and Eastern Greek Pottery and Terracottas.* Copenhagen 1973; H. Thrane, *Sūkās IV. A Middle Bronze Age Collective Grave on Tall Sūkās.* Copenhagen 1978; P.J. Riis, *Sūkās VI. The Graeco-Phoenician Cemetery and Sanctuary at the Southern Harbour.* Copenhagen 1979; E. Oldenburg & J. Rohweder, The Excavations at Tall Daruk (Usnu?) and 'Arab al-Mulk (Paltos). Copenhagen 1981. M.-L. Buhl, *Sūkās VII. The Near Eastern Pottery and Objects of Other Materials from the Upper Strata.* Copenhagen 1983; J. Lund, *Sūkās VIII. The Habitation Quarters.* Copenhagen 1986; P. J. Riis, Quelques problèmes de la topographie phénicienne: Usnu, Paltos, Pelléta et les ports de la région, in: P.-L. Gatier, B. Helly & J.-P. Rey-Coquais, *Géographie historique au Proche-Orient (Syrie, Phénicie, Arabie, grecques, romaines, byzantines).* Paris 1988, 315-324; J. Lund, The Northern Coastline of Syria in the Persian Period – A Survey of the Archaeological Evidence, *Transeuphratène* 2 1990, 13-36.

*14. Tall Sailun/Shilo, the West Bank (1926, 1929, 1932 and 1963).*
*Direction:* H. Kjær; in 1963: Sv Holm-Nielsen.
*Architects:* Ch. Christensen, Sv. Beck, C. G. Schultz.
*Financial support:* The excavation was funded by private means. The publication was financed by the H.P. Hjerl Hansen Memorial Foundation for Danish Palestine Research, the Rask-Ørsted Foundation, and the Research Council for the Humanities.
*Goal:* To document Biblical Shiloh.
*Result:* The finds show that the site was settled from the Chalcolithic/Early Bronze Age period on; the Iron Age Periods (especially Iron Age II) were well documented in the pottery finds. A destruction seems to have occurred in the latter part of the 8th century and again in the first part of the 6th century. The site was re-occupied in Late Hellenistic times and architectural remains from the Roman Period were in evidence. The town is believed to have expanded in the Byzantine period, when two churches, the so-called pilgrim's church and a basilica, were constructed.
*Bibliography:* M.-L. Buhl & S. Holm-Nielsen, *Shiloh, The Danish Excavations at Tall Sailūn, Palestine* in 1926, 1929, 1932, and 1963. Copenhagen 1969; F. G. Andersen, *Shiloh, The Danish Excavations at Tall Sailūn, Palestine in 1926, 1929, 1932 and 1963, II, The Remains from the Hellenistic to the Mamlūk Periods.* Copenhagen 1985.

*15. Umm Queis, Jordania (1977-1983).*
*Direction:* Sv. Holm-Nielsen, the University of Copenhagen. The Danish excavation is part of an international project.
*Financial support:* The Danish Palestinian Exploration Fund.
*Goal:* To document the archaeology of ancient Gadara.
*Result:* The Danish excavations centered around a Roman bath constructed in the 4th century A.D. It underwent several building phases before it became defunct in the Byzantine period. The western part of the structure was rebuilt as a private dwelling after the Arabic conquest of the area in 636 A.D. This phase ended in an earthquake in 746 A.D. after which the structure was abandoned.
*Bibliography:* F.G. Andersen & J. Strange, Bericht über drei Sondagen in Umm Qes, Jordanien im Herbst 1983, *Zeitschrift des Deutschen Palästina-Vereins* 103 1987, 78-100; S. Holm Nielsen, I. Nielsen & F.G. Andersen, The Excavation of Byzantine Baths in Umm Qeis, *Annual of the Department of Antiquities of Jordan* 30 1986, 219-232.

*16. Ma'agan Michael, Israel (1984).*
*Direction:* Th. Schiøler and M. Artzy.

*Architect:* A. Billund.
*Financial support:* The Carlsberg Foundation.
*Goal:* To investigate and date the remains of watermills built into a Roman gravity dam north of Caesarea Maritima.
*Result:* One of the mills could be referred to the Roman period. A C14 analysis of its mortar yielded the date: 345-380 A.D. The other mills were hardly more than two hundred years old.
*Bibliography:* M. Artzy & Th. Schiøler, Dæmningen ved kibbutzen Ma'agan Michael i Israel, in: *Museum Tusculanum* 56 1984-1986, 331-336 (with an English summary).

## Iran and the Persian Gulf

*17. Survey in the Hulailan valley, Luristan, Iran (1973)*
*Direction:* P. Mortensen, the Institute of Prehistory and Ethnography at the University of Aarhus in collaboration with the Iranian Center for Archaeological Research.
*Financial support:* The Carlsberg Foundation and the Iranian Center for Archaeological Research.
*Goal:* To determine the location of archaeological sites in the Hulailan valley and to conduct a few sondages aimed at the study of the changing settlement patterns in the Zagros mountains, especially in prehistoric times.
*Result:* Besides the studies in prehistoric archaeology material was gathered from the Hellenistic, Parthian, Sassanian and Islamic periods: settlements, burial grounds, remains of road systems etc. were identified and mapped.
*Bibliography:* P. Mortensen, A Survey of Prehistoric Settlements in Northern Luristan, *Acta Arch* 45, 1974, 1-47; E. Haerinck, Four Stucco-fragments from the Hulailan Valley (Luristan, Pish-i Kuh, Iran), *IrAnt* 12 1977, 167-173; I. D. Mortensen & P. Mortensen, On the Origin of Nomadism in Northern Luristan, in: *Archaeologica Iranica et Orientalis. Miscellanea in Honorem Louis Vanden Berghe.* Gent 1989, 929-952.

*18. Excavations at Ras al Qala'a, Bahrain (1953-1954; 1955-1960; 1961-1962; 1962-1963; 1964-1965; 1970 and 1978).*
*Direction:* P. V. Glob and T. G. Bibby of the Prehistoric Museum, Aarhus.
*Financial support:* The excavations were sponsored by the Government of Bahrain, the Bahrain Petroleum Company. Thanks to a grant by the Carlsberg Foundation the results are now being prepared for a final publication by H. Hellmuth Andersen and Fl. Højlund.
*Goal:* To investigate the metropolis of Bahrain in ancient times.
*Result:* Widespread settlement remains were uncovered dating i.a. from the Hellenistic period.
*Bibliography:* Annual excavation reports in English in the Danish journal *Kuml*; G. Bibby, *Looking for Dilmun.* New York 1969; O. Mørkholm, A Hellenistic coin hoard from Bahrain, *Kuml* 1972, 183-202.

*19. Excavations at the island of Failaka/Ikaros, Kuwait (1958-1963).*
*Direction:* Aa. Roussell and E. Albrechtsen (1958-59), K. Jeppesen, the Institute of Classical Archaeology at the University of Aarhus and P. Kjærum of the Prehistoric Museum, Aarhus (1960-1963).
*Financial support:* The excavations were sponsored by the government of Kuwait; the publications were supported by the Carlsberg Foundation.
*Goal:* The work began following an invitation from the government of Kuwait to P.V. Glob; the goal was to enlarge our knowledge of the archaeology of Failaka.
*Result:* A Greek fortified sanctuary with two temples was excavated at Tell Sa'aid (site F 5). The central temple is thought to have been constructed early in the 3rd century B.C. by one of Alexander the Great's successors. The enclosed area seems gradually to have been built over by private dwellings, the earliest of which may be dated from coin finds to about 200 B.C. An important Greek inscription dated to 73 (?) B.C. was found here giving the ancient name of Failaka as Ikaros. At another site (F 4) a workshop for the manufacture of terracotta figurines was unearthed.
*Bibliography:* H.-E. Mathiesen, *Danish Archaeological Investigations on Failaka, Kuwait. Ikaros,*

## DANES OVERSEAS – A SHORT HISTORY

*The Hellenistic Settlements 1, The Terracotta Figurines.* Copenhagen 1982; L. Hannestad, *Danish Archaeological Investigations on Failaka, Kuwait. Ikaros, The Hellenistic Settlements 2, The Hellenistic Pottery.* Aarhus 1983; K. Jeppesen, *Danish Archaeological Investigations on Failaka, Kuwait. Ikaros, The Hellenistic Settlements 3, The Sacred Enclosure in the Early Hellenistic Period.* Aarhus 1990.

20. *Survey and excavations in Saudi Arabia (1968).*
*Direction:* T. G. Bibby, The Prehistoric Museum, Aarhus.
*Financial support:* The Arabian American Oil Company.
*Goal:* To investigate the prehistory of Saudi Arabia.
*Result:* A large number of burials and settlements were put on the map; a sounding was dug in Hellenistic Thaj.
*Bibliography:* T.G. Bibby, *Preliminary Survey in East Arabia 1968.* Copenhagen 1973.

21. *Excavations at ed-Dur, The United Emirates (1987-1989).*
*Direction:* The Danish excavations were part of an international undertaking in which Scotland, Belgium and France took part. The leader of the Danish team was D. Potts, the Carsten Niebuhr Institute of the University of Copenhagen.
*Architect:* T. Neble.
*Financial support:* The Danish Research Council for the Humanities.
*Goal:* To investigate the comparatively unknown history of the area in the Roman period.
*Result:* The Danish expedition uncovered several small, rectangular buildings in a scattered settlement covering an area of ca. 1.5 x 4 km 2. Most of the buildings could be dated to the 1st century A.D. on the basis of finds of Roman pillar molded glass bowls and Parthian as well as Mesopotamian pottery. In the area a number of semi-subterranean tombs were excavated; in one of these a Roman glass beaker was found.
*Bibliography:* D. T. Potts, The Danish Excavations, *Mesopotamia* 34 1989, 13-27.

## Egypt and Tunisia

22. *Excavations at Mons Claudianus, Egypt (1987-).*
*Direction:* An international Committee, of which the Danish member is the papyrologist A. Bülow Jacobsen, University of Copenhagen.
*Financial support:* The funding was international. From Danish sources: the Foundation of Queen Margrethe and Prince Henrik, the Danish Research Council for the Humanities.
*Goal:* To investigate a refuse heap from a complex of buildings near the granite quarry at "Mons Claudianus" – especially in the hope of finding ostraca.
*Result:* Walls from two building phases were uncovered and in the associated fill numerous finds were made, of which the more than 4000 ostraca in Greek (and about 100 in Latin) are of exceptional interest. Some of the inscriptions are dated to the period between 106 and 111 A.D., thus confirming a period of use for the quarries which had been suspected earlier. However, it is clear that the quarry continued to be used after the reign of Trajan. Some of the inscriptions were meant to identify the content of the vessels on which they were written, others were added on sherds of broken pots. The latter group comprises i.a. private letters or texts dealing with the administration of the quarry: lists of names of workmen, the distribution of supplies etc. When the material is fully studied it will reveal a wealth of information about the organization of work (there is as yet little or no evidence of slaves working in the quarry) and about the military units present at the site. Among the many other interesting find groups is an important group of textiles.
*Bibliography:* J. Bingen, Première campagne de fouille au Mons Claudianus. Rapport Préliminaire. Avec une Annexe par Bodil Mortensen, Le secteur I, *Bulletin de l'Institut francais d'archéologie orientale* 87 1987, 52-54; A. Bülow-Jacobsen, Mons Claudianus. Roman Granite-Quarry and Station on the Road to the Red Sea, *ActaHyp* 1 1988, 159-165. L. Bender Jørgensen, Textiles from Mons Claudianus. A Preliminary Report, in this volume.

*23. Excavations at Carthage (1975, 1977, 1978, 1981, 1984).*
*Direction:* S. Dietz, the Department of Near Eastern and Classical Antiquities at the Danish National Museum.
*Architect:* E. Andersen.
*Financial support:* The Danish Research Council for the Humanities, the Carlsberg Foundation, the Tuborg Foundation, the Generalkonsul G. Enbom Foundation and Simon Spies.
*Goal:* In connection with the UNESCO-project "Pour Sauver Carthage" excavations were conducted on a site previously dug by the Dane C.T. Falbe in 1838, who had found a mosaic depicting a Nereid, which is now kept in the Danish National Museum. The purpose was to ascertain the context of this find.
*Result:* The excavation revealed a sequence of archaeological horizons beginning with a destruction layer associated with the sack of Carthage by the Romans in 146 B.C. In the 1st century A.D. the area was reoccupied as part of Roman Carthage and several buildings, presumably seaside villas were constructed here. In the Vandal Period (439 to 533 A.D.) occupation had ceased and several chambers were re-used as communal tombs. In the Byzantine period the area was reoccupied, but it fell into disuse after the Arab conquest.
*Bibliography:* S. Trolle, Danemark, *CEDAC Carthage, Bulletin* 1 1978, 9; S. Dietz & S. Trolle (eds.), *Premier rapport préliminaire sur les Fouilles Danoises à Carthage.* Copenhagen 1979; S. Dietz, Fouilles Danoises à Carthage 1975-1984, *Cahiers des Études Anciennes* XVI 1984, 107-118; Lund 1986; E. Poulsen, Tombs of the IVth-Vth Centuries AD in the Danish Sector at Carthage, *Cahiers des Études Anciennes* XVIII 1986, 141-160; J. Lund, Two Late Punic Amphora Stamps from the Danish Excavations at Carthage, *Studia Phoenicia* VI, 1988, 101-112; F.O. Hvidberg-Hansen, The Interpretation of Two Late Punic Amphora Stamps from Carthage, *Studia Phoenicia* VI 1988, 113-118.

*24. Survey and excavations in the Segermes-region, Tunisia (1984, 1987-1989).*
*Direction:* The project is the result of a collaboration between the Institut d'Art et Archéologie de Tunisie and Danish archeologists and historians. The Danish part of the project was directed by S. Dietz of the Danish National Museum, E. Poulsen as well as by H. Tvarnø and P. Ørsted from the Institutes of History at the Universities of Odense and Copenhagen.
*Architects:* C. Gerner Hansen, T. Neble, Th. Kampmann.
*Financial support:* The Carlsberg Foundation and the Danish Research Council for the Humanities; Simon Spies.
*Goal:* The purpose of the project was to investigate the interrelationship between the Roman municipium Segermes and its surrounding area.
*Result:* A survey was carried out, supplemented with excavations at selected spots, and architects drew plans of the ancient structures which were encountered. As a result of this work, it has been established that the Segermes region was uninhabited until the 4th/3rd century B.C., when it was drawn into the Punic sphere of influence. Some of the Punic sites -including presumably Segermes itself – survived into the Roman period. The staple agricultural produce of the surrounding land seems to have been olive and grain.
*Bibliography:* Lund & Sørensen 1988; F. Bejaoui & P. Pentz , En nyfunden basilika i Nordafrika, *ArbejdsmarkKøb* 1990, 47-60; J. Carlsen & H. Tvarnø, The Segermes Valley Archaeological Survey (Region of Zaghouan). An Interim Report, in: *L'Africa romana* 7. Sassari 1990, 803-813.

## Italy
*25. Excavations at the Baths of Trajan, Rome, Italy (1970, 1981-1983).*
*Direction:* K. de Fine Licht.
*Architect:* K. de Fine Licht.
*Financial support:* The Carlsberg Foundation and the Comune di Roma.
*Goal:* To investigate the cistern called Sette Sale in order to throw light on the use and disposition of the area, which had earlier been a part of the Domus Aurea.
*Result:* Two vaulted corridors along the western and eastern sides of the cistern excavated as was one wing of a four-winged complex. The corridor contained a large amount of potsherds and other

finds showing that it had become defunct in the 6th century A.D. indicating that the Baths had by then ceased to function.
*Bibliography:* K. de Fine Licht, Untersuchungen an den Trajansthermen zu Rom, *ARID 7. Suppl.* 1974; K. de Fine Licht, Marginalia on Trajan's Baths in Rome, in: *Studia romana in honorem Petri Krarup.* Odense 1976, 87-95; K. de Fine Licht, Scavi alle Sette Sale, *ARID 10; Suppl.* 1983, 186-202; K. de Fine Licht, Untersuchungen zu den Trajansthermen zu Rom II: Sette Sale, *ARID 19 Suppl.* 1990.

*26. Excavations at Monte Becco, Etruria, Italy (1971-1972, 1976-1977).*
*Direction:* I. Strøm, the University of Odense (in collaboration with the Danish Academy at Rome).
*Chief architect:* J. Fogh.
*Financial support:* The Danish Research Council for the Humanities, the Carlsberg Foundation, the University of Odense, Queen Ingrid, the Foundation of Queen Margrethe and Prince Henrik and various private foundations.
*Goal:* To clarify the archaeological history of the site.
*Result:* Three occupational phases were detected: 1) from 700 B.C. to ca. 480 B.C., 2) from ca. 425 B.C. to ca. 300 B.C. and 3) about 300 B.C. The finds reflected the changing conditions of life in a small rural community at the outskirts of the areas of the major Etruscan cities Vulci and Volsinii. The finds did not support a previous hypothesis identifying Monte Becco with Fanum Voltumnae.
*Bibliography:* I. Strøm, *ARepLondon* 1979-1980, 64.

*27. Southern Etruria, Investigations along Via Clodia, Italy (1972-1974).*
*Direction:* J. E. Skydsgaard, N. M. Saxtorph and M. Poulsen, the Institute of History at the University of Copenhagen.
*Financial support:* The Danish Research Council for the Humanities.
*Goal:* To map the course of the Via Clodia.
*Result:* The investigation showed the probable course of the road from Norchia via the Rocca di Rispampani and Tuscania further towards the north.
*Bibliography:* J. E. Skydsgaard, N. M. Saxtorph & M. Poulsen, Ancient and Modern Road-Systems near Tuscania, Continuity or Discontinuity, *ARID* 8, 1977, 19-38.

*28. Excavations at Monte Cugno/Ficana, Latium, Italy (1976-1980, 1983).*
*Direction:* The excavations were carried out as a joint Italian-Scandinavian project directed by V. Santa Maria Scrinari, Soprintendente alle Antichità di Ostia. The Danish fieldwork was directed by T. Fischer-Hansen, the Danish Academy in Rome.
*Architects:* G. Ahlgreen-Ussing and S. Karlsson.
*Financial support:* The Nordic Council for the Humanities, the Danish Research Council for the Humanities and the Soprintendenza archeologica di Ostia. The Carlsberg Foundation and the Bikuben Foundation have helped to cover the costs of the publication.
*Goal:* To throw light on the history of the settlement of Monte Cugno, which is identified as ancient Ficana, especially the process of urbanization and the circumstances surrounding the abandonment of the site.
*Result:* Material was found spanning the period from the Late Bronze Age to the Roman Empire; however, the larger part of the finds date from the 8th to the 6th centuries B.C. Remains of an impressive defense system with an agger and groups of huts of various sizes and types could be referred to the older settlement phase; in the 7th century B.C., rectangular houses with tiled roofs were built on stone foundations. In the Republican period a large area was included in a fortress with walls of ashlar blocks.
*Bibliography: Ficana – una pietra miliare sulla strada per Roma.* Roma 1981 (with bibliography); C. Thune Malmgren, Ficana in: *Enea nel Lazio, archeologia e mito.* Rome 1981, 102-104; A. Rathje, A Banquet Service from the Latin City of Ficana, *ARID* 12, 1983, 7-29; M. Cataldi, Ficana: campagne di scavo 1980-1983, *QuadAEI* 8, 1984, 91-97; G. Algreen-Ussing & T. Fischer-

Hansen, Ficana, le saline e le vie della regione bassa del Tevere, *QuadAEI* 11, 1985, 65-71; J. Rasmus Brandt, Ficana. Alcune osservazioni su capanne e fosse, *QuadSoprArchLazio* 1 1988, 12-28; Tobias Fischer-Hansen con la collobarazione di Gregers Algreen-Ussing e con un contributo di Carlo Pavolini, *Scavi di Ficana I. Topografia Generale.* Roma 1990.

*29. Excavations at La Giostra, Italy (1976-1978).*
*Direction:* M. Moltesen, the Danish Academy in Rome.
*Financial support:* The Danish Research Council for the Humanities.
*Goal:* To carry out a thorough examination of the town wall and to draw a plan of the buildings located within it.
*Result:* The ceramic material from the site was extremely homogeneous and could be dated between 350 and 250 B.C. The investigations revealed that we are dealing with a military stronghold constructed in connection with the expansion of Rome to the south at the time of the Samnite wars.
*Bibliography:* L. Quilici, Tellenae in: *QuadTopAnt* I, 1964, 33-40; M. Moltesen, La Giostra – Tellenae?, *QuadAEI* 1, 1977, 60-63; J. Rasmus Brandt, La Giostra – un esempio di urbanistica medio-republicana?, *QuadAEI* 3, 1979, 50-53; M. Moltesen, La Giostra, *NSc* XXXIV, 1980 (1981), 51-58.

*30. Excavations at Monte Castello di Procchio, Elba, Italy (1977-1986).*
*Direction:* A. Maggiani and M. Nielsen.
*Financial support:* The excavation was supported by Italian funds.
*Goal:* To investigate an Etruscan fortress on the island of Elba.
*Result:* A square building complex dating from about 300 B.C. was uncovered. A destruction layer yielded rich finds of pottery throwing light on the interaction between Elba and the surrounding areas.
*Bibliography:* A. Maggiani, in: *L'Elba preromana.* Pisa 1979, 5-29; A. Maggiani, in: *L'Etruria Mineraria, Atti del XII Convegno di Studi Etruschi e Italici,* Firenze 1981, 173-192; A. Maggiani, ie 1981, 173-192; A. Maggiani, in: *Studi e Materiali* 5 1982, 363; M. Cristofani, in: *StEtr* 51 1983, 214 no. 18; A. Maggiani, *StEtr* 51 1983, 433; G. Camporeale ed., *L'Etruria Mineraria,* Portoferraio 1985, 24 and 118; A. Giovannini, Tipologia strutturale e costruttiva delle fortezze d'altura, *Studi Classici e Orientali* 35 1985, 283-306.

*31. Excavations at the Baths of Mithras, Ostia, Italy (1978).*
*Direction:* Th. Schiøler.
*Financial support:* The Carlsberg Foundation.
*Goal:* To investigate the building history of the Baths.
*Result:* I. Nielsen and Th. Schiøler established that the baths were constructed at the time of Hadrian and functioned until the early 4th century A.D.
*Bibliography:* I. Nielsen & Th. Schiøler, The Water System in the Baths of Mithras in Ostia, *ARID* 9, 1980, 149-159.

*32. Excavations in the Villa Adriana, Tivoli, Italy (1978; 1980).*
*Direction:* N. Hannestad, the University of Aarhus.
*Architect:* Kj. Kjeldsen.
*Financial support:* The Danish Research Council for the Humanities.
*Goal:* To test a hypothesis of H. Kähler, that the tomb of Antinoos was to be sought at the western side of the so-called Canopus basin in Hadrian's villa.
*Result:* The sounding revealed that a smaller structure had previously been built into the slope, but that it had been torn down in Late Antiquity and replaced by a primitive garden. No evidence was found to support Kähler's hypothesis.
*Bibliography:* N. Hannestad, Über das Grab des Antinoos, *ARID* 11 1982, 69-108.

*33. Excavations at the Baths of Caracalla, Rome, Italy (1980).*
*Direction:* Th. Schiøler and Ö. Wikander, Dept. of Classics, the University of Lund.
*Financial support:* The Danish Research Council for the Humanities.
*Goal:* To excavate an ancient water mill located in the Baths of Caracalla.
*Result:* The investigation showed that the mill was part of the original Baths, constructed between 212 A.D. and 235 A.D.; a conflagration occurred soon after its construction. The mill was reconstructed in the last quarter of the 3rd century A.D. and ceased function in the 5th century A.D.
*Bibliography:* Th. Schiøler & Ö. Wikander, A Roman Water-mill in the Baths of Caracalla, *OpRom* 14, 1983, 47-64.

*34. Excavations at the Temple of Castor and Pollux, Rome, Italy (1983-1985 and 1987).*
*Direction:* Archaeologists from Denmark, Sweden, Norway and Finland collaborated in the project; the overall leader was C. Nylander, Director of the Swedish Institute, Rome. The Danish effort was directed by J. Zahle and I. Nielsen.
*Architects:* Cl. Persson and Kj. Aage Nielson.
*Financial support:* The Carlsberg Foundation, the Soprintendenza archaeologica di Roma.
*Goal:* To examine the temple in its context, to analyze the architecture and establish the chronological phases as a basis for restoring and preserving the building.
*Result:* The excavations carried out by Danish archaeologists in the area of the temple showed that we are dealing with a sequence of three temples superimposed on one another: the oldest one dates from 484 B.C., the middle one from 117 B.C. and the latest one from the time of the emperor Augustus: 6 A.D. These three main phases were known from ancient texts and their dating was confirmed by the excavation. In excavation trenches along the eastern side of the temple an intact stratigraphy from the 7th century B.C. to the time of Augustus was encountered. Furthermore, the excavations have shown, that the plans of the three temples were more similar than hitherto believed.
*Associated fieldwork:* Elisabeth Nedergaard investigated and measured the nearby foundations of the Triumphal arch of Augustus. As a result, it now seems clear that the remains can be dated between 29 B.C. and 6 A.D. and that they had not been built on top of the so-called Actium arch from 30 B.C., as had previously been believed.
*Bibliography:* I. Nielsen & J. Zahle, The Temple of Castor and Pollux on the Forum Romanum. A Preliminary Report on the Scandinavian Excavations 1983-1985 (I), *ActaArch* 56 1985, 1-29; P. Guldager & K. Slej, Il tempio di Castore e Polluce, *Archeologia Viva* April 1986, 24-37; I. Nielsen, Ultime indagini al tempio dei Castori (con appendice di C. Grønne), *QuadAEI* 14 1987, 83-87; S. Sande & J. Zahle, Der Tempel der Dioskuren auf dem Forum Romanum, in: *Kaiser Augustus und die verlorene Republik*. Berlin 1988, 213-224; E. Nedergaard, Zur Problematik der Augustusbögen auf dem Forum Romanum, *op. cit.*, 224-239; eadem, Nuove indagini sull'arco di Augusto nel Foro Romano, *QuadAEI* 16 1988, 37-43; B. Poulsen & C. Grønne, Ricerche nel Vicus Tuscus lungo il lato ovest del Tempio dei Castori, *QuadAEI* 16 1988, 27-31; I. Nielsen, The Temple of Castor and Pollux on the Forum Romanum, A Preliminary Report on the Scandinavian Excavations 1983-87 (II), *ActaArch* 59 1988, 1-14; B. Ginge & M. Becker & P. Guldager, Of Roman Extraction, *Archaeology* 42 1989, 34-37; K. Slej, in this volume; C. Grønne, Fragments of Architectural Terracottas from the First Temple of Castor and Pollux on the Forum Romanum. A Preliminary Report, *ARID* 19 1990, 105-117; I. Nielsen, The Forum Paving and the Temple of Castor and Pollux, *ARID* 19 1990, 89-104.

*35. Excavations at Pontecagnano, Italy (1987, 1989, 1990).*
*Direction:* I. Strøm, The Institute of Prehistoric and Classical Archaeology at the University of Copenhagen.
*Financial support:* The Carlsberg Foundation.
*Goal:* To excavate a local settlement in Etruscan Campania, which judging from the associated cemeteries was in use from the 9th to the 4th century B C., and to study the urban development of a local town in South Italy.

*Result:* Below a level of destruction from the Roman Imperial period remains of walls were found, and it has proved possible to document the layout of the streets and the town plan from the 4th to the 3rd century B.C.; finds of *graffiti* show that the inhabitants were Greek-speaking. Furthermore, remains were uncovered of a street level from early Augustan times. Finds of pottery dated to the 8th to 6th centuries B.C. have raised hopes of uncovering the habitation layers from which this material originates.

*Associated fieldwork:* Four students from the Institute of Prehistoric and Classical Archaeology at the University of Copenhagen: H. Horsnæs, S. Bernth, M. von Mehren and U. Helvig Petersen are engaged in the publication of 55 tombs from the 7th to the 4th centuries B.C. with financial support from the University of Copenhagen and private foundations. H. Horsnæs is furthermore working on the publication of a cemetery at Arenosola.

*Bibliography:* H. Horsnæs, in this volume.

## NOTES

1. This paper is dedicated to Mr. Poul Christensen, former draughtsman at the Institute of Prehistoric and Classical Archaeology at the University of Copenhagen, whose skill is surpassed only by his acute critical sense.
2. P.O. Brøndsted (see infra) is often credited with having discovered about 1828 that the heads in question originate from the Parthenon. However, the connection had been made earlier by the German art critic C.F. v. Rumohr and published in the journal *Kunst-Blatt* 3.11 1825, and it seems more than likely that Brøndsted had read this paper; at any rate he was the first to publish the two heads in Copenhagen and to document their relationship with the Parthenon in full (ROHDE 1985, 204-209).
3. The preserved parts of P.O Brøndsted's diaries, letters and other material, to which reference is made in the following, are kept at the Royal Library of Copenhagen and the Royal State Archives. It is to be hoped that this treasure trove of information about the early exploration of Greece will soon be made fully public also for a non-Danish audience.
4. If Walsingham was an assumed name, then it may be guessed that it was chosen in honour of Sir Francis Walsingham, Elizabeth I's secretary of state, who "ran and largely financed a small, underpaid secret service" (ANDREW 1986, 21).
5. Numbers in brackets refer to the catalogue of sites in the appendix.
6. With prehistorians and near eastern archaeologists, classical philologists, historians, art historians, theologians, papyrologists, architects – not to speak of palaeobotanists, geologists, cultural geographers and other representatives of the natural sciences.

## BIBLIOGRAPHY

| | |
|---|---|
| ANDREASEN, Ø.1935 | Kardinal Borgia og de danske i Rom, in: L. Bobé ed., *Rom og Danmark gennem tiderne*. København, 268-314. |
| – ed. 1967 | *Georg Zoëga: Briefe und Dokumente*. Copenhagen. |
| ANDREW, Ch. 1986 | *Secret Service, The Making of the British Intelligence Community*. London. |
| *Athènes* 1985 | *Athènes Affaire Européenne, du 12 octobre au 2 décembre 1985 au Zappeion Megaron à Athènes*. Athènes. |
| BENDTSEN, M. 1990 | The Acropolis and the Athenian City-Plan, *ActaHyp* 2, 209-218. |
| BERGHAUS, P. & SCHRECKENBERG, Ch. 1983 | *Katalogteil, in: Der Archäologe, Graphische Bildnisse aus dem Porträtarchiv Diepenbroick*. Münster, 129-340. |

| | |
|---|---|
| BERNAL, M. 1987 | *Black Athena, The Afroasiatic Roots of Classical Civilization, Volume 1: The Fabrication of Ancient Greece 1785-1985.* London. |
| BOARDMAN, J. 1988 | Classical archaeology: whence and wither, *Archaeology* 62, 795-797. |
| BOBÉ L. 1933 | *Moritz Hartmann MDCLVI-MDCXCV, Dansk og Venetiansk Orlogskaptajn, Ridder af San Marco og Gouverneur i Trankebar. Danmarks forbindelser med republikken Venedig.* Copenhagen. |
| BRACKEN, C.P. 1975 | *Antiquities Acquired, The Spoliation of Greece.* London. |
| BREITENSTEIN, N. 1951 | Christian VIII's Vasecabinet, in: *Antik-Cabinettet 1851, udgivet i hundredaaret af Nationalmuseet.* Copenhagen, 57-176. |
| BRØNDSTED, P.O. 1826 | *Reisen und Untersuchungen in Griechenland, nebst Darstellung und Erklärung vieler neuentdekten Denkmäler Griechischen Styls,* I. Stuttgart and Paris. |
| – 1830 | *Reisen und Untersuchungen in Griechenland, nebst Darstellung, und Erklärung vieler neuentdekten Denkmäler Griechischen Styls,* II. Stuttgart and Paris. |
| – 1844 | *Reise i Grækenland* 1-2. Copenhagen. |
| – 1861 | Udgravningen af Templet ved Phigalia. Efter P.O. Brøndsteds uudgivne Afhandling, ved M. Hammerich, *Nordisk Universitets-Tidsskrift* 7.1, 65-86. |
| BUCAILLE, R. & PESEZ, J.-M. 1978 | s.v. cultura materiale in: *Einaudi Enciclopedia* 4. Torino, 271-305. |
| BUHL, M.-L., DAL, E. & COLDING, T.H. 1986 | *The Danish Naval Officer Frederik Ludvig Norden, his Travel in Egypt 1737-38 and his Voyage... I-II, Copenhagen 1755 with Plates by Marcus Tuscher.* Copenhagen. |
| – 1990 | Frederik Ludvig Norden à Alexandrie en 1737 et 1738, in: E. Keck & S. Søndergaard & E. Wulff eds., *Living Waters, Scandinavian Orientalistic Studies Presented to Professor Dr. Frede Løkkegaard on his Seventy-Fifth Birthday, January 27th 1990.* Copenhagen, 31-42. |
| CLARKE, D.L. 1968 | *Analytical Archaeology.* London. |
| DESITTERE, M. 1984 | Contributo alla storia della paletnologia italiana, in: Ch. Morigi Gori & G. Sassatelli, *Dalla Stanza delle Antichità al Museo Civico.* Bologna, 61-85. |
| DIETZ, S. & TROLLE, S. 1974 | *Arkæologens Rhodos.* Copenhagen. |
| DYGGVE, E. 1943 | Recherches et explorations archéologiques danoises dans la péninsule des Balkans, en Égypte et dans le Proche Orient, *Le Nord* VI 1943, 133-164. |
| – 1948 | Oriental and Classical Archaeology, in: *The Humanities and the Sciences in Denmark during the Second World War.* Copenhagen, 55-63. |
| FABRITIUS, A., FRIIS, F. & KORNERUP, E. 1973 | *Kong Christian VIII.s dagbøger og optegnelser II, 1. Halvbind, 1815-1821.* Copenhagen. |
| FALBE, C.T. 1833 | *Recherches sur l'emplacement de Carthage.* Paris. |

| | |
|---|---|
| FISCHER, E. 1964 | Melchior Lorck, en dansk vagants levnedsløb i det 16. aarhundrede, in: *Fund og Forskning i det Kgl. Biblioteks Samlinger* 11, 33-72. |
| FISCHER-HANSEN, T. 1990 | Sizilien und Dänemark, *ActaHyp* 2, 169-188 |
| GALLAY A. 1989 | Logicism: a French view of archaeological theory founded in computational perspective, *Antiquity* 63, 27-39. |
| GLAMANN, K. 1990 | *Bryggeren J.C. Jacobsen på Carlsberg.* Copenhagen. |
| GUNDESTRUP, B. 1990 | Egyptian, Greek and Roman Antiquities in the oldest Royal Kunstkammer Collection in Denmark, *ActaHyp* 2, 43-56. |
| HANSEN, P.A. 1977 | *A Bibliography of Danish Contributions to Classical Scholarship from the Sixteenth Century to 1970, Danish Humanist Texts and Studies Edited by the Royal Library, Copenhagen* 1. Copenhagen. |
| HAUGSTED I. 1990 | Im Paradies. Die Athen-Reise des Architekten Jørgen Hansen Koch, *ActaHyp* 2, 189-207. |
| HAUSMANN, U. 1969 | *Allgemeine Grundlagen der Archäologie*, Handbuch der Archäologie. München. |
| HERMANSEN, V. 1951 | Fra Kunstkammer til Antik-Cabinet, in: *Antik-Cabinettet 1851, udgivet i hundredaaret af Nationalmuseet.* Copenhagen, 9-56. |
| HELK, V. 1971 | Dänische Romreisen von der Reformation bis zum Absolutismus (1536-1660), *ARID* 6, 107-196. |
| HIMMELMANN, N. 1976 | *Utopische Vergangenheit.* Berlin. |
| JANTZEN, U. 1986 | *Einhundert Jahre Athener Institut 1874-1974.* Mainz. |
| JOHANSEN, K. FRIIS 1935 | Georg Zoëga og Rom, in: L. Bobé ed., *Rom og Danmark gennem tiderne* I. København, 223-267. |
| – 1943 | Klassisk arkæologi, in: *Danmarks Kultur ved Aar 1940* VII. Copenhagen, 165-174. |
| KJØLSEN, F. H. 1965 | *Capitain F. L. Norden og hans rejse til Ægypten (1737-1738).* Copenhagen. |
| KRARUP, P. 1976 | Due Archeologhi danesi: Georg Zoëga e Peter Oluf Bröndsted, in: *Mélanges d'histoire ancienne et d'archéologie offerts à Paul Collart*, Lausanne, 277-284. |
| LIVENTHAL, V. 1986 | C. T. Falbe – søofficer og arkæolog, *Museum Tusculanum* 56 1984-1986, 337-361 (with an English summary). |
| LUND, J. 1986 | The archaeological activities of Christian Tuxen Falbe in Carthage in 1838, *Cahiers des Études Anciennes* XVIII, 8-24. |
| LUND, J. & SØRENSEN, L.W. 1988 | Vejen til Segermes, C. T. Falbes rejse gennem Tunesien i 1838, *ArbejdsmarkKøb* 1988, 9-23 (with an English summary). |
| – forthcoming | La visite de C. T. Falbe à Kasserine en 1838, in: J.-M. Lassere & P. Trousset, *Le mausollé des Flavii à Kasserine.* Rome. |
| LUNDBAK, H. 1989 | *Det danske Institut i Rom: Oprettelse og virksomhed indtil 1987.* Rom, to be published in: *Speculum Mundi, Roma – Centro internazionale di ricerche umanistiche*, Roma 1991. |
| MARTELS, Z.R.W.M. 1989 | *Augerius Gislenius Busbequius, Leven en werk van de keizerlijke gezant aan het hof van Süleyman de Grote.* Groningen. |

| | |
|---|---|
| MOLTESEN, M. 1989 | Danske udgravningsprojekter i Italien, in: J. Moestrup & E. Nyholm eds., *Italien og Danmark: 100 års inspiration*. Copenhagen, 96-107. |
| MÜLLER-HAAS, M.-M. 1989 | Ein Künstler am Bosporus, Melchior Lorch, in: G. Sievernich & H. Budde eds., *Europa und der Orient 800-1900*, Berlin, folding page between p. 240 and 241-244; 794-798. |
| OTZEN, B. 1978 | En orientrejse på Christian IV's tid, Jacob Ulfeldts og Christian Barnekows rejse til Palæstina og Ægypten 1588-89, *Convivium 1978*, 84-97. |
| PAPANICOLAOU-CHRISTENSEN, A. 1985 | *Athens 1818-1853, Views of Athens by Danish Artists*. Athens. |
| PIPLOVIC, S. 1987 | Istrazivanje graditeljskog nasljeda u Dalmaciji od strane danskog fonda i E. Dyggve (with an English resumé), *Vjesnik za arheologiju i historiju Dalmatinsku* 80, 93-130. |
| POULSEN, V. 1933 | Eine archäologische Zeichnung von Melchior Lorck, ActaArch 4, 104-109. |
| RASMUSSEN, S. 1986 | *Carsten Niebuhr und die Arabische Reise 1761-1767, Ausstellung der Königlichen Bibliothek Kopenhagen im Zusammenarbeit mit dem Kultusminister des Landes Schleswig-Holstein*. Heide in Holstein. |
| – ed. 1986 | *Den Arabiske Rejse 1761-1767 – set i videnskabshistorisk perspektiv*. København. |
| RENFREW, C. 1980 | The Great Tradition versus the Great Divide: Archaeology as Anthropology, *AJA* 84, 287-298. |
| RIIS, P.J. 1970 | *Sukas I. The North-East Sanctuary and the First Settling of Greeks in Syria and Palestine*. Copenhagen. |
| – 1979 | Klassisk og nærorientalsk arkæologi, in: *Københavns Universitet 1479-1979*, IX, 1979. Copenhagen, 121-160. |
| ROHDE, H.P. 1985 | Et ufuldendt storværk med perspektiver, in: Den røde tråd: Boghistoriske studier. Herning, 191-209. |
| SCHEPELERN, H.D. 1971 | *Museum Wormianum* (with an English summary). Odense. |
| SNODGRASS, A.M. 1985 | The New Archaeology and the Classical Archaeologist, *AJA* 89, 31-37. |
| – 1987 | *An Archaeology of Greece, The Present State and Future Scope of a Discipline*. Berkely, Los Angeles, London. |
| SØRENSEN, L.W. 1986 | Med professor Doerpfeld på Peloponnes 1893, Et foredrag af M.J. Goldschmidt (1854-1924), *Museum Tusculanum* 52-55 (1983), 5-50. |
| TILLEY, Chr. 1989 | Excavation as Theatre, *Antiquity* 63, 275-280. |
| TROJA, MYKENE 1990 | *Troja, Mykene, Tiryns, Orchomenos, Heinrich Schliemann zum 100. Todestag*. Athen. |
| TSIGAKOU, F.-M. 1981 | *The Rediscovery of Greece, Travellers and Pointers of the Romantic Era*. New York. |
| USSING, J.L. 1906 | *Af mit Levned*. København. |

| | |
|---|---|
| VILLADSEN, V. 1990 | "Close Encounter": Theophilus Hansen – Architect and Archaeologist in Greece, *ActaHyp* 2 1990, 219-227. |
| WATERHOUSE, H. 1988 | The British School at Athens, The First Hundred Years, *BSASuppl.* vol. 19. Oxford. |
| WHITLEY, J. 1987 | Art History, Archaeology and Idealism, The German Tradition, in: I. Hodder ed., *Archaeology as long-term history*. Cambridge, 9-15. |
| WINSTONE, H.V.F. 1982 – 1985 | *The Illicit Adventure*. London. *Uncovering the Ancient World*. London. |
| ZAHLE, J. 1986 | Dansk arkæologi i Middelhavslandene 1973-1984, in: *Museum Tusculanum* 56 1984-1986, 11-46. |

# ARCHAIC AND CLASSICAL GRAVES AT HALIEIS: A SUMMARY

BIRGITTE RAFN

The graves treated in this article belong to the cemetery outside ancient Halieis (near modern Porto Cheli) in the Southern Argolid of the Peloponnese, Greece. They were located along a road east of the town in an area with other graves found in 1958[1]. Excavation took place in 1973-75 and 1979 (RUDOLPH 1973-1974, 1975, 1979), and a total of 28 graves were found covering a period from the early 6th century B.C. through the 5th to the beginning of the 4th century B.C. Two thirds of the burials were from the 6th century, predominantly in the first half, while the 5th century graves were more equally dispersed over the century. *Fig. 1*

In general the graves were of a very simple kind, earth pits dug into the ground. Sometimes, however, the depth was considerable, and secondary cuttings were made halfway down on the long sides. In a few

Fig. 1. Aerial view of the graves excavated in 1974-1975. From S.

cases, large amounts of earth covered the pits, forming a mound with large rubble stones on top, and these graves also contained a considerable number of pots and other gifts. One grave was covered by slabs of shelly sandstone and another was partly covered by a layer of pebbles, but as a rule there was nothing to protect the pit but earth, sometimes with a couple of upright stones or slabs to mark the grave. In one case, a large *pithos* with a coarse-ware tub as lid was used as the receptacle for two adult people, and a smaller *pithos* and a coarse-ware *hydria* contained the remains of children.

The lay-out of the cemetery did show some deliberate planning in a long row of nine graves from the 6th century B.C. lying side by side, while greater irregularity was seen in the area dominated by 5th century graves, which also had an example of a grave placed immediately above another. This was probably due to a long wall running north-east, forming a boundary between this part of the necropolis and the graves further east. If the wall protected a family plot, it explains the crowded state inside it (GARLAND 1985, 106-107). The burials were all inhumations, except one cremation from the latter part of the 5th century B.C., and the skeletons were placed in a supine position, the majority

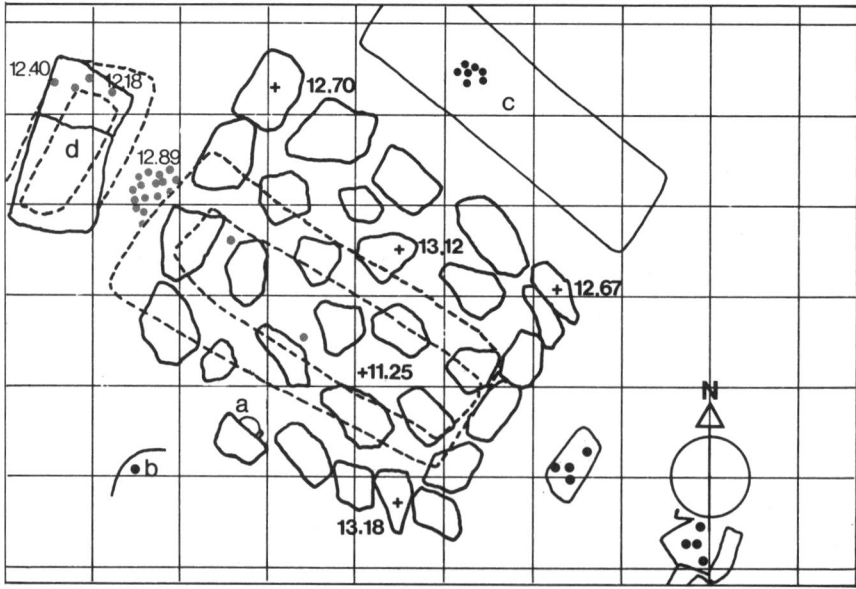

Fig. 2. Archaic grave surrounded by offerings. a: *chytra*, b: bone, c: grave pit, d: offering table. Black and grey dots indicate pots (Drawing by Poul Christensen).

Fig. 3. Archaic grave with skeleton and two pots.

with their heads facing east, the others toward west or north. As far as the skeletal material can be identified, there are 12 male burials, 9 female, 1 adult (cremation) and 6 children, one of these a neonate[2].

Nearly all the graves had grave goods, mostly pottery which was very unevenly distributed. The graves from the 6th century B.C. were as a rule sparsely endowed with pots, but contained several objects of metal, especially dress pins of iron and a couple of bronze rings, so they were by no means poor burials.

One of the graves, however, differed from the rest in its construction, as well as in the amount and quality of its pottery. The top of the *Fig. 2* grave mound had the form of a rectangle and was made mainly of large rubble stones with a packing of smaller stones within the rectangle; below a layer of earth nearly two metres thick was the burial itself – the skeleton of a young child about 9-10 years old, presumably a boy. Inside the grave pit were only a Corinthian *aryballos* and a small un- *Fig. 3* glazed bowl, but outside the mound a vast amount of pottery was

59

Fig. 4. Group of gifts outside the Archaic grave.

found in different spots. Close on 60 pots had been deposited, either in groups near the mound lying unprotected in the soil, or further away placed under stone slabs or on a tray-like structure that was surrounded by a mud-built edge and covered with slabs of limestone. A few single pots were placed here and there, one pot beside a large bone. Four of the pots were imports of very good quality, a Laconian cup painted by the Boread painter (RUDOLPH 1976), a Corinthian *aryballos* with a plastic female head (CATLING 1976, 13 fig. 17), and two Attic black-glazed cups of Komast shape (BRIJDER 1983, 89 K 109, 92 K 149). The main bulk of the pottery comprised normal-sized pots of standard ware like Corinthain *kotylai* and unglazed miniatures of local manufacture. Parallel with the grave was a pit of the same type and size as the other grave pits, containing a cluster of seven pots but no skeleton. Six of the pots were of the above-mentioned local fabric, the seventh an *aryballos* made of faience. The pit has tentatively been interpreted as a cenotaph, perhaps for a male relative of the child who died away from home, but the offerings could also be just another group of gifts for the boy.

The double burial of two adults, a man and a woman, in one *pithos* (RUDOLPH 1979, pl. 32a), shows that a well-built grave not necessarily did demand a large amount of grave goods. Not only was a large coarse-ware *pithos* procured, but the pit in which the *pithos* was placed was filled up with rocks of a considerable size acting as support for the *pithos* lying in an oblique position in the pit. Thus, after much painstaking labour, the two deceased, who must have died at the same time, were deposited in the *pithos* with no other objects than three iron pins, no doubt fastened to their dresses or shrouds.

Another *pithos* contained two children of about 5-6 years, this time an example of the more widespread habit of burying children in large pots (GARLAND 1985, 78). Their grave gifts consisted of a miniature *oinochoe* and a terracotta ram.

The graves of the 5th century B.C. showed an increasing amount of pottery, although seldom of outstanding craftsmanship, combined with a likewise larger selection of metal objects. One grave especially, from the secound quarter of the century, allows a general comparison with the rich grave about a hundred years earlier. It was built in almost the same way, although the stones used were smaller. A metre and a half below a rectangular mound was the pit with the skeleton, but this time the offerings were placed in the mound itself, and the buried person was

*Fig. 5*

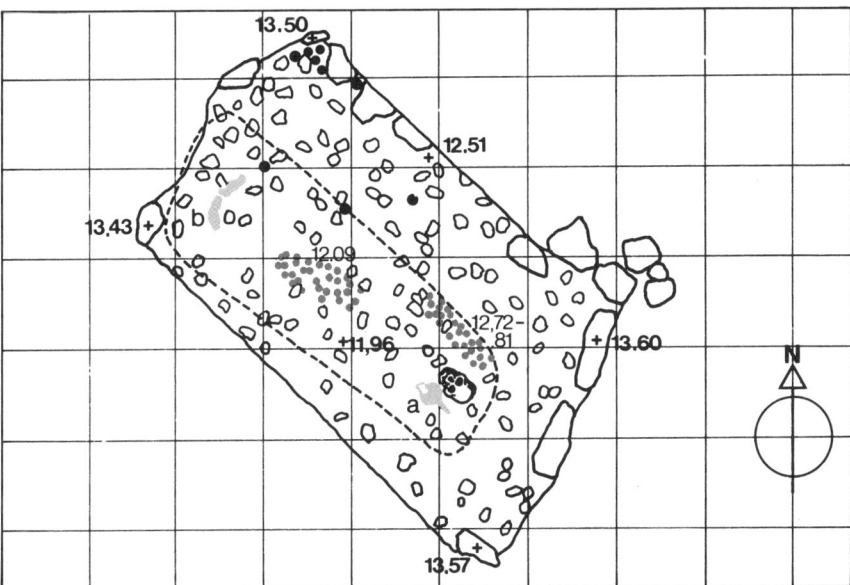

Fig. 5. Classical grave with skeleton and grave goods. a: mirror, b: sandals. Black and grey dots indicate pots (Drawing by Poul Christensen).

Fig. 6. Classical grave with skeleton and offerings.

not a child but an adult woman, who was found with a wealth of personal belongings and grave gifts such as pins of iron or silver-coated bronze, two *pyxides* and a mirror of bronze lying around her, and at her feet a pair of wooden sandals reinforced with iron. Besides 17 pots placed directly above and around the skeleton, there was another large group of offerings higher up the mound comprising 12 pots, two finger rings of iron, and egg-shells. Moreover, single pots were placed here and there, and at the bottom of the northwest corner were four pots. Nearly two thirds of the pottery comprised Corinthian *kotylai* and *pyxides* of various types, one third Attic black-figure or pattern *lekythoi*, all of mediocre quality, a notable contrast to the choice and valuable objects of metal.

*Fig. 6*

Outside the burial area limited by the wall and not far from the graves excavated in 1958 was the only cremation burial of the 5th century B.C. found in the cemetery so far. In the pyre were the remains of an adult, presumably a woman for a coarse-ware *hydria* with the bones of a neonate was found just beside the pyre pointing to a mother buried with her child. Near the pyre and *hydria* was a large cooking pot, a *chytra* with the half of a smaller *chytra* as lid carefully covered with rocks, while a third *chytra* was found on the opposite side of the pyre. East of the *hydria* were 35 pots divided into six different groups, lying on a line within a distance of three and a half metres from the *hydria*. Two of these groups were protected by two Corinthian pan tiles placed lengthwise; a third cluster was below a couple of large worked slabs of limestone, while the remaining three were unprotected by tiles or slabs. The greater part of the pottery formed a rather homogeneous collection of Corinthian pattern *kotylai* and small *pyxides* of various types painted in bright colours, moreover a few Attic

*Fig. 7*

*Fig. 8*

Fig. 7. In the middle the *hydria* used as urn, in front stones covering the *chytra*, in the background the upright tiles.

Fig. 8. Pots in front of tiles.

*lekythoi* and local miniatures. Around the large *chytra* and all over the area with the two burials were the fragments of an Attic band cup from the latter half of the 6th century B.C. Its presence in connection with burials from the 5th century is not quite clear but its fragmentary and scattered state (only two thirds of it were retrieved) could mean that it originally belonged to another grave, now lost.

Some 300 pots were found in connection with the 28 burials, representing about 40 different shapes and probably six different wares. Corinthian pottery was evidently the most favoured product, since more than 50 per cent of all the pots were from Corinth. Surprisingly, this import did not diminish during the 5th century B.C. to be replaced by Attic pottery; on the contrary the amount of Corinthian pots in the 5th century graves outnumbers the Attic pots by far.

The preferred shape among the Corinthian pots was the pattern *kotyle* (*Corinth* XIII, 1964, pl. 40, 285-1,2), followed by the ray *kotyle* (*Corinth* XIII, 1964, pl. 35, 252-2), and if the black-glazed, semiglazed and miniature pattern *kotylai* are added to these, an amount of 80 is reached, which clearly shows the popularity of the various versions of the *kotyle* for funeral purposes.

The second-largest group consists of pots of local fabric, and as the third comes the Attic pottery, among which the stemmed drinking cup and the *lekythos* are the best represented shapes. Laconian pottery was also found, although not in any great quantity compared with the Corinthian and Attic imports, but one of the finest pots from the cemetery was the above-mentioned cup by the Boread painter. As already stated, it was customary at Halieis to place many of the offerings outside or above the graves, either heaped together in groups, or as single pots placed at a greater or lesser distance from the grave itself. Where the graves lay close together, it was sometimes difficult to decide to which grave the gifts belonged. The outside offerings nearly always consisted of pottery, with a few exceptions like terracottas, which were not well represented in the cemetery at all.

It seems natural to ask whether certain types of pots were found in the graves but not outside them and vice versa, but in no case could such a difference be pointed out. The four preferred shapes, *kotylai*, *lekythoi*, convex *pyxides* and *lekanis pyxides*, were all placed both inside and outside the graves. This applies also to the many miniature pots found mainly in association with the well-furnished child's grave mentioned above.

Careful examination of the skeletal material allows the grave goods to be studied in relation to the sex and age of the occupant of each grave. Although it is necessary to make reservations in cases where the skeletons were too badly preserved to allow an indisputable identification, enough certainty remains to establish a certain pattern in the distribution of offerings in male, female and child burials.

The finds in general confirm the observations from other cemeteries in Greece dating from the same periods, as for example that most jewellery is found in graves of women, and toys in those of children (*Corinth* XIII, 1964, 83-84). On the other hand there were no weapons or strigils in the male graves. As for the terracotta figurines, the material mostly comprised standing females or heads and birds like doves and cocks, all coming from three graves of adult women.

The amount and variation of the pottery allow more conclusions and throw some light on the funerary practices at Halieis. There was a predominance of drinking vessels, whereas closed shapes like *oinochoai* and other pitchers were extremely rare. An interesting fact is that drinking cups of the stemmed type associated with *symposia*, here Attic palmette cups and black-glazed cups of Attic or Laconian fabric, to-

Fig. 9. Archaic male grave with two stemmed cups.

gether with local imitations, were found inside men's graves but not in these of women. Where drinking cups of the stemmed type were connected with female burials, they were outside offerings; no woman had such a cup within her grave. A counterpart to the stemmed cup was probably the cup-*skyphos*, black-figured or black-glazed, as it was found in four female graves (*Corinth* XIII, 1964, pl. 43, 295-4,5). Another type of pot associated exclusively with men is not surprisingly the *aryballos*, a palaistra requisite, found in seven examples all from 6th century graves. Two of these were the graves of children between 9 and 12 years of age, and the presence of the *aryballoi* may secure an identification of the children as boys (KURTZ & BOARDMAN 1971, 208).

On the other hand, no male grave contained *pyxides* of the powder, tripod or *lekanis* type (*Corinth* XIII 1964, pl. 88, 168-8, 194-3; pl. 90, 291-3). At Halieis these small vessels of Corinthian ware were numerous in women's graves, probably because they also in daily life contained objects that were considered typically feminine, as for example jewellery and cosmetics. The much larger convex *pyxis* (PAYNE

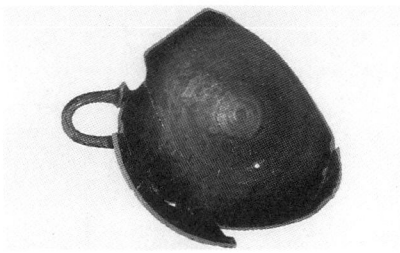 

Fig. 10. Attic black-glazed cup of Komast type. Inv. no. HP 2302.

Fig. 11. Laconian flat-based cup. Inv. no. HP 2729.

1931,323 fig. 164), a container of foodstuffs and a typical product of Corinthian workshops in the 6th and 5th centuries, was found in two male graves, although the majority of the convex *pyxides* came from women's graves.

Another notable aspect of the funerary rites practised in the cemetery is the presence of pots with pierced bases (RAFN 1984, 305-308). They are not many compared with the total amount, but 21 pots had a hole in the base intentionally made after firing. In most cases this hole was punched, and of a size ranging from 0.8 to 2.0 cm. A few had much smaller drilled holes, 0,2 to 0.3 cm. The punched holes could be almost circular, but most of them were of irregular shape. They were placed either right in the middle of the floor or off centre. The pots were mainly normal-sized drinking cups of various types, *kotylai*, *skyphoi* or stemmed cups. The latter had solely drilled holes, but also pattern *kotylai* had been pierced, and in one case the lower part of a full-size Laconian *krater* with a large irregular hole was found above a grave from the 6th century B.C. Far from all burials had pots with pierced bases: 21 examples found in association with nine graves mean that two thirds of the graves had no such pots. All pots but one were found outside or above the grave, often inverted. The exception was a flat-based cup of normal size inside the grave of a young adult, possibly male. It was the only drinking cup present in the grave and very likely a personal possession of the dead (RAFN 1984, 306 fig. 3).

There were no strict rules apparently, for the pots were connected with the burials of adults as well as of children, and sometimes there was only one pot outside the grave and sometimes several; the grave of the woman with the sandals had only one although it was otherwise so well furnished. There is no chronological distinction either, for pierced

Fig. 12. *Chytra* outside the Archaic grave, cf. *fig.* 2 a.

pots are found alike in the 6th and in the 5th century B.C. They must have been meant for pouring liquid into the ground (GARLAND 1985, 113-115) and were brought from home to the cemetery ready for the rites performed at the funeral itself or in connection with offerings made afterwards. That they were not indispensable is shown by the fact that they were found only with one third of the burials.

Precisely what rites took place at or after a funeral is difficult to say with certainty today. It is, however, presumed that some kind of meal was served for the dead (GARLAND 1985, 110-113). The presence of several large *chytras* in the cemetery confirms that food did play a part in the funerary ritual. These were found outside the graves standing *Fig. 12* upright or lying on their sides, sometimes sealed with a stone slab, or with another pot, and some of them had blackened undersides. In the vicinity of one of the graves was a hearth filled with ashes that may have played a part in the preparations of such a repast, to the extent that this was not done at home.

It is generally agreed that many of the pots used for drink offerings were broken afterwards, but it is very difficult to establish certain evidence of this custom (GARLAND 1985, 115, 170). When pots are found in fragments in a grave, the broke state could be due to the fact that they were dropped from above by the mourners (perhaps a ritual in itself) or that they broke during the filling in of the grave. Over the centuries the weight of the earth may have contributed to the breaking of the vessels, especially at their weak points at the foot, neck or handles. At Halieis there is only one undeniable case of deliberate breaking in an Attic black-glazed *skyphos*, the fragments of which were found in three different places at the lower end of a grave. Some of the fragments were even hidden under a stone. In another grave, a black-figured *skyphos* was found in fragments in two places also at the lower end but in this case the deliberate breaking seems less convincing. In a third case, fragments of the same Corinthian *kotyle* were found on either side of the mound above the boy's grave, and it is hard to imagine that this happened by accident, since the sherds were far apart, on different levels, and separated by a mound.

We know that commemorative visits were paid to the grave at certain intervals after the funeral, also that once a year there was a memorial

Fig. 13. Pots on the so-called offering table outside the Archaic grave. From N. Cf. *fig.* 2d (the second offering table is not illustrated).

festival in honour of the dead ancestors (HUMPHREYS 1980, 100-101). No doubt rites were then performed which also included the offering of pots. This is probably demonstrated at Halieis by pots deposited near graves much earlier than the pots themselves. Outside some of the Archaic graves were Corinthian miniature *kotylai* which definitely belong to the 5th century B.C., and one of them was carefully placed beside a stone.

As mentioned above, six groups of pots were found leading up to the cremation burial; of these the two farthest away were later than the rest by at least 25 years. The fact that it had been possible to place the later offerings directly in line with the others show that the tiles and stones slabs erected for protection were still easily seen.

*Fig. 13*   Near the well-furnished grave of the boy and near the row of 6th century graves were two tray-like structures with pots on top called offering tables. The pots were assembled at one end of the table thus leaving most of it empty. In both cases, a pot with pierced base was lying on top of the slab that covered the table. Most of the pots were Corinthian pattern *kotylai* not easily datable within a narrow period, but an Attic *lekythos* of Little Lion shape points to a date around 500 B.C., which is considerably later than the graves nearby. It is tempting to see the tables as places where offerings of food and drink were presented to the occupants of the graves and afterwards sealed by stone slabs with pots left below.

A total of 28 burials from a time span of two centuries does not create a firm base for general conclusions about the funerary customs practised at Halieis in the Archaic and Classical periods. It is striking to notice among the relatively few graves not only the differences in the normal pit grave type with respect to depth and superstructure, but also the examples of pot burials and cremation. Add to this the variety of grave goods and the uneven distribution of it among the graves, and a picture emerges of a provincial town whose citizens buried their dead not only according to common practice but also to individual preferences and family traditions.

Institute of Prehistoric
and Classical Archaeology,
University of Copenhagen
DK-1467 Copenhagen K

## NOTES

1. I should like to thank Professor Wolf Rudolph, Indiana University, Bloomington, for kindly allowing me to publish this summary study of the graves at Halieis. – The graves from 1958 were excavated by N. Verdelis and published by C. Dengate, *ADelt* 31 A, 1976, 274-324. Apart from a cremation burial dated late 7th century B.C., the graves, all inhumations, belong to the 5th and 4th centuries B.C.
2. The study of the skeletal remains was undertaken by Professor Marshall Becker, West Chester University, Pennsylvania.

## BIBLIOGRAPHY

| | |
|---|---|
| BRIJDER, H. A. G. 1983 | *Siana Cups I and Komast Cups*. Amsterdam. |
| CATLING, H. W. 1976 | Archaeology in Greece 1975-76, *ARepLondon* 22. |
| *Corinth* XIII 1964 | C. W. BLEGEN, H. PALMER, R. S. YOUNG, The North Cemetery. *Corinth* XIII. Results of Excavations Conducted by the American School of Classical Studies in Athens. Princeton. |
| GARLAND, R. 1985 | *The Greek Way of Death*. London. |
| HUMPHREYS, S. C. 1980 | Family Tombs and Tomb Cult in Ancient Athens – Tradition or Traditionalism?, *JHS* 100, 96-126. |
| KURTZ, D. C. & BOARDMAN, J. 1971 | *Greek Burial Customs*. London. |
| PAYNE, H. 1931 | *Necrocorinthia*. Oxford. |
| RAFN, B. 1984 | The Ritual Use of Pottery in the Nekropolis at Halieis, in H. A.G. BRIJDER, ed., *Ancient Greek and Related Pottery. Proceedings of the International Vase Symposium*, Amsterdam, 305-308. |
| RUDOLPH, W. W. 1973-1974 | Excavations at Halieis (Porto Cheli) 1973, *ADelt* 29 B2, 267-268. |
| 1975 | Final Report: Halieis, *ADelt* 30 B1, 72-73, pl. 43c. |
| 1976 | HP 2310: A Lakonian Kylix from Halieis, *Hesperia* 45, 240-252, pl. 59. |
| 1979 | Excavations in the Nekropolis of Halieis, *ADelt* 34 B1, 128-129, pl. 32a-b. |

## ABBREVIATIONS

| | |
|---|---|
| *ADelt* | Ἀρχαιολογικὸν Δελτίον |
| *ARepLondon* | *Archaeological Reports* |
| *JHS* | *The Journal of Hellenic Studies* |

# OUT OF TARQUINIA
# A NOTE ON ANOTHER PAINTED TOMB AT BLERA

## ERIK POULSGAARD MARKUSSEN

"Die zweite bemalte Kammer ist etwas kleiner, als die Grotta dipinta, ihr Grundriß noch gestreckter. Eine Säule ist nicht vorhanden. Beide Kammern stimmen in der Anordnung der schmucklosen Totenbänke und in der Dekoration der Wände vollständig überein. Die Decke ist hier sicher weiss stuckiert; die Bemahlung der Wände, in den Massen kleiner, sehr schlecht erhalten." (KOCH, VON MERCKLIN & WEICKERT 1915, 266).

Besides indicating the relation to the surroundings and mentioning some fragments of pottery, this short description of a lesser known painted tomb at Blera is all we learn from Koch, von Mercklin &

Fig. 1: Tomba Dipinta and surroundings: Grotta Penta is in the upper right corner, to the right of the moulded cube tomb façade.

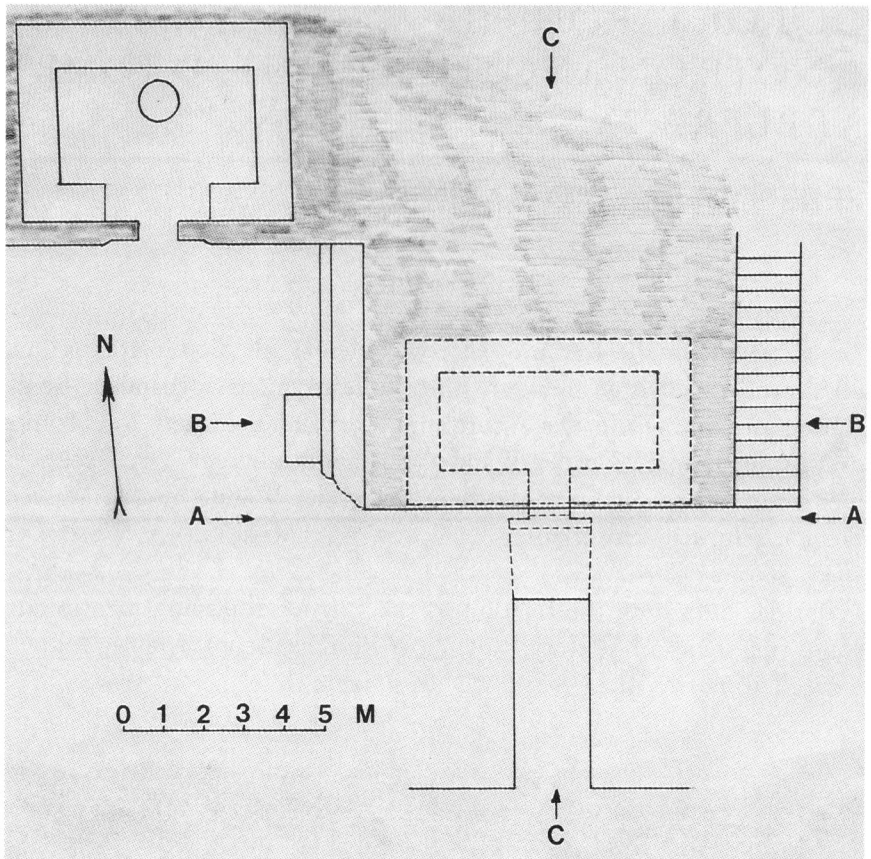

Fig. 2: Plan of the Tomba Dipinta and surroundings: Grotta Penta is in the upper left corner.

Weickert, who in 1915 published an overall report on the Etruscan necropoleis at Blera, now a small village south of Vetralla but in the Etruscan period a local centre in the Tarquinian territory (POULSGAARD MARKUSSEN 1985, 17-19. for Blera in general. A thorough topographical account is found in QUILICI GIGLI 1976. See also SANTELLA 1981). While the more interesting of the two painted tombs, the *Grotta Penta*, has been dealt with by the author in an earlier paper (POULSGAARD MARKUSSEN 1985; for references to the Grotta Penta cf. POULSGAARD MARKUSSEN 1979, 50 no. 1), this is devoted to its smaller, unnamed sister. Due to this last fact and for the sake of clarity, I shall afterwards refer to it as the *Tomba Dipinta*.

*Fig. 1*   Isolated the Tomba Dipinta is quite unimportant, architecturally as

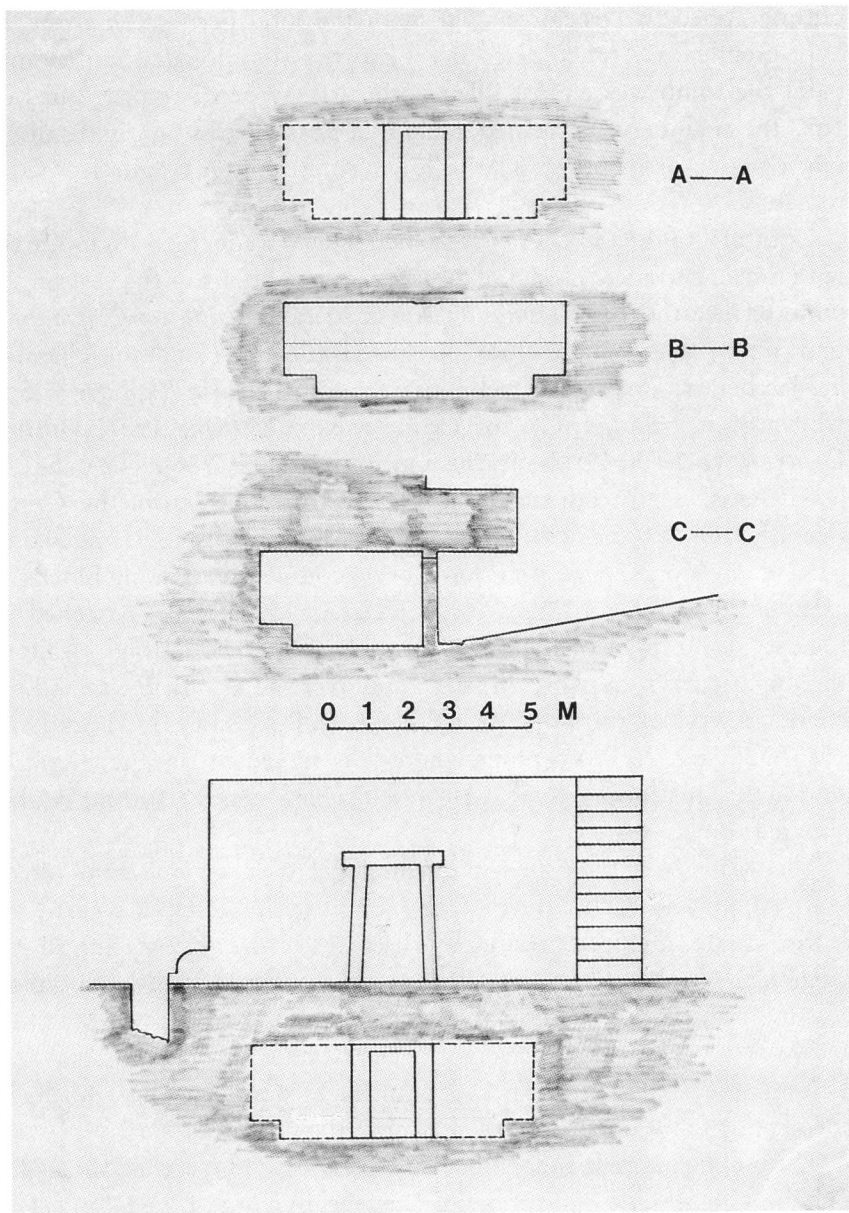

Fig. 3: Sections through Tomba Dipinta – cf. Fig. 2. Penta is in the upper left corner.

well as artistically. But to improve the statistics it deserves to be remembered as yet another example of the influence from Tarquinia, the main centre for this memorial practice. The tomb was measured and photographed in December 1986 with the kind permission from the Soprintendenza Archeologica per l'Etruria Meridionale; at that moment the tomb was almost filled with earth. When I returned in July 1987 the chamber was cleaned, making it possible to study in detail the few remains of painting. The following description results from this research.

Contrary to the *Grotta Penta*, which had a façade (now disappeared) with a true entrance (closed of course), its neighbour to the east on the same terrace the *Tomba Dipinta* was a so-called *cube tomb* (tomba a semi-dado) with a false door on the visible front and the chamber hidden below. This type is well know from the *Etruria Rupestre* area to which Blera belongs (Cf. for example ROSI 1925 & 1927; DEMUS-QUATEMBER 1958; OLESON 1982 and ROMANELLI 1986). The cube is a hewn massive protruding c. 6.40 m. towards south from the *Grotta Penta* façade, 9.10 m. wide and c. 5.75 m. high. Badly preserved, some part of the upper edge may have been composed of joint blocks as implied by Kock, von Mercklin & Weickert (1915, 263). Attached on the east side a flight of stairs (c. 1.60 wide, steps 0.40 m. high) leads to the upper surface, a platform stretching over the *Grotta Penta* and the chamber west of this (the West Chamber: POULSGAARD MARKUSSEN 1985, 30f., fig. 22.) to a point where it is served by another flight of stairs; this platform may have formed a new terrace for the higher situated tombs.

*Fig. 2-3*

The west side of the cube – in a right angle to the *Grotta Penta* façade – is resting on a rock-cut moulding composed of 2 steplike parts, the lower square, the upper rounded. The front of the cube (facing south) originally seems to have been adorned by a cut-out false door, a typical feature in the rock-cut tomb architecture. At least Kock, von Mercklin & Weickert speak of "ganz verwaschene Reste einer Scheintür mit vertieftem Spiegel" (1915, 263). Today no traces remain of this embellishment nor of any upper blocks crowning the cube.

The real chamber is hidden below the cube and is reached through a 6.50 m. long *dromos* cut out below the level in front of the façade. This 1.85 m. wide *dromos* is under open air the first 4½ m., then broadening to c. 2 m. almost below the front of the cube. At this point the smaller door (1 m. wide, c. 2 m. high) leads to the chamber. Just outside the door the *dromos* ends with 2 flat steps (18 cm. and 15 cm. high, 53 cm. and 40 cm. wide), and holes in the sidewall may indicate a door locking.

Fig. 4: The central part of the back wall.

The chamber is c. 7 m. wide and 4 m. deep with its long axis transverse to the *dromos*. The ceiling is almost flat, only parted on the *dromos* axis by a 0.60 m. wide *columen*. Its diminutive height of 2 cm. makes it possible that it was added in stucco. Leaving the entrance free the walls were encircled by a bench for the corpses, c. 0.80 m. wide and 0.45 m. above floor level. Traces of the stucco which covered the walls, benches, ceiling and possibly the floor, can still be seen, including part of the painted decoration. *Fig. 4*

Small pieces of this decoration still remain intact and even the colour is discernible here and there. The painting consisted of a horizontal frieze in the middle of the wall composed of a blue wave ornament (this *Fig. 5-6*

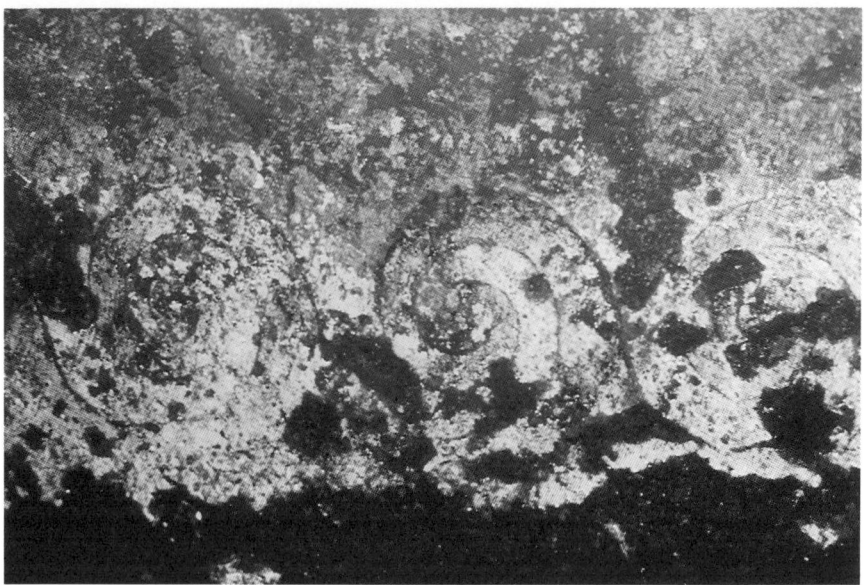

Fig. 5: Part of the wave ornament.

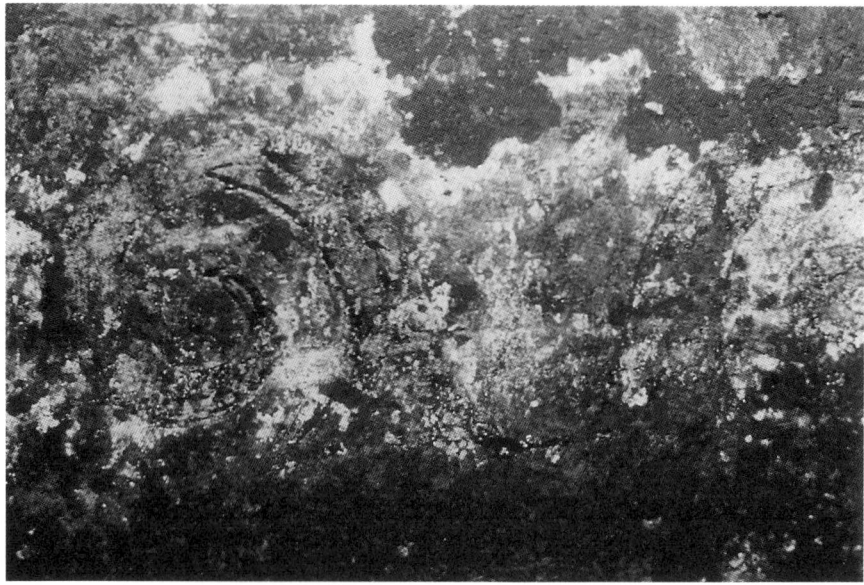

Fig. 6: The central part of the wave ornament.

Fig. 7: Incised lines on the back wall.

motif cf. POULSGAARD MARKUSSEN 1985, 27-30) on a white ground bordered on the upper side by a double band, the upper red (3 cm.) and black (or blue) (2 cm.) separated by white (1.5 cm.), while the lower border probably was the red painted base; there may have been a black line here too, resembling the upper band. This base is 0.46 m. high measured from the bench, while the lower border of the waves is 0.49 m. above the bench and the black (or blue) band 0.60 m. The waves are c. 10 cm. high and the distance between the crests about c. 11.5 cm. This makes it an almost exact copy of the one in *Grotta Penta* except for the central lotus, which is missing here: from the middle of the back wall the waves ran to each side continuing on the side wall and probably the entrance wall. Just beneath the ceiling there are traces of another horizontal band, identical with the one above the waves: from below black (or blue) (2.5 cm.), white (2.5 cm.) and red up to the ceiling (height varying from 3 cm. to 8 cm.); the red stops at each side of the *columen*. Between these bands the walls show no remnants of decoration; there may have been, but this area could as well have been left for non-painted adornments (i.e. shields hung on the wall) or the presumed artistic urge of the descendants (though unfulfilled). Two thin vertical lines, closely incised under the *columen*, may belong to the original design and indicate some sort of layout (Cf. WIT 1929 for incisions as part of the layout in the tomb paintings).

*Fig. 7*

In the chamber fragments of *2 vases* were found by the Germans (KOCH, VON MERCKLIN & WEICKERT 1915, 266, Abb. 63): 4 fragments from an amphora(?) in fine, red-yellow clay with orange to black slip, decorated with palmettes, circles and part of a 4-string lyre; and small pieces of a red-figured kylix with a meander framing the tondo.

The stylistical affinity to the *Grotta Penta* makes it almost certain to assume the same painter behind the two tombs. And one is even tempted to imagine a family tomb complex with a pater familias ("the former merchant from Tarquinia" – POULSGAARD MARKUSSEN 1985, 32) aware of the artistic fashions in the capital city. Chronologically the pottery is of less importance, indicating only a date between the Archaic and Roman time, but the tight connection to the *Grotta Penta* both topographically, architecturally and artistically points to a similar intimacy in time: somewhere at the beginning of the 4th century B.C.

Søndre Boulevard 27
DK-4930 Maribo

## NOTES

1. I would like to thank Dott. Paola Pelagatti from the *Soprintendenza Archeologica per l'Etruria Meridionale* (Villa Giulia) for the necessary permissions, the *Archeoclub di Blera* for making the tomb accessible, and the *Accademia di Danimarca* in Rome for accommodation and equipment; lecturer *Lars Johnsen* kindly adjusted the linguistic errors. Drawings and photographs are by the author. For M&M.


## BIBLIOGRAPHY

| | |
|---|---|
| DEMUS-QUATEMBER, M. 1958 | *Etruskische Grabarchitektur: Typologie und Ursprungsfragen* (Deutsche Beiträge zur Altertumswissenschaft 11) Baden-Baden. |
| KOCH, H., VON MERKLIN E. & WEICKERT, C. 1915 | Bieda, *RM* 30, 161-310. |
| OLESEN, J. P. 1982 | *The Sources of Innovation in Later Etruscan Tomb Design (ca. 350-100 B.C.)* (Archaeologica 27). Roma. |
| POULSGAARD MARKUSSEN, E. 1979 | *Painted Tombs in Etruria – A Bibliography.* Odense. |
| 1985 | Out of Tarquinia: The Grotta Penta at Blera, *ARID* 14, 17-36. |
| QUILICI GIGLI, S. 1976 | *Blera. Topografia antica della città e del territorio* (DAI Rom, Sonderschriften 3) Mainz am Rhein. |
| ROMANELLI, R. 1986 | *Necropoli dell'Etruria rupestre. Architettura.* Viterbo. |
| ROSI, G. 1925 | Sepulchral Architecture as Illustrated by the Rock Façades of Central Etruria. Part I, *JRS* 15, 1-59. |
| ROSI, G. 1927 | Sepulchral Architecture as Illustrated by the Rock Façades of Central Etruria. Part II, *JRS* 17, 59-96. |
| SANTELLA, L. 1981 | *Blera e il suo Territorio.* Blera. |
| WIT, J. de 1929 | Die Vorritzungen der etruskischen Grabmalerei, *JdI* 44, 31-85. |

# TEXTILES FROM MONS CLAUDIANUS
# A PRELIMINARY REPORT

## LISE BENDER JØRGENSEN

*Introduction*
The site of Mons Claudianus was introduced to the readers of *Acta Hyperborea* in the very first volume of the series (BÜLOW-JACOBSEN 1988). Since then, three excavation seasons in 1988, 1989 and 1990 have added much new information, and large quantities of finds of many categories. Textiles are one such; and although only a small sample of these has been investigated as yet, it is already clear that the Mons Claudianus textiles will be a key to the understanding of the Roman textile industry.

*The site*
First a few words on the site. Mons Claudianus is a Roman quarry, or rather a group of 130 small quarries, situated in the mountains of the Eastern Desert of Egypt, some 600 km south of Cairo. The quarries supplied stone for, for example, the Forum of Trajan, and pillars of the Pantheon, both in Rome; and for part of Diocletian's palace at Split. The administrative centre of the quarries was a defended settlement or fort in the Wadi Umm Hussein. Excavations have been centered around this settlement; a large *sebakh* or rubbish deposit south of the fort has been fully excavated, and in 1990 three areas within the fort itself have been dug. Since 1988, a survey of the quarry field has been carried out too.

*Fig. 1*

The most important find group is the *ostraca*; by now ca. 6.000 have been found. The *ostraca* supply the chronological framework of the excavations – for example the *sebakh* south of the fort is dated to the first decades of the 2nd century, and another *sebakh* in the SE corner of the fort seems datable to the middle and last half of the 2nd century AD – and they give us detailed information on the administration of the quarries, on food supplies, and on daily life. Other important artefact groups are well-preserved organic remains like leather, basketry, cor-

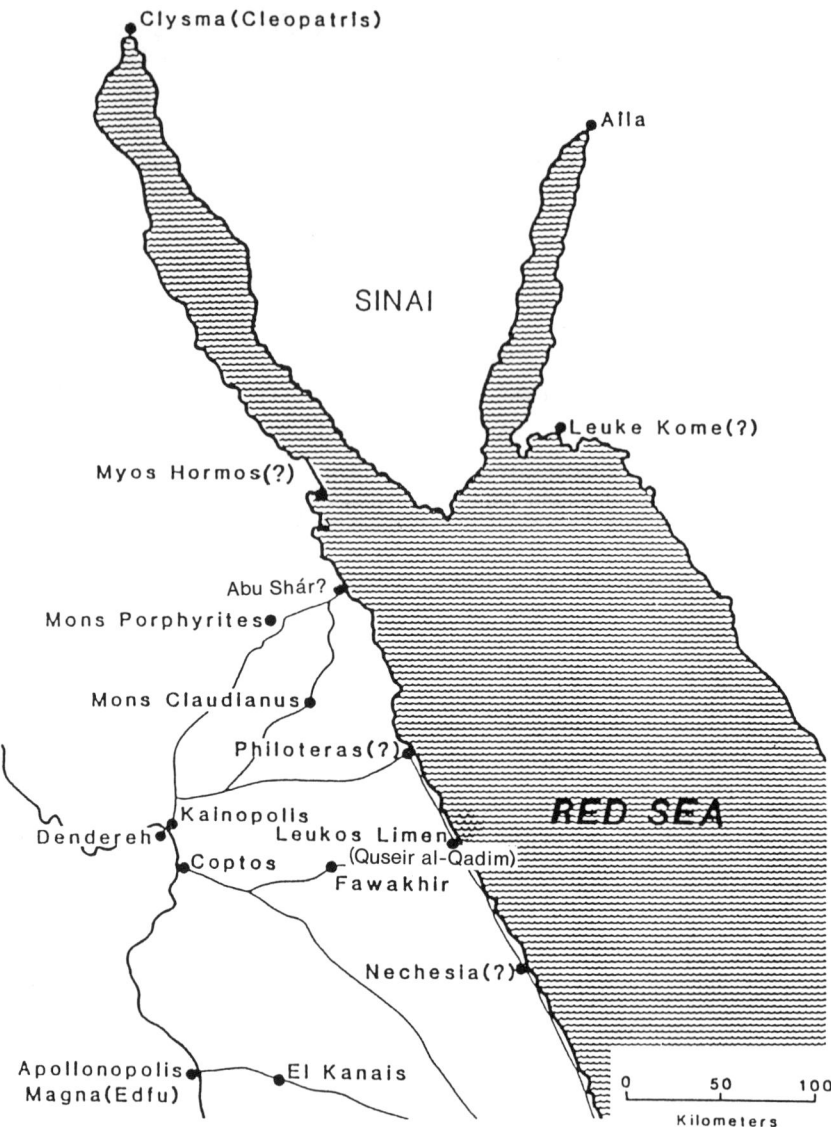

Fig. 1. Map of Egypt with the position of Mons Claudianus.

dage, paryrus fragments, food remains and textiles, and to these can be added "normal" non-perishable objects like pottery, metals and glass. Each of these adds its story to that of the *ostraca* (BÜLOW-JACOBSEN 1990, PEACOCK & MAXFIELD 1990).

## The textiles
In 1990 a sample of almost 500 textiles was recorded by the author. This number is estimated as about 10% of what was found during the campaign. The three earlier excavation seasons had yielded even larger amounts of textiles, and this means that by now somewhere between 25,000 and 50,000 textiles have been excavated at Mons Claudianus. Considering the narrow chronological framework furnished by the dated *ostraca*, the scientific value of this material is very high indeed.

## Recording methods, first aid and storage
The textiles excavated were crumpled up, and very dirty. Therefore, to facilitate examination, it was necessary to clean them and straighten them out.

First, they were put on a framed net and soaked in water. The water supply of the excavation was fetched from a pipeline, one hour's drive to the west, and this meant that the same water had to be used for several batches of textiles, and that no rinses could be made. This treatment is, of course, not ideal, and must be considered as a 'first aid'. Nonetheless, it did make it possible to perform an examination.

After soaking, the textiles were straightened out on a sheet of plastic, and left to dry in the shade. After drying, they were examined with a binocular microscope, mainly at 10-15x magnification. Details like size, shape, hems, selvedges, weave, spin, count, fibre and colour were recorded. At the close of the season, the washed textiles were stored between acid-free tissue-paper in a metal box. Unwashed textiles, like those from earlier campaigns, were put in plastic bags, and packed into metal boxes. All the textiles are deposited in the storerooms of the Egyptian Antiquities Service in Denderah.

## Technical description
### Fibres
Three types of fibre have been found at Mons Claudianus: sheep's wool, vegetable fibre (basts), and goathair. It has not yet been possible to make fibre analysis of the bast fibres to see whether they are flax or hemp. Other fibre types known from contemporary sites are cotton, camel hair and palm fibres, but these have not yet been observed at Mons Claudianus.

The majority of the textiles (more than 80%) are made of sheep's wool; only about 10% are basts, some 7% are goathair. These numbers most likely reflect differential conditions of survival rather than reflecting the true proportion between the fibres. Textiles from the southern *sebakh* were almost exclusively of wool. The part of the *sebakh* excavated in 1990 was the last vestiges of it, and the *ostraca*, for example, were notably weatherworn compared to those from the preceeding years. This, most likely applies to the textiles too, and vegetable fibres are more easily disintegrated than animal fibres. Those textiles which came from the SE corner of the Fort had a much higher proportion of bast fibres; still, they were stiff and brittle, indicating that conditions for survival of bast fibres are not ideal at this site.

## Colours

The colour range observed at Mons Claudianus compromises red, blue, purple, green, orange and yellow, and natural-coloured wool (white and brown). Goathair is blackish-brown; but here, too, some yellow, red and whitish threads have been found. Dye analyses have not yet been made; however, it is most likely that the reds derive from madder (*Rubia tinctoria*), blue from indigo (*Indigofera*) or woad (*Isatis tinctoria*); the purple may well be madder and indigo/woad mixed together, although other dyes are possible too; green similarly is most likely indigo/woad plus yellow; yellow can be obtained from many sources. These colours are well known from other Roman sites; nearby Quseir al-Qadim, a Roman port on the Red Sea coast, has yielded the same range of colours and dyes as the Mons Claudianus site (EASTWOOD 1982).

Most of the colours are found in tapestry bands (*clavi*) on undyed ground weave; some fabrics, however, are red with blue stripes or checks, or blue with red stripes/checks. One fabric is a sample of "shaded band"; the ground weave is green and orange; at the transition between the two colours is a "rainbow-band" of purple, orange and green. Similar fabrics have been found at various Roman sites in the Crimes, Syria, Israel, Nubia as well as at nearby Quseir al-Qadim (EASTWOOD 1982); they are thought to correspond to a reference in the *Periplus of the Erithraean Sea* to ζῶναι σχιωταί (XXIV, 15).

## Spinning

*Fig. 2* Spinning is basically s for single yarns, Zs for plied yarn; this is the

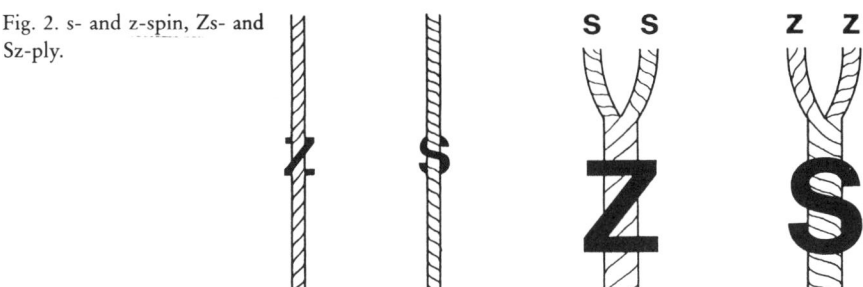

Fig. 2. s- and z-spin, Zs- and Sz-ply.

normal twist in Egypt and most other parts of the Near East. However, z-spun, og Sz-plied yarns appear too. Most textiles (some 70%) have s-spun yarn in both warp and weft; the rest are mostly s/z og z/z, only a few are from plied yarn. Sewing yarn is generally plied (Zs), but occasionally paired single yarn (ss).

## Weaves

Many different weaves have been found. The majority are tabbies, either well balanced (with an equal amount of threads in warp and weft), or weft-faced (with a tighter weft than warp). Other varieties are half-basket weave, generally with a paired weft; basket weave, with paired warp and weft; and tapestry bands, which technically belong to the tabbies as well. The latter are usually found on balanced or weft-

*Fig. 3*

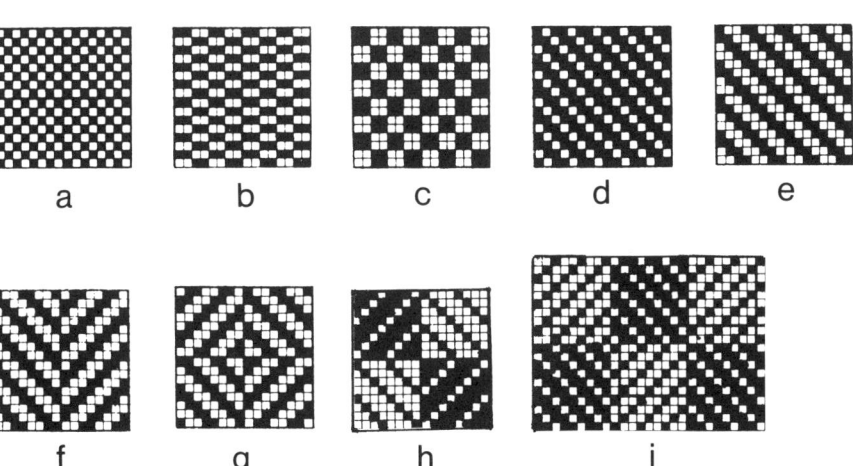

Fig. 3. Weaves found at Mons Claudianus. a: tabby; b: half-basket weave; c: basket weave; d: 2/1 twill; e: 2/2 twill; f: 2/2 broken twill; g: 2/2 diamond twill, h: 3/1 diamond twill; i: 2/1 damask twill.

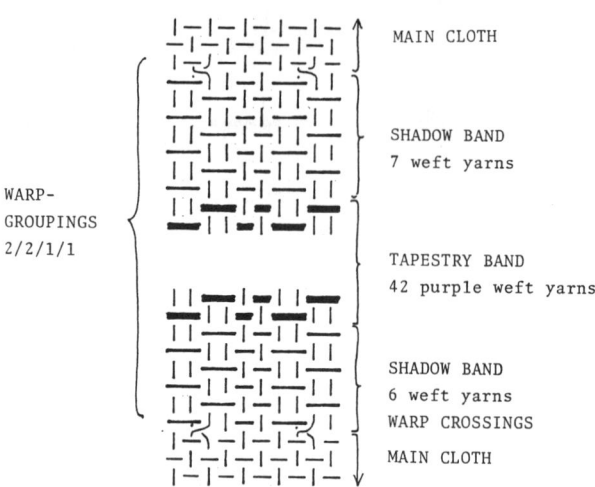

Fig. 4. Diagram of tapestry band with warp-crossings, warp-grouping, and shadow band.

faced tabbies; almost always a crossing of warp-threads can be observed at the transition between ground weave and tapetry band, followed by a "shadow band" of around 10 undyed picks, a band of dyed (purple, blue or red) picks, and finally another "shadow band", ending with a warp-crossing. Between the two warp-crossings a re-arrangement of the warp-ends can be seen. The warp is grouped in a wide variety of ways, e.g. 2/1/1/1/1/1, 2/2/2/2/2/2/1/1, 2/1/2/1 or 2/2/1/1. This feature has recently been investigated by D. De Jonghe & M. Tavernier in Coptic tapestries (1983); they conclude that the phenonomen indicates a certain weaving procedure, using a very simple loom with a heddle rod plus a shed rod for the basic weave, but inserting a second shed rod for the tapestry band. At that time, the earliest samples of this technique noted were from Palmyra (3rd century AD). Tapestry bands are quite common at Mons Claudianus: about 15% of the textiles had this kind of decoration. They derive both from the early 2nd century *sebakh* and from the SE corner of the Fort (mid/late 2nd century).

A small group of about 20 fabrics are twills. There are several varieties: 2/1 twills, 2/2 twills, 2/2 broken twills, 2/2 diamond twills, diamond twill 3/1, and a 2/1 damask twill. Finally two piled weaves can be listed.

The range of weaves found at Mons Claudianus corresponds well

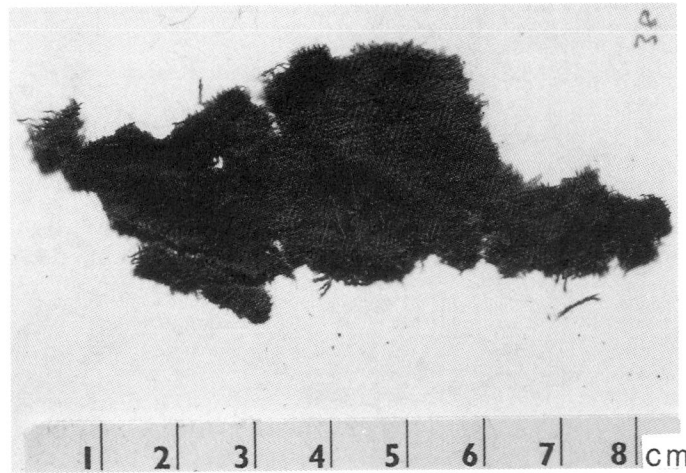

Fig. 5. Fragment of 2/1 damask twill from Mons Claudianus. Date: Mid/late 2nd century AD.

with contemporary sites like Quseir al-Qadim (EASTWOOD 1982), At-Tar in Iraq (FUJII et al. 1976, 1980), and Masada in Israel (YADIN 1966). The tabbies and tabby variants are the basic weaves at all these sites, with a sprinkle of 2/1 and 2/2 twills; the 3/1 twills have an only parallel at Quseir al-Qadim. The 2/1 damask twill at the moment seems to stand alone. It has its best parallels in a group of silk 3/1 damask twills from the 3rd and 4th centuries (see e.g. DE JONGHE & TAVERNIER 1977/78, 1981, and WILD 1984); however, the Mons Claudianus piece differs from these in several respects: it is of wool, not silk; and it is a 2/1 damask, not a 3/1 one. The appearance of a 2/1 wool damask in a 2nd century context may perhaps indicate that this kind of weave had a longer background in the Near East than hitherto believed.

Two 2/2 diamond twills deserve some comment too. One is a diamond twill z/s with a repeat of 20/18; thus it is a typical sample of the Virring type, which occurs commonly in North Europe during the Roman Period, both inside and outside the frontiers of the Roman Empire. The present author has discussed the Virring type and its origin (see BENDER JØRGENSEN 1986, and WILD & BENDER JØRGENSEN 1988). A result of the discussion is that the Virring type must have been produced in NW Europe around the Roman border, and was used both by Roman soldiers and Germanic and Scandinavian princes. The

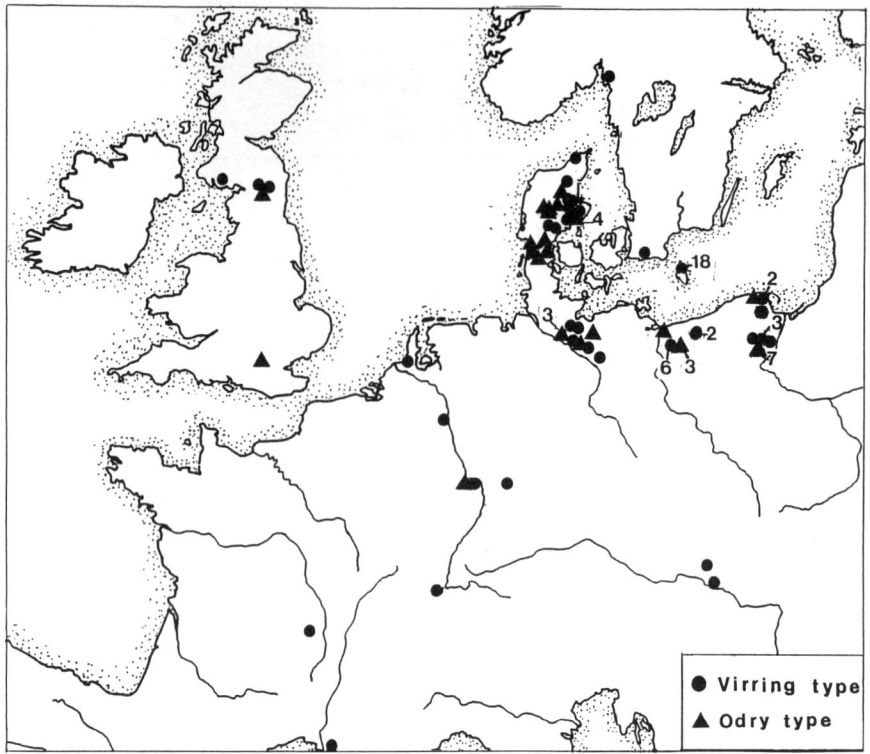

Fig. 6. Distribution map of the Virring- and Odry types in the 2nd century.

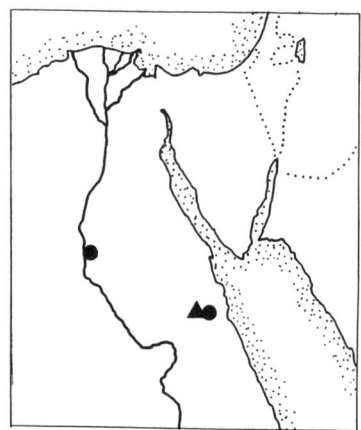

appearance of a sample of this type at Mons Claudianus emphasizes that the Virring type had a wide distribution within the Roman Empire. A second diamond twill is spin-patterned, and can be grouped with

Fig. 7. Sock in "Coptic knitting" from Mons Claudianus. Date: Mid/late 2nd century AD.

another North European cloth type, the Odry type. Like the Virring type, it occurs both on the Roman frontier (in Mainz, London and Vindolanda) and (more commonly) in the *Germania Libera* (BENDER JØRGENSEN forthcoming). Again, everything indicates that this piece was produced in Northern Europe.

*Fig. 6*

## Non-woven fabrics

Non-woven fabrics occur too; felt is quite common, and seems to have been used for padding in quilted garments or rugs. A particularly interesting piece is an almost complete knitted sock, found in the SE corner of the Fort in an Antonine/Severan context, i.e. mid/late 2nd century AD. It is so-called "Coptic knitting", i.e. cross-looped knitting, made

*Fig. 7*

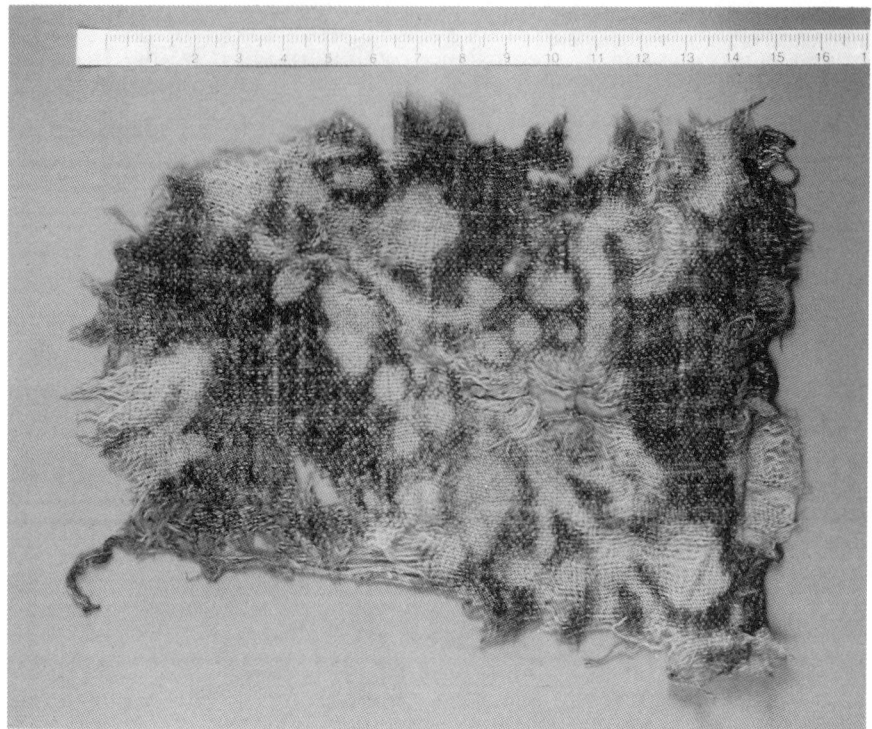

Fig. 8. Polychrome resist block printed wool fabric from Mons Claudianus. Date: Early 2nd century AD.

with a single pin (BURNHAM 1972). Similar fabrics have been found at many places in Egypt and the Near East; until now, a piece from Dura-Europos in Syria, dated to the 3rd century AD, has been the earliest.

## Constructional details

Hems and edges occur in many varieties. Simple selvedges (the weft turning and continuing in the next shed) are frequent; another common form is reinforced selvedges, made over three groups of warp threads. Cordeline finishing borders have been found in several instances, i.e. the warp ends are wound together in a cord-like border. The most common hem types are raw or rolled edge whipping, and rolled hems. Many textiles show heavy repairs, mainly in the form of patching.

## Decoration

The most common type of decoration found at Mons Claudianus is the tapestry bands described above. Most of them can probably de interpreted as *clavi*, as can be seen frequently in mummy paintings from the Fayoum. Two tapestry bands are evidently *gammas* or H-shapes, something that is well known both from Roman art and from preserved Roman textiles. No samples of so-called "Coptic tapestries" have been found at Mons Claudianus.

One sample of shaded band has alreay been mentioned; another piece worth mentioning is a purple band on a green background. Unlike the tapestry bands, it has no shadow band, andd no warp crossings. Instead of warp-grouping, part of the warp floats on the reverse of the band.

Two piled weaves were found. One was a looped, shaggy pile in undyed yarn, the other a polychrome rug with a meander-like design.

Finally a small group of resist block-printed wool fabrics deserve some attention, one polychrome (red and blue on undyed wool), two monochrome (blue on undyed). The best-preserved (polychrome) piece *Fig. 8* has a design of tendrils carrying vine-leaves and trefoil leaves in one derection, cable ornament with dots in another; this appear in natural colour against a blue background, with two unidentifiable red motifs. The two monochrome prints are more fragmented, and their designs cannot be reconstructed. The Mons Claudianus prints are the earliest samples of resist block printed textiles in the Roman world; a piece from At-Tar in Iraq (FUJII *et al.* 1976, p. 189) is the only published parallel of possibly comparable date. Pliny's Natural History (XXXV, 150) describes a method of dying with mordants that may well have been used for the pieces in question: "They (the Egyptians) first thoroughly rub white fabric and then smear them not with colours but with chemicals that absorb colours. When this has been done, the fabrics show no sign of treatment, but after being plunged into a cauldron of boiling dye, they are drawn out a moment later dyed, and the remarkable thing is that although the cauldron contains only one colour, it produces a series of different colours in the fabric, the hue changing with the quality of the chemicals employed, and it cannot afterwards be washed out".

## Uses/functions

The textiles from Mons Claudianus are all very much fragmented; many are evidently rags, torn or cut from originally larger pieces. Only rarely is it possible to determine, or even to guess, the original function.

The polychrome rug mentioned above is perhaps the most certain piece as regards its original use: it must derive from a floor covering, or perhaps a bedspread. The polychrome printed fabric is another, where a guess is possible: the motif suggests a wall-hanging or curtain rather than a piece of clothing.

Clothes must be richly represented among the rags; but only a few can be determined. One large piece may be the remains of a sleeve, patched three times. Most of the fabrics with tapestry bands probably derive from tunics, the bands being the *clavi* on each shoulder. The two samples of gamma or H-signs more likely come from cloaks. One fragment of a girdle was found. The goat hair fabrics are best interpreted as saddle cloth or bags.

Frequently the textiles from Mons Claudianus were in Antiquity cut into squares or rectangles of some 10/15 cm. As mentioned in the introduction, the textiles are crumpled up and very soiled when found, and as they furthermore derive from a large midden, the thought that many textiles found an end use as a kind of "toilet paper" presented itself. The theory cannot be proven yet; but similar suggestions have been put forward, for instance for textiles found at the contemporary Roman fort of Vindolanda in Britain, and for textiles from several medieval rubbish deposits in Europe. Other possible end uses for some of the Mons Claudianus rags are as jar stoppers or draught stoppers.

## Acknowledgements

Thanks are due to the 1st Dept. of the National Museum of Denmark for the generous loan of a microscope, and to the British Academy for financing my participation in the excavations. G. M. Vogelsang-Eastwood, Leiden, and J. P. Wild and W. Cooke, both Manchester, have given me much help and advice in discussing the Mons Claudianus with me, and I owe them a debt of gratitude for this.

Konservatorskolen
Esplanaden 34
DK-1263 Copenhagen K.

## BIBLIOGRAPHY

| | |
|---|---|
| BENDER JØRGENSEN, L. 1986 | *Forhistoriske textiler i Skandinavien. Prehistoric Scandinavian Textiles (Nordiske Fortidsminder,* Ser. B, 9). København. |
| forthcoming: | *North European Textiles until AD 1000 (Nordiske Fortidsminder).* |
| BURNHAM, D. 1972 | Coptic Knitting: An Ancient technique, *Textile History* 3, 116-124. |
| BÜLOW-JACOBSEN, A. 1988 | Mons Claudianus. Roman Granite-Quarry and Station on the Road to the Red Sea, *ActaHyp.* 1, 159-65. |
| 1990 | Mons Claudianus – et stenbrud i Ægypten, *Sfinx* nr. 1, 10-15. |
| DE JONGHE, D & M. TAVERNIER 1977/78 | Die spätantike Köper 4-Damaster aus dem Sarg des Bischofs Paulinus in der Krypta der St. Paulinus-Kirche zu Trier, *TrZ,* 40/41, 145-174. |
| 1981 | Les damasses de Palmyre, *BTextilAnc* 54, 20-51. |
| 1983 | Le phenomene du croisage des fils de chaine dans les tapisseries Coptes, *BTextilAnc* 57/58, 174/186. |
| EASTWOOD, G. M. 1982 | Textiles, in D. Whitcomb & J. Johnson: *Quseir al-Qadim 1980. Preliminary Report.* Malibu. |
| FUJII, H. (ed.) 1976 | *Al-Tar I. Excavations in Iraq, 1971-1974.* Tokyo. |
| 1980 | *Al Rafidan (Journal of Western Asiatic Studies) I. A Special Edition on the Studies on Textiles from At-Tar Caves, Iraq.* Tokyo. |
| PEACOCK, D. P. S. & V. A. MAXFIELD 1990 | *Archaeological reports from Mons Claudianus 1990.* Southampton. |
| WILD, J. P. 1984 | Some early silk finds in Northwest Europe, *The Textile Museum Journal* 1984, 17-23. |
| WILD, J. P. & L. BENDER JØRGENSEN 1988 | Clothes from the Roman Empire. Barbarians & Romans, in: L. Bender Jørgensen, B. Magnus & E. Munksgaard (eds.): *Archaeological Textiles (Arkæologiske Skrifter* 2), København, 65-98. |
| YADIN, Y. 1966 | *Masada.* London. |

# THE DANISH ARCHAEOLOGICAL EXCAVATIONS AT AYIOS KONONAS, CYPRUS
# A PRELIMINARY REPORT OF THE FIRST SEASON OF WORK (1989)

JANE FEJFER, NIELS HANNESTAD AND
HANS ERIK MATHIESEN

The first campaign at the settlement of Ayios Kononas on the northwestern part of the Akamas Peninsula took place in September and October 1989[1]. The site investigated, the central area of which measures c. 240 by 200 m, is situated 1.7 km from the coast on the gentle, western slopes of the Akamas ridge between the chapel of Ayios Kononas and the Medieval church of Ayios Yeoryios, about 75-85 m above sea level. From the chapel of Ayios Kononas, a fertile valley stretches towards the sea. The site also comprises a ruined chapel supposed to have been dedicated to Ayia Irini and, according to older maps, a collapsed church of Ayios Epiphanios, the ruins of which seem to have been incorporated in a farm house. The site is named after Saint Konon (the name being changed in modern times into Kononas), who is recorded to have suffered martyrdom in the middle of the 3rd century during the persecution of the Christians in the reign of Emperor Decius.

*Fig. 1*

Within the area are the remains of a deserted village, of which some partly ruined houses made of re-used ancient building material are still standing. In parts of the terrain, soil erosion has exposed the bedrock, while in others the soil was protected by limestone walls or foundations of houses of which substantial remains are still visible on the surface. In some parts of the site, walls are preserved to a height of 1.5 m, or even more, while in others only the bottom foundation layers remain. The area is also characterized by large amounts of limestone in heaps or strewn over the area – apparently much-eroded ancient building material. Judging from the remains, the habitation would seem to have been

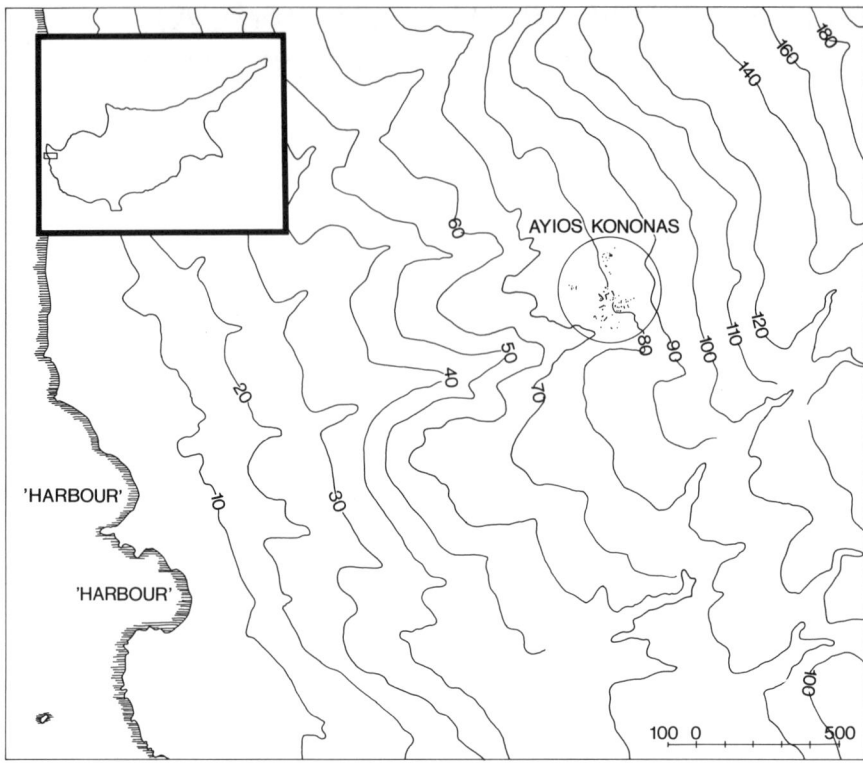

Fig. 1. Ayios Kononas is situated on the western side of the Akamas Peninsula. The site proper is within the circle.

situated primarily in a line from the church of Ayios Yeoryios towards the south, beyond the 'Ayia Irini' chapel. From here it spreads to the west, around a depression in the ground which proved to be a quarry.

In an area delimited by large irregular stones placed edgeways, in the northwestern part of the locality, large quantities of metal slag attest a metal production. No traces of habitation could be demonstrated in this area, and the stretch between the slag area and the site proper consists of open bedrock.

Today, the site of Ayios Kononas is deserted, apart from a seasonal sojourn of shepherds from the villages on the eastern side of the Akamas ridge in the old village houses. Most of the surrounding land is covered by scrub and bushes, *maki*, with only a few isolated fields, now disused. Scattered in the area one still finds some olive trees from the period of continuous habitation.

## THE DANISH ARCHAEOLOGICAL EXCAVATIONS AT AYIOS KONONAS

Archaeological investigations and reports from the Ayios Kononas area are sparse. The site is mentioned by Hogarth[2], and in the guidebook by the English traveller R. Gunnis from the beginning of this century there is a mention of "the ruins of a large town...; an area of about half a square mile is covered with ruins... Behind the village and in the thick scrub is a vast Hellenistic-Roman necropolis... The harbour of this ancient town can still be traced, and several black marble mooring pillars remain *in situ*"[3]. In recent years the area has been incorporated in three general surveys of the Akamas Peninsula, which is known traditionally as the land of the 101 churches[4]. The first survey was carried out in 1946 by J.S. Last[5], the next survey, by the Department of Antiquities, Cyprus, took place in 1960[6], and in 1981-82 an American team surveyed primarily the northern and eastern parts of the peninsula[7]. The material from these surveys showed a range of sites mainly of

Fig. 2. Fragmentary funerary stele of the Late Classical or Hellenistic period with a relief of an enthroned female figure. The stele was found near the church of Ayios Yeoryios.

the Neolithic, Hellenistic and Late Roman/Byzantine periods. However, no investigation has taken place previously at the site itself.

The main purpose of the first campaign at Ayios Kononas was to establish through a series of trial trenches the period of habitation of the settlement and its physical extent, to locate its core, and to define the character of the settlement.

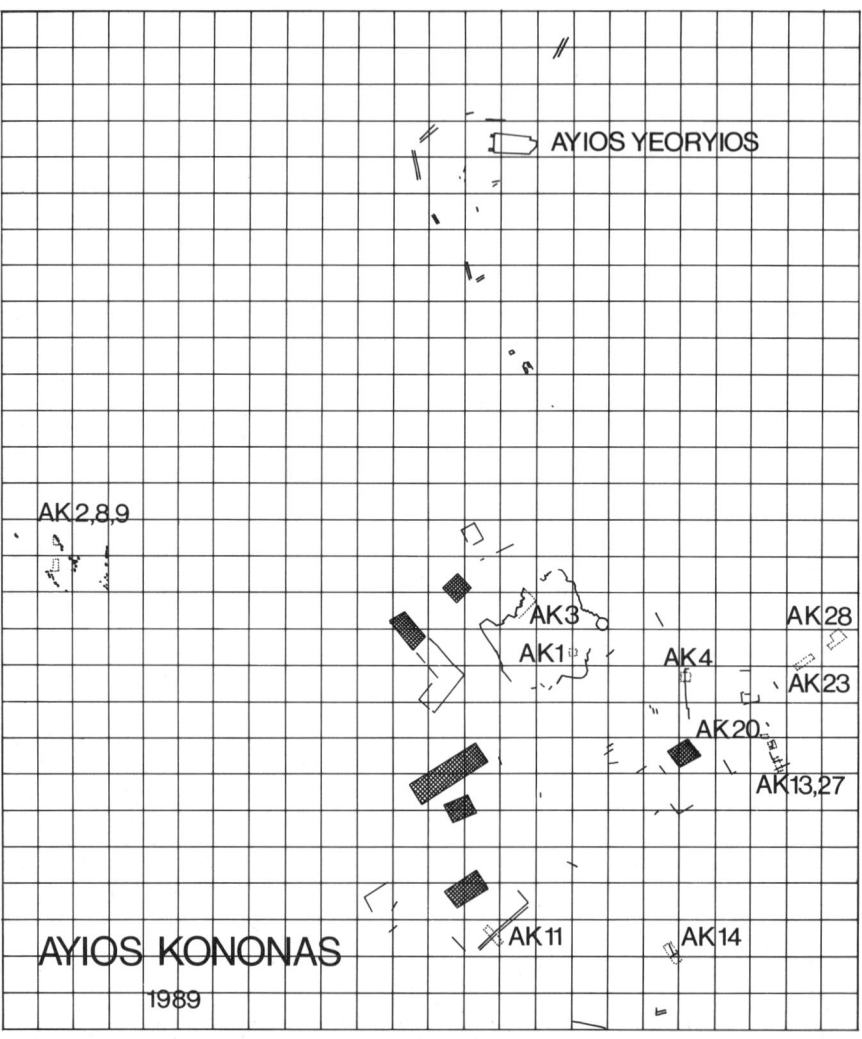

Fig. 3. This map of the site was drawn in 1989. The lines indicate visible ruins while the modern houses are cross-hatched. The numbers refer to trial trenches the outlines of which are indicated with dot-and-dash lines.

## THE DANISH ARCHAEOLOGICAL EXCAVATIONS AT AYIOS KONONAS

The campaign started with a survey of the site proper, including a registration of surface finds, above all pottery. Of great interest are also a sundial, architectural profiles, a fragmentary grave stele with a relief of an enthroned woman of the Late Classical or Hellenistic period[8], a Roman domestic miniature altar, pieces of slabs of Proconessus marble, olive presses and several fragments of grain mills of grey lava-stone. It is notable that prehistoric surface finds are scarce, that the Archaic period is missing and the Classical period so far is represented only by the grave stele. Further, there is hardly any glazed Islamic pottery.

*Fig. 2*

In addition, a new map of the site with the visible remains, supposed to be ancient, and the more recent village houses was drawn. This

*Fig. 3*

Fig. 4. The quarry (Trench AK3).

directed the placing of 13 trial trenches (AK 1, 2, 3, 4, 8, 9, 11, 13, 14, 15, 20, 23, 28). The provisional results of the excavation of some of these trenches will be described below.

Also the surroundings were examined, to decide whether it would be practicable to undertake a thorough surface survey in this very rough and difficult country. With a certain reservation concerning the problem of the partially impenetrable *maki*, which calls for special methods, the answer to this question would seem to be in the affirmative.

## AK 3, The Quarry

*Fig. 4*  AK 3 was laid out at the northern limit of a depression in the limestone bedrock in the middle part of the site. Here step-like cuttings indicated the existence of a quarry.

The excavation reached the bottom in this marginal part of the quarry, but this may not be the deepest level of the whole quarry. The quarry was filled with stones, chippings from the removal of blocks, masses of pottery and earth. It does appear that when the quarry became defunct, apparently in the Byzantine period, it was used as a refuse dump, and stone and other material was cast into it. Through the ages, earth from the surroundings silted, or was blown into it, starting with the ancient surface soil, the 'terra rossa', and followed by the *Fig. 5* lower levels. Thereby a kind of 'reversed chronological' stratigraphy emerged, and some Hellenistic sherds were found in the upper levels of the quarry, above Byzantine material.

The limestone of the quarry is relatively soft and easy to work. On the other hand, it erodes easily. To lift a block, a vertical channel was cut around the edges to the depth required and then the block was cut

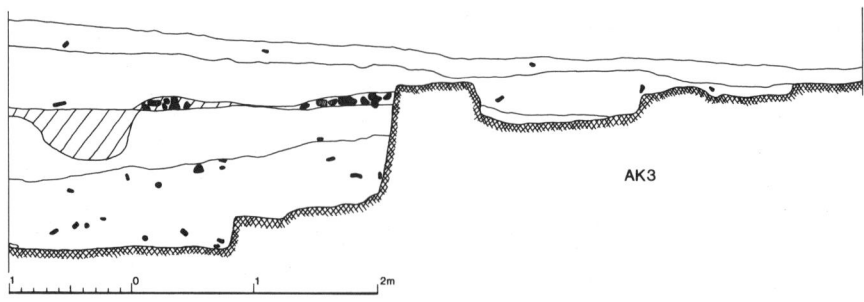

Fig. 5. Section from the quarry (Trench AK3).

## THE DANISH ARCHAEOLOGICAL EXCAVATIONS AT AYIOS KONONAS

Fig. 6. The church of Ayios Yeoryios.

loose by horizontal chiseling from the free side or sides. There seems to have been no standard scantlings, but to judge from the cuttings left in the rock, some of the blocks were of substantial size, at least up to c. 0.80 m.

The quarry measures c. 28 by 28 m and would seem to have been of only local importance. Probably most of the stones for the buildings at Ayios Kononas came from it. However, there is at least one other small quarry in the area.

## AK 4

This trench covers the northwestern corner of a large building with a smaller extension to the north, the walls of which were visible on the surface. The western wall of the larger building consists primarily of very large limestone ashlars, while the north wall of this building and those of the extension are of less regular stones. The excavation also revealed a small part of a wall running west from the northwestern corner of the larger building.

Apart from a limestone female ex-voto breast and a fragment of an architectural profile found in the surface layer, the corner of the larger building contained very few finds. In contrast, many fragments of glass and 7 copper coins (or 8; the last one may, however, be just a small disc) and a large quantity of tiles were found in the extension, which showed traces of fire. The coins are very eroded, and have not yet been examined after cleaning, but to judge from their physical appearance – they are small and very thin – they might be of the Late Roman or, perhaps rather more likely, of the Byzantine period.

The original use of this complex must remain uncertain until further excavation has been performed, but the female ex-voto breast would seem to indicate a religious function.

To the east of the large building, or at its eastern end, the chapel of 'Ayia Irini' has been built of re-used material, including several architectural profiles and at least one small column base.

Also the Medieval church of Ayios Yeoryios in the northernmost part of the site is constructed primarily of ancient stones, among these again several architectural profiles. The exact date of Ayios Yeoryios and 'Ayia Irini' is not known, but it seems likely that they were erected in the first centuries of the 2nd millennium AD. A small relief of a Maltese cross in the Ayios Yeoryios church perhaps should be taken to indicate that this church was built during the time of the crusaders. That would connote that the buildings from which the material originally came had collapsed at a previous time.

*Fig. 6*

Fig. 7. The slag area (Trenches AK2, 8, 9).

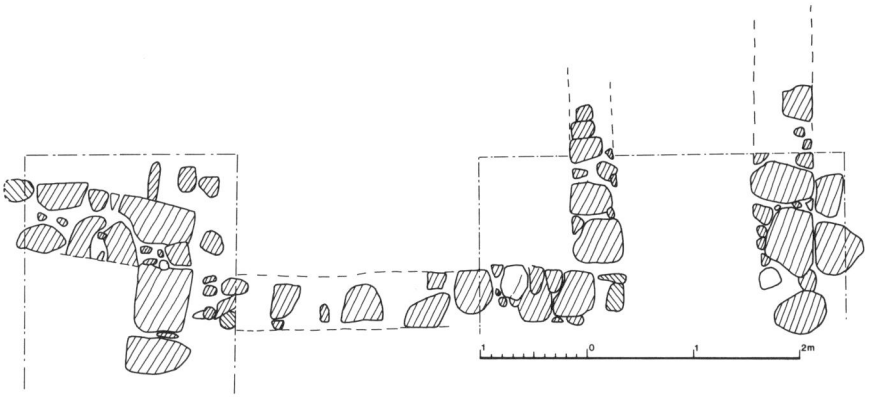

Fig. 8. Trench AK13 (to the right) and AK27. The coin of Emperor Constans was found in the corner of AK13.

## AK 2, 8, 9, The Slag Area

Trenches AK 2, 8 and 9 were laid out in an area with an abundance of metal slag lying on the surface. Single pieces of slag are found all over the site, but the main bulk is in the northwestern part, in an area surrounded by 'walls' of very large, irregular stones placed in two almost straight lines with a possible extension at a somewhat different angle to the east. As yet it is not clear whether these 'walls' were made contemporaneously with the metal production or whether they are of an earlier period.  *Fig. 7*  *Fig. 8*

Trench AK 2 covers a circle of stones with a depression in the middle visible on the surface in the southern part of the slag area. The examination showed that the circle had been placed on top of metal slag, the stones showed no traces of fire, and thus the circle probably was in no way connected with melting of metal. Still, in Layer 2 a single piece of wattle-and-daub with traces of fire and some charcoal, indicating that a melting did take place here, were found. The upper layer yielded a metal slag fused to a piece of coarse pottery. On the surface proper lay a few Byzantine sherds, but apart from these, the excavation, which was taken to bedrock, only about 0.50 m below the surface, gave no material immediately datable by ordinary archaeological methods.

The piece of pottery with an adhering slag, some other slags and some charcoal have been brought to Denmark for further, technical examination and dating by the thermolumiscence and accelerated radiocarbon method respectively. The results are not yet available, but one slag has been subjected to X-ray fluorescence by *Jysk Teknologisk Institut*. This examination suggests that the slags are of iron or copper, and their structure is as follows[9]:

Aluminium (Al) 9.5%
Silicon (Si) 17 %
Potassium (K) 0.1%
Calcium (Ca) 2.2%
Titanium (Ti) 0.2%
Manganese (Mn) 15 %
Iron (Fe) 12 %
Copper (Cu) 1.1%
Zinc (Zn) 0.1%

Besides, there are traces of vanadium, chromium, molybdenum and lead – all under 0.05%. The ore possibly came from deposits located on the Akamas ridge[10].

Trenches AK 8 and 9, which were placed on the 'walls' around the slag area, revealed that the large stones were placed directly on the bedrock, but otherwise gave no further information about the dating of the complex.

## AK 13, 27

The purpose of Trench AK 13 was to examine the remains of a wall running north-south and visible on the surface. At the southern end of this wall is another wall running east-west and, at a certain distance, yet another with the same orientation. To the west of these walls, the landscape slopes down towards the west, and to their south is a steep cliff some metres high.

The two southern walls may have been part of one complex, which, to judge by the pottery found between them, was erected in the Byzantine period. Although one of these walls seems to create a 'corner' with the northern wall, the latter may not originally have been part of this complex. It may even have been built in an earlier period; its quality is far better than that of the other walls, and the angle of the 'corner' is not quite 900, nor is there any bond between the two walls. Behind the wall running north-south, i.e. to the east of it, two coins apparently of the same type were found. So far only one of them has been positively

*Fig. 9* identified, and it was struck by Emperor Constans in 347/348 AD. A

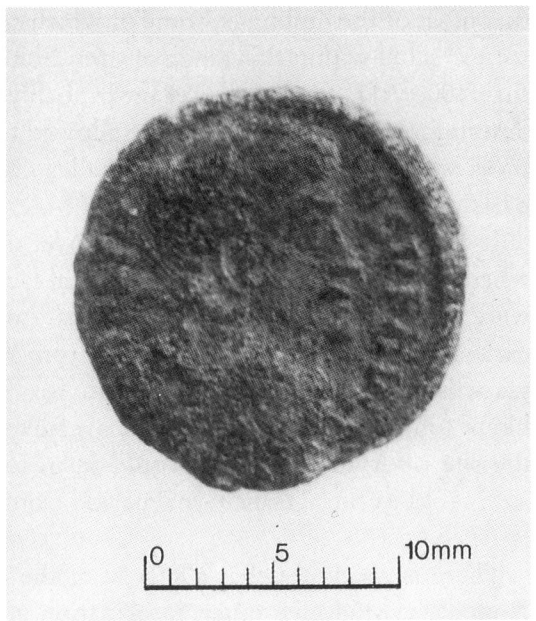

Fig. 9. Coin of Emperor Constans struck in AD 347/348.

similar date should most likely be suggested for the building to which the wall belonged.

The purpose of Trench AK 27 was to follow the northern extension of the north-south wall of Trench AK 13. However, after 2 m this wall was interrupted by a corner of a building, which was situated on the western slope of the hill. As a consequence of this siting, parts of the walls have tumbled down the slope. Until further investigation has been undertaken, the dating of this house is uncertain, but according to the finds of pottery it might be Byzantine.

## Conclusion and perspective

Although the understanding of the habitation at Ayios Kononas must remain extremely fragmented and random after only one season of work, which uncovered no more than a very small percentage of the ruins, some conclusions can already be drawn. Thus, the finds make it clear that the area was continuously inhabited from the Late Classical or Early Hellenistic to the Byzantine period. The heyday of the settlement was probably in the Late Roman or Byzantine period, when it reached its greatest extent, probably because people from the surrounding areas moved to the settlement at Ayios Kononas. It does seem likely that most of the buildings, some of which are of impressive dimensions, were erected within this range of time. Somewhat later, but hardly later than 1000 AD, a recession set in; probably most of the settlement was deserted, the large buildings were allowed to collapse and material from them was taken to erect much smaller Christian edifices in different parts of the site.

It would be of great interest to uncover the reasons for this recession; whether it was occasioned by ecological factors, or whether the reasons were of a more immediate, disastrous kind. Probably, stratigraphical excavations in the valley stretching from Ayios Kononas towards the sea will provide an approximate date for the soil erosion, which most likely followed deforestation and over-exploitation of the land. Thus, the site of Ayios Kononas would seem to be most suitable as a case study to the crucial transitional period from late Antiquity to the Middle Ages.

There is no doubt that a survey of the country surrounding Ayios Kononas would give much information about the dating of scattered settlements, patterns of habitation, and possibly also about lines of communication – the historical topography – in this part of Cyprus. It is hoped that this work will provide material for a more general study of the Akamas Peninsula as well as the interrelations between the Ayios Kononas site and the rest of the Akamas, i.e. also the town of Cape Drepanon in the south and the east coast of the peninsula, and even between this part of Cyprus and the southern regions of Asia Minor.

Future investigations should also include some of the many tombs, which are found all over the surrounding area, but especially to the south and east, and one or two bays on the sea which in all likelihood served as harbours for the settlement at Ayios Kononas, as indicated by many fragments of pottery, especially coarse ware and amphorae, both on land and in the water and by the remains of walls along the coast line. In the shallow waters of the northern part of the southern bay, stands a stone column the dating and purpose of which are unknown.

Department of Classical Archaeology,
University of Aarhus,
Denmark

## BIBLIOGRAPHY

| | |
|---|---|
| BROWN, V. TATTON 1986 | Gravestones of the Archaic and Classical Periods: local production and foreign influence, in: *Acts of the International Archaeological Symposium Cyprus between the Orient and the Occident*. Nicosia. |
| GUNNIS, R. 1948 | *Historic Cyprus* 2nd. ed. London. |
| HADJISAVVAS, S. 1977 | The Archaeological Survey of Paphos. A Preliminary Report, *RDAC* 1977, 222-231. |
| HOGARTH, D.G. 1889 | *Devia Cypria*. Frowde. |
| LAST, J.S. | Report on a Preliminary Archaeological Survey of the Western Part of the Akamas Peninsula (April 1946), unpublished. |
| WALLACE, P.W. 1984 | The Akamas Promontory of Cyprus, *RDAC* 1984, 341-347. |
| ZWICKER, U, ROLLIG, H. & SCHWARZ, U. 1972 | Investigations on Prehistoric and Early Historic Copper-Slags from Cyprus (Preliminary Report), *RDAC* 1972, 33-45. |

## NOTES

1. The members of the expedition, which was sponsored by The Carlsberg Foundation, Copenhagen, were the following: Jane Fejfer, Niels Hannestad, Anna-Elisabeth Jensen, Peter J. Crabb, Peter Hayes, Susanne Bang Nielsen, Leif Erik Vaag, Jette Geert-Jørgensen, Inge Hvolmsgaard Sørensen, Vincent Gabrielsen, Hans Erik Mathiesen.

2. HOGARTH 1889, 13f.
3. GUNNIS 1947, 382.
4. WALLACE 1984, 347, note 23.
5. LAST 1946.
6. HADJISAVVAS 1977, 222, note 2 (this work is unpublished). File 166/38/4 in The Cyprus Museum, Nicosia.
7. WALLACE 1984, 341 ff. and, especially, 345.
8. Cf. BROWN 1986, 439, pl. 50.
9. Cf. ZWICKER, ROLLIG & SCHWARZ 1972, 34 ff.
10. Mines are recorded in the Akamas by Pliny in his *Natural History*, XXXVI, 137.

# TERRACOTTA HORSES AND HORSEMEN OF ARCHAIC BOEOTIA*

## JAN STUBBE ØSTERGAARD

'The development of Boeotian institutions and society (in the Archaic period) remains obscure until the latter part of the sixth century'; those were the words of J. S. Buck in 1979[1] and they are true still. A glance at his references will show how little the archaeology of Archaic Boeotia has to offer. Yet it is from the archaeological evidence that advances are to be expected, since the epigraphical and literary sources so assiduously studied are hardly likely to multiply to the necessary extent. Alas, the archaeology of the period is at a virtual standstill, not from lack of finds, but from the lack of publication thereof; well excavated and thoroughly published sites are pitifully few. If undeterred and on the lookout for ways of making a contribution in the meanwhile, one must turn to the burials which constitute the bulk of the archaeological evidence for the society of Archaic Boeotia[2].

In the often richly furnished Archaic Boeotian tombs[3] the contents consist chiefly of vases and terracotta figurines[4]. Among the latter, the socalled idols are dominant together with horses and horsemen. Interest has centered on the former[5], while the latter have not been comprehensively dealt with since P. N. Ure's indispensable publication of the figurines from Rhitsona in 1934[6]. Though confined almost entirely to the finds from Rhitsona and only sparsly illustrated, Ure's very condensed treatment of the subject has remained the ultimate basis for ascribing and dating the horses and horsemen. Apart from the intrinsic merits of the work, this is due also to the fact that no material of comparable scope has been made available since then.

The number of know figurines of this type has never the less multiplied over the years. Major collections of terracottas have been published[7] and many individual pieces have appeared in museum catalogues and journals as well as in the publications of art market[8]. Most importantly, a number of finds from more recent excavations in Boeotia have been published, though only summarily[9].

Excellent use has been made of this fact by M. Szabo in the 1970's, in studies of some early groups of horses and horsemen poorly represented at Rhitsona[10]. Published in French in Hungarian periodicals these articles have not received the attention they deserve. Language barriers have also prevented the no doubt detailed discussion of the archaic horses and horsemen in his monograph, in Hungarian, on archaic Boeotian terracottas from reaching a wider audience[11].

In view of this, and of the fact that a growing number of figurines later than the ones dealt with by Szabo find no place in Ure's scheme of things, time seems ripe for a renewed inspection of the horses and horsemen, the aim being to clarify the increasingly blurred picture we have of these little works.

For lack of archaeological context, this inspection will of necessity be primarily concerned with style. The modelling and decoration of these handmade figurines will be examined in some detail in order to identify any stylistic groupings. Such an approach has already been taken to the Boeotian 'idols'[12] and for the horses and horsemen, the beginning made by Szabo is promising[13]; it is encouraging that working independently of him on the same material I came to very similar conclusions[14]. I also note that in recent research on the Attic Geometric horse-pyxides from the Kerameikos, the style and technique of the handmade horses on the lids form the basis of the attribution of the pyxides to individual hands and workshops[15]. In 1939, Grace was of the opinion that attributing the Boeotian 'idols' to individual hands would be 'a perfectly possible work of supererogatory erudition'[16]; for the history of art that may be, but in the present context a more positive attitude is justified.

The horses and horsemen considered here are those which I have either seen or had photographs of; though autopsy is always preferable, the features relevant to my purposes are visible in most ordinary illustrations. Many pieces are without documented contexts and in those cases I have taken no account of the given provenances, even when one may argue in favour of them[17]. Certainty is required. As for warnings that such objects may be 'unrealiable', they may be countered by pointing out that the low esteem in which our figurines have been held serves to make forgery on any scale very unlikely; only when we come to the Hellenistic period does that problem arise[18].

Before proceeding, some limitations on the scope of this exercise must be mentioned. I have not attemted a comparative study involving other types of Boeotian terracottas and contemporary vases, though called for; the relevant bodies of material are too extensive for me in this connection. Nor have I found it possible to examine the relations of Boeotian terracotta horses and horsemen with those of other parts of the Greek world[19]. There are points of similarity with Cypriot, Rhodian and Attic versions of the motif[20], but the Boeotian figurines are sufficiently distinct from others to be studied on their own.

## Geometric beginnings and the 'black' groups A-C

Although I intend to restrict myself to a muster of freestanding single horses and horsemen – thus excluding teams of horses – I begin by mentioning the horses serving as handles on the lids of Boeotian Late Geometric pyxides[21]. They are the earliest Boeotian terracotta horses known to me, belonging around 700 B.C. The idea is Attic in origin [22] and the horses look Attic too: heavy, black animals with reserved decoration, tails and legs vertical. They are earlier by a century or more than the first horses to appear at Rhitsona, to which we now turn.

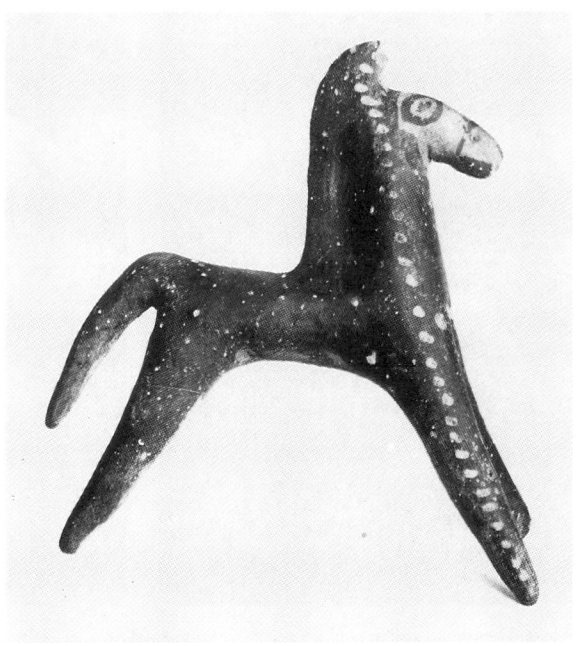

Fig. 1. Thebes, Archaeological Museum, Rhitsona 145.94. H.12,5cm. Group A (A1).

## Group A

Earliest are figurines from the series of graves named 'Corinthian c' by Ure and dated c.590-570 B.C. They belong to the 'primtive' class and most are striped in black glaze on the clay ground ('black on browns') or in red on a white ground ('red on whites')[23]. But we look first at a lone black horse (A1)[24]. The head is reserved, but noseband, eye, and the rest of the body are in black glaze. On the black, the horse carries rows of white dots: a row up the front of each foreleg, continuing right up to the crest of the mane, a row across the chest and one down the length of the back. The tail has white cross bars. The conical, pointed legs are extended and the tails is raised at an angle. The barrel is short and cylindrical, the neck very upright with the front continuing the line of the extended forelegs so that is almost seems inclined backwards. The mane is thin, set off from the neck, and tapers into a high crest. The large head has a bulge under the eye.

*Fig. 1*

A number of horses share these features to form group A[25]:

Fig. 2. Denmark, private. H.15,0 cm. Group A (A3).

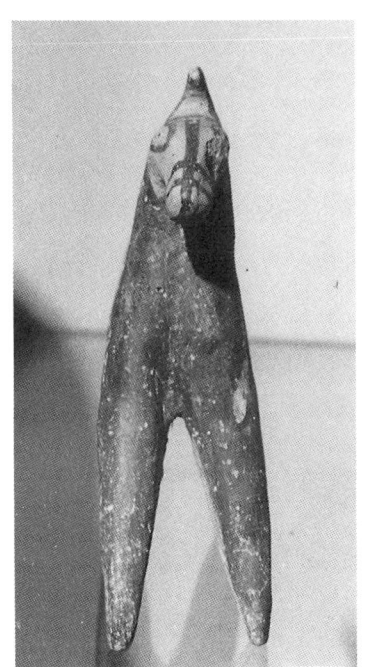

Fig. 3. University of Newcastle, Greek Museum inv.no. 73. H.14,2cm. Group A (A6).

Fig. 4. University of Newcastle, Greek Museum inv.no. 73. H.14,2 cm. Group A (A6).

## A

1. Rhitsona 145.94. URE 1934, 61 pl. XV. Horse.     *Fig. 1*
2. Basle, market. *MuM Sonderliste E August* 1964, no. 21. Horse.
3. Denmark, private. *Louisiana Årbog* 1958, 13 fig. 5; 26 fig. 15 left. Horse[26].     *Fig. 2*
4. Geneve, Musée d'Art et d'Historie 10.939 *Le Musée d'Art et d'Historie* 1919-1960; *Geneve* s.a. 23 pl. 19 right. Horse.
5. London, British Museum 73.8-20.577. HIGGINS 1954, no. 771. Horse.
6. Newcastle upon Tyne, University, Greek Museum inv. 73. Unpublished. Horse[27].     *Fig. 3-4*

Related:

7. Manchester, Manchester Museum 40242. Unpublished. Horse[28].

The similarity between A1 and A5 was recognized by Ure and Higgins, while Szabo added A2 and A4[29]. Members of the group, so far all horses, have in common their shape as described for A1. They also share the reserved head with painted details. A1-3 have rows of white dots, whereas A4 has incised zigzags enclosed by lines up each foreleg. A5 is apparently without any decoration on the black. A1 probably has the reserved belly and inside of legs found in the rest of the group.

As pointed out by Szabo, a number of Boeotian plastic vases and terracottas may be connected with group A[30].

Fig. 5. Malibu, J.Paul Getty Museum inv.no. 82.AD.84. H.12,7 cm. Group B (B1).

## Groups B, Ba and Bb

Fig. 5  The use of white decoration on the black glaze recurs on a horseman in the J. Paul Getty Museum in Malibu, but it is applied in a scheme as different as the modelling from that found in group A. The horse is of a more powerful build, with thick pillar-like forelegs and quite naturalistic hind legs showing hock-joints and fetlocks. The tail is thick and curves down into a vertical position. The body of the horse is quite long from rump to thrust-out chest and on it is set a neck of triangular

Fig. 6. Copenhagen, National Museum inv.no. 4731. H.17,5 cm. Group B (B2).

profile, very deep at the root. The mane ends in a low forelock, of triangular shape when seen from above. The ears are pricked up attentively, there is a slit for the mouth and the nostrils are indicated by holes.

As for the rider, he sits well back on the horse and has very thick arms extended towards the neck and similar, bent, legs. His hands are vertically pierced, probably for reins which would have run through the slit mouth. The trunk of his body continues without a break into

Fig. 7. Munich, Antikensammlungen inv.no. 6598. H.9,5 cm. Group B (B5).

Fig. 8. Athens, Kanellopoulos Museum inv.no. 1774. H. 11,5 cm. Related group B (B7).

Fig. 9. Tübingen, Antikenmuseum inv.no. 5455/28. H.12,0 cm. Related group B (B8).

the head, dominated by a huge nose. Details such as fingers, eyes, hair and the riders wreath are in black glaze. There are white dots on the wreath and on the black chiton. The horse is all black except for the reserved belly and inside of the legs (the left painted all round). On top of the forelock is a white zigzag and the long hair of the mane is shown as vertical white zigzags. White is also used for the noseband, cheek-straps and eyes as well as for the dot rosette on the chest.

It's fine piece and it has several companions making up group B:

### Group B

*Fig. 5* 1. Malibu, J. Paul Getty Museum 82.AD.84. *GettyMusJ* 12, 1984, 93, 94 figs. 1a-d. Horseman.
*Fig. 6* 2. Copenhagen, National Museum 4731. BREITENSTEIN 1941, no. 149. Horseman[31].

3. Brunswick, Bowdoin College, Warren Collection 1913. 3. K. HERBERT, *Ancient Art in Bowdoin College*. Cambridge MA 1964, 92 f. no. 277, pl. 30. Horseman, warrior[32].
4. New York, Pomerance Collection. *Pomerance* 1966, 86 no. 100. Horseman.
5. Munich, Antikensammlungen 6598. SZABO 1979, 7, 12 fig. 8. Horse[33].   *Fig. 7*
6. Toronto, Royal Ontario Museum 919×13.6. Unpublished. Horse[34].
Related:
7. Athens, Kanellopoulos Museum 1774. Unpublished. Horse[35].   *Fig. 8*
8. Tübingen, Antikensammlung d. arch. Inst. 5455/28. Unpublished. Horseman[36].   *Fig. 9*
9. Berlin, private. GEHRIG 1975, no. 126. Horse.
10. Copenhagen, National Museum 7057. BREITENSTEIN 1941, no. 150. Horse.

This group, comprising both horses and horsemen, was first established by Szabo, who brought together B2, B3, B5, B7, B9 and B10[37]. B1-B6 are very much alike, B1-B2 so much so that they must be by the same hand. Besides their zigzag manes we have within the group the verticals of B5-B6. Both types of mane are found among the related pieces B7-B10. They deviate in the less naturalistic hind legs and shorter, slanted tails of B7-B10, the hooved legs and thinner curved neck of B10, the forward curving legs of B8. One notes the use of added red on B2 and B8.

We are also indebted to Szabo for having seen the relationship between this group and some distinctive Boeotian plastic vases in the shape of rams and 'sphinxes'. The connection is one of both decoration and modelling. He notes a ring vase with rams head spout as belonging to the same sphere[38].

As being of less demanding workmanship and more abstract shape, but clearly associated with group B, Szabo draws attention[39] to some figurines which I think may be ordered – with some pieces added – in two distinct groupings:

## Ba

1. Athens, National Museum A 18770. SZABO 1979, 7, 14 fig. 11a-b. Horseman[40].   *Fig. 10*
2. Athens, National Museum no. ? *BCH* 14, 1890, 218 fig. 6. Horseman.
3. Oxford, Ashmolean Museum 1893. 110. C. E. VAFOPOULOU-RICHARDSON 1981, 7 no. 5a.   *Fig. 11*
Horse.[41].
4. Thebes, Archaeological Museum 5362. ANDREIOMENOU 1985, 116f. to photo 19; 126 photo 19 middle. From Tanagra. Horse.

In shape and decoration the figurines of group Ba remain dependent on group B, repeating its characteristic features in less careful execution; only the fetlocks of the hind legs have completely disappeared as has the realistic position of the riders legs, now curved forward like B8[42].

Fig. 10. Athens, National Museum inv.no. 18770. H.14,6 cm. Group Ba (Ba1).

Fig. 11. Oxford, Ashmolean Museum inv.no. 1893.110. H.10,5 cm. Group Ba (Ba3).

Bb

Fig. 12   1. Munich, Antikensammlungen 6595. SZABO 1979, 7, 13 fig. 9. Horseman[43].
2. Switzerland, private. BLOESCH 1974, 29 no. 166. Horseman.
Fig. 13   3. Bochum, Antikenmuseum S 533. KUNISCH 1972, 14 no. 10. Horse.

The technique of decoration is that of group B, but the scheme is new. Horizontal white elements have replaced vertical ones on the neck, alternating straight and wavy stripes on Bb1-2, only stripes on B3. On

Fig. 12. Munich, Antikensammlungen inv.no. 6595. H.14,0 cm. Group Bb (Bb1).

Fig. 13. Bochum, Antikenmuseum der Ruhr-Universität inv.no. S 533. H.10,3 cm. Group Bb (Bb3).

Fig. 14. Houston, Museum of Fine Arts inv.no. 34-139. H.15,6 cm. Group C (C1).

Fig. 15. York, York City Art Gallery inv.no. 1082. H.11,5 cm. Group C (C2).

Fig. 16. Stuttgart, Württembergisches Landesmuseum inv.no. 2.689. H.10,8 cm. Group C (C21).

Bb1-2, the uppermost stripe continues along the head of the horse to form eye and cheekstrap.

Little remains of the forms found in group B, really only the plastically rendered ears and forelock. The horses have grown slimmer, with legs approaching a conical shape, the tail raised at an angle, the neck of more or less the same width along its length and not very deep. The horses head no longer has the large heaviness of group B, but tapers to a point. The riders are legless, with arms reduced to mere stumps and the large noses are raised to the sky.

Three figurines may seem slender evidence for a group, but Bb1-2 must be by the same hand and such similarity in handmade objects would seem to imply production in considerable numbers.

## Group C

We come now to a third group of 'blacks', assembled by Szabo under the heading 'cavaliers à vernis'[44], my group C. It is less homogenous, especially in shape, than those hitherto met with. The common features may be illustrated by the horseman in Houston which heads my list. It is painted in a brownish black glaze, with belly and inside of legs reserved. There is no use of added white. The legs are of identical slender conical shape and quite long, extended both lengthwise and sideways. The tail is missing, but the preserved root indicates a downwards slant. The barrel is thin, the neck curves forwards diminishing only slightly in width. The crest of the mane rises to a point over the small, featureless head – the extremity is missing. Finally the rider, legless with highly stylized facial features – nose and beard – sitting far foreward on his mount, clasping the neck.

*Fig. 14*

*Fig. 14*
*Fig. 15*

C
1. Houston, Museum of Fine Arts 34-139. HOFFMANN 1970, 249 no. 133. 250 (ill.). Horseman.
2. York, York City Art Gallery 1082. *City of York Art Gallery Preview* 17, 1964, 626 pl. 3 left. Horseman.
3. Thebes no. ? *ADelt* 26, 1971, Chron 223 no. 3, pl. 196Beta alpha. From Boeotia. Horseman.
4. Berlin, Antikensammlung TC8414. K. SCHIFNER, *Griechische Terrakotten* Leipzig 1959, 23 no. 1, pl. 1. Horseman, warrior.
5. Thebes no. ? *ADelt* 26, 1971, Chron 223 no. 1, pl. 196Alpha alpha. From Mourikion Thebon. Horseman (rider missing).
6. Thebes 5132. ANDREIOMENOU 1985, 116 to photo 18. 126 photo 18 right. From Tanagra. Horse.
7. Thebes 5128. *ADelt* 32, 1976, Chron 121, pl. 93 gamma. From Tanagra. Horseman.
8. Thebes no. ? *ADelt* 26, 1971, Chron 223 no. 2, pl. 196 Alpha beta. From Boeotia. Horseman (rider missing).
9. Basle, market. *MuM Sonderliste W* 1987, 5 no. 7 (ill.), 7 no. 7. Horse.
10. Munich, Antikensammlungen 6592. Unpublished. Horseman[45].
11. Munich, Antikensammlungen 6593. Unpublished. Horseman[46].
12. Olympia K 167. SZABO 1973, 18 no. 14; 15 fig. 12. Horseman.
13. Thebes 5130. ANDREIOMENOU 1985, 116 to photo 18; 126 photo 18 middle right. From Tanagra. Horseman.
14. Thebes no. ? *ADelt* 26, 1971, Chron 223 no. 4, pl. 196Beta beta. From Boeotia. Horseman.
15. Thebes 5140. *ADelt* 31, 1976, Chron 121, pl. 93 gamma right. From Tanagra. Horseman.
16. Thebes 5139. ANDREIOMENOU 1985, 116 to photo 18; 126 photo 18 left. From Tanagra. Horseman.

17. Athens, National Museum 3887. Zervos 1934, pl. 128 middle. Horseman, warrior.
18. Olympia no. ? Szabo 1973, 18 no. 13; 14 fig. 11. Horseman.
19. Budapest, Museum of Fine Arts 51.137. Szabo 1973, 18 no. 15; 16f. fig. 13-15. Horseman.
20. Thebes 5364. Andreiomenou 1985, 116 to photo 19; 126 photo 19 left. From Tanagra. Horse.
21. Stuttgart, Württembergisches Landesmuseum 2.689. Unpublished. Horseman.[47].

*Fig. 16*

Having viewed these horses and horsemen some further comments on group C are called for. The horses may be covered completely in glaze or have belly and inside of legs reserved. In two instances the use of reservation is more extensive: C19 has the tail reserved and decorated with three transverse and one lengthwise stripe in glaze; on C4 the tail carries a more complex scheme of five lengthwise stripes combined with crosshatching and other areas are reserved as well – mane, head of horse and parts of the rider. The prominent nose and beard of this rider are a regular feature in group C, but here elaborate headgear is added and legs are shown as well. A bulge indicates his sex. The arms, too, are exceptionally elaborate and the right hand is pierced to hold a weapon. The horse has also received additional plastic detailing, the ears; and like the rider the horse has other features added in glaze in the reserved areas. At the core both rider and horse are however of the C-breed, representing the high end of a spectrum af quality. Individual details occur on other figurines of the group, headgear and raised right arm on C17, ears on the horses C12 and C15. The lower end is made ud of such horsemen as C10 and C11 whose heads are featureless protrusions. The latitude of modelling within the group is exemplified by C6, C7, C13, C15 and C16 all from tomb Epsilon 17 at Tanagra – necks may be more or less curved, crests more or less prominent, some heads heavier and larger than others. In the tomb series just mentioned C7 and C13 on the one hand, C15 and C16 on the other, are very like one another, C6 representing a third variety. As more figurines become available, the diversity of group C may turn out to be less haphazard than it seems.

## Groups A-C; style and chronology

A review of these groups of 'blacks' shows that they are related to one another primarily by the extensive use of black glaze in their decoration. Stylistically, groups A and C are clearly closer to each other than they are to group B, having in common the conical, pointed legs without anatomical details, extended sideways as well as lengthwise. The use of reservation in the heads of group A is parallelled by C4 and reservation is used on the tail of C4 and C19. The scheme of crossbars on the tail of the latter reminds one of the crossbars on the tail of A11 and both point foreward to later groups where this scheme is standard practise[48]. In shape, both group A and group C have a general affinity with the level of abstraction of such later groups. In the use of added white on the black glaze group B and its subsidiaries Ba and Bb are connected with group A. Looking at the shape of first group B, a gulf divides it from A and C. Here a relative naturalism, there abstraction. Only late in the 6th century is something comparable found, but in quite a different tenor[49]. Antecedents are as distant in time, but closer in appearance, namely the horses on the lids of the Late Geometric Boeotian pyxides[50]. On the basis of style, one would regard A and C as more or less contemporaneous, B as earlier. On this view, group Ba would be seen as the less competent companion of group B and group Bb as a possible bridge between B and A, combining features from both groups.

Turning now to the external evidence for the chronology of groups A, B and C, we find A with only the context of A1 to go on, grave 145 at Rhitsona dated c.580 B.C.[51] This is an ante quem; considering the fact that no figurines of the group were found in later graves at Rhitsona one might regard c.580 B.C. as being near the lower end of the time range for group A. For the stylistically related group C we are slightly better off. We have the evidence of C20 from tomb Lampda 9 at Tanagra, dated to the 1st quarter of the century[52], and of the tomb series C6, C7, C13, C15, C16 from tomb Epsilon 17 on the same site, dated c.570[53]. On this evidence, the similarity in style of group A and C seems one of date as well.

We have no context, alas, for group B, but the excavator of the Akraiphia graves states that figurines belonging to the group have been found in contexts dated to the early 6th century[54]. What we do have is an approximate date for the horse Ba4, found at Tanagra in a tomb of the 1st quarter of the 6th century, namely tomb Lampda 9 mentioned above for its C-figurine, C20. This suggests a certain overlap between groups Ba and C. A date very early in the century for group B is supported by the stylistically related plastic vases in the shape of rams and 'sphinxes' and the ring vase in Berlin, all given a date of c.600 B.C.[55].

So far then, the evidence points towards a date in the 1st quarter of the 6th century for groups A, B, Ba and C. That we should not go much higher than c.600 B.C. is also supported by the information that at Akraiphia no terracotta figurines have been found in graves of the 7th century[56].

The archaeological contexts for groups C and Ba given above was not available to Szabo, who argued on stylistic and technical grounds that group C must at least partially belong to the 2nd half of the 7th century B.C., comparing the facial profiles of certain C-riders with those found in his 'atelier des centaurs' which in their turn are dated to the 2nd half of the 7th century by reason of their similarity to terracottas from the Proto-Attic deposit from the Agora of Athens, of c.640 B.C.[57] In my opinion the likeness is of too general a nature to permit chronological conclusions. Untill archaeological evidence proves otherwise, I prefer to see the 'atelier des centaurs' – whose stylistic cohesion and connection with group C I accept – as belonging to the 1st quarter of the 6th century B.C.[58]

Finally a word on group Bb. Though its close relations in style to the groups already discussed makes a date similar to theirs more or less certain, another piece of evidence that this is in fact so must be mentioned. In grave Lampda 9 at Tanagra, of the 1st quarter of the century, the figurines C20 and Ba4 were found together with a series of horses of the black on brown variety[59]. They belong to my group Ha, to be dealt with later. On the neck, these horses have a scheme of alternating straight and wavy horizontals very like that of Bb1 and Bb2.

## *The early 'black on browns'; groups D-F*

After the 'blacks', it is time to look at the two main divisions of Ure's 'primitive' class. I start with those whose stripes in black glaze on the clay ground have earned them the name of 'black on browns'. They do not appear earlier nor in greater number at Rhitsona than the 'red on whites' but they cease to be made just after the middle of the century, whereas the 'red on whites' continue down to its end[60].

## *Groups D and Da*

Two sorry looking steeds from grave 101b may be the first by a small margin to appear at Rhitsona[61]. Although they are somewhat alike, they do not have the degree of similarity which makes more of the same kind likely. We turn instead to grave 145, which also contained the fine

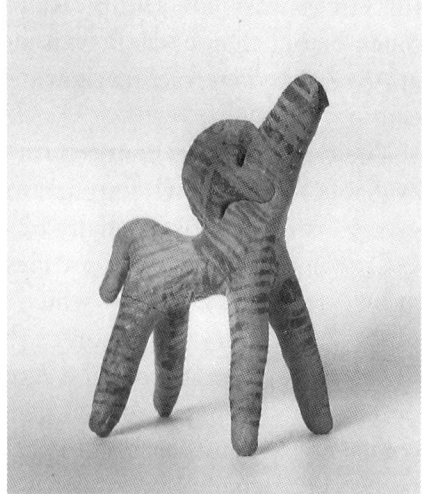

Fig. 17. Munich, Antikensammlungen inv.no. 6594. H.10,0 cm. Group D (D3).

Fig. 18. Uppsala, Gustavianum inv.no. 814. H.10,7 cm. Related to group D (D8).

horse A1. Two horsemen from this grave go together with others into group D:

D

1. Rhitsona 145.96. URE 1934, 62 pl. XV. Horseman.
2. Rhitsona 145.97. URE 1934, 62 pl. XV. Horseman.

*Fig. 17*  3. Munich, Antikensammlungen 6594. Unpublished. Horseman[62].

Related:

4. Zürich, market. *Galerie H. Vollmoeller I. Auk.* 1975, no. 30. Horseman.
5. Thebes no. ? *ADelt* 26, 1971, Chron 223, pl. 196Alpha gamma. From Boeotia. Horse.
6. Budapest, Museum of Fine Arts 81.88A. *BMusHong* 46/47, 1976, 16 fig. 7 (SZABO). Horse.
7. Once Dresden, Slg. Fiedler. *AA* 1891, 21 Abb. 3. Horseman.

*Fig. 18*  8. Uppsala, Gustavianum 814. Unpublished. Horseman, warrior[63].

9. Oklahoma, Stovall Museum C45-46/6. A.J. HEISSERER, *Classical Antiquities. Stovall Museum* (Oklahoma 1986), 84 no. 131. Horseman, warrior.
10. Frankfurt-am-Main, Liebighaus. *StädelJb*, NF 10 (1985), 318 Abb. 58. Horse.

Like C, this is a rather heterogenous assembly and really not very pretty. Legs are thick and slightly extended; tails are vertical and hang close to the hind legs. Necks droop forward with crests barely indicated and small pointed heads with no features. The riders are almost shapeless protrusions on the necks, their eyes indicated by a hole – passing right through the head in case of D2. On D2, toes and fingers are indicated by incision. The striping may look as if 'laid on in any and all directions'[64], but in fact we can discern a scheme of verticals on the barrels and horizontals on legs and neck – those on the neck continuing across the rider.

Szabo brought together D1, D2, D3, D5 and D6 and pointed out that there are Corinthian figurines somewhat like them[65]. To him this implies relations between the coroplastics of Corinth and Boeotia; if so, it remains an isolated case as far as the horses and horsemen are concerned. Certainly, the connection is not as clear as in the case of the early 6th century Boeotian idols with moulded faces of Corinthian type[66].

In Boeotia, the figurines of group D have much in common with the socalled squatting apes of which a great number exists[67].

Among the figurines belonging a general way in this undistinguished company[68], I think one may set apart the following as a group:

## Da

1. Rhitsona 110.119. URE 1934, 62 pl. XV. Horse.
2. Rhitsona 50.391. URE 1934, 62 pl. XV. Horse.
3. Berlin, private. GEHRIG 1975, no. 127. Horse.
4. Aarhus, Antikmuseet K 562. Unpublished. Horseman[69]. *Fig. 19*
5. Cambridge MA, Arthur M. Sackler Museum of Archaeology 25.30.114. Unpublished. Horseman[70]. *Fig. 20*

Fig. 19. Aarhus, Antikmuseet inv.no. K 562. H.9,5 cm. Group Da (Da4).

Fig. 20. Cambridge MA, Arthur M. Sackler Museum inv.no. 25.30.114. H.8,5 cm. Group Da (Da5).

Fig. 21. Thebes, Archaeological Museum, Rhitsona 145.95. H.16,5 cm. Group E (E1).

Fig. 22. Kassel, Staatliche Kunstsammlungen, Antikenabteilung inv. no. T 418. Group E (E2).

Fig. 23. Denmark, private. H.21,5 cm. Group E (E5).

The short, thick legs are more strongly extended than in D and the tails are raised at an angle. The short necks have prominent, pointed crests. The scheme of striping is that of group D.

## Group E

Yet another figurine from grave 145 at Rhitsona introduces the next group of black on browns[71]. It is a horseman, but the rider has not survived. The horse has legs tending towards the conical and almost vertical. The tail is flat, vertical and attached to the left hind leg, falling from hindquarters set so low that the barrel of the horse rises at an angle towards the neck. The neck is broad all along its length and has a slight forwards inclination. The mane ends in a high rounded crest. The head is an insignificant projection without facial features. Remains of the riders hands show that he clasped the neck on a level with the head of the horse. The glaze stripes of the decoration are organized according to the scheme already met with: the two verticals indicating the crest of the mane are a novel feature.

*Fig. 21*

A little troop of horsemen share these characteristics:

E

1. Rhitsona 145.95. URE 1934, 62 pl. XV. Horseman.
2. Kassel, Staatliche Kunstsammlungen, Antikenabteilung T418. SINN 1977, 37 no. 59, pl. 21. Horseman.
3. Paris, Louvre CA322, MOLLARD-BESQUES 1954, 18 no. B106, pl. 13. Horseman[72].
4. Winterthur, Archäologische Sammlung. H. BLOESCH, *Antike Kleinkunst in Winterthur* I (1964), 17 no. 38, pl. 11. Horseman.
5. Denmark, private. Unpublished. Horseman[73].
6. Budapest, Museum of Fine Arts T8. SZABO 1986, 53, fig. 52. Horseman.

*Fig. 21*

*Fig. 22*

*Fig. 23*

The figurines of group E, all horsemen, are quite the biggest we have met so far. The horses' tails are all attached to left hind leg. The riders have elongated bodies and sit pressed up against the horses neck clasping it high up with both arms. In E3 – E5 riders are very similar to one another, with clay discs for eyes[74] and large noses, and short bent legs. E6 has the same face, but only stumps for legs like the rider of E2, whose face is more stylized but retains the clay discs for the eyes. On E3 and E5 the horses mouth is incised.

The authors publishing E2 and E3 note that the glaze decoration is applied on a slip of a paler colour than the clay of the figurine (E2: 'Grundierung beigefarben'; E3: 'engobe blanc'). In the case of E2, we

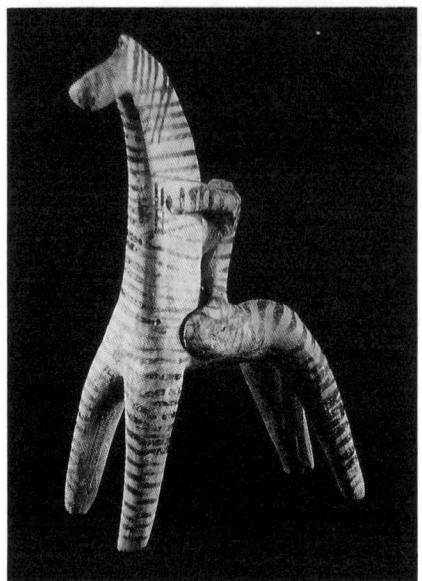

Fig. 24. Aarhus, Antikmuseet inv.no. K 547. H.18,3 cm. Group F (F2).

Fig. 25. Boston, Museum of Fine Arts inv.no. 19.312. H.18,0 cm. Group F (F3).

may be confident that we have to do with a slip of the clay used for the figurine itself, since the author distinguishes it from white ground proper ('Weisser Überzug'); in the Louvre-catalogue, however, the term 'engobe' is the only one used. Considering the importance in the classification of Boeotian archaic terracottas of the technical difference between 'black on brown' and 'red on white' attention must be paid to this aspect when describing the figurines[75].

## Groups F and Fa

Fig. 24

A pale whitish buff clay slip characterizes the majority of pieces in a group related in other ways as well to group E. It is group F, introduced by a horseman in Aarhus[76]. The horse is an imposing animal, standing on thick legs that are almost vertical when seen in profile but very bowlegged from a frontal point of view. The tail is broad and flat and vertical, attached to the right hind leg. The really conspicous feature is of course the enormous neck, broad from front to back at the root and of triangular cross-section, the front being quite flat. The neck curves gently forwards, becoming slimmer and ending in a small triangular crest over the relatively small, featureless head. The rider sits close to the neck, but clear of it. His torso is very elongated and the head just a protruding knob. Massive arms are held straight out to clasp the neck and the legs are bent double to point backwards.[77]. The striped decoration is set in the now familiar scheme.

F
1. Amsterdam, Allard Pierson Museum 6323. *Selected Pieces in the Allard Pierson Museum 1976*, 58 pl. 24. Horseman.
2. Aarhus, Antikmuseet K 547. Unpublished. Horseman[78].
3. Boston, Museum of Fine Arts 19.312. Unpublished. Horseman[79].
4. London, market. *Sotheby's 6.12.1971*, no. 112 pl. 15. Horseman.
5. Athens, National Museum no. ? ZERVOS 1934, pl. 127 left. Horseman.
6. Switzerland, private. BLOESCH 1974, 28f. no. 164, pl. 27. Horseman, warrior 27[79a].
7. Houston, Ménil Collection. HOFFMANN 1970, 252 no. 115, 253 (ill.). Horse.
8. Athens, National Museum 4229. ZERVOS 1934, pl. 127 right. Horse.
9. Athens, National Museum 4232. Unpublished. Horse.
10. New York, market. *Royal Athena Galleries Catalogue no. 44* (1965), 4 no. 9. Horse.
11. Zürich, market. *H. Vollmoeller 1988*. Unpublished. Horse.
12. Chalcis, Museum 1362 (?). *ADelt 27*, 1972, Mel. 170f., pl. 57 gamma upper right. From Chalcis. Horse (fragment).
13. Chalcis, Museum 1363alpha (?). *ADelt 27*, 1972, Mel. 170f. pl. 57 gamma, upper left. From Chalcis. Horse (fragment).
14. Basle, market. *MuM 34*, 1967, 25 no. 51, pl. 14. Horse.
15. Princeton, The Art Museum 29-107. Unpublished. Horse[80].
16. Denmark, private. Unpublished. Horse[81].

*Fig. 24*
*Fig. 25*

Fig. 26. Cambridge MA, Arthur M. Sackler Museum inv.no. 25.30.93. Group Fa (Fa3).

Fig. 27. Athens, Kanellopoulos Museum inv.no. 1786. Group Fa (Fa4).

This is a very homogenous group, as group E, with which it is clearly associated. To the description given above we may add that the tail is found attached to the left as well as to the right hind leg. The horizontal stripes on the neck are usually divided into two or more sections set at different angles and criss-crossing where they meet. F3 for example has three and also has the vertical stripes on the head found in several other figurines of the group. The fact that the whitish slip may be confused with proper white ground makes me think that a horse from Rhitsona may belong to this group, though listed under 'red on whites'[82]. A horse once on the art market in Zürich appeared at first to be merely a lone outsider on the fringe of group F, but has since been joined by others to form a well defined subsidiary:

Fa
1. Zürich, market. *H. Vollmoeller April* 1987, no. 4. Horse.
2. Athens, National Museum 4233. Unpublished. Horse.

*Fig. 26*    3. Cambridge MA, Arthur M. Sackler Museum of Archaeology 25.30.93. Unpublished. Horse[83].
*Fig. 27*    4. Athens, Kanellopoulos Museum 1786. Unpublished. Horseman[84].

Like those of group F, these are uniformly large figurines and have quite similar legs, tails and barrels. The rider of Fa4 has the shape and posture characteristic of F-horsemen. The technique and sheme of decoration is also that of F, except that horizontals on the neck all have the same orientation. The shape of the necks is the distinguishing feature of group Fa, being shorter and deeper, with heads that have plastically rendered ears.

### *Dating groups D-F*

In dating groups D, Da and E a pointer is given by figurines excavated at Rhitsona. D1 and D2 come from grave 145 of c.580 B.C.[85] and considering the lack of black on browns in any number from earlier graves one would tend to see this ante quem as being nearer the upper than the lower limit of the group. Some support for this view may be had from the date of graves 50 and 110, containing the stylistically related Da1 and Da2; both belong to the middle of the century[86].

As for group E, grave 145 at Rhitsona also furnished us with E1, suggesting a date to some extent contemporaneous with group D.

The 'squatting ape'-figurines which have features in common with both D, Da and E were found at Rhitsona in graves from the first half

Fig. 28. Kassel, Staatliche Kunstsammlungen, Antikenabteilung inv.no. T 364. H.14,0 cm. Group G (G4).

Fig. 29. Bochum, Antikenmuseum der Ruhr-Universität inv.no. S 1000. H.12,6 cm. Group G (G11).

of the 6th century, one in the same grave as a horse belonging in a general way with group D[87].

No informative archaeological context is available for groups F and Fa[88], but a date in the vicinity of group E is likely for stylistic reasons – the shape and stance of the legs, the elongated torsos of the riders, the considerable size of the figurines and the character of the decoration are much alike.

## 'Black on browns' of the mid sixth century B.C.; groups G-H

I now turn to a very large group indeed, consisting almost entirely of horsemen deemed sufficiently alike by Ure to warrant the term 'standardised' og 'regulars'[89]. This is group G, comprising what to most people must be the typical archaic Boeotian terracotta horsemen.

It might have been thought sufficient to refer to some representative members of the group, as is usually done. However, readers who care to actually view the pieces listed below may agree that assembling them all has not been an altogether futile exercise. I think an unsuspected diversity is revealed. We certainly have cases of figurines produced by the same hand and with time other variations may prove to reflect local and regional traditions. Some major divisions are tentatively indicated by spacings in the list.

G

1. Rhitsona 86.275. URE 1934, 62 pl. XV. Horseman.
--------------

2. London, British Museum 1912. 6-26.271. HIGGINS 1954, no. 782. Horseman.
3. London, British Museum 1912. 6-26.270. HIGGINS 1954, no. 783. Horseman.

*Fig. 28* 4. Kassel, Staatliche Kunstslg. Antikenabteilung T364. SINN 1977, 37 no. 60 pl. 21. Horseman.
5. Toronto, Royal Ontario Museum 919×13.4. Unpublished. Horseman[90].
6. Amsterdam, Allard Pierson Museum 1318. *Selected Pieces Allard Pierson Museum* 1976, 58, pl. 24 left. Horseman.
7. Birmingham, City Museum 57'43. Unpublished. Horseman.
8. Amsterdam, market. *Christie's Amsterdam 10.12.1987*, 13 no. 39. Horseman.
9. Leiden, Rijksmuseum van Oudheiden I 1947/12.1. LEYENAAR-PLAISIER 1979, 26f. no. 39; II pl. 7. Horseman.
10. Budapest, Museum of Fine Arts 50.296. SZABO 1986, 53f. 142 n. 110, fig. 53. Horseman.

*Fig. 29* 11. Bochum, Antikenmuseum S1000. N. KUNISCH, *Antiken d. Slg. Julius C. und Margot Funcke. Zweite Stiftung* (1980), 12 no. 161. Horseman.
12. London, market. *Sotheby's 13.7.1970*, 59 no. 95. Horseman, warrior.

*Fig. 30* 13. Athens, National Museum 4213. Unpublished. Horseman.
14. Athens, Kanellopoulos Museum 1970. BROUSKARI 1985, 52. Horseman.
15. Athens, National Museum 3885. Unpublished. Horseman.
16. Chalcis, Museum 2744. *AEphem* 1974, 240 no. 20, pl. 77 gamma. Horseman.
17. Great Britain, private, J. Chesterman Coll. 125. J. CHESTERMAN, *Classical Terracotta Figures* (1974), 35 fig. 23; 94 no. 23. Horseman.

*Fig. 31* 18. Tübingen, Antikensammlung 5562. *Tübinger Antiken* (1962), 21 no. 45 Horseman.
19. Great Britain, private. NICHOLSON 1968, 22 no. 62, pl. 9. Horseman.
20. Netherlands, private. *Klassieke Kunst uit particulier bezit* (1975), no. 245 fig. 104. Horseman.
21. Athens, National Museum 4225. Unpublished. Horseman.

Fig. 30. Athens, National Museum inv.no. 4213. Group G (G13).

Fig. 31. Tübingen, Antikenmuseum inv.no. 5562. H.14,5 cm. Group G (G18).

# TERRACOTTA HORSES AND HORSEMEN OF ARCHAIC BOEOTIA

Fig. 32. Uppsala, Gustavianum inv.no. 813. H.10,8 cm. Group G (G31).

Fig. 33. Reading, Ure Museum of Greek Archaeology inv.no. 22.ix.8. H.12,0 cm. Group G (G33).

Fig. 34. Uppsala, Gustavianum inv.no. 2224. H.11,0 cm. Group G (G42).

---

22. London, British Museum 1907. 12-20.3. HIGGINS 1954, no. 787. Horse.
---
23. Federal Republic of Germany, private. *Antiken aus rheinischem Privatbesitz. Rheinisches Landesmuseum* (1973), 175 no. 258 pl. 116. Horseman.
24. Athens, National Museum ST33. HOLMBERG 1963, 110 no. 60 pl. 17. Horseman.
25. Rhitsona 50.389. URE 1934, 62; GRACE 1939, fig. 47. Horseman.
26. Frankfurt-am-Main, Museum für Vor- und Frühgeschichte, Beta 165. *Antikensammlung. Ausgewählte Werke. Archäologische Reihe* 5 (1984), 36 no. 24. Horseman.
27. London, British Museum 1929.4-22.1. HIGGINS 1954, no. 786. Horseman.
28. London, British Museum 1949.7-10.1. HIGGINS 1954, no. 785. Horseman.
29. Great Britain, private. F. NICHOLSON, *Greek, Etruscan and Roman Pottery & Small Terracottas* (1965), 53 fig. 50. Horseman.
30. Athens, Kanellopoulos Museum 1820. BROUSKARI 1985, 52. Horseman.
31. Uppsala, Gustavianum 813. Unpublished. Horseman[91].
32. Rhitsona 110.116. URE 1934, 62.63, pl. XV. Horseman.

*Fig. 32*

Fig. 35. Princeton, The Art Museum inv.no. 37-338. H.14,5 cm. Group G (G55).

Fig. 33
33. Reading, Ure Museum of Greek Archaeology 22.ix.8. Unpublished. Horseman[92].
34. Rhitsona no. ? Rhitsona grave 49. URE 1934, 62 49.421-425. Horseman.
35. Rhitsona no. ? Rhitsona grave 49. URE 1934, 62 49.421-425. GRACE 1939, fig. 49. Horseman[93].
36. Thebes no. ? *Magna Graecia* 20 no. 5, 1985, 3 fig. 3 right. From Tanagra. Horseman.
37. London, market. *Sotheby's 10.7.1979*, no. 180. Horseman.
38. Switzerland, private. *Antike Kunst aus Privatbesitz Bern-Biel-Solothurn* (1967). 128 no. 313. Horseman.

39. Rhitsona 51.308. URE 1934, 62; GRACE 1939, fig. 51. Horseman.
40. Toronto, Royal Ontario Museum 919x13.7. Unpublished. Horseman.
41. Toronto, Royal Ontario Museum 919.5.76. Unpublished. Horseman[94].
42. Uppsala, Gustavianum 2224. Unpublished. Horseman[95].
43. Thebes 5261. ANDREIOMENOU 1985, 116 to photo 16; 125 photo 16 right. From Tanagra. Horseman.
44. Thebes 5262. As above, photo 16 left. Horseman.
45. Thebes 5263. As above, photo 16 middle left. Horseman.
46. Thebes 5264. As above, photo 16 middle right. Horseman.
47. Vienna, Kunsthistorisches Museum, Antikensammlung V 2812. K. MASNER, *Die Sammlung antiker Vasen u. Terracotten* (1892), 85 no. 786 (not ill.). Horseman[96].
48. Thebes 5120. *ADelt* 31, 1976, Chron 121, pl. 93 delta left. From Tanagra. Horseman.
49. Thebes 5121. As above, pl. 93 delta right. Horseman.
50. Thebes 5124. As above, pl. 93 delta middle. Horseman.

*Fig. 34 34*

------------

(various)
51. Federal Republic of Germany, private. *Kunst der Antike. Museum für Kunst u. Gewerbe Hamburg* (1977), 119 no. 90. Horseman.
52. Switzerland, private. *Art Antique. Collections privées de Suisse Romande* (1975), no. 169. Horseman.
53. Würzburg, Martin v. Wagner Museum H3884. SIMON 1975, 65 (not ill.). Horseman.
54. Louvain-la-Neuve, Musée FM33. *Des Animaux et des Hommes. Crédit Communal Bruxelles* (1989), 198 no. 238. Horseman.
55. Princeton, The Art Museum 37-338. Unpublished. Horseman[97].

*Fig. 35*

------------

Add: Near no. 36 but no rein, Thebes No. ? *Loc. cit. ad* no. 36, fig. 3 left. From Tanagra. Horseman.

Near no. 33, but no eye or rein, Rhitsona 50.390 (Thebes 6044). URE 1934, 62. Horseman.

One should, finally, note the existence of a number of irregulars' connected with group G by shape or decoration[98].

*Fig. 36-37*

Fig. 36. Athens, Kanellopoulos Museum inv.no. 1831. Connected group G.

Fig. 37. Athens, Kanellopoulos Museum inv.no. 1816. H.17,5 cm. Connected group G.

Horsemen dominate in group G, the only horse being G22. The legs of the horses are extended slightly lengthwise as well as sideways; tails curve outwards and slant downwards on a line parallel to the hind legs. The length of the barrel corresponds to that of the legs and neck, the latter having a forwards inclination and ending in a pointed crest. The head is relatively small and highly stylized with no modelled features except for rare cases where ears are shown (G1, G4, G55). The riders are legless (stumps on G1, G4 and G55) with arms stretched out to touch each side of the neck; this position of the arms is already familiar to us, but group G gives us an explanation of it, many figurines having the reins painted in (G32-G47)[99]. As for the riders heads, they are turned to the sky with prominent noses and beards. G-riders are occasionally identified as monkeys[100], but they are undoubtedly human, often with eyes, beard and hair (or headdress?) painted in. In one case the rider is a helmeted warrior (G12).

The striped decoration on figurines of group G is generally applied with greater care than on the black on brown groups met with so far. The basic scheme is the familiar one of horizontals on legs, tails and necks[101], verticals on barrels. There are two novelties: along the flanks the horses have a horizontal stripe which continues down each side of the crossbars on the tail, and, on the chest, G-horses regularly carry an ornament – usually two or three horizontal rows of dots between stripes (grid-pattern on G48-G50; field of dots on G18). A ladder pattern runs down the horses' heads, rarely lengthwise striping instead (as on G55); eyes are in many cases painted in, set well back on the neck and round or lozenge in shape. The riders have a few horizontal bars on the body and along the arms (vertical stripes on G4, G55).

Apart from those already mentioned, variations in shape and decoration exist which suggest two major divisions within the group:

*G2-G22*: Relatively long, slender legs, hind legs often more strongly extended lengthwise than forelegs. Barrel slender, neck slender and curved. Stripes on flank and across back have equal spacing and width. Neither reins nor eyes shown. Within the subgroup, stripes are generally thinner, more closely spaced and more numerous on *G2-G13* than on *G14-G21*. *G2-G3* probably by the same hand. Not represented at Rhitsona.

*G23-G50*: More thickset in build than preceding; shorter legs, neck deeper and shorter approaching triangular profile. Stripes across back

Fig. 38. Leipzig, Antikenmuseum der Karl-Marx-Universität inv.no. T 2342. H.10,2 cm. Group H (H1).

Fig. 39. Athens, Kanellopoulos Museum inv.no. 1782. H.12,0 cm. Group H (H2).

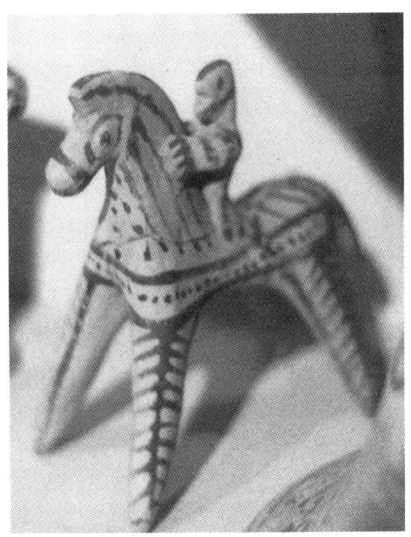

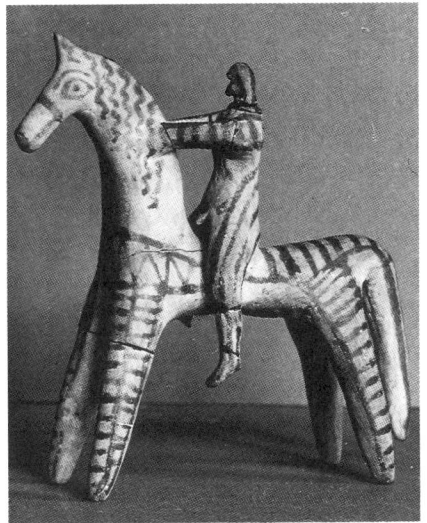

Fig. 40. Athens, National Museum inv.no. 4220. Group H (H7).

Fig. 41. Copenhagen, National Museum inv.no. 7312. H.12,6 cm. Group H (H9).

fewer, thicker and more widely spaced than those on flank. Horses *G23-G26* have eyes, no reins, and a set of vertical stripes on the shoulder *above* the horizontal along the flank: this latter feature is not found on *G27-G31*, which are otherwise similar. *G32-G47* have both eyes and reins: within the narrow confines of group G, these figurines have variety in shape and decoration. *G43-G46* are from a grave at Tanagra are by the same hand. Finally *G48-G50*, by the same hand, have neither reins nor eyes.

These divisions were originally established on the basis of relatively few figurines. The advent of much new material has not made a reorganization necessary and very few pieces remain under the heading 'various'. It may well be that publication of the numerous G-figurines which surely remain unknown will serve not only to strengthen but also to diversify the picture given above.

Assessing the significance – if any – of such subgroups will only be possible when much more extensive archaeological documentation becomes available. In this respect, the largely unpublished and quite inaccessible finds from the graves recently excavated in the necropoleis at Tanagra and Akraiphia will be of decisive importance. For some preliminary remarks, the reader is referred to the section on interpretation which concludes this study.

## Groups H, Ha and Hb

Before discussing the chronology of group G, which comprises several figurines from Rhitsona, it would be useful to consider another large group of 'black on browns', related to group G, but not represented at all at Rhitsona.

Within the criteria used to assemble it, this group, group H, is heterogenous in the extreme. It might in fact seem advisable to split it up already at this stage, but I have preferred to wait untill further material becomes available and proceed instead as when dealing with group G. Spacings denote the subdivisions as I see them:

### H

*Fig. 38* 1. Leipzig, Antikenmuseum der Karl-Marx-Universität inv. T 2342. E. PAUL, *Antike Welt in Ton* (s.a.), 63 no. 14; pl. 7. Horseman.
*Fig. 39* 2. Athens, Kanellopoulos Museum 1782. Unpublished. Horseman[102].
3. London, British Museum 83.6-20.2. HIGGINS 1954, no. 772. Horse.
4. Thebes, Archaeological Museum inv. ? ANDREIOMENOU 1985, 116 to photo 17; 126 photo 17 right. From Tanagra. Horseman.
5. Thebes, Archaeological Museum inv. ? ANDREIOMENOU 1985, 116 to photo 17; 126 photo 17 left. From Tanagra. Horseman.
6. Athens, National Museum 4218. SZABO 1986, 50 fig. 44. From Tanagra. Horseman.
*Fig. 40* 7. Athens, National Museum 4220. Unpublished. Horseman.

Fig. 42. Athens, Kanellopoulos Museum inv.no. 1754. H.10,0 cm. Group H (H12).

Fig. 43. Athens, Kanellopoulos Museum inv.no. 1761. H.10,5 cm. Group H (H13).

Fig. 44. Boston, Museum of Fine Arts inv.no. 14.762. H.10,6 cm. Group H (H14).

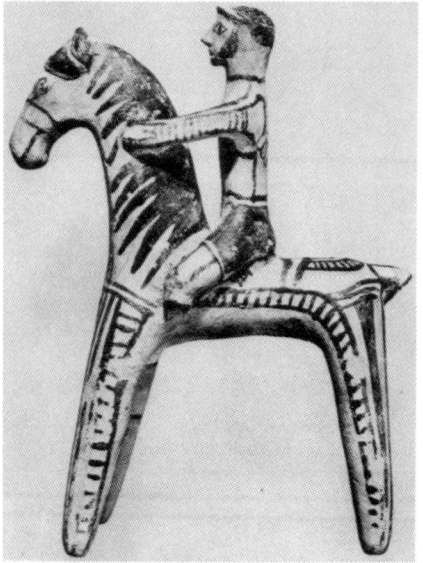

Fig. 45. Athens, Kanellopoulos Museum inv.no. 1965. Circle on chest. Group H (H18).

Fig. 46. Athens, National Museum inv.no. ST 32. H.16,8 cm. Group H (H26).

8. Athens, National Museum 3881. Unpublished. Horseman.
-------------
*Fig. 41*  9. Copenhagen, National Museum 7312. BREITENSTEIN 1941, no. 151. Horseman.
10. London, market. *Sotheby's 7.11.1977*, no. 176. Horseman, warrior.
11. Athens, National Museum no. ? *BCH* 14, 1890, 219 fig. 7. Horseman, warrior.
*Fig. 42* 12. Athens, Kanellopoulos Museum 1754. Unpublished. Horseman.
*Fig. 43* 13. Athens, Kanellopoulos Museum 1761. Unpublished. Horse.
*Fig. 44* 14. Boston, Museum of Fine Arts 14.763. Unpublished. Horse[103].
15. Hamburg, Museum für Kunst und Gewerbe 1955.30. *AA* 1960, 94 no. 20, Abb. 34b. Horseman, warrior.
-------------
(related to H9-H15, less closely interconnected)
16. U.S.A., private. SZABO 1986, fig. 47. Horse.
17. London, market. *Sotheby's 19.7.1961*, no. 169. Horseman.
*Fig. 45* 18. Athens, Kanellopoulos Museum 1965. Unpublished. Horse.
19. Oxford, Ashmolean Museum 1893.112. VAFOPOULOU-RICHARDSON 1981, 8 no. 5c, fig. 5c. Horseman.
20. Hannover, Kestner-Museum 1966.10. LIEPMANN 1975, 50 no. T25. Horseman.
21. Budapest, Museum of Fine Arts T11. SZABO 1986, fig. 46. Horseman, warrior.
22. Denmark, private. *Antik kunst i dansk privateje. Ny Carlsberg Glyptotek* (1974), 36 no. 208, fig. 208. Horseman (rider missing).
23. Denver, University of Colorado Collection 22333. *ADelt* 28, 1973, Meros A 197, pl. 102 c. Horseman.
24. Dresden, Skulpturensammlung ZV1482. M. RAUMSCHÜSSEL, *Antike Terrakotten* (1969), 43 no. 4, Abb. 4. Horseman, warrior.
-------------
25. Munich, Antikensammlungen, Slg. Schoen 122. LULLIES 1955, 74 no. 122 Tf. 51. Horse.
*Fig. 46* 26. Athens, National Museum ST32. HOLMBERG 1963, 109f. no. 59 pl. 18. Horseman, warrior.
27. Athens, National Museum 4017. J. SWEENEY ET AL. (edd.), *The Human Figure in Early Greek Art* (1987), 112-113 no. 32. Horseman.

Fig. 47. Stuttgart, Württembergisches Landesmuseum inv.no. 2.688. H.12,7 cm. Group H (H36).

Fig. 48. Athens, Kanellopoulos Museum inv.no. 1485. H.10,5 cm. Group H (H40).

Fig. 49. Athens, Kanellopoulos Museum inv.no. 1775. H.10,5 cm. Group H (H45).

28. Athens, National Museum 4208. ZERVOS 1936, pl. 140. Horseman, warrior.

---

(More loosely interconnected):
29. Heidelberg, Antikenmuseum 58/2. R. HAMPE ET AL., *Neuerwerbungen Heidelberg 1957-1970* (1971), 13 no. 25 Tf. 14. Horseman.

30. London, market. *Sotheby's 4.12.1979*, no. 60. Horseman.
31. Amsterdam, market. *Christie's 10.12.1987*. Horseman.
32. New York, private. D. v. BOTHMER, *Ancient Art from New York Private Collections* (1961), no. 164 pl. 62. Horseman.
33. Thebes, Archaeological Museum 163 (?). *AEphem* 1976, Chr. 21 no. 9; pl. K delta right. Horse.
34. Würzburg, Martin v. Wagner Museum HA1625. Unpublished. Horse.
35. Karlsruhe, Badisches Landesmuseum B1518. *Badisches Landesmuseum Karlsruhe. Meisterwerke* (1959), 47 no. 6, pl. 6. Horseman.

*Fig. 47* 36. Stuttgart, Württembergisches Landesmuseum 2.688. Unpublished. Horseman[104].
-------------
37. Amsterdam, Allard Pierson Museum 3295. Unpublished. Horseman (rider missing)[105].
38. Thebes, Archaeological Museum no. ? ANDREIOMENOU 1985, 117 to photo 21; 127 photo 21 middle. From Tanagra. Horse.
39. Thebes, Archaeological Museum no. ? ANDREIOMENOU 1985, 117 to photo 21; 127 photo 21 right. From Tanagra. Horse.

*Fig. 48* 40. Athens, Kanellopoulos Museum 1485. Unpublished. Horse.
41. Copenhagen, National Museum 4716. BREITENSTEIN 1941, no. 152 pl. 16. Horseman.
42. Oxford, Ashmolean Museum 1893.163. Unpublished. Horseman.
-------------
(various)
43. Munich, Antikensammlungen 5234. Unpublished. Horseman[106].
44. Athens, National Museum 4316. SZABO 1986, fig. 48. Horseman.

*Fig. 49* 45. Athens, Kanellopoulos Museum 1775. Unpublished. Horseman, warrior[107].
46. Athens, National Museum 4154. A. ROES, *Oorsprong der geometrischen Kunst* (1931), 120 fig. 124. Horseman.
47. Athens, National Museum no. ? ZERVOS 1934, pl. 128. Horseman.

Horsemen are predominant in group H, though not as markedly as in G. Modelling varies greatly, but there is some consistency within the suggested subgroups. A pale clay slip is frequently used.

What all figurines here have in common are certain elements of their decoration, not found in other groups. As in group G, the decoration is generally applied with some care, relative to groups D, E and F.

On the legs of the horses, figurines of group H have vertical stripes, often combined with horizontals to form ladder or herringbone patterns (row of dots between verticals on H10, H21 and H22). Along the flanks, the horizontal stripe found in group G is usually replaced by a double line, often framing another motif such as crossbars (as H 14, or forming ladders as H13), dots (as H15), chequers (as H24) or zigzags (as H41). Finally, we have on the neck not the horizontals of the other black on brown groups, but rather more or less stylized versions of the vertical fall of the hair of the mane from just a single wavy zigzag (as H34), to series of wavy lines (as on H9) and very elaborate, naturalistic coiffures (as H26).

I have the following comments on the proposed subdivisions:

*H1-H8*: Legs of horses quite strongly extended; strong, deep necks. Riders legless. Herringbone pattern on legs, mane indicate by long ondulating verticals following the curve of the neck, those furthest forward being cut off by a crossbar to create triangular space for eye (not H2). Usually field of dots on chest (not H1, H2) and single horizontal along flank, unlike other group H figurines (double line with row of dots on H7).

H4 and H5 probably same hand. A centaur in Berlin belongs with this subgroup. A Scythian horseman in Munich is related[108].

*H9-H15*: Slender more or less curved necks. Numerous wavy lines fall from edge of mane. Within the subgroup, H9-H11 are very close, H9-H10 possibly by same hand. Similarly H12-H14, where H12-H13 seem by same hand.

*H16-H24*: Share one or several of the characteristics of the abovementioned subgroup.

*H25-H28*: Very elaborate figurines, in both decoration and modelling. Distinguishing feature plastically rendered ears and forelock. A dog in Athens belongs here[108a].

*H29-H36*: Little cohesion in this subgroup, but generally highly stylized manes and in all cases reins indicated. Some very sloppy work. Reins are indicated and sometimes divide the decoration of the mane into two different sections (as *H29, H30, H35*). Verticals on front legs often continue up each side of neck.

*H37-H42*: Only verticals on legs; horizontal double lines on flanks without 'fill' (zigzag on H41). Mane in solid glaze with fringe of 'frills'.

The criteria by which group H has been assembled makes it necessary to exclude some stylistically related figurines. They clearly belong together and I therefore list them as a group:

## Ha

1. Thebes, Archaeological Museum 5363. ANDREIOMENOU 1985, 117 to photo 20; 127 photo 20 middle right. From Tanagra. Horse.
2. Thebes, Archaeological Museum 5367. ANDREIOMENOU 1985, 117 to photo 20; 127 photo 20 left. From Tanagra. Horse.
3. Thebes, Archaeological Museum 5368. ANDREIOMENOU 1985, 117 to photo 20; 127 photo 20 right. From Tanagra. Horse.
4. Thebes, Archaeological Museum 5369. ANDREIOMENOU 1985, 117 to photo 20; 127 photo 20 middle left. From Tangara. Horse.
5. Denmark, private. *Louisiana Årbog* 1958, 26 fig. 15 third from left. Horse.

Fig. 50. Boston, Museum of Fine Arts inv.no. 14.764. H.10,4 cm. (right); inv.14.765. H.11,2 cm. (left). Group Ha (Ha10-Ha11).

    6. Thebes, Archaeological Museum 5361. ANDREIOMENOU 1985, 116-117 to photo 19; 126 photo 19 right. From Tanagra. Horse.
    7. Philadelphia, market. *Hesperia Art Bulletin* 13 (s.a.), 19 no. 177. Horseman.
    8. Athens, National Museum 4317. SZABO 1986, fig. 45. Horseman.
    9. Athens, Kanellopoulos Museum 1755. Unpublished. Horse.

*Fig. 50*   10. Boston, Museum of Fine Arts 14.764. Unpublished. Horse.
*Fig. 50*   11. Boston, Museum of Fine Arts 14.765. Unpublished. Horse.
*Fig. 51-52*   12. Brooklyn, The Brooklyn Museum 22.11. Unpublished. Horse.
*Fig. 53*   13. Manchester, Manchester Museum 1983.1205. Unpublished. Horseman[109].

The legs of these horses are identical, conical, and extended both lengthwise and sideways. Tails are raised. The shape of the neck and the head are the distinguishing feature of the modelling: the necks are long and slender of more or less equal width along their length and curve gently forward. The crest of the mane is made of a separately applied piece of clay forming an overhang over the head and giving a bonnet-like impression. The head is small and tends to droop downwards. The riders have prominent, drooping noses and the top of their head is flat. They are legless.

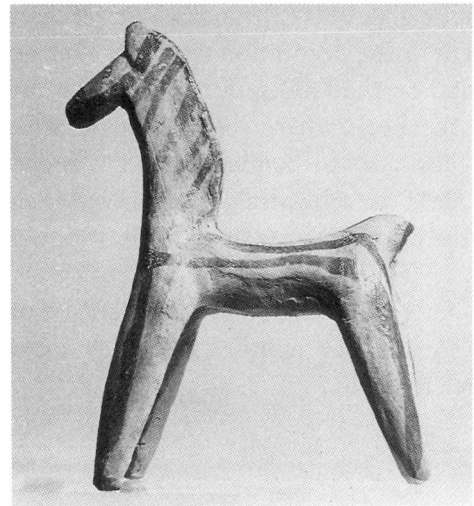

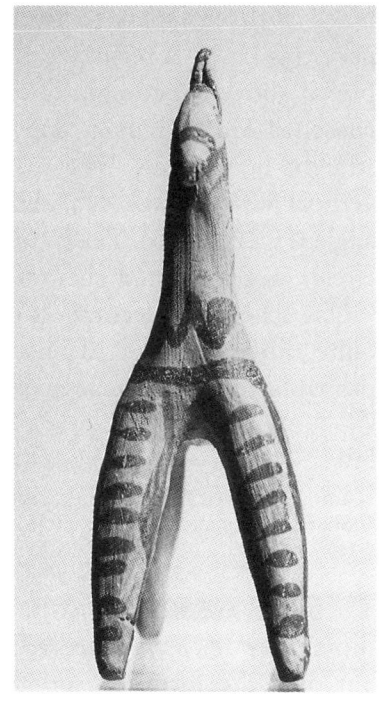

Fig. 51. Brooklyn, The Brooklyn Museum inv.no. 22.11. H.11,0 cm. Group Ha (Ha12).

Fig. 52. Brooklyn, The Brooklyn Museum inv.no. 22.11. H.11,0 cm. Group Ha (Ha12).

Fig. 53. Manchester, The Manchester Museum inv.no. 1982.1205. H.10,0 cm. Group Ha (Ha13).

Though it is the bonnet-crest and the otherwise identical modelling which is the common distinguishing feature of the group, the decoration is also distinctive. All are black on browns and have the basic scheme of group H (except all-black Ha6), with verticals on the legs and one or two horizontals along the flank. The verticals may by combined with crossbars to form ladders (as Ha12), and wavy verticals occur (as Ha9). A recurring element of the decoration is a wavy zigzag, placed above the straight horizontal on the flanks, occasionally on the chest (as Ha11, Ha12), and on the neck where they alternate with straight horizontals. The mane may also be rendered with a broad vertical dash of glaze (Ha7, Ha8, Ha11) or with straight stripes set at an angle (Ha12, Ha13). The head of the horses carries an eye (dot or dot in circle), nosestrap and cheekstrap.

The scheme of decoration just described recurs on two horsemen of quite different shape. They are so like one another that they most probably form the nucleus of a related group:

Hb
1. Athens, National Museum no. ? SZABO 1986, fig. 49. Horseman.
2. Amsterdam, market. J. SCHULMAN, *13. Antique Dealers Fair Delft* (1961), 6 no. 42. Horseman.

The horses are of a heavier build than Ha, with thicker, conical legs and short, deep necks inclined a little forwards. The crest of the mane juts out over the forehead and the ears are very prominent, almost like horns. The riders are legless, with arms reduced to stumps extended outwards. Their heads are very highly stylized, being just a pointed, bullet-like projection set on the neck.

The glaze decoration is like that of Ha, with verticals on legs and a horizontal along the flanks, combined with wavy zigzags. On the neck Hb1 has alternating straight and wavy horizontals, Hb2 just the latter.

*The style and chronology of groups G, H, Ha and Hb*
It is now time to discuss the chronology of groups G, H, Ha and Hb. Starting with group G, an ante quem is given by the horseman G1 from grave 86 at Rhitsona, the latest of the tombs belonging to Ure's 'Corinthian c'-series and usually dated c.580-570 B.C.[110] This series is followed by the one called 'Boeotian Kylix A'[111], comprising Ure's 'mid-sixth-century' graves. Several G-figurines were found in them: G25 (grave 50), G34-G35 (grave 49), G39 (grave 51) and G32 (grave 110). Most authors date these graves as Ure did, to the years c.560/550 or slightly later[112]. The presence in the typologically earliest graves, 49 and 50, of Attic black figure lekythoi of the Blackneck Class may argue in favour of a date after rather than before 550 B.C.[113] This would

create an akward gap between the latest Corinthian C grave, grave 86, and the earliest Boeotian Kylix A graves. I know of no attempt to bridge this, the date of grave 86 being difficult to lower; it depends on black figure kantharoi of Boeotian make which reflect the style of Attic Comast cups, usually dated 585-570 B.C.[114] It may be that the sequence of graves excavated is simply not chronologically representative. In this connection, one may note that it has not been possible to ascertain the presence at Rhitsona of figurines belonging to the first of my two subgroups within group G (G2-G22); is their more slender build, and their lack of eyes and reins a sign of earlier date? Or of regional differences? We have but to wait for the archaeological context which we miss for that subgroup.

Among the stouter steeds of my second subgroup (G23-G50) we have figurines excavated by A. Andreiomenou at Tanagra. G43-G46 are horsemen from Tomos E tomb 16, dated '3rd quarter 6th century'. They are very similar indeed to the horsemen G34-G35 from tomb 49 at Rhitsona. A date in the 3rd quarter of the 6th century is also given to Tomos E tomb 15, in which G48-G50 were found; this tomb contained an Attic black figure lekythos of the Blackneck Class[115].

At Rhitsona, no grave later than the ones cited above had black on brown horses or horsemen of any kind, whereas the red on white figurines to be dealt with below continue to the end of the century and a little beyond.

All in all, a date of the 2nd and 3rd quarter of the sixth century must be given to group G. The possibilty of further refinement of the internal chronology of the group remains open.

It is a striking fact that no member of our very large black on brown group H appears to have been found at Rhitsona. Fortunately, a tomb at Tanagra containing four H-figurines has been partially published by A. Andreiomenou. This tomb, Tomos Sigma grave 51, had terracottas belonging to two different subgroups within group H, namely H4-H5 and H38-H39. The date given by the excavator is the 3rd quarter of the 6th century[116].

From a stylistic point of view, there can be no doubt that of the black on brown groups met with so far, group G offers the closest parallels in both shape and decoration. Compared to those of groups D-F, the figurines of groups G and H have proportions that are much alike and group H has a fair number of big nosed, legless riders, cousins of those in group G. Both groups have the horizontal decorative element along the flanks, often combined with stripes across the back. It would be tempting to give group H a date range similar to that of group G.

An indication that group H does in fact belong at least partially to the 2nd quarter of the 6th century as well as to the 3rd, is given by remarks made by F. Grace on the horseman H27. He compares the head of the horse to that found as handle on a Boeotian miniature saucer and rightly finds it 'remarkably similar'. By virtue of the Late Corinthian origin of its decoration, the saucer is dated to the 2nd quarter of the century[117].

Confirmation that group H is contemporary with group G may be had from group Ha, to which I now turn. Its relations with group H have been described above. The scheme of decoration which predominates in group Ha is one of alternating straight lines and wavy zigzags, and it is closely parallelled by that found in in group Bb (Bb1-Bb2, Bb3 having stripes set like Ha12). On stylistic grounds, the 'black' group Bb has been dated to the 1st-2nd quarter of the 6th century. Furthermore, the necks of group Ha are reminiscent of those in group C, a connection which is strengthened by the horse Ha6, all black except for the reserved belly and inside of legs as is the case for a majority of figurines in group C, also belonging to the 1st-2nd quarter of the century.

We are fortunate in having for group Ha archaeological data which bear out these stylistic considerations. From Tomos Lampda tomb 9 at Tanagra Andreiomenou has published 7 horses. Of these, five belong to group Ha (Ha1-Ha4, Ha6), one to group C (C20) and one to Ba (Ba4). The tomb is dated to the 1st quarter of the 6th century[118].

Thus, group Ha must by all accounts belong to the earlier part of the 1st half of the 6th century, making a date range which includes the 2nd quarter of the century likely for group H.

Finally, group Hb must be dated in the light of its close relations with group Ha.

## The 'red on whites'; groups I-J

The second main division within Ure's class of 'primitive' horses and horsemen are the 'red on whites', decorated in applied red – sometimes in black and yellow as well – on a white ground[119]. The earliest come from graves of his 'Corinthian c' series, a lone horse with the rider

Fig. 54. Thebes, Archaeological Museum, Rhitsona 86.277. H.13,0cm. Group I (I1).

Fig. 55. Thebes, Archaeological Museum, Rhitsona 49.438. H.15,0cm. Group Ia (Ia1).

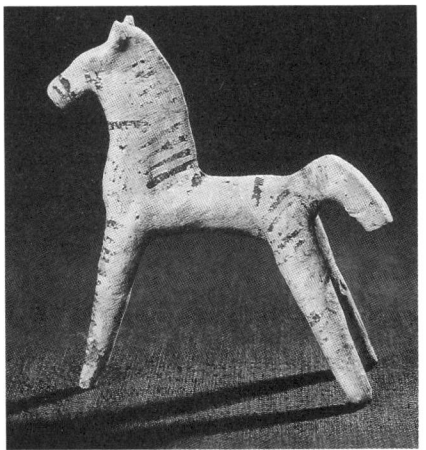

Fig. 56. Reading, Ure Museum of Greek Archaeology inv.no. 87.2.1. H.12,0cm. Group Ia (Ia2).

Fig. 57. Stuttgart, Württembergisches Landesmuseum inv.no. 2.687. H.14,6 cm. Group Ia (Ia8).

sitting sidesaddle from grave 125d being perhaps marginally the oldest. This grave is dated c.590-580 B.C., just preceding the latest tomb of the series, grave 86[120].

## Group I

Grave 86 contained eight red on white horses of what Ure terms 'the normal early type'[121]. Only one of these is actually illustrated by him, and it heads the following list of what is probably a much larger group:

## I

*Fig. 54*
1. Rhitsona 86.277. URE 1934, 63, pl. XVI. Horse.
2. Great Britain, private. NICHOLSON 1968, 23 no. 66. Horse.
3. Hamburg, Museum für Kunst und Gewerbe 1917. 996. *AA* 1928, 367; 368 fig. 82. Horse.

These red on whites have relatively slender legs of identical, conical shape more strongly extended lengthwise than sideways. Tails are long, raised and gracefully curved, almost on a level with the back. The barrel is thin and stretched to the point where it begins to sag in the middle. Necks are set very upright and have manes curving into a small plastically rendered crest on the forehead. In the modelling of the head there is some attempt at naturalism.

The painted decoration follows the general scheme met with among the black on browns, but there is no horizontal element along the flanks. In comparison to the black on browns, stripes are thinner and more closely spaced, except on the barrel which has fewer, thicker bands. On the neck, the horizontals do not go all the way across, except for a broader band at shoulder height. The horse I1 has herringbone-pattern on the tail.

### Group Ia

According to Ure, the red on whites of my group I continue in his 'Boeotian Kylix A' graves of the mid 6th century B.C.[122] Of the fifteen pieces mentioned from these graves, just one is illustrated. I see it as clearly related to, but nevertheless distinct from, group I. A number of other figurines may be grouped with it:

Ia

*Fig. 55* 1. Rhitsona 49.438. URE 1934, 63 pl. XVI. Horse.
*Fig. 56* 2. Reading, Ure Museum of Greek Archaeology 87.2.1. Unpublished. Horse[123].
3. Belgium, private collection. *Marbres Helléniques. De la carriére au chef-d'oeuvre* (Crédit Communal, Bruxelles 1987), 127 no. 40; 120 to nos. 26-27; 130 to no. 27 (colour). Horse[124].
4. Berlin, private. GEHRIG 1975, no. 129. Horse.
5. Thebes, Archaeological Museum no. ? *ADelt* 30, 1975, Chr. 128; pl. 75 beta From necropolis at Akraiphia. Horse.
6. Berlin, private. GEHRIG 1975, no. 130. Horse.
7. Basle, market. *MuM Sonderliste A Mai 1953*, no. 7. Horse.
---
*Fig. 57* 8. Stuttgart, Württembergisches Landesmuseum 2.687. Unpublished. Horseman, warrior[125].
9. London, market. *Sotheby's 10/11.6.1983*, no. 212. Horseman, warrior.
*Fig. 58* 10. Athens, Kanellopoulos Museum 1837. Unpublished. Horseman.
*Fig. 59* 11. Athens, Kanellopoulos Museum 1835. Unpublished. Horseman[126].
12. Thebes, Archaeological Museum no. ? (Room B, case 13). Unpublished. Horseman.
13. Thebes, Archaeological Museum no. ? (Room B, case 13). Unpublished. Horseman[127].

Fig. 58. Athens, Kanellopoulos Museum inv.no. 1837. H.10,0 cm. Group Ia (Ia10).

Fig. 59. Athens, Kanellopoulos Museum inv.no. 1835. H.15,8 cm. Group Ia (Ia11).

Fig. 60. Munich, Antikensammlungen inv.no. 5334. H.15,2 cm. Group Ia (Ia16).

Fig. 61. Boston, Museum of Fine Arts inv.no. 01.8011. H.13,0 cm.

14. Würzburg, Martin v. Wagner Museum H5278. SIMON 1975, 56. Horse.
15. Houston, Ménil Collection no. ? HOFFMANN 1970, 249 no. 114, 251 (ill.). Horse.
16. Munich, Antikensammlungen 5334. Unpublished. Horseman[128].

*Fig. 60*

Before commenting on the subdivisions indicated in the list, I point out some common denominators of the group. In shape, the figurines differ from I in having legs generally shorter and thicker in relation to the whole. Barrels are also shorter and tend to be broader than they are high. Most tails are raised, at the root often of almost rectangular cross section and as broad as the barrel. The heads of the horses invariably have plastically rendered ears set on each side of the crest of the name and bulges where the eyes are painted in. As for the decoration, the technique of applied, matt colours on white ground makes for generally poor preservation: to make matters worse, incrustation of the surface is for some reason more frequent as is discolouring due to fire. The general scheme is that of group I, but black and yellow are more in evidence, especially in the broader stripes around the barrel and across the base of the neck. The striping on legs and tails is usually herringbone[129].

It seems to me that within the group one may discern two major subdivisions by differences in the modelling of the horses' heads:

*Ia1-Ia7*: Relatively heavy heads with long muzzles that do not taper appreciably. They are in fact somewhat like the heads seen in group A. Ia5 and Ia6 have in common a projection added to the top of the crest of the mane. An interesting figurine in Boston of a satyr playing the double-flutes whilst reclining back to front on what is probably a mule rather than a horse belongs here[130].

*Fig. 61*

*Ia8-Ia16*: Heads of more naturalistic shape, with shorter, pointed muzzles. Within the subdivison, Ia14-Ia16 have been set apart because the horses have the same heavy hindquarters combined with a barrel which grows very thin towards the neck. They also share a detail of decoration, the uppermost stripe on the hindlegs being curved. That other types of figurines may be connected with this subdivision is indicated by a ram riding warrior, once on the art market in Munich[131]. The curved uppermost stripe recurs on a red on white horse from Rhitsona, intermediate in shape between groups I and Ia and with thin red striping very widely spaced[132].

## Group Ib

What may be an independent group of red on whites related to the two just described should be mentioned here. The figurines concerned come from both the 'Boeotian Kylix A' and the 'Boeotian Kylix B' series of graves at Rhitsona:

Ib

1. Rhitsona 49.434. URE 1934, 64, 65 pl. XVI. Horseman, warrior.
2. Rhitsona 31.370. BURROWS & URE 1907/08, 208; pl. 12e. URE 1934, 65 and 66. Horseman, warrior.
3. Rhitsona 12.90. BURROWS & URE 1909, 317 fig. 6. Horseman, warrior.

Fig. 62. Zurich, Leo Mildenberg Collection inv.no. M 267. H.15,6 cm. Group J (J5).

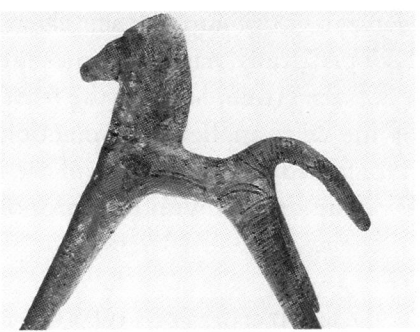

Fig. 63. Athens, Kanellopoulos Museum inv.no. 1901. H.15,3 cm. Group J (J6).

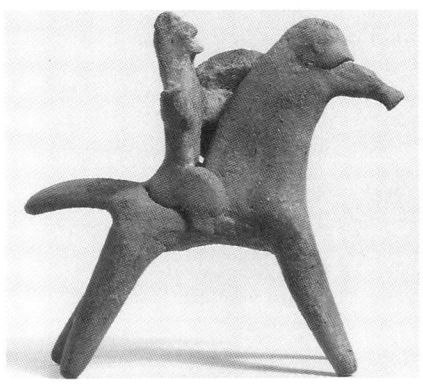

Fig. 64. Kassel, Staatliche Kunstsammlungen, Antikenabteilung inv.no. T 524. H.13,6 cm. Group J (J11).

Fig. 65. Denmark, private. H.15,2 cm. Group J (J13).

According to Ure these figurines were accompagnied in each grave by several similar ones. Their distinguishing feature is their slender build, with very long legs in a comparatively upright stance, and the riders with their characteristic headgear – called 'cavalier's caps' by Ure, but more likely helmets[133]. The riders all have rudimentary legs 'wrapped' around their mounts. The highly stylized rider of a horse in Amsterdam has just such 'legs', while the horse is closely related to Ia in shape[134].

## Group J

Quite a number of red on white figurines illustrated by Ure remain without definite interconnections, apart from the similarity of technique. Others again are not illustrated and described too briefly to warrant an opinion on their character. We do however in the 'Boeotian Kylix A' graves have one other type of red on white horse belonging to a definite group, heading the J-list below. It is the only piece illustrated of the thirteen figurines mentioned by Ure as representative of the 'typical red on white horse of the mid-sixth century'[135]. I muster group J, before dealing with the chronology of the red on whites:

## J

1. Rhitsona 117.6. URE 1934, 64 pl. XVI. Horse.
2. Thebes, Archaeological Museum 6137. From Rhitsona grave 49. Horse[136].
3. Heidelberg, Antikenmuseum TK11. NEUTSCH 1948, 29 no. 5; pl. 16. Horseman, warrior.
4. Berlin, private. GEHRIG 1975, no. 128. Horseman (rider missing).

*Fig. 62*    5. Zürich, Leo Mildenberg Collection M267. KOZLOFF, MITTEN & SGUAITAMATTI 1986, 43 no. II.56. Horse.

*Fig. 63*    6. Athens, Kanellopoulos Museum 1901. Unpublished. Horse[137].

7. Würzburg, Martin v. Wagner Museum H5279. SIMON 1975, 56. Horseman, warrior[138].
8. London, British Museum 1912.6 – 26.259. HIGGINS 1954, 211 no. 788: pl. 105. Horse.
9. Bern, Antikensammlung des Bernischen Historischen Museums 22532. I. JUCKER, *Aus der Antikensammlung des Bernischen Historischen Museums* (1970), 77 no. 118. Horse[139].
10. New York, Pomerance Collection. *Pomerance* 1966, no. 101. Horse[140].

*Fig. 64*    11. Kassel, Staatliche Kunstsammlungen, Antikenabteilung T524. SINN 1977, 36-37 no. 57; pl. 20. Horseman, warrior.

12. Switzerland, private. BLOESCH 1974, 29 no. 167; pl. 27. Horseman, warrior.

*Fig. 65*    13. Denmark, private. *Louisiana Årbog* 1958, 24; 26 fig. 15, fourth from left. Horseman[141].

14. Basle, market. *MuM Sonderliste P Februar 1976*, no. 6. Horseman[142].

The typical J-horse stands on long, slender, conical legs, strongly extended both sideways and lengthwise. The tail is very broad at the root and raised high. Barrels are short, necks broad from front to back. The head is pointed, bulging in the region of the eyes, and surmounted by a forelock made of a separately applied piece of clay[143]. The stylized, racy elegance of the finest J-horses make them perhaps the most esthetically pleasing of the 'primitives'.

The riders of the group have legs (traces on J4, rudimentary on J13-J14). They are a militant lot, 4 out of the 6 preserved being warriors armed with shields, J12 with a helmet as well.

Where preserved, the painted decoration shows use of black and yellow as well as red in a scheme like that of group Ia. A noticeable departure from that norm is seen on J6 which has a horizontal double line along the flank.

My comments on the suggested subdivions within the group:

*J1-J6*: The neck continues the line of the extended forelegs; the heads are short and pointed. A team of two horses in Paris belongs here[144]. This subdivision contains the typical mid-sixth century red on whites as described by Ure.

*J7-J14*: Necks close to vertical or inclined forwards; heads elongated in comparison to J1-J6 and with very long muzzles (as J11). Examples of this subdivision are mentioned, but not illustrated, by Ure, describing them as 'snouty' with bottle-like heads[145].

Summing up the stylistic connections between the red on white groups discussed above, they have in common their technique of decoration. The scheme of the striped decoration has the same overall character. In shape, I and Ia are clearly closely related, while the tentative grouping Ib has more to do with the two other I-groups than with group J, which stands apart. Comparing group J with the Ia-figurines, some riders are somewhat alike (J13, Ia11-Ia13) and the basically triangular profiles of the horses heads on J1-J6 have something in common with those of Ia8-Ia13. In group I, the stance of I2 is not unlike the J's, and like I1, this horse also has the gracefully curved, flying tails met with in group J.

## *The style and chronology of groups I, Ia, Ib and J*

Looking back to the black and black on brown groups presented earlier, we cannot point out any one group as an obvious relation or precursor. Resemblances in shape and decoration exist, but do not coincide. The stride and rakish set of the neck in J1-J6 reminds one of group A[146]: but the heads of the horses in that group are like Ia1-Ia7, heavy built and with bulging eyes. A comparison between A1, Ia1 and J5 is instructive (figs. 1, 55 and 62). In the context, the modelling of the riders and the horses heads in groups I, Ia and J have a degree of naturalism comparable to that of certain figurines in group H (H25-H28) – in the context, that is, of the abstraction seen in other groups. In technique of decoration there is evidently a decisive difference, though the use of a pale clay slip in groups of black on browns should be kept in mind (E, F, Fa and H). The scheme of striping and its generally careful execution is closest to groups G and H; the differences are well explained by Ure[147].

There is, finally, one respect in which the red on white may also be linked with groups G and H. It is the occurrence of what may be brands, limited so far to horses of groups G, H, I, Ia and J. This subject is discussed in Appendix A.

A review of the external archaeological evidence for the chronology of the red on white groups must open with the horse I1 from Rhitsona, grave 86, of c.580-570 B.C.[148] It would be premature to suggest a date range on that basis, but dates available for the stylistically related group Ia may help. In fact, there is just the horse Ia1 from Rhitsona grave 49 to go on. It is dated c.550 B.C. or perhaps a little later[149]. The figurines said by Ure to be like Ia1, but not illustrated and therefore not included come from other graves in his Boeotian Kylix A series similarly dated (50, 110). This suggests that group I has a date range extending towards the middle of the century, rather than its beginning, developing into Ia. Ia1 belongs then, to the years around 550 B.C., perhaps especially after[150] – though not continuing towards the end of the century, because on the tenous evidence available this would seem to be the period to which group Ib belongs. Ib1 was found with Ia1 in grave 49 at Rhitsona, but the other two figurines of the group come from the later, Boeotian Kylix B graves, 31 and 12, one being typologically early, the other late, in the series. Ure dated grave 31 c.520 B.C., grave 12 c.500 B.C., but as we shall see in connection with the late archaic group L below, this may be too high a chronology[151]. Suffice it to say that group Ib covers the 2nd half of the 6th century B.C., bringing to an end the story of the 'primitives'.

What, now of group J? Well, the indications we have come again from Rhitsona, J1 and J2, from graves 117 and 49 respectively. The date of grave 49 has already been discussed and 117 belongs with it. Group J must then be seen as a contemporary of Ia. The warrior horseman cited above[152] for its parallel to the plastic forelocks of group J is decorated in the polychrome, naturalistic manner of of the late archaic group L, below, suggesting that J-figurines may have continued down through the 3rd quarter of the 6th century B.C.

In my earlier article I reluctantly established a *group K*, whose point of departure was a horseman from Boeotia, but otherwise was made up of teams of horses. Further study has made it clear that it is advisable to stick to the original plan of dealing with freestanding horses and horsemen only. I hope to follow up the lead on teams so ably given by Szabo on a later occasion[153].

Fig. 66. Munich, Antikensammlungen inv.no. 5206. H.10,4 cm. Group L (L3).

Fig. 67. Heidelberg, Antikenmuseum inv.no. TK 15/2. H.11,8 cm. Group L (L9).

JAN STUBBE ØSTERGAARD

*The Late Archaic figurines; groups L and La*
My muster of groups of horses and horsemen belonging to Ure's 'primitive' class has come to an end and I therefore turn to his other main class, the 'late archaic'[154].

*Group L*
Among the terracottas of this class found at Rhitsona one was a horseman. It heads the list of figurines in my group L. Suggested subdivisions are indicated in the usual manner:

L
1. Rhitsona 31.378. URE 1934, 69: pl. 18. *Archaeological Museum of Thebes. Guide* (1981), 62: pl. 31 (colour). Horseman.
   ------------
2. Once Paris, market. W. FRÖHNER, Collection Hoffmann I. Terres cuites antiques, verreries et bijoux d'or, Auc. Drouot (1886), 5 no. 7. 6 (ill.). Horseman.

*Fig. 66*  3. Munich, Antikensammlungen 5206. *AA* 1913, 19, 2 no. 3b (not ill.). Horseman.
4. Toronto, Royal Ontario Museum 919 x 13.13. Unpublished. Horseman[155].
   ------------
5. London, British Museum 1875.3 – 9.12. HIGGINS 1954, 215 no. 804; pl. 109. Horseman.
6. London, British Museum 1875.3 – 9.13. HIGGINS 1954, 215 no. 805; pl. 109. HIGGINS 1986, pl. IV (colour). Horseman.
7. Athens, National Museum 4737. Unpublished. Horseman[156].
8. Berlin, Antikensammlung TC7090. KNOBLAUCH 1937, 205 no. 511. Horseman.

*Fig. 67*  9. Heidelberg, Antikenmuseum TK 15/2. R. HAMPE & H. GROPENGIESSER, *Aus der Sammlung des archäologischen Instituts der Universität Heidelberg* (1967), 54. 105. pl. 21. Horseman[157].
*Fig. 68* 10. Munich, Antikensammlungen, Slg. Schoen 146. LULLIES 1955, 53 no. 146. pl. 52. Horseman.
11. London, market. *Christie's 23.7.1936*, 25 no. 66. Horseman, warrior.
   ------------
12. Amsterdam, Allard Pierson Museum 645. R. A. LUNSINGH SCHEURLEER, *Grieken en het Klein. Allard Pierson Museum* (1986), no. 22. Horseman.
   ------------
13. Solothurn, private. SCHEFOLD 1960, 230 no. 278. 182 (ill.). Horseman.
   ------------
*Fig. 69* 14. Athens, Kanellopoulos Museum 1791. Unpublished. Horseman[158].
15. Kassel, Staatliche Kunstsammlungen, Antikenabteilung T532. SINN 1977, 37-38 no. 6. pls. III (colour) and 21. Horseman.
16. Leiden, Rijksmuseum van Oudheiden I 1957/8.1. LEYENAAR-PLAISIER 1979, 27 no. 40. pl. 7. Horseman.
*Fig. 70* 17. Munich, Antikensammlungen 5207. Unpublished. Horseman[159].
   ------------
Related:
18. New York, market. *The Ernest Brummer Collection* III (1979), 389 no. 739. 388 (ill.). Horseman, warrior.

Group L consists entirely of horsemen and compared to figurines in our other groups – with the exception of B – they are very lifelike. The stance of the horses is naturalistic in as much as forelegs are generally

Fig. 68. Munich, Antikensammlungen inv.no. Slg.Schoen 146. H.11,0 cm. Group L (L10).

Fig. 69. Athens, Kanellopoulos Museum inv.no.1791. H.11,3 cm. Group L (L14).

Fig. 70. Munich, Antikensammlungen inv.no. 5207. H.9,2 cm. Group L (L17).

more perpendicular than the hind legs, and care is taken to show the swelling of thing and rump. In the case of L1, the joints of the hindlegs are rendered, on L2-L4 those of the front legs as well. L1, L11 and L18 stand on rectangular plaques to ensure stability. On to the tails, which vary from from the quite naturalistic version of L11 to the more stylized of horses like L15. Barrels are still more or less unarticulated cylinders, but in several cases the transition from barrel to leg is indicated (i.e. L14-L17). Chests, necks and heads have a new vitality. In modelling, volume and proportions they form coherent wholes (L5 less so): chest and throat swell forewards and we see examples of the musculature of the shoulders being indicated (as L3), the cheek of the head is set off from the throat, ears are carefully modelled as pricked up or slanted backwards, positions seen in real life. Eyes are rendered plastically or painted in, sometimes both. Heads are carefully shaped and tend to be long and rather flat, nostrils and mouth are shown. The hogged manes are set off from the neck and curve forewards into a high crest. This crest is a hallmark of the group, spatulate in form and at its base as wide as the head from which it tapers forward into a rounded point.

The riders of these mounts sit well forward and are modelled in some detail. Their riding posture is good, with legs bent and hands holding the reins low in the lap or higher with hands touching the mane. We have both youths and grown, bearded men variously attired; some are naked (as L5), others wear short chitons (as L9) occasionally a chlamys as well (L6). L6, L7 and L9 sport fine petasoi and one, the related figurine L18, is a warrior with helmet and a shield slung on his back. Wherever shown, hair is short and thick, beards long and pointed.

L-figurines are painted with matt, dusty colours on a white ground. The polychromy is naturalistic. They are solid and handmade except for the faces which were made by means of a mould, a practise widespread in Boeotian coroplastics of the 6th century B.C.[160] The use of facemoulds (whole head: L1, L13?) on our horsemen is generally overlooked, but was noted by Knoblauch who established workshops on the basis of the different matrices used[161].

I have the following comments on the divisions within the group:

*L1*: Rather larger than the average L-figurine (but cp. L18). Front of muzzle flat, hock-joints shown. Whole head of rider from mould.

*L2-L4*: Horses gallup, joints shown on all legs. Head of horse L4 cp. L14-L17. Riders like L5-L11.

*L5-L11*: Joints of legs not shown, legs rather short. Horses and riders of compact build.

*L14-L17*: Very alike, perhaps same hand. Lower legs set like matchsticks in heavy thigs and shoulders. Strong necks and very characteristic heads, long and flat. Moulded faces of riders small, set in large high-domed heads.

## Group L and the Boeotian 'genre groups'

In technique and character of shape and decoration these figurines are intimately connected with the numerous depictions in terracotta of scenes from Boeotian daily life known as 'genre groups', a sphere to which figurines inspired by comedy and a host of animal studies also belong[162]. The relation is one of context as well, if we dare trust the information given in the publication of L9 (found in a grave containing a goat and a woman at work). A study of this complex of late archaic Boeotian terracottas would be useful – and probably both interesting and enjoyable too, since the quality is high and the subject matter so diverse.

## Group La
Before considering the date of group L, I present a little troop of horsemen riding a little apart from the main body:

La
1. Copenhagen, Ny Carlsberg Glyptotek 3628. ØSTERGAARD 1986, 81-82. 84-87 figs. 2-4. 107. *Fig. 71-73*
   Horseman.
2. Athens, Kanellopoulos Museum 1824. Unpublished. Horseman[163]. *Fig. 74*

Fig. 71. Copenhagen, Ny Carlsberg Glyptotek inv.no. 3628. H.8,4 cm. Group La (La1).

Fig. 72. Copenhagen, Ny Carlsberg Glyptotek inv.no. 3628. H.8,4 cm. Group La (La1).

Fig. 73. Copenhagen, Ny Carlsberg Glyptotek inv.no. 3628. H.8,4 cm. Group La (La1).

## TERRACOTTA HORSES AND HORSEMEN OF ARCHAIC BOEOTIA

Fig. 74. Athens, Kanellopoulos Museum inv.no. 1824. H.9,5 cm. Group La (La2).

Here the horses' legs, barrel and tail are stylized in the manner of earlier groups. Legs are extended, short and conical, the tail massive and raised high, the barrel extremely short. Quite at odds with the advanced modelling of the horses' neck and head, and of the rider. The powerful, proud neck carries a head of heavier and less elongated build than seen in group L. Mouth, nostrils and eyes are plastically rendered[164], as are the pricked up ears. The mane ends in a crest quite unlike that of the L's, being square cut and projecting out low over the forehead; a distinct groove at the level of the ears sets its off from the mane. The rider sits in a relaxed posture, leaning back a little and holding the reins in his lap. The moulded heads are closest to that of L1 and L5. Where preserved, the decoration is as in group L. A donkey carrying produce in baskets slung across its back, in Würzburg, is like the La horsemen[165].

165

## The chronology of the Late Archaic groups L and La

The archaeological evidence for the date of group L is limited to L1, from grave 31 at Rhitsona, which in Ure's relative chronology is typologically the earliest of his Boeotian Kylix B series of interments. Only once does Ure venture to give an absolute date for the grave, of 'about 520 B.C.', though without stating precisely why[166]. A lower date was proposed by Haspels on the basis of the Attic black-figure lekythoi and skyphoi found in the tomb which in her opinion indicated a date of c.500 B.C.[167] In her review of Haspels work, A.D. Ure pointed out that the consequence of the proposed dates for the earliest and latest grave in the Boeotian Kylix B series (c.500 for grave 31, c.490 for grave 18) was to create a gap in relation to the Boeotian Kylix A series and to compress the development of the Boeotian ceramic material in the Boeotian Kylix B graves within a decade, which she found hard to imagine[168]. The adjustment suggested by Haspels has apparently met general approval, 'c.500 B.C.' or 'early 5th century B.C.' being the date given by authors publishing L-horsemen – though none have entered the discussion. In his review of the published material from Rhitsona, Sparkes gives grave 31 the date 'c.515 B.C.' and K.Kilinski discusses the chronology of Boeotian black-figure vasepainting within the framework given by Ure 'as a convenience'[169]. Since the absolute dates of the Boeotian Kylix B tombs must ultimately depend on the Attic vases found in them, I choose to follow the date given by Boardman for the latest of the well-defined groups of Attic black-figure lekythoi represented in grave 31. This is the lekythos 31.165 of the Class of Athens 581, dated 'early 5th century'[170]. It is to be hoped that the full publication of the tombs excavated comparatively recently by A.Andreiomenou at Tanagra and Akraiphia will provide the sorely needed supplement to the evidence from Rhitsona.

As the subdivisions suggested within group L do not afford evidence of any relative chronology, we must place the group as a whole around 500 B.C., and with it La. Parallels to the crests of the horses in group L and La seem to confirm this date. The crests of group L may be compared to that of the marble pegasus protome from the Herakleion at Thasos, dated c.500 B.C.: a terracotta horse with rider in Boston, said to be from Assos, is even closer, and is dated to the early 5th century B.C.[171] For the crests – or forelocks – of La, two parallels may be cited, one a bronze pegasus protome, the other a fragment of a marble relief

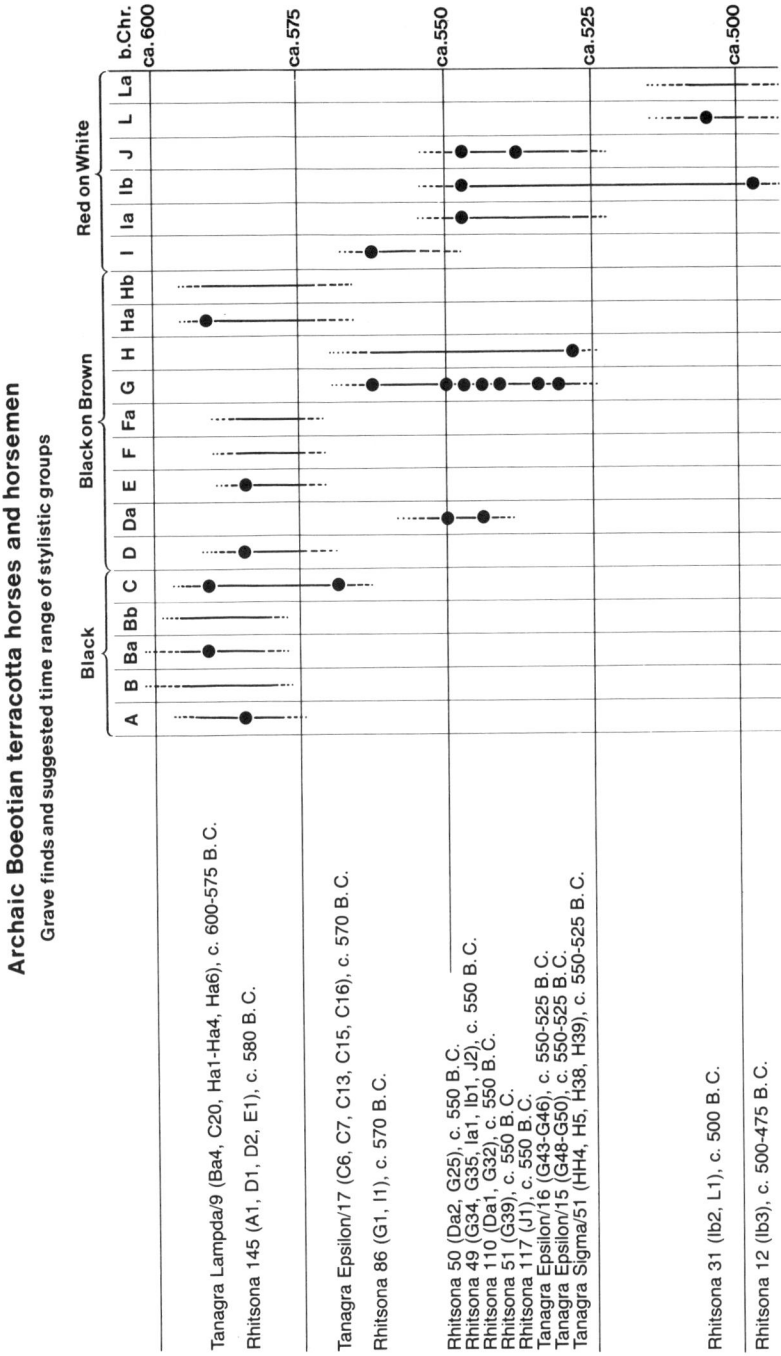

Fig. 75. Archaic Boeotian terracotta horses and horsemen. Diagram of suggested stylistic groups, their chronology and interrelations.

showing the neck and head of a horse. Both are in Athens; they come from the Acropolis and are dated to the last quarter of the 6th century[172].

## A review of the proposed groups

Having traced the ancestry of the horseman which brought about this study, La1, we see that it spans a period of roughly a century, at least. Readers may find a recapitulation useful, giving the salient points of the story and allowing me to add some observations resulting from such an overview.

*Fig. 75*

The early groups B, A and C – the 'blacks' – first recognized by Miklos Szabo, are seen as the opening chapter, belonging to the first quarter of the 6th century B.C. They evince a stylistic development from the relative naturalism of groups B and Ba, towards greater abstraction as in groups A and C, with Bb as a possible intermediary. Boeotian board idols provide a parallel in this respect. Groups B and A have relations to other terracottas and to plastic vases; these need closer study[173].

The 'blacks' are to a certain extent contemporary with the first groups of striped 'black on browns' – those decorated with glaze stripes on the clay ground. The earliest of the latter, groups D, E and Ha, are represented in graves containing figurines of groups Ba, A and C.

The three groups of black on browns just mentioned have been given a date of 1st-2nd quarter of the 6th century B.C.: a fourth, group F, belongs with them because stylistically related to E. Groups D, E and F[174] might reasonably be regarded as forerunners of the figurines assembled in group G, comprising what Ure called the 'standardized' or 'regular' black on browns. The bulk of this very large group belong to the middle and 3rd quarter of the 6th century. As for the early black on brown group Ha, it seems connected by virtue of its scheme of decoration with group H. This is a large group of black on browns running parallel to group G but far more heterogenous; it will in fact probably have to be split up into several independent groups.

Despite their apparent uniformity, the figurines of group G are, I think, worth a closer look. Gathered in large numbers differences become discernible and they can hardly be fortuitous. They certainly reflect individual hands and in all probability workshops and regional traditions as well. The variations seen may also turn out to have chronological implications[175].

Of the horses in matt colours – red, and also black and yellow – on a white ground, a very few belong to contexts dated to the 1st quarter of the 6th century. The first, so far, to form a group are the horses of group I, dated to the 2nd quarter of the 6th century. The direct descendants are groups Ia and Ib, appearing around the middle of the century, the former lasting through the 3rd quarter while the latter continues down to c.500 B.C. and possibly beyond. Branching off from I we have group J, contemporary of Ia. None of the red on white groups have really close connections with figurines of the black on brown variety, but there is some affinity between the black horses of group A and those of Ia and J[176].

With the advent of the horsemen of group L and La, we witness a radical change in decoration, naturalistic polychromy on white ground supplanting the abstract decoration of earlier groups. The latter continues however, as demonstrated by the horsemen of group Ib, one of whom (Ib2) comes from the same grave as L1, the horseman from Rhitsona. Figurines of groups L and La are handmade as hitherto, but a mould is used for the faces of the riders, or – exceptionally – for the head. In shape, the Late Archaic L- and La-horsemen do not in my view constitute as radical a departure from earlier groups as supposed by Ure on the basis of the lone horseman from Rhitsona, L1. In the rendering of the lower parts of the horses, modelling ranges from the highly stylized version of La, through varying degrees of naturalism in group L, L1 representing an extreme in the latter respect. As for the horses' forepart and the riders, they are indeed more advanced than any earlier, but among the figurines of group H the horses and horsemen H25-H28 are at least on the way towards the level reached in group L; further back along the line we have such horsemen as C4 and B1.

Groups L and La have been dated 'c. 500 B.C.' and with them the production of horses and horsemen seems to cease altogether in Boeotian workshops[177].

## Classification and terminology

My remarks on the relationship between the figurines of groups L-La and earlier groups calls into question the classification proposed by Ure for the figurines from Rhitsona, that of a 'primitive' class, followed by a 'late archaic' one. I would prefer to see all groups as belonging to a coherent tradition, simply termed 'Archaic', with classes established according to technique of decoration: blacks, black on browns, red on whites and the naturalistically polychrome.

The term 'primitive' was chosen by Ure to express his opinion of the quality of the figurines in question. On principle, this practise is unfortunate, quite apart from the fact that such a judgement seems unduly harsh if passed 'in toto' on the material now at our disposal. The more elaborate pieces in groups H, C, and B, referred to above, can hardly be described as 'lacking in artistic pretensions and technical skill'[178].

By doing away with a 'late archaic' class, referring to style, we may use 'late archaic' for groups L-La as well as for Ib, denoting their chronological position.

Whatever one thinks of the horses and horsemen studied here, accepting the groupings suggested implies acknowledgment of a diversity of style and of quality of execution which most accounts do not lead one to suspect.

*Stylistic diversity; region, workshop, craftsman*
The question naturally arises of what reality this diversity reflects – if any. The broad outlines of a development over time have been given, but many groups are contemporaneous. We may then attempt to explain differences by connecting groups with specific localities, all working within the framework of a common Boeotian style, distinct from that of other regions in Greece. This has been attempted, with a leading role being given to Tanagra and Thebes[179]. But the fact of the matter is that we are left clutching at straws for lack of proper archaeological documentation. There are good reasons for accepting the authenticity of the museum objects dealt with here, but we may as well set aside the information given on their place of discovery[180]. Our possibilities are determined by three sites from which reliable information has come: Rhitsona, Tanagra and Akraiphia. Of these, Rhitsona is the only one published with a degree of completeness, but even its usefulness is restricted: the excavators themselves are aware of the illicit digging prior to their arrival and of not having a proper idea of the extrent of the cemetery; they were not given the means to fully illustrate their finds and to make matters worse, the finds themselves are inaccessible today

because of the storage facilities available to the Museum of Thebes. In the case of Tanagra, the situation is strange. It is given as the provenance of a great number of terracottas – it is, and was, an enviable one. Some may be true[181], but what is needed is the scholarly publication of the many archaic graves excavated in our time. The glimpses we have had have been tantalizing. Even then, a full picture is not to be hoped for because of the enormous extent of earlier plunderings[182].

In the light of what has been said of Rhitsona and Tanagra, the crucial importance of the excavations at Akraiphia becomes apparent. In excess of 1300 tombs have been excavated to date since the inception of excavations in the 1970's, a major part of them being of the Archaic period. The archaeology of Archaic Boeotia will benefit enormously from their full and speedy publication, a task worthy of assistance[182a].

When viewing the figurines from the relatively well documented necropolis at Rhitsona on the background of the whole of the material presented here, one is struck first of all by the absence there of pieces comparable in quality with the best of our horses and horsemen. The horse A1 and, especially, the lone rider L1 are evident exceptions[183]. Secondly, there there is at Rhitsona a noticable lack of 'blacks', groups A-C, A1 being the exception. This despite the fact that graves of the period are quite numerous, belonging to the 'Corinthian C'-series. Finally, no representatives of the very large group H, black on browns of the mid 6th century, seem to have been found at Rhitsona. They have so far only appeared at Tanagra, together with figurines of group G, which are very much present at Rhitsona. And we have, on the other hand, groups known only from Rhitsona, such as D, Da, E, I and J. The trickle of information on terracottas found at Akraiphia includes the horse Ia5, joining a troop known from Rhitsona, but not Tanagra. Have red on white horses and horsemen been found at Tanagra at all?

At the risk of being hypercritical, I think it premature to advance hypotheses on localization[184], but I have no doubt that regional traditions existed. Hopefully, the stylistic analysis attempted here will be of some use, once a better archaeological record is established.

Diversity will then most probably be explained partly by different geographical origins. On the next level we must imagine one or several workshops adhering to that local tradition. Within such a tradition these workshops may well have their own peculiarities. And so we finally reach the primary source, the individual craftsman, atom of the trade and of society. We have met them, I believe, in groups B, Bb, G, H and L, spanning the period in which handmade terracotta horses and horsemen were produced in Boeotia in any numbers.

*The makers – potters or coroplasts?*
The virtually identical handmade figurines, such as B1-B2, Bb1-Bb2, must imply production in great numbers, by a single craftsman or by very close associates. This has a bearing on how the production of terracottas was organized. It is usually assumed that in 6th century Boeotia terracotta figurines were produced by people who made the pottery of the period[185]; coroplasts as craftsmen who have emancipated themselves from the vase-maker are supposed to appear only at the end of the century, on the evidence of such figurines as those of group L, according to Ure, or with the introduction of white ground decoration using several colours around the middle of the century, according to Higgins[186]. That the making of vases and figurines took place in the same workshop is very likely, having in common the raw materials, facilities for firing and an outlet for selling the finished products. But bearing in mind the sheer volume of production indicated by the number of figurines of various types which have come down to us from archaic Boeotia, as well as the degree of practise implicit in the almost identical pieces referred to above, the craft of making terracottas must at the very least have had a certain independence at quite an earlier date than hitherto supposed – if not actually its own specialized practitioners.

*Function of the figurines*
This study has only a very modest contribution to make towards an understanding of the part played by these horses and horsemen in the life and death of people in Archaic Boeotia. Wherever documented, the context is funerary[187], and various interpretations have been put foreward. They may be valid, but are always brief and uncorroborated: toys beloved in life, servants to assist the deceased, symbols of the heroic status attained beyond the grave or of the position actually held in society, images of theriomorphic deities and mythological ancestors of the Boeotians. These are qualified guesses. Even if no real headway is to be expected before we have the results of contemporary archaeological investigation conducted in Boeotia, a start ought to be made on the

evidence available from Rhitsona, if only to formulate hypotheses. Such basic information as the sex and age of the person buried is scanty at best, but even so there is something left to do. The Rhitsona publications do not attempt to analyse the graves in terms of society and beliefs, concentrated as they are on presenting and ordering basic excavational data. I think properly conducted analysis of the contents of the graves might be useful[188], providing that all the finds are made available for research.

All that is beyond the scope of this article. As it is, I conclude my contribution with some observations which may be of use.

There is for example the fact that in several instances figurines by the same hand have been found in a single grave[189]. Such pieces are likely to have been acquired specifically for use at the burial – they were hardly personal belongings or objects of everyday use, but must have been imbued with a meaning relevant to the funeral, the rite of passage.

We also find horses and horsemen of different groups laid down in the same grave. And in at least one case, the groups concerned are of distinctly different quality of craftmanship[190]. What the import of this is remains uncertain; it is tempting to see a reflection here of the composition of the group of people present at the funeral.

Finally, graves may contain not only a combination of different groups, some horses, some horsemen: the horsemen reviewed here are not alike, some are warriors, some have diadems, most are plain civilians in dress, and many are naked. In group L the variety is especially striking, and difference in age is shown, making it even more so. The significance of this escapes us, but being aware of it is a start.

This muster of Archaic Boeotian terracotta horses and horsemen ends with thoughts turning to a question not tackled at all: what circumstances determined the enormous output of these terracottas roughly within the confines of the 6th century B.C.?

# APPENDIX A

*Brands on Archaic Boeotian terracotta horses*
The painted decoration of Archaic Boeotian terracotta horses occasionally includes features which do not belong to any repertoire of decorative ornaments. They are usually found on shoulders or – more often –

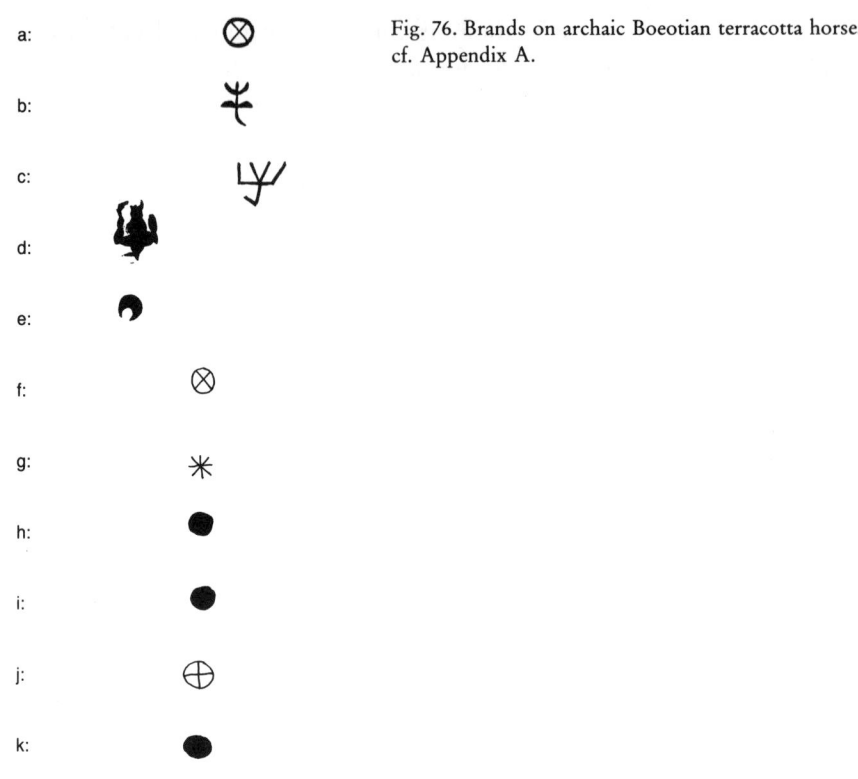

Fig. 76. Brands on archaic Boeotian terracotta horses, cf. Appendix A.

on the croup or the hindquarters. They are probably to be identified as brands. The use of brands on Greek horses is well attested, from Geometric to Classical times, cf. K.Braun, AM 85, 1970, 256-267 with earlier literature; BOHEN 1988, 10. 42. I note the following:

Fig. 76  Group G:   G30 (fig.76, a, on hindquarters, b, on croup)
                    G31 (fig.76, c, on croup)
                    G55 (fig.76, d, on croup, uncertain)[191]

        Group H:    H17 (fig.76, e, on shoulder, f, on hindquarters)

        Group I:    I3 (fig.76, g, two on hindquarters)

        Group Ia:   Ia1 (fig.76, h, on both shoulders, in yellow)

*Group J:*   J5 (fig.76, i, on both shoulders, in red)
J9 (fig.76, j, on shoulder, in red)
J13 (fig.76, k, on shoulder)

On the interpretation of brands, see K.BRAUN, *op.cit.*, 265-267.


# APPENDIX B

*Other known Archaic Boeotian horses and horsemen*
Here I briefly cite those figurines, which are known to me but have not been included in this study. I do so because the tendency has been for such 'loners' to find companions eventually. I note the surroundings in which they are likely to belong:

*'Blacks':* Thebes 5141. ANDREIOMENOU 1985, 126 photo 18 middle left; London, market. *Sotheby's 19.6.1961.* Both cp. group C.

*'Black on browns':* Early: Vienna, Kunsthistoriches Museum, Antikensammlung V1798. Unpublished. Horseman, warrior; York, York City Art Gallery 1081. *Connoisseurs Yearbook* 1965, 89. Both cp. groups E–F.
Mid sixth century(?): Tübingen, Antikensammlung 5561. *Tübinger Antiken* (1962) 22 no.46 (not ill.); London, British Museum 1912.6-26.273. HIGGINS 1954 no.770; Frankfurt an Main market. *Dr. K.Deppert Verkaufsliste* 11, 1959 no.11; ibid.no.12; Rhitsona 51.310. Ure 1934, pl.XV; Tübingen, Antikensammlung 1393. Unpublished; Netherlands, private. G.SCHNEIDER-HERMANN (ed.), *Eine niederländische Studiensammlung Antiker Kunst* (1974) 12 no.13; Hannover, Kestner-Museum 1966. 11. LIEPMANN 1975, 44 no.T16; Athens, National Museum 4313. ZERVOS 1934 pl.127 middle; Stuttgart-Munich, market. *H.H.Kricheldorff Liste* 56, 1961, 12 upper middle; Toronto, Royal Ontario Museum 971.154.40. Unpublished; Stuttgart-Munich, market. *H.H.Kricheldorff Liste* 56, 1961, 12 upper right. Athens, National Museum no.? ZERVOS 1934 pl.128 left; Stuttgart, market. *H.H.Kricheldorff Auk.IV,* 7.10.1957, 33 no.519.

'*Red on whites*': Early: Rhitsona 125d.3. URE 1934, pl.XVI.
Mid sixth century: Rhitsona 50.392, 110.118, 117.10, all URE 1934, pl.XVI; Erlangen, Kunstsammlung des archäologisches Institut der Universität inv.no. I406. W.GRÜNHAGEN, *Antike Originalarbeiten* (1948) 68 (cp. group Ia); Greifswald, Ernst-Moritz-Arndt-Universität, Archäologische Seminar. A.HUNDT & K.PETERS. *Greifswalder Antiken* (1961) 106 no.460 (cp.group Ia); market, Basel. *MuM Sonderliste E* (1962) no.25 (cp.group Ia); *MuM* 14/15.3.1975, 85 no.186; *ibid.*, no.187 (cp.group J); Vienna, Kunsthistorisches Museum, Antikenabteilung 2123. Unpublished (cp. group Ia); Denmark, private. *Louisiana Årbog* 1958, 27 right; Frankfurt, Liebighaus no.?. *StädelJb* NF 10, 1985, 318 fig.57; Frankfurt, Liebighaus St.P.411. P.BOL & E.KOTERA, *Bildwerke aus Terrakotta. Liebighaus Antike Bildwerke* III (1986) 26 no.13; market, Freiburg. *Galerie G.Puhze Katalog* 6, 14 no.137; Basle market. *MuM Auk*.34, 6.5.1967 no.53. pl.14.

## Acknowledgements

My warmest thanks go to the following institutions and individuals for kindly supplying me with information, photographs and publication permits: Antikmuseet, Aarhus (L.Hannestad); Allard Pierson Museum, Amsterdam (H.E.Frenkel, R.A.Lunsingh Scheurleer); Kanellopoulos Museum, Athens (M.Brouskari); H.M.Berg; Birmingham Museums and Art Gallery, (D.Symons); Antikenmuseum der Ruhr-Universität Bochum (N.Kunisch); Museum of Fine Arts, Boston (M.Padgett); Arthur M. Sackler Museum of Archaeology, Cambridge MA (D.G.Mitten); Szépmüveszeti Múzeum, Budapest (M.Szabo); The National Museum, Copenhagen (M.Køllund); Museum für Vor- und Frühgeschichte, Frankfurt am Main (J.v.Freeden); Hunterian Museum, Glasgow (L.Keppie); Museum für Kunst und Gewerbe, Hamburg (W.Hornbostel); Antikenmuseum des Archäologischen Instituts der Universität Heidelberg (H.Gropengiesser); Museum of Fine Arts, Houston (C.Young); Knud W. Jensen, Humlebæk; The Israel Museum, Jerusalem (U.Avida); Badisches Landesmuseum, Karlsruhe (M.Maass); Staatliche Kunstsammlungen Kassel; Liverpool Museum (R.Lang); The British Museum, London (D.Williams); The J.Paul Getty Museum, Malibu (K.Hamma); The Manchester Museum (S.Lawrance); L.Mildenberg; Staatliche Antikensammlungen, München (F.W.Hamdorf); University of Newcastle upon Tyne (B.Shefton); The

Brooklyn Museum, New York (R.Bianchi); The Metropolitan Museum, New York (J.Mertens); The Ashmolean Museum, Oxford (M.Vickers); The Art Museum, Princeton (R.Guy); Ure Museum of Greek Archaeology, Reading (J.Gardner); Württembergisches Landesmuseum, Stuttgart (M.Honroth); Archaeological Museum, Thebes (A.Andreiomenou); Royal Ontario Museum, Toronto (N.Leipen); Antikensammlungen, Universität Tübingen (B.v.Freytag gen. Löringhoff); Gustavianum, Uppsala (M.Blomberg); Kunsthistorisches Museum, Wien (A.Bernhard-Walcher); Martin von Wagner Museum, Würzburg (G.Beckel); York City Art Gallery (S.Northcroft); Archäologisches Institut der Universität Zürich (M.Sguaitamatti).

Support from the Ny Carlsberg Foundation made it possible for me to visit a number of museums in Europe and the United States of America; for this I express my gratitude.

Department of Antiquities
Ny Carlsberg Glyptotek
Dantes Plads 7
DK-1556 Copenhagen V

# NOTES

*This is a considerably expanded and revised version of an article published in *MeddelelsGlyptKøb* 42,1986,81-108 (in Danish, English summary). An appendix A on possible owners' marks has been added; Appendix B cites those Archaic Boeotian horses and horsemen which have yet to find company. Abbreviations used are those recommended by the *Archäologische Bibliographie des deutschen archäologischen Instituts and Archäologische Anzeiger* 1985, 757-765. Additional abbreviations are listed in the bibliography. *Please note!* On each page, illustrations are arranged in numerical order from left to right and from top to bottom.

1. BUCK 1979, 88.
2. For the social dimensions of burials: MORRIS 1988, 29-59.
3. I know of no separate account of Boeotian burial customs. For the Archaic period Tanagra and Rhitsona supply the best evidence: HIGGINS 1986, 44-49 (Tanagra); BURROWS & URE 1907/08, 242-250 and Ure 1934, 4-15 (Rhitsona).
4. For Archaic Boeotian terracottas in general: HIGGINS 1967, 45-47. 145; SZABO 1979, 3-4 (history of research); HIGGINS 1986, 64-65. 71-96; SZABO 1986.
5. URE 1934, 53-60; GRACE 1939, 21-48; PAUL 1958/59; HIGGINS 1986, 71-78.
6. URE 1934, 53-54. 61-66. 69 no.31.378.
7. Especially BREITENSTEIN 1941, HIGGINS 1954, MOLLARD-BESQUES 1954, Sinn 1977.
8. References given in connection with relevant figurines.
9. For references: HIGGINS 1986, 180 (Tanagra), 182 (Akraiphia). Add: A. ANDREIOMENOU, Jewelry and weapons from tombs at Akraiphia (830-500 B.C.). *Proceedings of the 6th International Boeotian Conference* 1989 (forthcoming). Precise references to individual pieces will be given in the course of presentation.

10. Szabo 1973, 1975 and 1979.
11. Szabo 1986. An English edition is needed.
12. Grace 1939, 21-48; Paul 1958/59 passim.
13. Cf. note 10.
14. Østergaard 1986, 87-90, groups A-C. P.114-125 below.
15. Bohen 1988, 41-76.
16. Grace 1939, 22.
17. Cf. Sparkes 1967, 117.
18. Cf. Higgins 1986, 72.
19. Introduction to Cypriot figurines with earlier literature: Monloup 1984, 40-41 with notes 8-21. For figurines from other parts of Greece (Rhodes, Samos, Crete, Argos, Corinth, Attica): Monloup 1984, 41-42 with earlier literature notes 22-29. Add Crouwell & Tatton-Brown 1988 and Guggisberg 1988. Being in Hungarian, the chapters in Szabo 1986 on Archaic terracottas from outside Boeotia are not accessible to me.
20. Cypriot origins suggested by Higgins 1986, 78. Attic connections proposed by Szabo 1973, 12 and passim. East Greek and Cycladic as well as Attic: Szabo 1979, 7-8. Rhodian parallels, reminiscent of my group Ia: B. D. Wescoat (ed.), *Syracuse. The Fairest Greek city. Emory University Museum* (1989) 116 no.42 with references.
21. Ruckert 1976, 31-33. pl.21,3.4.
22. Bohen 1988, 10.
23. Corinthian c graves: Ure 1934, 22-23. Primitive class: Ure 1934, 53-54. 63 (review of 'black on browns). 65-66 (review of 'red on whites'). Of the figurines dealt with by Ure, many come from graves published in earlier reports from Rhitsona; these should always be consulted, since they often contain information not given under the relevant numbers in Ure 1934.
24. The photograph of this piece is from the negative used for the illustration Ure 1934, pl.XV. Much of the material for Ure's plates is in the care of the Ure Museum of Greek Archaeology, Reading.
25. The letters of the alphabet used to designate groups do not carry chronological implications, but reflect the development of my work.
26. H.15,0 cm. Yellow brown clay. Thin reddish brown glaze. Belly and inside of legs reserved. Reserved head has two stripes for nosestrap and one stripe lengthwise down head. Nostrils pricked. Row of white dots up each foreleg, continuing on neck; row of white dots across chest. Break in left hind leg mended.
27. H.14,2 cm. Row of white dots down throat to chest. Tip of tail missing.
28. H.16 cm. Dark brown clay. Shiny black glaze. Belly and inside of legs reserved. Head not reserved. Neck very thin in cross section and of equal width along length.
29. Ure 1934, 61; Higgins 1954, 207 no.771; Szabo 1973, 16 with note 29; Szabo 1979, 8 with note 55 ('chevaux à la tête reservée').
30. Szabo 1979, 8 with note 58. 9 with notes 61-62. Add the terracotta stag, Munich, Antikensammlungen 6596. Unpublished. H.18,3 cm. Handmade. Shape and stance as A4, but with stags tail and antlers, and head turned sideways. Decoration in glaze on brown clay ground, crossbars on front legs and chest, hatched triangles between vertical zigzags on throat. On each flank horizontal zigzag between lines. Spots on back. On head nosestrap as A-horses. Related: Basle, market. *MuM Sonderliste A* (1953) no.1. Goat; and Athens, National Museum 12993. Szabo 1973, 6 no.3 (not ill.). Man with goat.
31. The top surface of the forelock painted white. The holes in the legs probably for wheels as on the warrior horseman Kanellopoulos Museum 1816, cf. note 98 below. Holes through forequarters possibly for mounting of breastplate, cf. Bohen 1988, 10, also found on B4. The head of the rider shown Szabo 1979, 12 fig.6 and Szabo 1986, fig.29 does not belong, cf. Breitenstein loc.cit.
32. Traces of white zigzags seem visible in publication photograph.
33. White triangle on top surface of forelock; short white line down back from root of mane; mouth incised.
34. H.14,0 cm. Decoration in white as on B5. A catalogue of Greek terracottas in the ROM is under preparation by Neda Leipen.

35. SZABO 1979, 7 note 41. H.11,5 cm. No fetlocks on hind legs. Decoration in white as B5, but white spots on top surface of forelock and white spots for nostrils.
36. H.12,0 cm. Reddish brown glaze. No fetlocks on hind legs. Vertical white zigzags on mane. White circle for eyes. Stripes in glaze and added red on rider, hair red, preserved left leg curves forewards.
37. SZABO 1979, 6-7 with notes 39-41.
38. SZABO 1979, 4-7. To ram vases add: Munich, Antikensammlungen 6396. Unpublished; U.S.A., private. *Ancient Art* 1954, 26 no.130, pl.XXVI; GEHRIG 1983, 95 no.95bis.
39. SZABO 1979, 7 with notes 42-44.
40. White chevron with crossbar on top surface of forelock.
41. Row of white dots down edge of mane. White chevron on top surface of forelock.
42. Parallels from Cyprus to this feature, i.e. London, British Museum 1876.4-9.91 and 1876.4-9.92; CROUWELL & TATTON-BROWN 1988, pl.XXVI 1-2.
43. H.13,3 cm. Belly and inside of legs reserved. Reddish black glaze. Only one wavy horizontal on right side of neck. Crossed bandoliers on chest and back of rider. Tips of arms and tail missing. As related to the B-groupings add: Stuttgart, Württembergisches Landesmuseum inv.arch.65/3 = *Ars Antiqua AG* (Luzern) 7.11.1964, 20 no.83. pl.XIX.
44. SZABO 1973, 15-19. Unpublished pieces listed, but not illustrated, by Szabo are not included. The terracottas at the museum in Skimatari are no longer accessible for study (1989).
45. H.9,6 cm. Reddish brown glaze. Legless rider pressed to neck. Head of horse cylindrical with two incised lines for mouth.
46. H.9,5 cm. As C10, but no incision for mouth of horse. Same hand?
47. H.10,8 cm. Inside of legs reserved, belly partially so.
48. Groups E-J below.
49. Group L below.
50. Cf. note 21. Horses on the lid of the LG pyxis *ADelt* 26,1971 Chron 217 pl.188 gamma have a band in added white around barrel (on exhibit Thebes Museum, Room B). ANDREIOMENOU 1985, 117 to photo 19 cites parallel to technique of white on black in LG pottery from Eretria.
51. URE 1934,59 'about 580 B.C.' without further argument. Contents of grave URE 1934, 89. pls.II.V.VII.XIII.XV. Date retained by SPARKES 1967, 128 (not argued).
52. ANDREIOMENOU as cited in list.
53. ANDREIOMENOU as cited in list. For vases from this grave see ANDREIOMENOU 1985, 115 to photo 11. 124 photo 11; *ASAtene* 59, 1981, 254-256, fig.7-11.
54. I thank A.Andreiomenou.
55. Above p.119. SZABO 1979, 6 with notes 31-38 for date.
56. As note 54.
57. SZABO 1973, 12. 15-16.
58. Concentrating as I do on horses and horsemen, I must refrain from the more lengthy discussion which Szabo's detailed argumentation invites.
59. Cf. group Ha below.
60. Cf. note 23.
61. URE 1934, 61 no.101b.38 and 101b.39, pl.XV.
62. H.9,2 cm. Rider has holes for eyes. Tail very short, almost triangular.
63. H.10,7 cm. Head of horse missing. Neck long as D5 but straight. Gridpattern on shield, cp. D9.
64. URE 1934, 63.
65. See D6 for reference. Some teams of horses also belong: Liverpool Museum 51.105.17. Unpublished. Team of four horses on a common base, one with rider; Basle, market. *MuM* 34, 1967 no.52. Team of three horses on a common base, one with rider.
66. PAUL 1958/59, 167-169.
67. As URE 1934, pl.XVIII no.59.53. Cf. PRESTON 1975. Connection seen by URE 1934, 62 to no.96.8.
68. Among which also the horses cited note 61. URE 1934, 62 nos.96.8 and 96.9 probably belong as well.

69. H.9,5 cm. Pale reddish brown clay (MUNSELL 7.5YR 7/4). Glaze stripes dark brown to red. Tip of crest of mane missing, head chipped.
70. H.8,5 cm.
71. E1 in the list below.
72. MOLLARD-BESQUES 1963, pl.V,2 for colour illustration.
73. H.21,5 cm. Clay reddish brown. Numerous breaks, some fragments turned grey (fire). Black glaze decoration badly preserved, but striped as other E's. Mouth of horse incised line. Rider has clay discs for eyes. Tail attached to left hind leg. Add as related to E: London, market. Sotheby's 10.7.1989 no.160. Horseman.
74. Clay disc eyes and incised mouth also seen on 'squatting ape' J.Paul Getty Museum 71.AD.133, PRESTON 1975, fig.1.
75. Cf. HIGGINS 1954, viii. 5-6 and PAUL 1958/59, 182. 187. From the colour photograph cited note 72, E2 has a cream coloured clay slip rather then white ground proper.
76. F1 in the list below.
77. There are parallels to this position from other areas and periods, i.e. terracotta horseman from Vari, KAROUZOU 1980,135; terracotta rider from Athens, *Hesperia* II,1933,617 fig.83 no.302 (both 7th cent.B.C.); CROUWELL & TATTON-BROWN 1988, pl.XXVI, 3 (Cyprus, 7th-6th century); LA ROCCA 1985, pl.XIV.XXII-XXIII (mounted amazon, marble, 5th cent.B.C.). An observation from real life? The rider of a Boeotian terracotta hippalektryon (Louvre CA1792, MOLLARD-BESQUES 1954, 19 no. B108; dated c.550-525 B.C.), has one leg in this position; in the light of the many parallels to the 'kneeling' position cited here the interpretation of the posture of the rider as being connected with burial rites is hardly tenable, cf. *RA* 1951, 166-167 (S.MOLLARD-BESQUES).
78. H.18,3 cm. Clay yellow brown (MUNSELL 2.5YR 7/4), pale clay slip, glaze stripes shading from purple to red. Head of rider missing. Tail attached to right hind leg.
79. H.18,0 cm. Whitish clay slip. Tail attached to right hind leg.
79a. Bloesch connects this piece with F5 and F8.
80. H.19,0 cm. Yellow brown clay. Buff clay slip.
81. H.24,4 cm. Yellow brown clay. Whitish buff slip and glaze stripes badly preserved. Incised line for mouth. Tail attached to right hind leg.
82. URE 1934, 63 nos.86.277-292 'one with very short barrel, enormous neck and absolutely flat in front'.
83. H.17,5 cm.
84. H.19,0 cm. Rider has nose and beard.
85. Cf. note 51.
86. See note 112.
87. Cf. notes 61 and 68.
88. Unless the horse referred to in note 82 belongs; grave 86 at Rhitsona dated c.570 B.C., cf. note 110 below. Under present storage conditions at the Museum of Thebes, the Rhitsona finds are unfortunately inaccessible.
89. URE 1934, 63.
90. H.13,1 cm. H. of G7 below: 12,5 cm.
91. H.10,8 cm. Fork-like pattern on back.
92. H.12,0 cm.
93. This and the preceding piece may from Ure's description be identified as one of the Rhitsona-figurines cited.
94. *G40*: H.10,2 cm. *G41*: H.10,0 cm.
95. H.11,0 cm.
96. Correct height 11,1 cm.
97. H.14,5 cm. Clay red-buff to gray. Forelock in separate piece of clay, ears rendered; rider has rudimentary legs. Fork-like pattern on back and zigzag behind rider. Parallels to the set of vertical stripes on the shoulder *above* the flank horizontal: G23-G26.
98. New York, market. *Sotheby's 24/25.11.1987* no.441. Horseman (indiscriminate striping); Chalcis, Museum 2745. *AEphem* 1974, 240 no.21, pl.77 gamma 2. Horseman (black blotches); Munich, Antikensammlungen Schoen 123. Unpublished. Horseman (h.10,3 cm., all black);

# TERRACOTTA HORSES AND HORSEMEN OF ARCHAIC BOEOTIA

Athens, Kanellopoulos Museum 1831. Unpublished. Horseman (fig.36); Athens, Kanellopoulos Museum 1816. BROUSKARI 1985, 24. 25 (ill.) (fig.37). Warrior horseman, horse on wheels. I can find no convincing Late Geometric Attic parallels for the shape, decoration and motif of this figurine. In shape both horse and rider are clearly closest to figurines of group G. The hole for the horses eye recurs in group D. The black glaze stripes, fired reddish brown, are in the scheme of group G and the field of dots on the chest is found on G18 as well as on a subgroup within the contemporary mid 6th cent. group H (H1-H8 in the list below). Mounted warriors are found among Boeotian terracotta horsemen throughout the 6th century, being especially numerous in groups H and J (see lists below). The use of wheels is attested by the early 6th century horseman B2 and a dog associated with group H (cf. note 108a).

99. GRACE 1938, 40 note 56 suggests that the presence of reins is a sign of relatively later date.
100. I.e Leyenaar-Plaisier to G9.
101. Row of dots between uppermost stripes on neck of G13 (fig.30). In the same position G3-G4 have wavy stripes.
102. H.12,0 cm. No spots on chest; eye not set in triangular space; relatively poor work.
103. *H12*: H.10,0 cm. Tail modern. On horse's throat vertical row of 3 dots over horizontal ladder on chest, under which 3 dots horizontally. *H13*: H.10,5 cm. On throat of horse large 'S'. 3 sets of double lines across back between which rows of dots. Ladder on tail. *H14*: H.10,6 cm.
104. H.12,7 cm.
105. H.11.8 cm. Clay orange brown, clay slip. Glaze reddish brown. Break shows missing rider contiguous with neck, cp. H41. Stripes along flank continue across chest. Ladder-pattern on tail.
106. H.15,4 cm. Rider has wedge shaped head with vertical stripes for hair and dot for eye, rudimentary legs. Herringbones on legs of horse, broad stripe along flank, wavy verticals on neck.
107. H.10,5 cm.
108. Staatliche Museen, Antikensammlung TC8413. WINTER 1907, 36:1; N.N.BRITOVA, *Greek Terracottas* (in Russian)(1969) 25 fig.19. The Scythian horseman archer Munich, Antikensammlungen S.L.80, J.SIEVEKING, *Die Terrakotten der Sammlung Loeb* (1916) 4. Tf.6,2, has hindquarters decorated much as H3, but different in shape. Spots abound on the rider and on the forepart of the horse, whose neck and head are close to H45 below. The attempted naturalism in the rendering of the legs of the horse in the Munich piece is parallelled by the Boeotian 'red on white' terracotta *hippalektryon* in the Louvre cited note 77, with a head reminiscent of H45 and a mane with 'frills' as H37-H42 below.
108a. National Museum 12995. SZABO 1986, fig.42. On its forehead an elaborate palmette with pendant bud (cp. chest of H27), legs have holes for wheels, cf. note 98.
109. *Ha9*: H.10,3 cm. Wavy and straight vertical on each front leg. On chest 3 verticals over horizontal. Alternating straight and wavy stripes on neck, wavy over straight horizontal along flank, stripe down middle of back, crossbars on tail. *Ha10*: H.10,4 cm. *Ha11*: H.11,2 cm. *Ha12*: H.11,0 cm. *Ha13*: H.10,0 cm. The wavy stripe along the flank and alternate stripes on neck are red (as opposed to dark brown), either applied red or diluted glaze (SCHMALTZ 1977/78, 60 briefly notes this practise in Boeotian'Vogelschalen' but does not refer to an example of it).
110. URE 1934, 22-23. 51-52; PAYNE 1931, 60. 320 to no.1263; HASPELS 1936, 4-5 (wrongly attributing grave 86 to the later Boeotian Kylix A-series); SPARKES 1967, 128; KILINSKI 1974, 123; SCHMALTZ 1977/78, 30 implies a higher chronology when dating graves 50, 51 and 31 'c.580 B.C.' (for mid 6th century date of graves 50, 51 and date c.515 B.C. for grave 31 see notes 111 and 166 respectively). No arguments or references are given, but found 'convincing' by B.FREYER-SCHAUENBURG in *CVA Kiel Kunsthalle, Antikensammlung I* (1988) 15 Pl.1-2.
111. BURROWS & URE 1907/08, 305-318; URE 1927, 12. 78-81; URE 1934, 22-23. 51-52.
112. URE 1934, 23. 51; GRACE 1939, 40 and note 56 (graves 49, 50, 51, 110); PAYNE 1931, 60 (graves 50, 51). 320 no.1262 (grave 49). For higher dates proposed by SCHMALTZ 1977/78 see note 110.
113. HASPELS 1936, 5. Commented by A.D.URE, *JHS* 57, 1937, 265.
114. URE 1934, 50-51. Date of Attic Comast Group: R.M.COOK, Greek Painted Pottery (2.ed.)(1972) 74. 78; BOARDMAN 1974, 18. PAYNE 1931, 199 and KILINSKI 1974, 79-81 discuss Boeotian imitations.
115. ANDREIOMENOU 1985, 116 to photo 14. 124 photo 14.

116. References in H-list.
117. GRACE 1939, 37-38. The saucer in question illustrated in KAROUZOU 1980, 131. The resemblance to H26 seems even greater. A date before 550 B.C. supported by *CVA Tübingen I* (1973) 85-86 Pl. 49, 1-7 (K.WALLENSTEIN).
118. References in Ha-list.
119. URE 1934, 53-54. 65-66.
120. URE 1934, 63 no.125d.3. pl.XVI. Not included in classification of Corinthian graves, cf.URE 1934, 22 note 1, but found under 'early sixth-century graves', p.63. Dated 'c.590-580 B.C.' by SPARKES 1967, 128 without arguments. Date of grave 86, see note 110.
121. URE 1934, 63 nos.86.277-284.
122. URE 1934, 65.
123. H.12,0 cm. Dark red on white ground. Closely spaced vertical stripes on chest. Rein shown.
124. No decoration is preserved; the piece is grey from fire cp.Ia4.
125. H.14.6 cm. Herringbones on legs. Brownish stripes on the riders back. Breaks indicate that the left arm originally carried a shield.
126. *Ia10*: H.12,0 cm. Heavy incrustation. The rider's face is reminiscent of the terracotta centaur Munich, Antikensammlungen 7631, SZABO 1973, 13 fig.9-10. His headgear is like that of the horseman H26. *Ia11*: H.15,8 cm. Black for outline of eye and for pupil; horizontals of mane red, edge of mane black; low on neck 5 horizontals go right across (red, yellow, red, black, red). Bearded rider wears petasos with radiating red stripes on top of brim. Narrowly spaced red horizontals on his body.
127. *Ia12* and *Ia13*: For shape of horse cp.Ia16. Plastic rendering of saddlecloth (?) behind rider. Legs of riders as Ia11. Faces mould made, cp. the horseman Louvre CA1506, MOLLARD-BESQUES 1954, 19 no. B107, related to Ia by shape of ears and crest as well as decoration.
128. H.15,2 cm. Left arm of rider missing, muzzle chipped. Red on center of *petasos*, rider wears red belt. No black or yellow.
129. The fire alluded to above is that of cremation burials, turning the clay grey, cf. URE 1934, 64 no.110.120-131. Authors publishing figurines should note this as well as the details of the distribution of the colours used in the decoration.
130. Boston, Museum of Fine Arts 01.8011. *AntK* 7, 1964, 70. pl.21.1 (H.HOFFMANN). That a mule is meant is suggested by the long ears, the lack of a crested mane and the fact that we have other Boeotian satyrs riding mules, but not horses, i.e. Boston, Museum of Fine Arts 08.290. *AntK* 7, 1964, 69-70. pl.21.2 (c.500 B.C.?), and U.S.A., private. W.RUDOLPH & A.CALINESCU, *Ancient Art in the V.G.Simkovitsch Collection* (1988) 166 no.161 (reclining back to front, 3rd century B.C.).
131. *Griechische Ausgrabungen. Auktion Galerie Helbing 27.-28.6.1910,* München (1910) 15 no.226. pl.4.
132. Thebes, Archaeological Museum 6046 (Room B, case 5) from Rhitsona grave 50. Must be of the series 50.393-398 described by URE 1934,65 as continuing the grave 86 type (Group I). There are faint traces of a horizontal stripe along the flanks, cf.J6 below (fig.63). To Ia list add Liverpool Museum 1968.189. Unpublished. Horse.
133. URE 1934, 66. No parallels are cited. More simply explained as a stylized rendering of a helmets crest, so also P.KNOBLAUCH 1937, 196 no.435 (Rhitsona 12.90).
134. Allard Pierson Museum 890. *BABesch* II,1,1927, 12 fig.2.
135. URE 1934, 65.
136. Room B, case 6. This must be one of the 3 red on white horses 49.442-444 described by Ure as typical of his mid-sixth century graves, cf.URE 1934, 65. Three bands around barrel (red, yellow, red); low on neck two thin black stripes above two broad red ones, going right across. Yellow dot for eye.
137. H.15,3 cm. Note curved double line on hind leg and double line along flank. Red blotch on shoulder; cp. BURROWS & URE 1907/08, 264 nos.50.393-402 for similar feature, of which 50.399-402 are like J6 according to URE 1934,65.
138. Neck upright, elongated head but muzzle not as snouty as the following. Build of horse very heavy.

139. The drooping tail of this piece looks odd in the context of group J. According to Jucker, the root of the tail is a modern addition – could a wrong angle have been chosen?

140. The mouldmade figurine of a woman sitting sidesaddle on this horse is of a type created on Rhodes in the early 5th century B.C. and imitated in Boeotia in the mid 5th, cf. HIGGINS 1954, 64 no.121 (Rhodes). 218 no.817 (Boeotia). Such a date is incompatible with that of the horse (mid 6th cent.). I doubt that the rider belongs.

141. H.15,2 cm. Several breaks, no missing parts. Incrustations, decoration badly preserved. For rudimentary legs pointing forewards cp. Rhitsona 117.10, URE 1934, 65. pl.XVI, and Ia11-Ia13.

142. Rider dwarfing horse as Rhitsona 110.118, URE 1934, pl.XVI. A very similar piece is Würzburg, Martin-von-Wagner-Museum K1922. E.SIMON (ed.), *Die sammlung Kiseleff II: Minoische und griechische Antiken* (1989) 153 no.243. pl.95. Horseman (rider missing).

143. I disagree with Sinn's interpretation (to J11) of this feature as a part of the horses headgear, a browband ('Stirnband'). A horseman (warrior) in Berlin has a similar forelock while the headgear is painted in: Berlin, Antikensammlung TC8334. ROHDE 1968, 39 no.11. pl.11 (colour). Plastic rendering of headgear is seen in Cypriot terracottas, cf. CROUWELL & TATTON-BROWN 1988, pl.XXVI, 1-2.

144. Louvre CA1136. MOLLARD-BESQUES 1954, 18 no. B105. pl.14. Cf.SZABO 1975, 18. 16 fig.10-12.

145. URE 1934, 65 nos.40.134, 50.399. From the description, it sounds as if some of the horses URE 1934, 64 nos.110.120-131 belong to this subdivision.

146. Cf. URE 1934, 64 nos.110.120-131 compared with 145.94 (A1); they are unfortunately not illustrated, but may belong to group J, cf. note 144.

147. Ure 1934, 65; add the absence of a horizontal element on the flanks found in groups G and H, as well as the type of mane characterizing group H (group not represented at Rhitsona).

148. For the date of grave 86, see note 110.

149. For dating see note 112 and 113.

150. Ia1-figurines may have been found in the typologically later Boeotian Kylix A grave 51, cp. BURROWS & URE 1907/08, 270 nos.312-316 said to be like 49.438 (Ia1), but not cited in the review of red on whites URE 1934,65. The horseman in Paris, Louvre CA1506, MOLLARD-BESQUES 1954, 19 no.B107. pl.14, may also serve to show that group Ia continues through the 3rd quarter of the 6th century. The modelling and decoration of neck and head relate it to group Ia, while the rest of the body is more like Ib. The horseman is dated 'c.510 B.C.' by Mollard-Besques, on the basis of the style of the mould made head of the rider. The closests parallels are the early kouroi of the 'Ptoon 20 Group', cf. G.RICHTER, Kouroi (1960) 126ff.

151. For the dates of grave 31 see note 166-68, of grave 12 URE 1909, 308; URE 1927, 80.

152. Note 143.

153. ØSTERGAARD 1986, 95-96; SZABO 1975.

154. URE 1934, 68-69.

155. L3: H.10,4 cm. KNOBLAUCH 1937, 205 no.510. 192 'Gruppe 2'. L4: H.10,0 cm. Tail missing. White ground, on which yellow for horse, naked rider red with black hair; mouth, nostrils and ear ducts of horse red.

156. H.c.10 cm. Tail and tips of ears on horse and left foot of rider missing. In shape closest to L5 –L6. Holes for nostrils of horse, groove for mouth. Horse white, its harness red. The skin of the rider is red, his short chiton white with red stripes, the *petasos* white.

157. Point of crest missing.

158. H.11,3. Decoration not preserved.

159. H.9,2 cm. Several breaks, left foot of rider missing. Horse piebald yellow on white with red in mouth, nostrils and earducts. Naked rider red with black hair.

160. Thus the 'mourning women' of c.600 B.C. listed SZABO 1973, 14-15. Also Boeotian female figurines ('pappades') as HIGGINS 1986, 74-75 figs. 74-76 (early 6th century, black on brown). 83 figs.84-86 (red on white, c.550-500 B.C.). The earliest example of a horseman with moulded face known to me: Ia12-Ia13, cp. also the Ia-related horseman Louvre CA1506 of c.510 B.C. cited in note 150.

161. KNOBLAUCH 1937, 191-192 'Zu F'. 202 no.484 (L1). 205 nos.509-511 (L3,L8,L9). He does

not distinguish between headmoulds and facemoulds. Observing the ridges and differences in surface character caused by the use of facemoulds requires very close examination. HIGGINS 1986, 91 notes the moulded head of L1 but sees L6 as handmade throughout. Ideally, publications of these figurines should include a detail photograph of the head.

162. HIGGINS 1986, 84-92 for introduction, 182 for bibliography; add: KNOBLAUCH 1937, 191-192 (Zu F). 202-206 nos.481-520. SINN 1977, 28 no.25. 45 no.93, and references.

163. H.9,5 cm. Decoration not preserved.

164. On La1 only left eye thus.

165. Martin-von-Wagner-Museum HA1689. SIMON 1975, 58 (not ill.). F.MUTHMANN, *Der Granatapfel* (Bern 1982) fig.43.

166. For published references to grave 31: SPARKES 1967, 129. The Boeotian Kylix B series and the position of grave 31: BURROWS & URE 1907/8, 305-318; URE 1927, 39-40, 80. Date c.520: URE 1934, 60 (cf.51 bottom).

167. HASPELS 1936, 108.

168. *JHS* 57, 1937, 265.

169. SPARKES 1967, 129. KILINSKI 1974, 120. 126 (c.515 B.C.).

170. ABV 496.178. BOARDMAN 1974, 148.

171. Thasos *protome:* Thasos Museum 4. *Guide de Thasos* (1967) 117 no.8. fig.58. Horseman in Boston: VERMEULE 1968, 9. figs.5-6.

172. Bronze *protome:* National Museum 6693. W.LAMB, *Greek and Roman Bronzes* (1929) 101. pl.38a; cf. CAROLINE V. WANGENHEIM, *Archaische Bronzepferde in Rundplastik und Relief* (Bonn 1988) 8-9 no.2. 12 (date). (She regards the groove in the mane as typical of late archaic Attica). Marble relief: H.SCHRADER, *Die archaischen Marmorbildwerke der Akropolis* (Frankfurt an Main 1939) 390 no.476. 394 (date). pl.200.

173. Groups A-C see p.114-125. Stylistic development of early board idols: PAUL 1958/59, 168. 170.

174. Groups D-F see p.125-133.

175. Groups G, H, Ha, Hb see p.133-150.

176. Groups I, Ia, Ib, J see p.150-158.

177. Groups L, La see p.160-168. A horseman (half-figure) in Boston, Museum of Fine Arts 97.348. VERMEULE 1968, 9. figs.3-4, with a horse's head reminiscent of H27 should be noted when considering antecedents of group L.

178. URE 1934, 53. 68. Cp. HIGGINS 1986, 78. Positive MONLOUP 1984, 42.

179. HIGGINS 1984, 8. HIGGINS 1986, 64. 72. 84 is rather contradictory. PAUL 1958/59, 168 is positive towards the possibility of localisation of terracotta idols on the basis of style, but not of the appearance of the clay. Localisation of Boeotian pottery: KILINSKI 1974, 114-118; A.ANDREIOMENOU, *To keramikon ergasterion tis Akraiphias* (Athens 1979). Localisation of Archaic Cypriot terracottas: MONLOUP 1984, 23 (Salamis); V.TATTON-BROWN (ed.), *Cyprus and the East Mediterranean in the Late Iron Age* (London 1989) 28-43 (Kition).

180. Cf. note 17 and 18.

181. Especially those figurines in the National Museum at Athens which may with certainty be connected with earlier Greek government excavations (as Ba 1, Ba 2, H27). The same goes for the material in the small museum at Skimatari, but this is not available for study.

182. As ANDREIOMENOU 1985. Consequences of illicit digging: HIGGINS 1986, 64.

182a. See note 9 for references. At the 6th International Boeotian Conference in 1989, many participants supported the idea of a moratorium on excavations other than those of rescue in order to concentrate on the publication backlog and improvement of facilities at the Museum of Thebes.

183. High quality board idols of the period are similarly rare, seen by PAUL 1958/59, 174 as a sign of the provincial status of Rhitsona.

184. HIGGINS 1984, 8 ascribes horses of group B to Tanagra because only found there. They have now been found at Akraiphia, cf. p.124 above.

185. URE 1934, 53 (same workshops). 54 (same people). 68 (same workshops, possibly same people). Also KILINSKI 1974, 115-116; HIGGINS 1986, 68 (same people).

186. URE 1934, 68; HIGGINS 1986, 69.

187. Higgins 1986, 64 assumes that the figurines were used in sanctuaries and private homes as well. Precise documentation of the position of the finds from archaic Boeotian graves are rarely found. I note the following photographs of our figurines in situ: *AAA* 7, 1974, 337 fig.20 (Akraiphia, team of horses related to Ia); *ADelt* 31,1976 Chr. pl.90 alpha (Akraiphia, horseman); HIGGINS 1986, 39 = 43 fig.25 (Tanagra, grave E/17, the horseman is probably C16).

188. MORRIS 1987 provides part of the theoretical framework and a comprehensive set of references for such work.

189. D1-D2 (?), Rhitsona grave 145; G43-G46, Tanagra grave E/16; G48-G50, Tanagra grave E/15. Many similar series have probably been found but not documented.

190. Rhitsona grave 145: A1, D1-D2, E1. Other group combinations from Rhitsona: Grave 86: G1, I1; grave 49: G34, G35, Ia1, Ib1, J2; grave 50: Da2, G25; grave 110: Da1, G32; grave 31: L1, Ib2. From Tanagra: Grave L/9: Ba4, C20, Ha1-4, Ha6; grave S/51: H4-5, H38-39 (from different subdivisions).

191. The motif on the croup of G30, G31 and G55 (?) probably represents a flying bird, cp. the more elaborate version on a recently acquired G-horseman in Copenhagen, Ny Carlsberg Glyptotek 3694.

# BIBLIOGRAPHY

| | |
|---|---|
| *Ancient Art* 1954 | *Ancient Art in American Private Collections.* Cambridge MA. |
| ANDREIOMENOU, A. 1985 | La Nècropole classique de Tanagra. *Colloques int. du CNRS 'La Béotie Antique'*, 109-127. Lyon (1983). |
| BLOESCH, H. (ed.) 1974 | *Das Tier in der Antike. Archäologisches Institut der Universität Zürich.* Zürich. |
| BOARDMAN, J. 1974 | *Athenian Black Figure Vases.* London. |
| BOHEN, G. 1988 | *Die geometrischen Pyxiden.* Kerameikos XIII. Berlin |
| BREITENSTEIN, N. 1941 | *Danish National Museum, Catalogue of Terracottas, Cypriote, Greek, Etrusco-Italian and Roman.* Copenhagen. |
| BROUSKARI, M. 1985 | *The Alexandra and Paul Kanellopoulos Museum.* Athens. |
| BUCK, J.S. 1979 | *A History of Boeotia.* Edmonton. |
| BURROWS, R. & P.N. URE 1907/08 | Excavations at Rhitsona in Boeotia, *BSA* XIV, 1907/08, 226-318. |
| 1909 | Excavations at Rhitsona in Boeotia, *JHS* 29, 1909, 308-353. |
| CROUWELL, J.H. & V.TATTON-BROWN 1988 | Ridden Horses in Iron Age Cyprus, *RDAC* 1988, 2, 77-85. |
| GEHRIG, U. 1975 | *Antiken aus Berliner Privatbesitz.* Antikenmuseum, Berlin. |
| 1983 | *Tierbilder aus vier Jahrtausende. Antiken der Sammlung Mildenberg.* |

| | |
|---|---|
| GRACE, F.<br>1939 | *Archaic Sculpture in Boeotia.* Cambridge MA. |
| GUGGISBERG, M.<br>1988 | Terrakotten von Argos. Ein Fundkomplex aus den Theater, *BCH* 112, 1988, 167-234. |
| HASPELS, C.H.E.<br>1936 | *Attic Black-Figured Lekythoi.* Paris. |
| HIGGINS, R.A.<br>1954 | *Catalogue of the Terracottas in the Dept. of Greek and Roman Antiquities, British Museum, I.* London. |
| 1967 | *Greek Terracottas.* Frome and London. |
| 1984 | A Boeotian Horseman, *GMusJ* 12, 1984, 7-9. |
| 1986 | *Tanagra and the Figurines.* London. |
| HOFFMANN, H.<br>1970 | Ten Centuries that shaped the West. Houston. |
| HOLMBERG, E.<br>1963 | Attic and Boeotian figurines and a Melian relief, *in:* ARMANDRY, P.(ed.), *Collection Hélène Stathatos III. Objets antiques et byzantins,* 109-112. Strasbourg. |
| KAROUZOU, S.<br>1980 | *The National Museum.* Athens. |
| KILINSKI II, K.<br>1974 | *Boeotian Black-figure Vase-Painting of the Archaic Period.* Ann Arbor (Diss.). |
| KNOBLAUCH, P.<br>1937 | *Studien zur archaisch-griechischen Tonbildnerei in Kreta, Rhodos, Athen und Böotien.* Bleicherode. |
| KOZLOFF, A., D.G. MITTEN & M.SGUAITAMATTI<br>1986 | *More Animals in Ancient Art from the Leo Mildenberg Collection.* Mainz am Rhein. |
| KUNISCH, N.<br>1972 | *Antiken der Sammlung Julius C. und Margot Funcke.* Bochum. |
| LA ROCCA, E.<br>1985 | *Amazonomachia. Le sculture frontonali del Tempio di Apollo Sosiano.* Roma. |
| LEYENAAR-PLAISIER, P.<br>1979 | *Les terres cuites grecques et romaines. Catalogue de la collection du Musée National des Antiquités à Leiden.* Leiden. |
| LIEPMANN, U.<br>1975 | *Griechische Terrakotten, Bronzen, Skulpturen. Bildkataloge des Kestner-Museums* XII. Hannover. |
| LULLIES, R.<br>1955 | *Eine Sammlung griechischer Kleinkunst.* München. |
| MAXIMOVA, I.<br>1927 | *Les vases plastiques dans l'Antiquité II.* Paris. |
| MOLLARD-BESQUES, S.<br>1954<br>1963 | *Museé National du Louvre. Catalogue raisonné des figurines et reliefs en terrecuite grecs, etrusques et romains I.* Paris.<br>*Les terres cuites grecques.* Paris. |
| MONLOUP, J.<br>1984 | *Les figurines de terre cuite de tradition archaïque (Salamine de Chypre XII)* Paris. |

| | |
|---|---|
| MORRIS, I.<br>1988 | Burial and ancient society. The rise of the Greek city-state. Cambridge. |
| NEUTSCH, B.<br>1948 | Welt der Griechen im Bilde der Originale der Heidelberger Universitäts Sammlung. Heidelberg. |
| NICHOLSON, F.<br>1968 | Ancient Life in Miniature. Birmingham City Museum & Art Gallery. Birmingham. |
| PAUL, E.<br>1958/59 | Die böotische Brettidolen, Wissenschaftliche Zeitschrift der Karl-Marx-Universität Leipzig 8, 1958/59, 166-205. |
| PAYNE, H.<br>1931 | Necrocorinthia. A Study of Corinthian art in the Archaic Period. Oxford. |
| POMERANCE<br>1966 | The Pomerance Collection of Ancient Art. The Brooklyn Museum. New York. |
| PRESTON, L.E.<br>1975 | Four Boeotian ape figurines from the J. Paul Getty Museum, GMusJ 2, 1975, 121-126. |
| ROHDE, E.<br>1968 | Griechische Terrakotten. Tübingen. |
| RUCKERT, A.<br>1976 | Frühe Keramik Böotiens, 10.Beih. AntK, 1976. |
| SCHEFOLD, K.<br>1960 | Meisterwerke der griechischen Kunst. Basel. |
| SCHMALTZ, B.<br>1977/78 | Zur Chronologie der böotischen Vogelschalen, MarbWPr 1977/78, 21-60. |
| SIMON, E.(ed.)<br>1975 | Führer durch die Antikenabteilung des Martin von Wagner Museums der Universität Würzburg. Mainz. |
| SINN, U.<br>1977 | Staatliche Kunstsammlungen Kassel. Antike Terrakotten. Kassel. |
| SPARKES, B.A.<br>1967 | The Taste of a Boeotian Pig, JHS 87, 1967, 116-130. |
| SZABO, M.<br>1973 | Contribution à la question de la coroplathie béotienne du VIIe siècle av.n.è., BMusHong 41, 1973, 3-19. |
| 1975 | Attelages de chevaux archaïques en terre cuite en Attique et en Béotie, BMusHong 45, 1975, 7-20. |
| 1979 | Vases plastiques et terrres cuites béotiennes à la fin du 7e et au début du 6e siècle av.n.è., ActaClDebrec 15, 1979, 3-16. |
| 1986 | Archaikus Agyagszobraszat Boiotiaban. Budapest. |
| URE, P.N.<br>1927 | 6th and 5th century pottery from Rhitsona. London. |
| 1934 | Aryballoi and Figurines from Rhitsona. Cambridge. |
| VAFOPOULOU-RICHARDSON, C.<br>1981 | Greek Terracottas. Ashmolean Museum. Oxford. |
| VERMEULE, C.<br>1968 | Archaic terracotta rider, AntPl VIII, 1, 7-11. Berlin. |

| | |
|---|---|
| WINTER, F.<br>1907 | Die Typen der figürlichen Terrakotten I. Berlin-Stuttgart. |
| ZERVOS, C.<br>1934 | L'Art en Gréce. Paris. |
| 1936 | L'Art en Gréce. 2nd ed. Paris. |
| ØSTERGAARD,<br>J.STUBBE<br>1986 | Heste fra den boiotiske stald, MeddelelsGlyptKøb 42, 1986, 81-108. |

Credit for illustrations:

Courtesy of the Antikmuseet, Aarhus: Fig.19, 24

Courtesy of the Kanellopoulos Museum, Athens: Fig.8, 27, 36, 37, 39, 42, 43, 45, 48, 49, 58, 59, 63, 69, 74

Courtesy of the Antikenmuseum der Ruhr-Universität, Bochum: Fig.13, 29

Courtesy of the Museum of Fine Arts, Boston: Fig.25 (neg.no.E3310), 44 (neg.no.E3309), 50 (neg.no.E3308), 61 (neg.no.E3311)

Courtesy of the Arthur M.Sackler Museum of Archaeology, Harvard University, Cambridge, Massachussetts, J.C.Hoppins Bequest: Fig.20, 26

Courtesy of The Brooklyn Museum, Brooklyn: Fig.51 (neg.no.22.11A), 52 (neg.no.22.11B)

Collection Stathatos III (1963) pl.18, no.59: Fig.46

Courtesy of the National Museum, Dept. of Near Eastern and Classical Antiquities, Copenhagen: Fig.6 (neg.no.T333), 41 (neg.no.T24)

Courtesy of Helle Damgaard Andersen, Copenhagen: Fig.10, 30, 40

Ny Carlsberg Glyptotek, Copenhagen: Fig.71 – 73

Courtesy of the Antikenmuseum, Heidelberg: Fig.67 (neg.no.N.S.877c)

Courtesy of the Museum of Fine Arts, Houston: Fig.14

Courtesy of Knud W. Jensen: Fig.2, 23, 65

Courtesy of the Staatliche Kunstsammlungen, Antikenabteilung, Kassel: Fig.22 (neg.no.AS1507), 28 (neg.no.AS1488), 64 (neg.no.AS1499)

Courtesy of the Antikmuseum der Karl-Marx-Universität, Leipzig: Fig.38

Courtesy of the J.Paul Getty Museum, Malibu: Fig.5

Courtesy of The Manchester Museum, Manchester: 53 (neg.no.4650/2)

Courtesy of the Antikensammlungen, Munich: Fig.7, 12, 17, 60, 66, 68, 70

## TERRACOTTA HORSES AND HORSEMEN OF ARCHAIC BOEOTIA

Courtesy of the Greek Museum, University of Newcastle, Newcastle: Fig.3-4

Courtesy of the Ashmolean Museum, Oxford: Fig.11

Courtesy of The Art Museum, Princeton: Fig.35

Courtesy of the Ure Museum of Greek Archaeology, Reading: Fig.1, 33, 54, 55, 56

Courtesy of the Württembergisches Landesmuseum, Stuttgart: 16 (neg.no.Ant.2753), 47 (neg.-no.Ant.2752), 57 (neg.no.Ant.2750)

Courtesy of the Antikenmuseum, Tübingen: Fig.9 (neg.no.1288b), 31 (neg.no.1289d)

Courtesy of the Gustavianum, Uppsala: Fig.18, 32, 34

York City Art Gallery Preview 66, 1964: Fig.15

Courtesy of Leo Mildenberg, Zürich: Fig.62 (neg.no.1369-2)

# THREE CORINTHIAN SHERDS FROM RHODES – A CASE STUDY

## LONE WRIEDT SØRENSEN

For some forty years the Department of Near Eastern and Classical Antiquities of the National Museum in Copenhagen has housed a number of objects acquired by the members of the Danish Archaeological Expedition to Rhodes. Among these are three vase fragments which probably all come from Middle Corinthian craters. For two of these fragments, the figure scenes they once formed part of may be reconstructed from comparisons with other and better preserved craters. The third fragment, however, seems to belong to a scene without immediate parallels. The largest amount of pottery from the Greek mainland has been found in Italy and Sicily, and studies of its distribution and significance have therefore focused on the western market, while the exchange of pottery between various Greek areas has received relatively little attention. The comparatively large amount of Corinthian craters found at Caere has been the subject of a recent paper which concludes that they were primarily produced for the aristocracy of this particular Etruscan city (DE LA GENIÈRE 1988). However, this suggestion leaves the finds of similar craters elsewhere unexplained. The present sherds from Rhodes offer an opportunity for a case study of the find situation in the eastern part of the Mediterranean and a comparison with the trends in the West.

The main objective of the Danish expedition in 1902 was to excavate the acropolis of Lindos, but other important investigations were carried out, both in the village of Lindos and at Exochi and Vroulia. The members of the expedition and especially K.F. Kinch, who spent a considerable time in Rhodes, also made frequent trips into the country and recorded meticulously everything of archaeological interest. Kinch's notebooks, which are preserved at the Danish National Museum, give an impression of the richness of the archaeology of the southern part of Rhodes, but also of the extent of the illicit exploitation going on at that time. A number of objects were purchased from the local contractors, but other items, probably including the three sherds concerning us here, were acquired through what today would be called a rescue excavation.

Together with other effects of the expedition, the sherds were stored in the building of the Carlsberg Foundation which generously financed the expedition. In 1947 the Foundation needed more space and donated the material to the National Museum. The inventory list made on this occasion mentions that the sherds probably come from Lindos, from a ruined necropolis between the village and Hagios Aemilianos. In his notebook from late January 1906, Kinch comments upon excavations which may be linked with the information on the above-mentioned inventory. Here we learn that a large deposit of sherds was excavated in

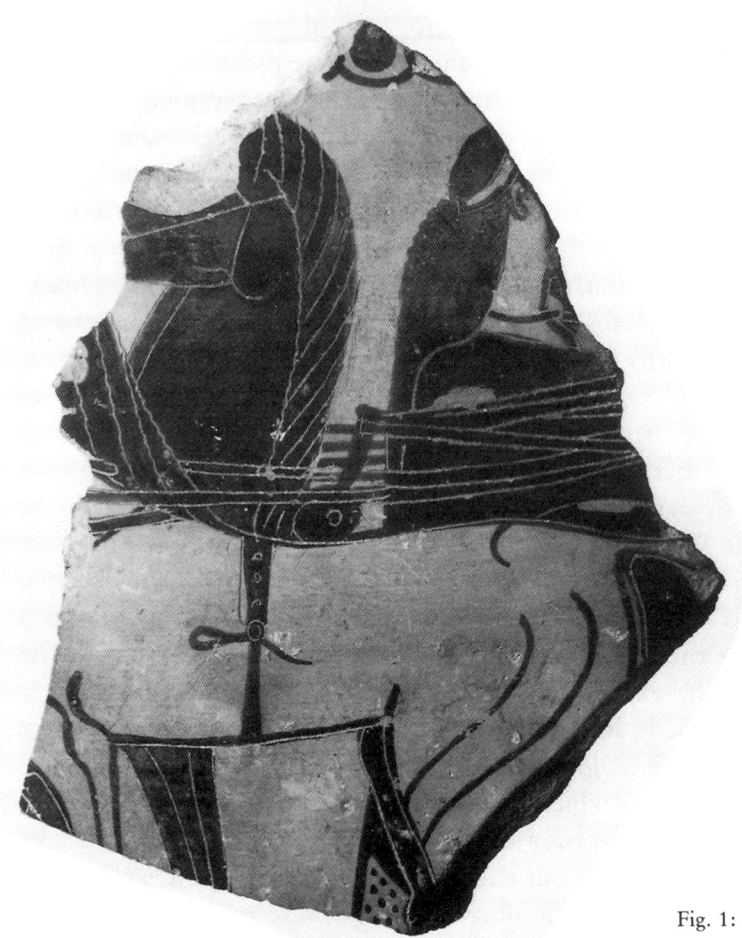

Fig. 1: Inv. no. 12350.

the road outside the house of a woman called Eumorphia or Phrono north-west of the village of Lindos. Kinch was evidently convinced that a necropolis was located on her property and tried to obtain her permission to carry out excavations there. Having failed, however, he notes that according to Phrono, her grand father had smashed the vases in question, and he adds in irritation that Phrono is half-witted and not to be believed. The deposit contained "sherds of several hundred vases, Attic, Corinthian and Rhodian (Milesian), almost all large vessels, bell craters, column amphoras, other types of amphoras but only very few small vessels". According to Kinch the vessels seemed to have been smashed on purpose, since the sections with figures were especially damaged, evidently because the figures were considered demons. 12 to 15 baskets of sherds were brought to Kinch's house at Lindos for further study, but Kinch never made another comment on them.

Although we cannot prove for sure that the sherds presented here formed part of the deposit in question, it is highly likely, since they correspond with Kinch's description. The name Eumorphia is furthermore written on the back of another sherd which was stored together with them.

1: Inv. no 12350. Shoulder sherd. Fine very pale brown (10YR 7/4) clay with tiny red and white inclusions, slip same colour, paint very dark grey (2.5YR N3/) and reddish brown (2.5YR 4/4). Inside painted. On outside, small section of a frieze of rays. Below this, part of two pole horses turned towards the left. In the background, part of a standing woman turned towards the right. The woman's ear and neckline and one of the horses are painted in outline, the rest in silhouette drawing with incised details.

*Fig. 1*

Although all three fragments may be placed within the general frame of the established typological system, they are unfortunately comparatively small and partly for this reason they are difficult to attribute to a specific painter. No. 1, which represents the best draftsmanship, needs little introduction. It was published together with a sherd in the Allard Pierson Museum in Amsterdam to which it joins and was attributed to the Three Maidens Painter, a personality who has in the meantime dissolved into several painters belonging to the Three Maidens Group or the so-called Gorgoneion Group (GJØDESEN 1963, 339; BENSON 1969; AMYX 1988, 194). This indicates how difficult it is to attribute even good quality work to specific painter personalities, and the problem becomes even greater when only a fraction of a given vase painting is preserved. F. Croissant has recently pointed out the eclectic character even within the same Corinthian works of art, and the changing quality is exemplified by sherd no. 2 from Lindos (CROISSANT 1988, but cf. also CARTER 1989, 376). However, the Copenhagen-Amsterdam crater no doubt belongs to the Gorgoneion Group, not only because of the style and technique, but also because of the subject matter. The couple standing in a chariot on the fragment in Amsterdam is repeated on other craters of this group, and in one case inscriptions identify the main characters as Helen and Paris (GJØDESEN 1963 pl. 70 fig. 7; AMYX 1989 pl. 79). It is, of course, tempting to assume that the possible mutual source of inspiration of the vase paintings was associated with this Homeric topic.

*Fig. 2*  2: Inv. no 12349. Shoulder sherd. Clay fine, very pale brown (10YR 8/3), slip same colour, paint very dark grey (5YR 3/1) and dusky red (10R 3/4). Inside painted. The paint appears somewhat diluted on the out-

Fig. 2: Inv. no. 12349.

side. On outside, part of two warriors towards the right. The foremost warrior wears a helmet with a tall crest-holder, his body is covered by a round shield decorated with a *Gorgoneion*, and the stroke along his back is probably a quiver. The warrior behind him carries a spear in his right hand and his shield on the left arm. It is seen from the inside. The decoration is worn.

In contrast to the previous sherd, where the figures are neatly drawn with a firm and able hand, the draftsmanship of no. 2 is at least in part mediocre. The figures are painted in silhouette with details indicated by incisions, and only the emblem of the shield, a *Gorgoneion* rendered in outline technique, seems to have received the painter's full attention. Actually, if it were found separately, one would not immediately associate the shield with the warriors, especially since it is carried on the foremost warrior's right arm. The two warriors may have formed part of a row of hoplites, which is a common motif in Corinth. A famous predecessor of this subject matter is one of the friezes of the Chigi *olpe* (SIMON 1981 pl. VII), which together with the other vases of the Protocorinthian polychrome group is believed to reflect major works of art, be it wall painting or ivory carving (ROBERTSON 1975, 54; CARTER 1989, 362). However, the warriors are painted with a great deal of overlapping the shields giving the impression of a sliced salami, while the figures on our sherd stand with so much space in between them that their shields hardly touch. The Chigi hoplites furthermore all carry their shields on their left arm, and this is also the case on the other famous Protocorinthian miniature renderings of hoplites. Rows of marching hoplites are a well-known subject in Corinthian vase painting, mainly on round *aryballoi*, but they also appear on other small shapes (PAYNE 1931, 116; AMYX 1988, 647). The warriors are often shown turned towards the right, carrying their shield on their right arm like the warrior on the Lindos sherd (AMYX 1988 pl. 72, 2). However, small-scale representations such as these are probably not immediately comparable with the paintings on larger vessels, since they are reduced to stock motifs, and the shields were probably added without much consideration, in order to finish the drawing as quickly as possible. Moreover, a row of standing or walking warriors was evidently not a motif favored by painters of larger vessels. On a crater by the Athena Painter, three hoplites are standing behind a chariot, but they are not immediately comparable with the Lindos warriors, although one of them also carries a shield decorated with a *Gorgoneion* (AMYX 1989 pl. 104, 1b). They are turned towards the left and the composition follows the early renderings with close set figures and overlapping shields. Otherwise hoplites are shown in battle scenes either with many participants or in a standard setting of a battle between two or four warriors – a single- or mixed double so to speak (for instance AMYX 1988 pl. 103, 1a; PAYNE 1931 pl. 41, 3; BENSON 1956 pl. 77 fig. 40). The idea of showing the shields on the Lindos sherd from alternating sides could have been influenced from these duels and used in order to break the monotony of a row of figures. Another explanation may be that the painter deliberately chose to represent the foremost warrior "left handed" in order to focus on the shield emblem and thereby single him out as a specific figure.

Although this particular painting cannot be restored and interpreted, the identity of the warrior with the *Gorgoneion* shield may be revealed from comparisons with other Corinthian representations, especially since his military outfit very much resembles that of Achilles lying in ambush on the bottle in Athens signed by Timonidas (AMYX 1988 pl. 84, 1). Typologically, the two *Gorgoneia* are furthermore very similar, although the eyes of the Lindos *Gorgoneion* are more rounded. The Damon Painter, rendering the fight between Achilles and Memnon on a Late Corinthian hydria, also chose to depict Achilles with the same gear (AMYX 1988, pl. 118, 2), and on two other late vase paintings a *Gorgoneion* likewise adorns his shield, which takes up a central position of both scenes (KOSSATZ-DEISSMANN 1981 no 478 and 897). However, Corinthian painters did not always decorate Achilles' shield with a *Gorgoneion*, and other heroes like Hippolitos or "Melanas" also used it as an emblem (KOSSATZ-DEISSMANN 1981 no. 558; AMYX 1988, pl. 79; pl. 123, 1). It furthermore reappears in other vase paintings where the identity of the figures is not immediately understandable. Not even the Kykla Painter's warriors fighting over a dead body can be named since several such duels took place in connection with the Trojan war (BENSON 1969, pl. 34 fig. 3; AMYX 1988 pl. 83, 1b; FRIIS JOHANSEN 1967, 57 and 191f). This brief survey has shown that in Corinthian vase painting the *Gorgoneion* was often used as Achilles' shield emblem (cf. also HALM-TISSERANT 1986, 252), and especially the comparison with Timonidas' drawing of Achilles lying in ambush makes an identification of the Lindos warrior with this renowned hero tempting. However, the evidence is not sufficiently supportive. As shown above, the *Gorgoneion* was not monopolized by Achilles, and the identity of the figure cannot be established through a reconstruction of the scene based upon comparisons with other Corinthian paintings. Moreover it may be argued that the *Gorgoneion* was a popular motif in Corinthian art (PAYNE 1931, 79; HALM-TISSERANT 1988) and that it was simply chosen for its decorative quality.

3: Inv. no 12347. Shoulder sherd. Clay fine, light yellowish brown (10YR 6/4), slip brownish yellow (10YR 6/6), paint very dark greyish

*Fig. 3*

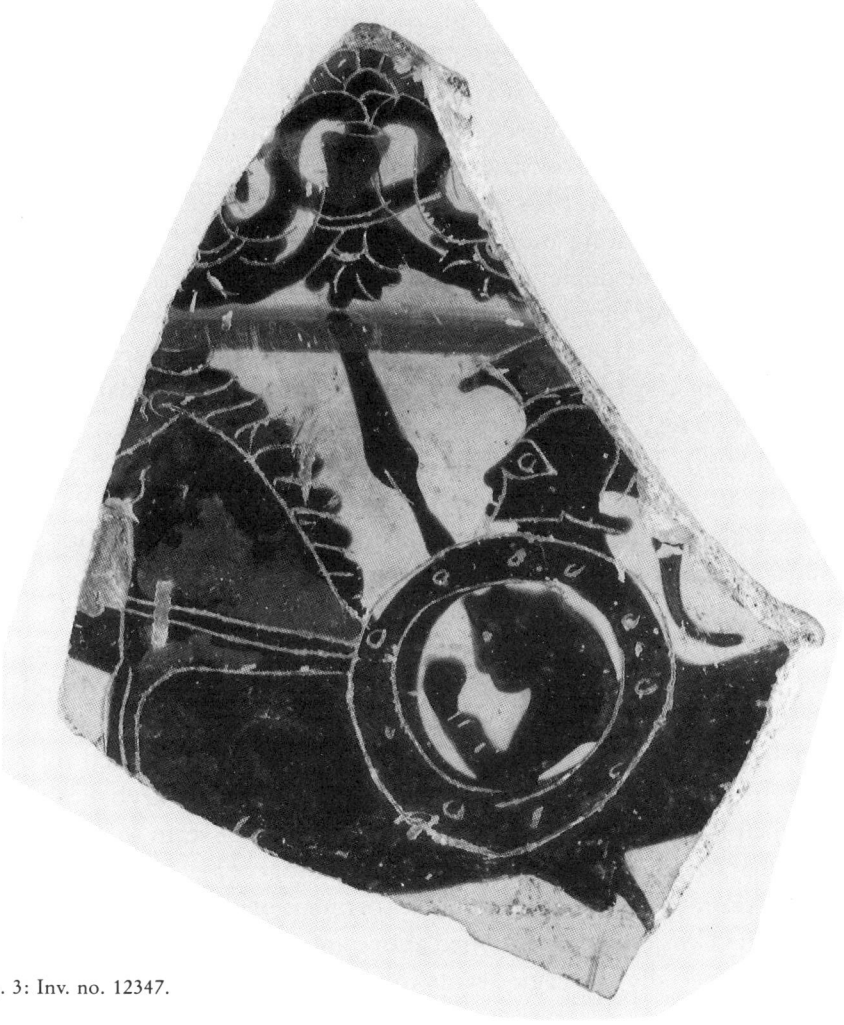

Fig. 3: Inv. no. 12347.

brown (10YR 3/2) and dark red (10R 3/4) added on crest and neck of horse. Inside painted. On outside, lotus frieze and part of mounted warrior towards the left. The figures are painted in silhouette with incised details. The warrior is wearing a crested helmet with cheek pieces, a spear and a shield with the front part of a lion on a reserved background. His leg is not indicated.

On the third fragment, no. 3, an armed horseman towards the left and a section of the ornamental frieze above him are preserved. The frieze consists of a lotus chain, which is not often seen on Corinthian craters, where tongues or rays are usually painted just below the neck, as on no. 1. However, it does appear occasionally, for instance on the Eurytios crater (PAYNE 1931 pl. 27), and a crater in the Louvre attributed to the Memnon Painter (BENSON 1956 pl. 76 fig. 36; BENSON 1969, 120; BAKIR 1974, 58; AMYX 1988, 234). On Corinthian craters horsemen appear as figures flanking a main theme such as a duel, or they are shown in a row as exemplified by another crater by the Memnon Painter (AMYX 1988 pl. 103). The mane of our horse is flying backwards indicating motion, and the fragment evidently belongs to the type of scene depicting only horsemen. A comparison with friezes of galloping horses on craters in the Louvre and in Brussels may furthermore help to explain the painted area below the fracture in front of the neck of the Lindos horse, together with the triangular extension below its body, as being parts of the tail of the horse in front (BENSON 1969 pl. 38). The two craters in question are attributed to the Detroit Painter or considered near him (BENSON 1969, 121; AMYX 1988, 197). Although they do have certain traits in common with the Lindos sherd, such as the somewhat squat warriors placed in the same unnatural position on their horses, the published photographs do not allow us to decide whether the same painter was responsible for decorating the crater which our sherd once belonged to. The shield emblem of the Lindos horseman is painted on a reserved background and was probably meant to represent the front part of a lion with a raised fore-leg, like the much better rendering on an Early Corinthian aryballos by the Käppeli Painter (AMYX 1988, pl. 47, 6). It does not seem to be repeated on other Middle Corinthian craters, and painters of larger vessels of this phase seem to have used a limited assortment of shield emblems. Apart from the Gorgoneion mentioned above and a strictly ornamental decoration, especially the eagle seems to have been popular.

The lists published by Payne and Amyx clearly show that the majority of Corinthian craters were shipped to the western part of the Mediterranean. J. de la Genière has advanced the theory that Corinthian craters were produced especially for the members of the Caeretan nobility, since more than 40% of the exported Corinthian craters with a known provenance were found at Caere, a single piece found at another Etruscan locality, and the rest spread over 15 sites with only a few concentrations (DE LA GENIÈRE 1988). As a further proof of the popularity of this particular shape at Caere, de la Genière points out that the only four extant column craters of a known provenance from an Etruscan workshop imitating Corinthian pottery were likewise found there. Although this theory may be partly true, it raises a couple of questions. The reason why such a large proportion of Corinthian craters ended up at Caere and almost exclusively at Caere within the Etruscan world is not immediately clear. Corinth seems to have had no particular relation with Caere; the story about Demaratos fleeing from Corinth to Tarquinia may contain a hint at more intimate connections between these two cities, but this is not reflected by the material evidence concerning us here. Moreover, the Etruscan imitative production of Corinthian pottery mentioned above seems to have been located at Vulci and not at Caere, where the only workshop producing Italo-Corinthian pottery apparently concentrated on making amphorae (COLONNA 1961; SZILÁGYI 1986).

The function of the crater and the introduction of the "banquet couché" has been discussed by various scholars (FEHR 1971; DENTZER 1982; SCHMITT & SCHNAPP 1982; RATHJE 1988) and de la Genière concludes that when using these craters for their symposia "le notable de Caere se sent ainsi introduit dans la sphère hellénique la plus sélecte, rapproché des héros de la légende". Since the general cultural development of the southern Etruscan centres was apparently rather uniform, the nobility of Tarquinia and Vulci might have been expected to pay an interest in achieving the very same set of symbols as their aristocratic peers at Caere and therefore also share their interest in, for instance, Corinthian craters for their symposia. However, this was apparently not the case, and it would seem that apart from a presumably mutual interest in table ware of precious metals, various places may have had different preferences in pottery substitutes, or contact was established with different Greek centres. Not only Corinthian but also Laconian craters accumulated at Caere, and it could be argued that Caere was simply a major consumer of Greek craters. However, according to Stibbe, unpublished material from Gravisca includes an important number of Laconian craters (STIBBE 1989, 71 and note 267), which may indicate a pattern of distribution slightly different from that of the Corinthian craters and at least partly answer the question concerning what types of vessels were used in the Tarquinian area, unless of course they belong to a period later than the first half of the 6th century B.C.

A research of the distribution of East Greek pottery, which until about the middle of the 6th century B.C. clearly dominates imported pottery in Etruria, supports the impression that various trends did exist from place to place (MARTELLI CRISTOFANI 1978; MARTELLI 1979 fig. 4). Studies of transport amphorae seem to confirm this, although conclusions based upon evidence concerning this type of vessel are less reliable (BOITANI 1985, 25). However, in order to define possible trends in the distribution of Greek pottery, comparative studies of find groups and especially their composition of pottery, foreign as well as local, may improve our knowledge of various kinds of interactions and help us distinguish between cases where one particular type of object may be considered important evidence for aspects such as contact/trade, acculturation, social status, etc., and when the appearance of a specific type of pottery has a random character. The two examples from the second quarter of the 6th century B.C. used by Martelli to illustrate the variety of pottery found together emphasizes the importance of studies of this kind (MARTELLI 1985, 177).

No doubt the majority of Corinthian craters were shipped to the West, where they were used for various banquets. However, the fact that our three sherds were found in Rhodes, which is not mentioned in de la Genières list of find-places prompts a short survey of the appearance of this and related products in the eastern Mediterranean. At first glance it seems that only a few other craters followed the ones presented here to Rhodes, where Corinthian pottery was otherwise popular enough for the local potters to copy the imported products (PAYNE 1931, 301; ROEBUCK 1959, 77; AMYX 1988, 677 and 684). Only a single handle plate from a Late Corinthian crater was illustrated from the excavations of the sanctuary of Athena Lindia but altogether 10 fragments were described, which apparently represent one vessel each (BLINKENBERG 1931, pl. 52, 1179). So Corinthian craters are fairly well represented at Lindos, while only a couple of fragments have been found elsewhere in Rhodes (PAYNE 1931, nos. 1188 and 1453A). Corinthian craters were also shipped to localities to the south of Rhodes, as proved by excavations at Naucratis and Tocra, although the number recovered here is smaller than in Rhodes (PAYNE 1931, nos. 1160, 1179, 1180, 1191, 1470B, 1485; BOARDMAN 1966, 23 no 233-35). It is, of course, tempting to suggest that this correspondence of finds between Rhodes and Naucratis was not entirely fortuitous, especially since other types of objects confirm interrelations between not only these two places, but also Cyprus, where it has been suggested that Greeks *en route* to Egypt stopped at Amathus (BOARDMAN 1980, 122, 125f; KARAGEORGHIS 1982, 139). In the present case, however, the material evidence from Cyprus does not support this. In Cyprus, where the amount of Corinthian pottery remains small, and is almost confined to *aryballoi* throughout the 7th and the early 6th century B.C., not a single crater fragment has been found (SØRENSEN 1988, 20 f.), and the finds become even more scattered when we move to the Levant, to judge from the material published from Tell Sukas, Ras el Bassit, Ras Ibn Hani and Sarepta (PLOUG 1973, 17-22; COURBIN 1986, 198; BOUNNI, LAGARCE & SALIBY 1978, 284; KOEHL 1985, 51). The absence of Corinthian pottery at Al Mina during the early part of the 6th century corresponds with the lack of evidence of other contemporary Greek pottery, a situation which was possibly caused by political circumstances (ROBERTSON 1940, 21; BOARDMAN 1980, 52; SØRENSEN 1988, 24). Unfortunately Greek pottery from Palestine is still largely unpublished, and although Corinthian products from the Archaic period are known to have been found, proper publication is needed before the significance of the material can be estimated (CLAIRMONT 1954-55, 100; WENNING 1981, 37). However, based upon the published material, we may conclude that Corinthian craters hardly played any role beyond Rhodes and Naucratis.

The present case also illustrates that, although Rhodes has an ideal geographical position for interconnections between Greece and the southeastern part of the Mediterranean, the island apparently did not act as a redistribution centre for all kinds of goods to destinations in Cyprus and the Levant, where the recorded finds demonstrate that Greek pottery was in demand. As in the West, East Greek products clearly dominate the ceramic finds from the first part of the 6th century

B.C., and various East Greek craters and *dinoi* may partly have fulfilled the demand for this type of vessel in finer pottery. It should be noticed, however, that apart from the omnipresent East Greek bowls and cups, the *oinochoe*, which is another important shape connected with banquets, appears to be more substantially represented, to judge from the finds from Cyprus, Tell Sukas and Bassit (PLOUG 1973, 54, 65; COURBIN 1986, 198; SØRENSEN 1988, 20, 22). At the moment, it is not possible to decide whether this reflects the pattern of production or the taste of the inhabitants, but it is interesting to note that according to a preliminary account of the ceramic finds from the Samian Heraion, East Greek craters and *oinochoai* likewise represent the predominant shapes of fine ware – next to Ionian bowls (ISLER 1978, 74). Although it should be taken into consideration that we are here dealing with sanctuary finds, they none the less testify to the popularity of the very same shapes at one of the major East Greek centres.

Moreover, the finds from the Samian Heraion show that pottery from the Greek mainland was not entirely ousted by East Greek products. The largest number of Laconian craters recovered from the eastern Aegean has also been found here, and it has been suggested that the popularity of Laconian pottery in Samos may reflect the political ties between the aristocracies of these two places (NAFISSI 1989, 73). About 600 B.C. Samos is thought to have played an important role in the trade of Laconian pottery, and based upon its distribution, a route Laconia-Cyrene-Egypt-Samos has been suggested (NAFISSI 1989, 72). Corinthian pottery has appeared along the same route, at Cyrenaica and in Egypt, and could have been shipped on some of the same ships, whether Samian or not, in analogy with the Giglio wreck which contained Etruscan, Corinthian, Laconian and Samian pottery (BOUND 1985).

However, at the moment an attempt to pin down exact trade routes for specific products seems premature, and a more meticulous registration of various types of artifacts is required in order to verify or reject theories concerned with this topic. The finds from Rhodes would seem to support this. Rhodes has so far not been included in the debate concerning the distribution of either Corinthian or Laconian craters. A comparison with the amount of Corinthian craters from most of the other find places shows that they are after all quite well represented in Rhodes, counting little less than half the number known from Caere.

According to the files from the Danish expedition, the same deposit in Lindos contained fragments of Laconian craters, raising their number to at least 13, which indicates that their presence in Rhodes should perhaps also be taken more seriously (SØRENSEN forthcoming). It may be argued that the actual number of finds from Rhodes is too small to allow for any kind of deductions, but we do not have standard procedures for evaluating a given frequency, and the material should not be ignored, especially in discussions concerning interrelations. This brief survey has furthermore shown that, although Corinthian craters travelled eastward, recent excavations in Cyprus and the Levant have reconfirmed the established picture that they did not reach beyond the Rhodes-Naucratis line. In the West, certain trends have been noticed between finds of Greek pottery at various locations, and this phenomenon seems to be repeated in the eastern Aegean. Based upon the published material, it appears that during the first part of the 6th century B.C. craters from the Greek mainland were shipped to specific areas in the eastern Aegean, where East Greek vessels serving the same purpose were also found, and that Laconian craters predominate in Samos, while a preference for one product over another is not detectable in Rhodes.

Institute of Prehistorical and Classical Archaeology,
University of Copenhagen,
Vandkunsten 5
1467 Copenhagen K

## BIBLIOGRAPHY

| | |
|---|---|
| *AGRP* 1988 | J. Christiansen & T. Melander eds., *Ancient Greek and Related Pottery*. Copenhagen. |
| AMYX, D.A. 1988 | *Corinthian Vase-Painting of the Archaic Period*. California. |
| BAKIR, T. 1974 | Der Kolonnettenkrater in Korinth und Attika zwischen 625 und 550 v. Chr., *Beitrage zur Archaeologie 7*. Würzburg. |
| BENSON, J.L. 1956 | Some Notes on Corinthian Vase-Painters, *AJA* 60, 219-230. |
| 1969 | The Three Maidens Group, *AJA* 73, 109-122. |
| BOARDMAN, J. 1980 | *The Greeks Overseas*. London. |
| BOITANI, F. 1985 | Cenni sulla distribuzione delle anfore da trasporto arcaiche nelle necropoli dell'Etruria meridionale, *CEA*, 23-26. |

| | |
|---|---|
| BOUND, M. 1985 | Una nave mercantile di età arcaica all'isola del Giglio, *CEA*, 65-70. |
| BOUNNI, A., LAGARCE, J. & SALIBY N. 1978 | Rapport préliminaire sur la deuxième campagne de fouilles (1976) à Ibn Hani, *Syria* 55, 1978, 233-301. |
| *CEA* 1985 | M. Cristofani, P. Moscati, G. Nardi & M. Pandolfini, *Il commercio etrusco arcaico*. (Quaderni del centro di studio per l'archeologia Etrusco-Italico 9). Roma. |
| CARTER, J.B. 1989 | The Chest of Periander, *AJA* 93, 355-378. |
| CLAIRMONT, Chr. 1954-1955 | Greek Pottery from the Near East, *Berytus* 11, 85-139. |
| COLONNA, G. 1961 | Il ciclo etrusco-corinzio dei Rosoni, *St.Etr* 29, 44-88. |
| COURBIN, P. 1986 | Bassit, *Syria* 63, 175-220. |
| CROISSANT, F. 1988 | Tradition et Innovation dans les ateliers corinthiens archaïques: Matériaux pour l'histoire d'un style, *BCH* 112, 91-166 |
| LA DE LA GENIÈRE, J. 1988 | Les acheteurs des cratères corinthiens, *BCH* 112, 83-90. |
| DENTZER, J.-M. 1982 | *Le motif du banquet couché dans le Proche-Orient et le monde grec du VIIe au IVe siècle avant J.-C.* Rome. |
| FEHR, B. 1971 | *Orientalische und Griechische Gelage*. Bonn. |
| FITTSCHEN, K. 1973 | Der Schild des Achilleus, *Archaeologia Homerica* II 1973 N, 1. |
| FRIIS JOHANSEN, K. 1967 | *The Iliad in the Early Greek Art*. Copenhagen. |
| GJØDESEN, M. 1963 | Greek Bronzes: A Review Article, *AJA* 67, 333-351. |
| HALM-TISSERANT, M. 1986 | La gorgonéion emblème d'Athena, *RA* 245-278 |
| 1988 | Sur l'évolution du Gorgoneion à Corinthe et à Athènes, dans la peinture du haut archaïsme, *AGRP*, 211-221. |
| ISLER, H.-P. 1978 | Samos: La ceramica arcaica, *CGE* 71-84. |
| KARAGEORGHIS, V. 1982 | *Cyprus from the Stone Age to the Romans*. London. |
| KOEHL, R.B. 1985 | *The Imported Bronze and Iron Age Wares from Area II, X, Sarepta III*. Beirut. |
| KOSSATZ-DEISSMANN, A.1981 | Achilleus. *LIMC* I, 1, 37-200. |
| *LIMC* | *Lexicon Iconographicum Mythologiae Classicae*. |
| MARTELLI CRISTOFANI, M. 1978 | La ceramica greco-orientale in Etruria, in: *Les céramiques de la Grèce de l'est et leur diffusion en occident*. Paris, 150-212. |
| MARTELLI, M. 1979 | Prime considerazioni sulla statistica delle importazioni greche in Etruria nel periodo arcaico, *St.Etr* 47, 37-52. |
| 1985 | I luoghi e i prodotti dello scambio. M. Cristofani ed., *Civiltà degli Etruschi*, Milano, 175-224. |
| PAYNE, H. 1931 | *Necrocorinthia*. Oxford. |

| | |
|---|---|
| PLOUG, G. 1973 | *Sukas II. The Aegean, Corinthian and Eastern Greek Pottery and Terracottas.* Copenhagen. |
| NAFISSI, M. 1988 | *Distribution and Trade*, in: Stibbe 1989, 68-77. |
| RATHJE, A. 1988 | Manners and Customs in Central Italy, *ActaHyp* 1, 81-90. |
| ROEBUCK, C. 1959 | *Ionian Trade and Colonization.* New York. |
| SCHMITT, P. & SCHNAPP, A. 1982 | Image et société en Grèce ancienne: les représentations de la chasse et du banquet, *RA* 57-74. |
| SZILÁGYI, J.Gy. 1986 | Etrusco-korinthische Vasen in Malibu. *Occasional Papers on Antiquities 2. Greek Vases in The J. Paul Getty Museum*, 1-16. |
| SIMON, E. 1981 | *Die griechische Vasen.* Munich. |
| STIBBE, C. M. 1989 | *Laconian Mixing Bowls.* Amsterdam. |
| SØRENSEN, L. WRIEDT 1988 | Greek Pottery found in Cyprus, *ActaHyp* 1, 12-32. |
| forthcoming | *Lindos IV.2. Excavations and surveys in Southern Rhodes. The Post-Mycenaean Periods.* Copenhagen. |
| WALTER-KARYDI, E. 1973 | *Samische Gefässe des 6. Jahrhunderts v. Chr. SAMOS* VI,1. Bonn. |
| WENNING, R. 1981 | Griechische Importe in Palästina aus der Zeit vor Alexander d. Gr. Vorbericht über ein Forschungsprojekt, *BOREAS* 4, 29-46. |

# CHARON'S FEE IN ANCIENT GREECE? – SOME REMARKS ON A WELL-KNOWN DEATH RITE

KELD GRINDER-HANSEN

Among the burial rites of ancient Greece the placing of a coin in the mouth of the deceased has a special place, due to the written tradition of the ancient myth about the ferryman Charon, who in exchange for a small fee ferried the souls of the dead across the River Styx to the Underworld. Finds of coins in Greek graves have traditionally been interpreted as Charon's fee (for instance KURTZ & BOARDMAN 1971, 211; VERMEULE 1979, 212, 7; GARLAND 1985, 23). In this paper the sources for this widespread assumption will be examined, in order to assess the probability of a connection between the notions of a transmigation of souls to the Underworld and the actual application of coins in the cult of the dead.

The starting-point for the discussion must be taken in the texts of the ancient authors, which point unambiguously towards the Charonmyth as the explanation for the custom. However, it has to be considered whether the references represent the Charon myth as a living concept in the Greek religious world, or describe it as a mere literary convention.

The representation of coins in the Greek graves must be examined to gain an impression of the frequency of coins in graves, their numbers, the selection of types, the precise find spot inside the graves and the general chronological framework for the practising of the coin rite. An answer to these questions could emerge only from a total examination of the known grave material from Greece, which is far beyond the scope of this study. The aim is merely to present some overall tendencies in this very scattered and complex archaeological source material. These tendencies must then be interpreted in the light of the evidence drawn from the written sources. Do they support the literary picture, or do they point to other explanations for the death rite? There are obvious methodological problems involved in applying inferences from archaeological finds to the thoughts and notions which have resulted in the placing of the death-coins, but the attempt must nevertheless be made. Finally, the information which can be deduced from the ritual use of coins in the cult of the dead from other cultures and periods must be taken into consideration, in order to approach the ancient coin practice from a somewhat different angle.

## *Charon's fee in the literary tradition*

Charon did not appear on the mythological scene until rather late, and he never attained an official place in Greek mythology (HERMANN 1954, 1042; SOURVINOU-INWOOD 1986, 210-12). On the other hand he seems to have enjoyed a certain popular renown throughout Antiquity, which gradually allowed for his intrusion into literature. There are relatively frequent references to the Charonmyth among the ancient writers, but it is remarkable that only a few of these originate in the Classical and Hellenistic periods. There are no references to Charon in Homer (8th century B.C.), even though Acheron – the River of Death – is mentioned. The earliest known description is found in the epic *Minyas* (end of the 6th or beginning of the 5th century B.C), where Charon appears as a local ferryman (Pausanias, *Description of Greece* X, XXVIII,2). Aschylus mentions Charon's boat – but not Charon himself – which the souls had to enter to reach the Underworld *(Septem contra Thebas*, 833-37). In an epigram of c. 500 B.C. from Teithronion in Phokis, Charon is used as a symbol for death itself (PEEK 1955, 414, no. 1384). This aspect of Charon as a deathfigure is also stressed by Euripides (*Heraclidea*, 430-34, *Alcestis*, 254, 361) and by Aristophanes in his parody of the latter (*Lysistrata*, 604-07), and was later to be all-important in both literature and iconography (SOURVINOU-INWOOD 1986, 210). In these early references Charon does not demand money from his passengers. This otherwise characteristic feature seems to be a later addition, which is first known from Aristophanes' comedy *The Frogs* (140, 270) from 405 B.C. Here Aristophanes mentions a fee of two obols. This increase in rates should probably be seen as an ironical comment on contemporary rises in prices in the Athenian society, since other writers mention a fee of only one silver coin, placed in the mouth of the dead. This coin is usually referred to as an obol or naulos, which simply translated means "passage-money". From the Hellenistic period Charon's fee is mentioned only by Callimachos (*Hecale* frg. 278). Most of the references to the death-coin rite belong to the centuries of the

Roman Empire (WASER 1898). The geographer *Strabo* (64/3 B.C. –21 A.D.) mentions that the inhabitants in the town of Hermione on the coast of Argolis did not place passage-money with their dead, because they had direct access to the Underworld through a chasm (Strabo, *Geography* 8, 6,12). *Lucian* (about 120 A.D. – after 180 A.D.) often refers to the Charon-myth. In a famous passage he speaks ironically of the familiar custom of placing a coin with the dead:

"So thoroughly are people taken in by all this that when one of the family dies, immediately they bring an obol and put it into his mouth, to pay the ferryman for setting him over. They do not stop to consider what sort of coinage is customary and current in the lower world, and whether it is the Athenian or the Macedonian or the Aeginetan obol that is legal tender there; nor, indeed, that it would be far better not to be able to pay the fare, since in that case the ferryman would not take them and they would be escorted back to life again." (*De luctu* X, translated by A.M.Harmon, *Loeb* 1925, IV, 119).

It is highly questionable whether Lucian is referring to living notions and customs, which formed part of the religious beliefs of Roman society. More likely he is presenting a literary tradition, which is based on the classical Greek authors. A remarkable uniformity in the description of the myth among the Roman authors confirms this impression. Charon is the grey-bearded grim old ferryman, who stands sentry over Styx, demanding a coin from all souls, in order to ferry them across to the Underworld (Lucian, *Cataplus* 4-6, 18, 19; *Menippus* 10, *Dialogi Mortuorum* 4, 10, 21; Propertius, *Elegiæ* V, 11,7; Juvenal, *Satira* 3, 264-7; Virgil, *Aeneid* 6, 298 ff.; Apuleius, *Metamorphoses*, 6, 17-20; 4,28,6, 24). Charon has become a literary convention, which the Roman satirists and moralists used as a symbol for the inevitability of death and the futility of striving for wealth and prosperity (GRINDER-HANSEN 1990).

The conclusions which can be drawn from the literary evidence are therefore limited. There are no references to the figure of Charon before the 5th century B.C. and the use of passage-money cannot be traced further back than to the last decade of this century. The general literary character and the fact that only very few of the references originate in the Classical and Hellenistic periods makes it highly difficult to use the written evidence as a direct source on the notions and the practice of the death-coin rite in ancient Greece.

## The archaeological evidence

On 5th century white-ground lekythoi, Charon is often depicted standing in his boat, receiving a deceased person, who has been brought to the ferry by Hermes (KURTZ 1975, 63-64, 66, 215, 218, 221, 283; Brommer 1969, 167-71; SOURVINOU-INWOOD 1986, 212-25, pls. 168-74). The dead are nearly always women or childen (BROMMER 1969, 170). The scene of Charon in his boat occurs also on a Greek funerary altar at Milan, and on other monuments (REINACH 1912, 60, no. 1). There are usually no references to Charon's fee on these pictures, apart from a rather dubious example of a lekythos, which should depict a coin in the hand of the deceased (POTTIER 1883, 37, no. 13; Fairbanks 1914, 153 pl. 31,4). The same motive is also found on a terracotta lamp (MÜLLER & WIESELER 1891, I, pl. LXIX, 871), whose authenticity, however, has been seriously questioned (BROMMER 1969, 171).

The general absence of figurative representations of Charon's fee could point to a far smaller spread of the use of passage-money than could be expected from the written evidence alone. On the other hand, the first known literary reference to the ferry fee originates in the last decades of the 5th century, that is later than most of the Charon pictures on lekythoi. Therefore the absence of the coins could be explained by the fact that this aspect of the myth first gained in importance in the following centuries – a theory which can find some support in the numismatic evidence from the grave material (see below). In this connection it should be noted that coins are not usually depicted in Greek iconography, except indirectly in the shape of purses (MEYER 1988).

There does not exist any comprehensive archaeological study of Greek coins found in graves. The information must be gathered from the scattered and rather unhomogeneously treated grave-coin material found in archaeological publications. The following survey is based only on samples from the comprehensive archaeological material.

A general orientation in the archaeological literature shows that the custom never obtained the central position among the Greek burial rites which could be expected from the descriptions by the ancient authors.

The first known graves with coins originate in the second quarter of the 5th century B.C (GRINSELL 1957, 262). The numbers of graves from this century are, however, very few. One example of this early ritual use of coins is found at the North Cemetery in Corinth, where a Corinthian silver obol was found near the mouth of a skeleton in a grave from the second quarter of the 5th century (BLEGEN et al. 1964, 84). In the 4th century B.C., a notable rise in the use of death-coins can be seen, which continues well into the 3rd century B.C. (BRUCK 1926, 145; ROBINSON 1942, 204-05). The use of coins in graves was never universal in the Greek world and in no period did the custom spread outside a very restricted group of the population. The percentage of graves with coins is generally very low in proportion to the total number of graves excavated. An example is the North Cemetery in Corinth, where about 500 graves mostly from the 6th-3rd century were examined. Coins occurred only in sixteen graves, that is in about 3% of the graves. One coin was found in each of the fifteen burials and six in a late grave. Ten of the coins were silver obols from Corinth (8 pieces), Argos (1), and Leukas (1) and one coin was a silver hemi-obol from Thebes. The others were locally struck bronze coins. The coins were in most cases found near or in the mouth of the skeletons. In one grave a bronze coin was found in a vessel at the foot of the dead. Most of the burials with coins originated in the 4th and 3rd centuries (BLEGEN et al. 1964, 83-84 and 88-89). Further examples of the existence of the death-coin rite in Corinth have emerged during recent excavations, for instance 4 Hellenistic burials with coins found either by the skull or at the south head end of the grave (PEMBERTON 1985, 272) and two 4th century burials from the sanctuary of Demeter, where a local Corinthian bronze coin and a bronze coin from Syracuse were found in the mouth of respectively a child and a woman (STROUD 1965, 13). The same pattern can be found at the necropole of Halae in Boeotia, 6th-3rd century B.C., where the majority of the grave-coins originated in the 4th and especially the 3rd century B.C. The coins were predominantly found near the head or in the mouth of the skeletons (GOLDMAN & JONES 1942, 370).

In Athens the general use of coins in the cult of the dead seems very limited. The excavations of the important Athenian necropole at Kerameikos have produced only very few examples of coins in graves, The Eridanos necropole could not furnish a single grave find (SCHLÖRB-VIERNEISEL 1966; KNIGGE 1966), while the excavations at the so-called "Südhügel" at Kerameikos produced coins in only three burials among the several hundred examined from the 6th-3rd century (KNIGGE 1976, 60). The introduction of the death-coin custom in Athens seems rather late. The known examples from Athenian graves all belong to the Hellenistic period (KURTZ & BOARDMAN 1971, 166).

The cemetery at Olynthus in Chalcidike stands as a contrast to Athens. 66 out of 644 burials (about 10% of the graves) from the 5th and 4th century B.C. contained coins. The coins were in at least 42 cases placed in the mouth, but they could also be found in the hands or on the body. Each person had from one to four coins in the graves. The number was generally one or four, rarely three. Most of them were small bronze coins of various denominations, but a few silver coins were also represented. The main body of the coins comprised locally produced bronze coins, but in all 14 different mints were represented. Only three coins date to the 5th. century and another three coins could be later than 348 B.C. The rest originate in the first five decades of the 4th century (ROBINSON 1942, 202-05). The Olynthus necropole reflects the extension of the death-coin custom among the inhabitants of a northern Greek town within a restricted period of time. This evidence is very important for the discussion of the death-coin practice, but must not be taken as a general expression of the spread of the custom in the whole of Greece. The Olynthus material stands alone with its documented widespread use of coins in the cult of the dead and must so far be considered an extreme regional variation inside the Greek world.

At the Hellenistic cemetery at Myrina in Aiolis (2nd and 1st century B.C.) 17 out of a total number of 116 graves contained coins, or c.15 % of the graves. The coins were found in the mouth of the skeletons in four burials and near the skull in one. The original placing of the coins could not be decided in the rest of the graves. The coins were nearly all locally made bronze coins from Myrina (POTTIER & REINACH 1888).

At Asine in Argolis three burials from around 300 B.C. were found with coins placed in the mouth of the skeletons. One of them contained a silver obol, while in the two others a 3/4 obol of Argos was found along with a bronze coin of Sikyon. It is interesting to note that the placing of the small bronze coin is found in the two cases where the silver coin represented only three quarters of the value of the traditional payment to Charon, as if the bronze coin should bring the value up to par (HÄGG & FOSSEY 1982, 101-03). This admittedly limited source material could indicate that there existed firm notions of the tariff for crossing the Styx. Similar thoughts could lie behind the different numbers of coins which were placed in the graves at Olynthus (ROBINSON

1942, 205). On the other hand, it is not unusual to find even larger numbers of coins in graves, which by far exceeded the sum necessary for paying Charon. For instance a grave at Nikesiani held 124 bronze coins and one gold (KURTZ & BOARDMAN 1971 211), and a burial at Lavovouni contained 11 bronze coins in the mouth and another in the hand of the skeleton (*ARepLondon* 1987-88, 14). The preferred coin types in graves seem to vary from place to place. In Corinth the small silver coins – obol and hemiobol, were most commonly used, while locally produced bronze coins dominated in Olynthus. Often small silver and bronze coins are represented side by side in the grave material. The more precious large silver and gold coins were seldom used as grave-coins. Pseudo-coins – "ghost-money"- made of gold blankets and sometimes bearing the impression of a real coin, may have replaced genuine coins. For instance a gold leaf impression of an owl-faced Athenian coin was found with a cremation in an urn at the Agora in Athens (*Hesperia* 6 1936, 363) and another example of a piece of gold foil pressed over the figure of an awl turned up in a burial in Athens (*Hesperia* 32 1963, 125). The use of "ghost-money" is especially documented in Sicily and South Italy, and later in Sicyon (KURTZ & BOARDMAN 1971 211), but is also known from Megalopolis in Arcadia (GARDNER 1892, 9).

The coins are normally found in the mouth of the skeleton, but can also be found in the hand or loose in the grave. In the earliest graves from the 5th century there seems to be a tendency towards a placing of the coins in the latter manner rather than in the mouth (ROBINSON 1942, 205). In the 4th century B.C. the classical position of the mouth is preferred.

Although the sex of the dead can rarely be determined accurately, men seem to have been furnished more frequently with coins than women (KURTZ & BORDMAN 1971, 166). At the North Cemetery in Corinth all but one of the graves containing coins were those of adults (BLEGEN et al. 1964, 84), whereas 21 of the burials at Olynthus belonged to children (ROBINSON 1942, 202).

*The death-coin rite in a cross-cultural perspective*
Before turning to the discussion of the ideas behind the Greek death-coin custom, it could be useful to take a short look at the comprehensive ethnographical literature on the ritual use of coins in the cult of the

dead. This cross-cultural material documents the existence of the custom from all parts of the world, with a great variety of conceptions connected (ANDREE 1889, 24; SARTORI 1899; MOSS 1925, 9-10, 110; FRAZER 1931, 19; BERNDT 1952, 131-32; TYLOR 1891, I 494). In Europe the death-coin custom has been practised throughout the Middle Ages up to recent times. The continuity from Antiquity is traceable in Macedonia and Greece, where the use of death-coins, placed in the mouth of the deceased, was connected to a post-Charon figure by the name of Charos, who was perceived as a kind of death demon (RODD 1892, 125-26). Outside the Mediterranean region, similar "post-Antiquity" interpretations of the death-coin rites are not found. Instead a great variety of other explanations emerge (SEGERSTEDT 1907; BORZA 1955; GRINSELL 1957, VEIT 1982; GRINDER-HANSEN 1988, GRINDER-HANSEN 1990). On the basis of these marked variations in the form of the death-coin practice and the rituals linked to its use, it must be considered if the grave-coins in ancient Greece can only be interpreted in close connection with the myth of Charon and his fee. In fact, this explanation does not fit in very well with the archaeological evidence. The earliest examples of grave-coins originate in the second quarter of the 5th century B.C., that is well before the first written mention of the custom. Of course, it is possible that popular notions of Charon have existed long before this time, but this can only be an *e silentio* conclusion. The tendency towards a placing of the coin in the hand or lose in the grave in the earliest phases of the death-coin custom also speaks against this assumption, as does the general lack of figurative representations on the lekythoi of the 5th century. In the 4th century, when the archaeological material shows a rise in the use of death-coins, we have nearly no reference in literature to the Charon myth. In fact most of the literary references were written after an interval of several hundred years from the time when the the death-coin rite was practised in Greece. In the Roman Empire the use of death-coins is universally found (GORECKI 1975; ALCOCK 1980), but hardly as a result of an adoption of the belief in the Charon myth (GRINDER-HANSEN 1990). The Romans have their own death-coin tradition, which goes back to about 1000 B.C. From that time on graves are found in Italy, where pieces of raw copper are placed in the hands of skeletons or loose in the graves, probably offered as a grave gift in line with other kinds of goods (WILLERS 1924; BERGONZI & PIANA AGOSTINETTI 1987). In Greece the find of ceremonial iron spears – the so-called oboloi – in graves could perhaps be seen as a parallel example of the ritual use of pre-monetary means of payment (DECHELETTE 1911; KRON 1971, 131-44) and also as one more argument against the linking together of grave-coins with the notions of Charon's fee. The mouth as the preferred position of the death-coin is in accordance with the myth, but this does not automatically mean an observance of the Charon custom. It is quite possible that other notions have underlain the placing of the coins (GRINDER-HANSEN 1988, 119-25).

The changing numbers of coins used in graves suggest different coin practices. When larger sums of money are found in the burials, it is more likely that they have been offered for their intrinsic value in the other world than for their capability to secure the deceased a better seat in Charon's boat. In this way they function as grave gifts along with other types of objects which the deceased could make use of in the life to come. A single coin in the mouth of a skeleton could indicate a Charon fee practice, but could also be seen, for example, as a symbolic dowry – a *pars pro toto*, which transfered the belongings of the dead to the bereaved without having to offer a large number of grave gifts (ROHDE 1925, 306-07). This theory can find some support in the interesting fact that coins became prevalent only at a time when other funeral furniture was reduced and in this way became a substitute for the more precious and numerous offerings of an earlier date (GOLDMAN & JONES 1942, 370).

Finally the use of coins in the cult of the dead can be seen simply as a means of protecting the living against the evils of the dead. This is a phenomenon known from many cultures. The coins are often put with the dead in order to avoid haunting. The placing of coins in the mouth of the corpse is in many cultures connected with the desire to block the entrance for the return of the soul to the body. The coins are also found in the corpse's hand, on its chest, under its head and on its eyes (SEGERSTED 1907, 45-53).

It is not possible on the basis of the existing source material to reach any conclusive solution to the problems concerning the ritual use of coins in graves. However it can be established that there is very little evidence in favour of a connection between the Charon myth and the death-coin practice. Therefore it must be urged that the expression "Charon's fee" should be removed from the vocabulary of archaeologists and be replaced by the more correct name death-coin, which can stand for a number of different coin uses and notions.

National Museum
Frederiksholm Kanal 12
DK-1220 Copenhagen K.

# BIBLIOGRAPHY

ALCOCK, J.P. 1980 — Classical Religious Belief and Burial Practice in Roman Britain, *The Archaeological Journal* 137 50-85.

ANDREE, M. 1878 — *Ethnographische Parallelen und Vergleiche*. Stuttgart.

BERGONZI, G. & PIANA AGOSTINETTI, P. 1987 — L'"obolo di Caronte". "Aes rude" e monete nelle tombe: La Pianura Padana tra mondo classico e ambito transalpino nella seconda età del ferro, *Scienze dell' Antichità, Storia Archeologia Antropologia* 1, 161-223.

BERNDT, R.M. 1952 — *The first Australians*. Sydney.

BLEGEN, C.W., PALMER, H. & YOUNG, R.S. 1964 — *The North Cemetery, Corinth* XIII. Princeton.

BORZA, H. 1955 — La mythe de l'obole à Charon et le symbolisme actuel de la monnaie dans le cerceuil, *Orbis (Bulletin Internationale Documentation Linguistique)*, IV,1, 134-48.

BROMMER, F. 1969 — Eine lekythos im Madrid, *MM* 10, 155-71.

BRUCK, E.F. 1926 — *Totenteil und Seelgerät*. München.

DECHELETTE, J. 1911 — Les origines de la drachme et de l'obole, *RevNum* 15, 1911, 1-59.

FAIRBANKS, A. 1914 — *Athenian White Lekythoi*. New York.

FRASER, J.G. 1931 — *Garnered Sheaves*. London.

GARDNER, E.A. 1892 — *Excavations at Megalopolis 1890-91*. London.

GARLAND, R. 1985 — *The Greek Way of Death*, New York.

GOLDMAN, H. & JONES, F. 1942 — Terracottas from the 1942 necropolis at Halae, *Hesperia* 11, 365-421.

GORECKI, J. 1975 — Studien zur Sitte der Münzbeigabe in römerzeitlichen Körpergräbern zwischen Rhein, Mosel und Somme, *BerRGK* 56, 179-468.

GRINDER-HANSEN, K. 1988 — Penge til færgemanden, Mønter i dødekulten?, *ArbejdsmarkKøb*, 115-25.

1990 — De dødes penge – En begravelsesritus og dens meningsbetydning i Romerriget. *Antikken, Den jyske historiker*, nr.51-52, 81-92.

## CHARON'S FEE IN ANCIENT GREECE?

| | |
|---|---|
| GRINSELL, L.V. 1957 | The ferryman and his fee, *Folklore*, LXVIII, 257-69. |
| HERMANN, C. 1954 | s.v. Charon, in: T. Klauser ed., *Reallexikon für Antike und Christentum* 2, 1040-61. |
| HÄGG, I. & FOSSEY, M. 1982 | Kharon's Fee and Relative Coin Values, *NumZ* 96, 1982, 101-103. |
| KNIGGE, U. 1966 | Eridanos-Nekropole II, *AM*, 81, 112-135. |
| 1976 | *Der Südhügel, Kerameikos* IX. Berlin. |
| KRON, U. 1971 | Zum Hypogäum von Paestum, *JdI* 86, 131-148. |
| KURTZ, D.C. & BOARDMAN, J. 1971 | *Greek Burial Customs*. London. |
| 1975 | *Athenian White Lekythoi*. Oxford. |
| MEYER, M. 1988 | Männer mit Geld. Zu einer rotfigurigen Vase mit Alltagsszene", *JdI* 103, 87-125. |
| MOSS, R. 1925 | *The Life after Death in Oceania*. Oxford. |
| MÜLLER, C.O. & WIESELER, F. 1856 | *Denkmäler der Alten Kunst* II. Göttingen. |
| PEEK, W. 1955 | *Griechische Vers-Inschriften* I. Berlin. |
| PEMBERTON, E.G. 1985 | Ten hellenistic graves in ancient Corinth, *Hesperia* 54, 271-307. |
| POTTIER, E. 1883 | *Étude sur les Lécythes Blanc Attiques*. Paris. |
| POTTIER, E. & REINACH S. 1888 | *La necropole de Myrina*, Paris. |
| REINACH, S. 1912 | *Répertoire de Reliefs Grecs et Romains* III. Paris. |
| ROBINSON, D.M. 1942 | *Necrolynthia, Excavations at Olynthos* XI. Baltimore. |
| RODD, R. 1892 | *Customs & Lore of Modern Greece*. London. |
| ROHDE, E. 1925 | *Psyche, Seelencult und Unsterblichkeitsglaube der Griechen*. Tübingen. |
| SARTORI, P. 1899 | Die Totenmünze, *Archiv für Religionswissenschaft* 2, 205-25. |
| SCHLÖRB-VIERNEISEL, B. 1966 | Eridanos-Nekropole II, *AM* 81, 4-111. |
| SEGERSTEDT, T. 1907 | *Mynts använding i Dödskulten*. Lund. |
| SOURVINOU-INWOOD, C. 1986 | s.v. Charon I, in: *LIMC* III,1, 210-25. |
| STROUD, R.S. 1965 | The Sanctuary of Demeter and Kore on Acrocorinth, *Hesperia* 34, 2-24. |
| TYLOR, E.B. 1891 | *Primitive Culture. Researches into the Development of Mythology, Philosophy, Religion, Language, Art and Custom* 1-2, 3.ed. London. |
| VEIT, L. 1982 | Die Münze in Totenkult, *Münzen in Brauch und Aberglauben*. Mainz, 94-95 and 101-04. |
| VERMEULE, E. 1979 | *Aspects of Death in Early Greek Art and Poetry*. Los Angeles. |
| WASER, O. 1898 | Charon, *Archiv für Religionswissenschaft* I, 1898, 152-82. |

WILKE, G. 1925      Charonspfennig, in: M. Ebert ed., *Reallexikon der Vorgeschichte* 2, 1925, 302-03.

WILLERS, H. 1925      Das Rohkupfer als Geld der Italiker (Etwa 1000-343), *Zeitschrift für Numismatik* 34, 193-283.

# THE AGER PICENTINUS[1]

## HELLE W. HORSNÆS

This article discusses the *Ager Picentinus* from the late 8th to the beginning of the 6th cent. B.C. In this period we see the formation of a number of important cities in Campania, such as the Etruscan (or Etruscanized) cities Pompeii, Nola, Capua and Pontecagnano, and the Greek cities Cumae/Neapolis and Poseidonia. It is my conviction that a better understanding both of the cities themselves and of the interaction between them can be obtained by examining the development in the territory around the sites in the formative period immediately before the urbanization occurred.

A study of the territory of Poseidonia in the period after the foundation of the colony was furnished by E. Greco in 1979, but neither the previous period nor the area to the north of the river Sele – the *Ager Picentinus* – were treated there. In the following I shall attempt to give an outline of the archaeological evidence from this area. The article is divided into two parts: a summary of today's knowledge of the two most important sites in the *Ager Picentinus*, Pontecagnano and Arenosola, and a short survey of sites in the southern part of the Sele Plain in the orientalizing period.

The *Ager Picentinus* is here defined as the almost triangular plain *Fig. 1* enclosed by the Tyrrhenian Sea, the Picentini Mountains and the river Sele. The landscape is flat, rising gently from the sea towards the Picentini Mountains. Geologically it consists of a travertine plateau covered by alluvial soil. Today the whole plain is almost cross-hatched by the rivers Tusciano and Picentini and by a large number of smaller rivers and canals.

The general outline of the coast seems to have changed only a little since Antiquity. The *Ager Picentinus* itself has not been the subject of geological research, but Schmiedt (1972) and Fleming (1974) conclude that the absolute level of the whole Tyrrhenian Sea has changed less than 0.50 m during the last 2000 years. Schmiedt's results, however, have to be taken 'cum grano salis', as he totally excludes the area between the Ponza Islands and Velia from his study, and thus takes into

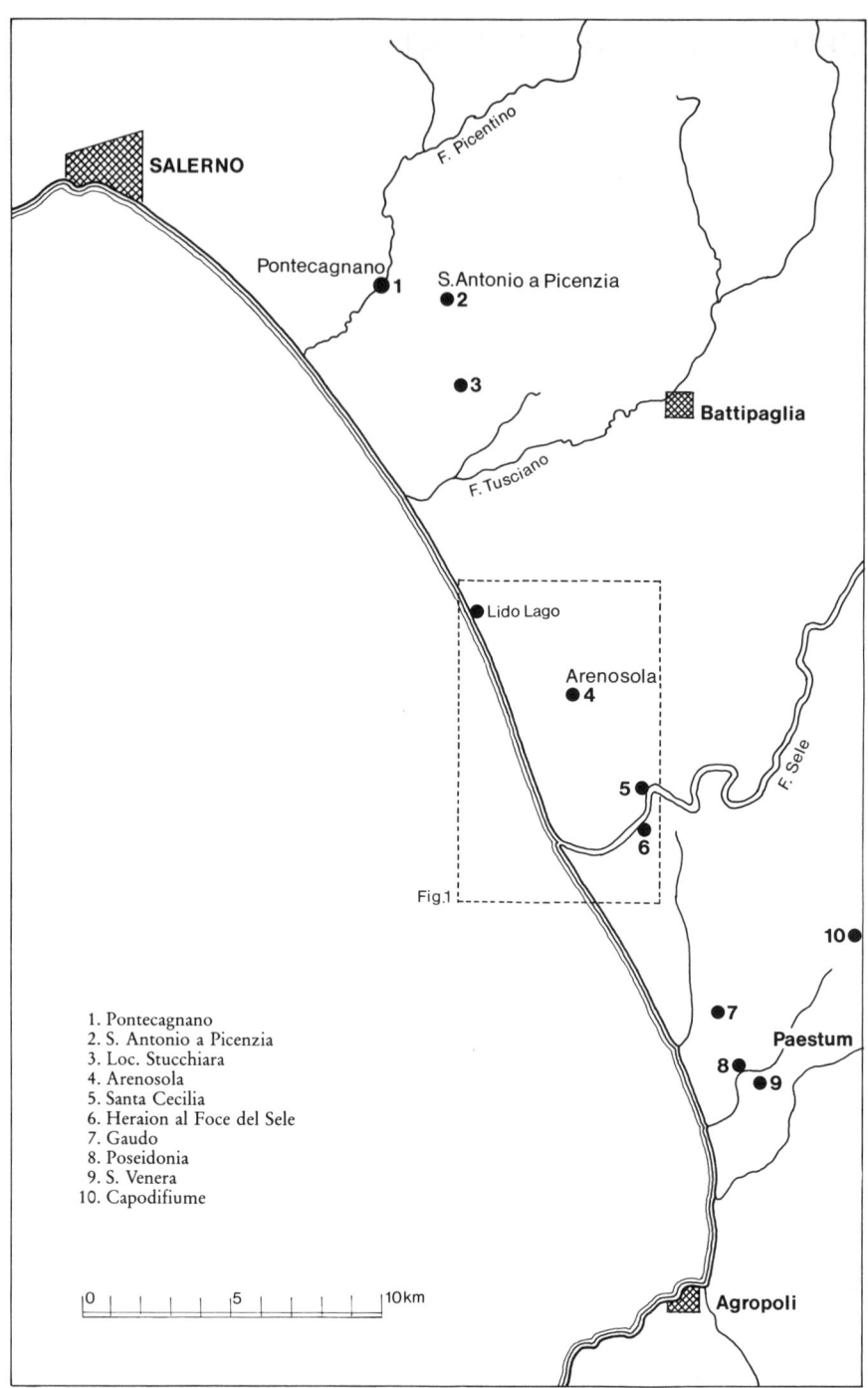

Fig. 1. The *Ager Picentinus*.

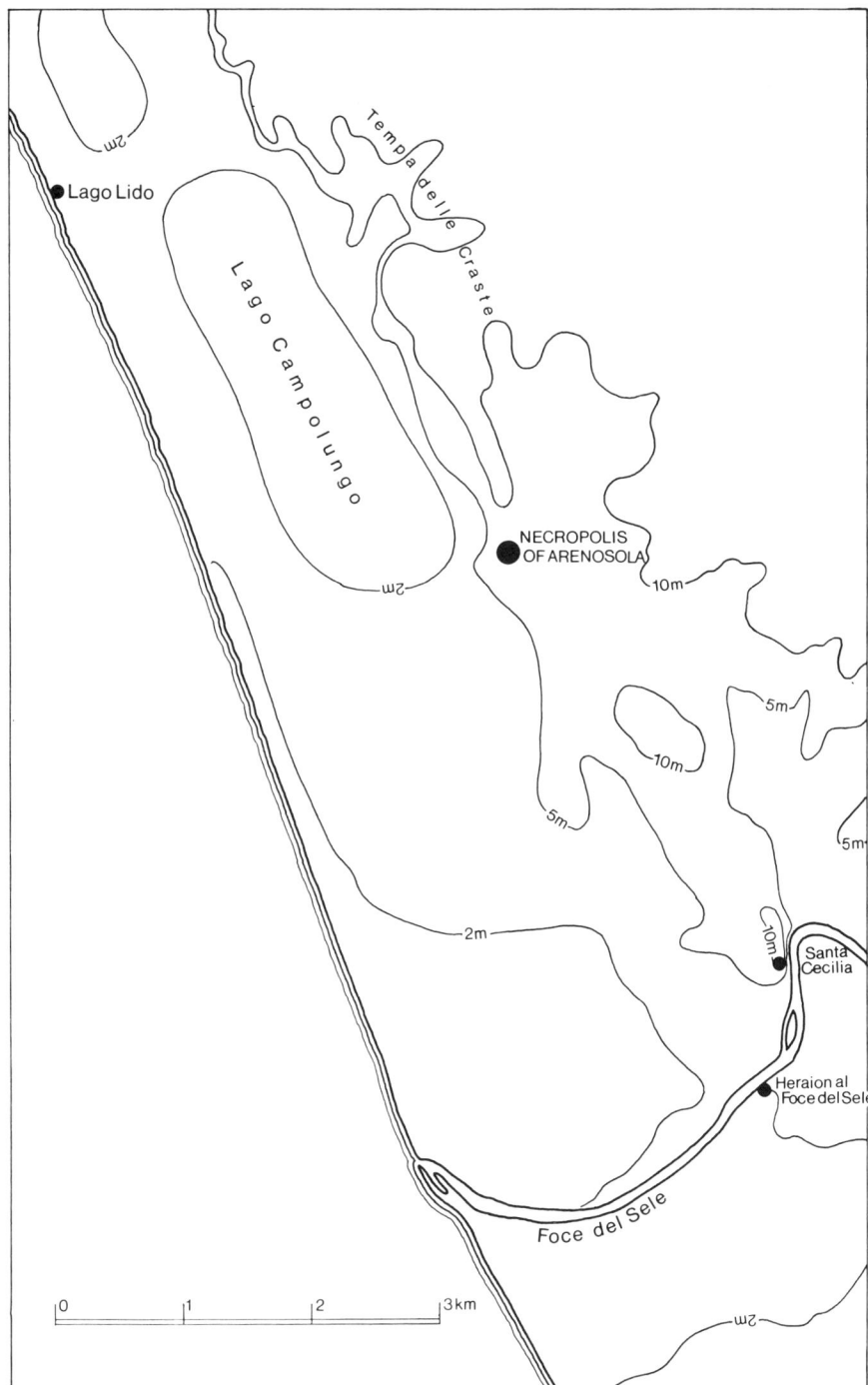

Fig. 2. The topography of Arenosola and environments.

consideration neither the volcanic activity and bradyseism in the Bay of Naples, nor the alluvial deposits of the many rivers of the *Ager Picentinus* and Sele itself.

Extensive modern building activity in the area since the Second World War has brought many changes to the *Ager Picentinus*. Until the 1930s, when intensive draining was started, malaria was still rife in the area, and little agricultural work was undertaken in the now so fertile plain.

Pontecagnano is undoubtedly the best known archaeological site in the *Ager Picentinus*. Finds from Pontecagnano have been known for more than a century,[2] but it was only when intense building activity in the early 1960s revealed tombs at Pontecagnano that large-scale archaeological research on the site was undertaken (SESTIERI 1960a; BAILO MODESTI 1984, 217). During the last 30 years, excavations and research in the *Ager Picentinus* have mainly concentrated on Pontecagnano. The rich archaeological finds date from the beginning of the 9th cent. B.C. until the late Roman period. Of great importance are the many tombs dating from the 9th to the 6th cent. B.C. They show that in this period Pontecagnano had close contacts with the Southern Etruscan area, and it has become increasingly obvious that the passage in Pliny (*NH* III, 70), *A Surrentino ad Silarum amnem XXX m.p. ager Picentinus fuit Tuscorum*, is based on historical fact (NAPOLI 1965, 666).

*Fig. 2* In 1929 another necropolis was discovered during some of the first agricultural works at Arenosola[3] in the southern part of the *Ager Picentinus*, less than 4 km from the Sele river. The tombs were found on the south-western edge of a small plateau, 9-13 m above normal sea-level, stretching southwards like a tiny promontory over the surrounding plains (*Map IGM Foglio 197 I, S.E. (Aversana)*, 95.55E/86.35N). The necropolis was partly excavated by Prof. A. Marzullo during three campaigns from 1929 to 1931 (MARZULLO 1938). A total of 139 tombs was unearthed, the greater amount of which (133 tombs) is from the orientalizing and early Archaic period (c. 700-575 B.C.), while the remaining 6 tombs can be dated to the 4th cent. B.C. (PANEBIANCO 1937, 189 fig. 5; TRENDALL 1987, cat. nos. 2/582, 3/207 and 3/77 from T 4, cat. no. 2/437 from T 17, and cat. no. 3/94 from T 2).

In 1950 further excavations at Arenosola were conducted by Prof. P.C. Sestieri. They revealed 11 tombs from the late 8th cent. B.C., and

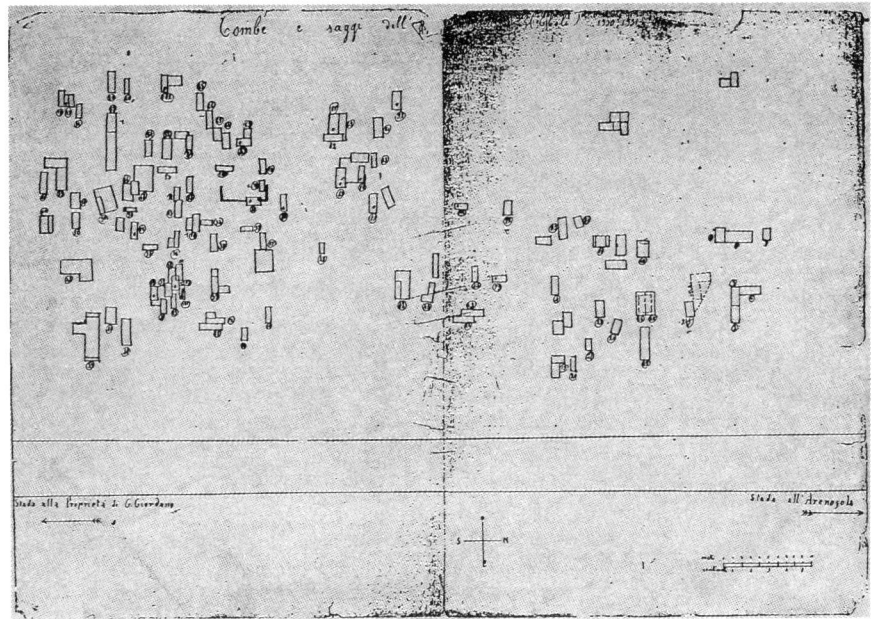

Fig. 3. Arenosola, original sketch of the excavation area.

a number of Roman tombs (SESTIERI 1950; VOZA 1962a). Unfortunately, no exact information is given as to their exact location.

The excavation by Marzullo was well documented, and the excavation notebooks as well as a plan of the excavation area are preserved in the archives of the Museo Provinciale di Salerno. Unfortunately, the plan is rather schematic. It was made at the beginning of the campaign of 1931 and covers only the excavations in 1930 and 1931, whereas no plan was ever made for the campaign of 1929. The plan shows that the extent of the principal excavation area was c. 35 x 65 m, but the excavation notebooks reveal that a number of tombs that cannot be found on the plan were discovered and excavated up to 60 m beyond this zone (e.g. T 73, excavated in 1930), which means that the full extension of the necropolis still has to be defined. Therefore, it is not possible, for the time being, to get an idea of the number of inhabitants of the Arenosola settlement (contra HOLLOWAY 1981, 119).

The orientalizing tombs are very similar to the contemporary ones from Pontecagnano (D'AGOSTINO 1968): they are all inhumation tombs in a *fossa*, often lined with stones and with the bottom paved with pebbles. Almost all the tombs were covered by a heap of stones

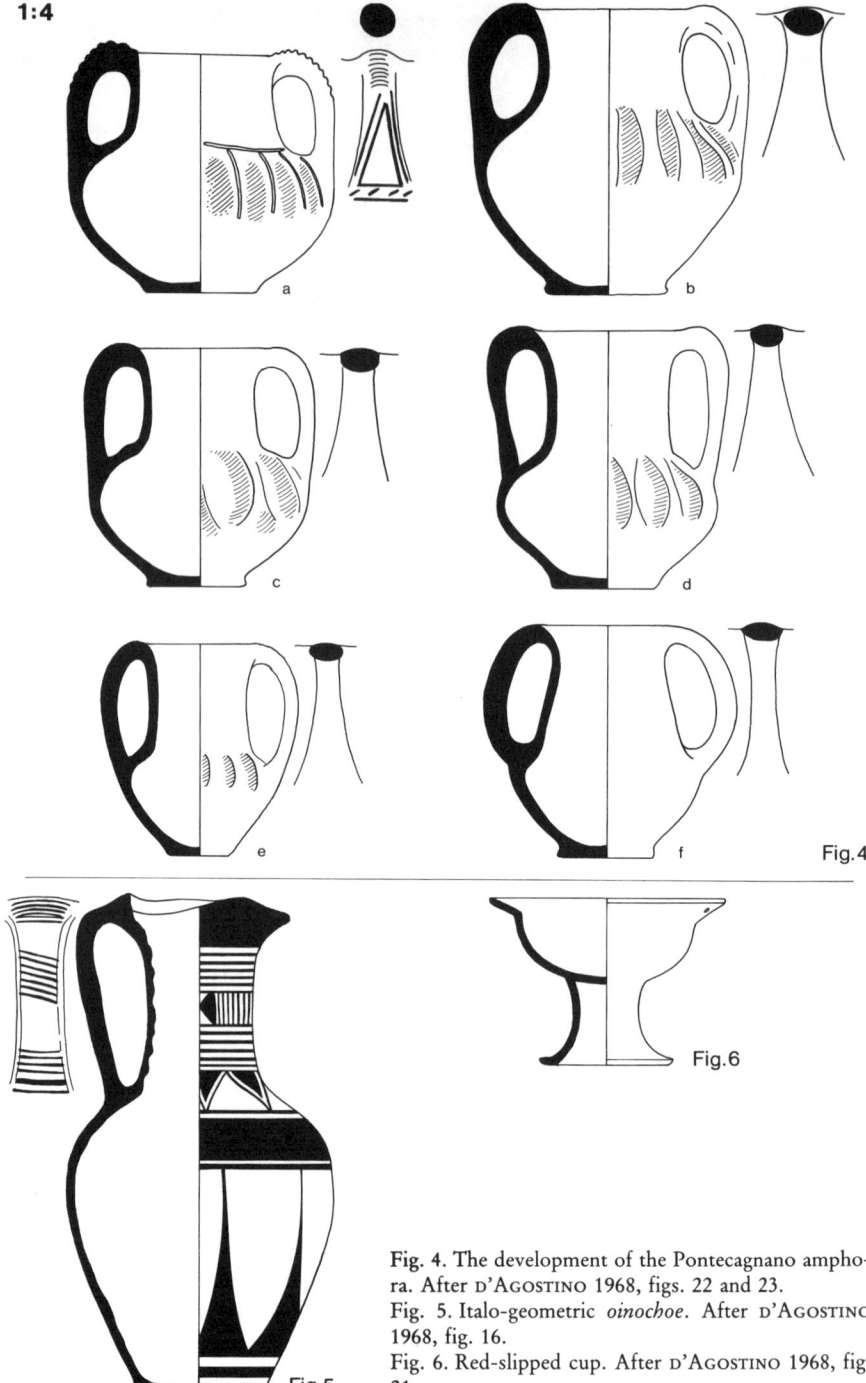

Fig. 4. The development of the Pontecagnano amphora. After D'AGOSTINO 1968, figs. 22 and 23.
Fig. 5. Italo-geometric *oinochoe*. After D'AGOSTINO 1968, fig. 16.
Fig. 6. Red-slipped cup. After D'AGOSTINO 1968, fig. 21.

("cumulo di sassi"). As in Pontecagnano, most have an east-west orientation; although the very strict east-west – or in some cases north-south – orientation seen on the plan reflects a general tendency rather than a rule. All the bodies were lying supine with the legs extended. Often the body was placed with the head to the east. At Pontecagnano the tombs can in some cases be shown to be part of family groups (D'AGOSTINO 1982, 210-213; CERCHIAI 1987, 44-45), but this cannot be proved for the tombs from Arenosola; partly because it is not possible to be certain that all tombs within the principal excavation area have been discovered – according to the excavation notebook for 1929 no systematic search for tombs was undertaken – partly because the plan of the excavation area and the excavation notebooks provide diverging information as to the exact location of the individual tombs.

As a rule, the tombs at Arenosola were well preserved. Bracelets and finger-rings were normally found still *in situ* around the bones of the forearms and the fingers, and the fibulae were lying at the shoulders or on the stomach of the body. Weapons, e.g. lances and axes, were placed alongside the body, and the grave-goods – mostly pottery – were lying at the feet and along the legs of the deceased.

The close connections to Pontecagnano are most clearly shown by the grave goods. The most common find from both sites from the 7th cent. B.C. is the "Pontecagnano amphora" of dark *impasto*, first classified by B. d'Agostino (1968, 109). The typological development of this class of pottery forms the framework for relative chronology in the *Ager Picentinus* from the late 8th to the beginning of the 6th cent. B.C. This typology, established by d'Agostino, was based on 38 tombs from the necropolis of S. Antonio at Pontecagnano (D'AGOSTINO 1968, 109-113). It shows a development from an amphora with a low neck and a very broad belly ('tipo 41') towards an amphora with a higher neck and generally slimmer proportions ('tipo 45 and 46'). Applied to the Arenosola material, where the Pontecagnano amphora was found in 110 of the 133 orientalizing tombs, d'Agostino's general typology is still valid. His earliest chronological group (D'AGOSTINO 1968, 193, no. 1) is not attested at Arenosola among the tombs excavated by Marzullo, but the chronological stage corresponding to the transition of Pontecagnano phase II-III is represented by the tombs excavated at Arenosola by P.C. Sestieri (VOZA 1962a). The distribution of the Pontecagnano amphora – so common in the *Ager Picentinus* – is restricted

*Fig. 4*

to Etruscan Campania, which is undoubtedly its centre of production.

Apart from the Pontecagnano amphora, a number of other types of pottery found both at Arenosola and at Pontecagnano seem to have been produced locally. Among these are, for example, a certain group of Italo-Geometric *oinochoai* of Protocorinthian form.

*Fig. 5* An example of this group is the *oinochoe* from Pontecagnano T 691 (D'AGOSTINO 1968, 98-99 cat. no. XXIII,24). The clay has been identified as Cumaean, but there is reason to believe that it was produced locally. The *oinochoe* is decorated in the characteristic Italo-Geometric style: the lip is painted; and on the neck a horizontal frieze consisting of vertical lines alternating with butterflies is bordered by two groups of horizontal lines. On the shoulder there are rays of solid triangles with outline drawing. The broadest point of the belly carries a large horizontal band between two horizontal lines, and the lower part of the belly is covered by long rays. At the base there are two reserved horizontal lines, and the handle is decorated with three groups of horizontal lines.

The decoration has been described in some detail, because exact parallels are common at Arenosola. Of a total of 44 *oinochoai* of Protocorinthian type found at Arenosola, 11 (25%) are decorated like those described above (D'AGOSTINO 1968, cat. no. XXIII,24), varying only in details: the central 'butterfly' of the frieze on the neck is at times replaced by an hour-glass ornament or horizontal zig-zag lines, and the number of reserved lines at the base varies from one to three.

Only one other example of *oinochoai* with this scheme of decoration is known to me, from Pontecagnano T 1377 (STRØM et al., forthcoming), whereas no examples are found at Cumae. The decoration scheme of rays with outline drawing on the shoulder is also unknown at Cumae.

*Fig. 6* Another type worth mentioning is d'Agostino's 'tipo 34' (1968, 105), a small cup on a high pedestalled foot, completely covered by a coral red slip. 5 examples of this type have been found both at Arenosola and at Pontecagnano: they are from Arenosola T 3 (two examples), T 20, T 23, T 78; and from Pontecagnano T 183 (D'AGOSTINO 1965, 680 and pl. CXXXVII,a), T 243 (unpublished, exhibited in the Museo Nazionale dell'Agro Picentino), T 605 and T 608 (D'AGOSTINO 1968, 105), and T 1402 (STRØM et al., forthcoming).

The cups display little variation in the form, and in fact the cups from Arenosola T 3, T 20, T 23, and from Pontecagnano T 183, T 243, and T

608 are so alike that one is reminded of modern industrialized production. All the cups from Arenosola are made of yellowish, soft clay, whereas d'Agostino mentions two different types of clay for the cup from T 605 and T 608 from Pontecagnano. The clay used for the cup from T 605 is local (D'AGOSTINO 1968, 86 and 105 cat. no. XXII,28), whereas the cup from T 608 is made of a type of clay which d'Agostino proposed for imported Ionian pottery (D'AGOSTINO 1968, 86). The 'tipo 34' is closely connected with the handleless cup with banded decoration that is common in Campania in two varieties: either with flat base or with high pedestalled foot (D'AGOSTINO 1968, 105, 'tipo 27'-'tipo 33'). It is usually made of local clay, but the decoration scheme has close parallels in the Rhodian banded dishes (HAYES 1966, cat. no. 681-713; HAYES 1973, cat. no. 1998-2007). Monochrome red-slipped cups, however, are not found in the East Greek area. Although the East Greek influence on the Italic pottery should not be underestimated, I feel it is safe to assume that the pedestalled cups with coral red slip were made in the *Ager Picentinus*.

These few examples should give an idea of the close – and not unexpected – affinity between the material from Pontecagnano and Arenosola in the orientalizing period, which is seen to be even more pronounced, when the material from Arenosola is considered as a whole. The archaeological finds show that the same craftsmen were active in both Pontecagnano and Arenosola, goods were imported from the same areas (especially Southern Etruria), and the dead were buried according to the same rites. The inhabitants of the two sites must therefore be regarded as belonging to the same cultural sphere.

Although a very large number of tombs is known from the 7th cent. B.C. in the *Ager Picentinus*, we still know next to nothing about the 7th cent. B.C. habitations in the area. At Pontecagnano the extension of the urban area has been established for the later periods (BAILO MODESTI 1984), but few finds from habitation areas are dated to before the 6th cent. B.C.: From the Greek sanctuary of Apollo in Via Verdi a kiln and a votive deposit containing pottery, dated respectively to the 2nd half and to the end of the 7th cent. B.C. (CERCHIAI 1984, 248), have been found. In Proprietà Negri-Sessi south-east of the Via Verdi sanctuary, a 7th cent. B.C. well has been found (CERCHIAI 1984, 247). A preliminary report mentions the find of 9 more kilns with associated Italo-Geometric pottery close to the necropolis at S. Antonio di Picenzia dated to Pontecagnano phase I-II (*Eubei* 1978, 300-301). But so far, Pontecagnano has revealed no structures securely identified as belonging to habitation areas antedating the 6th cent. B.C. Some post-holes found in Via Bellini, however, might belong to huts dating to the end of the 8th cent. B.C. (GRECO 1984, 264).

At Arenosola no archaeological finds give hints as to where the habitation areas are to be found. Immediately to the west of the plateau, where the necropolis was excavated, is Lago Campolungo, only 1 m above normal sea-level, which on early maps (MAGINI 1620; ZANNONI 1808, map 19) is seen as a lagoon with an outlet at modern Lido Lago. It is thus highly unlikely that any ancient habitation area should be found between the sea and Arenosola itself. In Antiquity, however, the lagoon may have served as shelter for smaller boats, which could be pulled up at its mouth.

In the neighbourhood of Arenosola there are a number of sites that may possibly shed new light on the cultural development in the southern part of the *Ager Picentinus*.

On the north bank of the Sele, c. 1 km north of the Foce del Sele there is a hillock known as Santa Cecilia. This rises 16 m above normal sea-level; this is not much, but it is the highest point found within a radius of 3 km. Already the excavators of Foce del Sele noted many surface finds on Santa Cecilia (ZANOTTI-BIANCO 1940, 895; ZANCANI MONTUORO & ZANOTTI-BIANCO 1951, 22).[4] The topography of the site, controlling all traffic on the Sele, overlooking a greater part of the Sele Plain, and with easy access to the sea, makes it very likely that Santa Cecilia was of great importance. Zancani Montuoro and Zanotti-Bianco also noted a big, unexplored necropolis "ad est del fiume", which they tried to identify as belonging to the habitation on Santa Cecilia (ZANOTTI-BIANCO 1940, 895; ZANCANI MONTUORO & ZANOTTI-BIANCO 1951, 22). However, they gave no more information, either on the exact location of the necropolis – it was probably not far from Santa Cecilia and on the same side of the river – or on the date of the tombs. It is not unthinkable that the habitation area of the Arenosola necropolis is to be found at Santa Cecilia. The two places are located at almost the same distance from the sea, just above the marshlands. At Tarquinia, which must be considered the best known site in regard to the relation between habitation area and necropolis in the late 8th to the 7th cent. B.C., no necropolis has been located more than 3 km from the habitation area on the Pian di Città (HENCKEN 1968, fig. 2; BONGHI JOVINO 1986, 63-65). The distance between Arenosola and Santa Cecilia is slightly greater, almost 4 km, but still not excessive. However, the possible existence of another necropolis, perhaps even closer to Santa Cecilia, should be kept in mind. An interesting toponym is Tempa delle Craste – the "Hill of Sherds" – c. 3 km north of Arenosola, which indicates that sherds used to be found there. Only a survey of the area will tell us whether this is in fact an archaeological site, and if so, of which period. Exactly the same toponym is also found on the north bank of the Sele c. 8 km from the sea (*Map IGM Foglio 198 III, N.O.*).

Returning to Pliny, it is thus clear that Etruscans were present not only at Pontecagnano in the northern part of the *Ager Picentinus*, but also – at least in the 7th and the beginning of the 6th cent. B.C. – at Arenosola, close to the Sele River, mentioned explicitly by Pliny (*NH* III, 70) as the limit of Etruscan penetration into the south.

Based on literary sources, the river Sele seems to have been the cultural or administrative frontier between Greeks and Etruscans in the *Ager Picentinus* after the foundation of the sanctuary of Hera Argiva at Foce del Sele and the colony of Poseidonia c. 600 B.C.

In the period preceding the colonization, Southern Villanovan culture, which must be considered Proto-Etruscan[5], characterizes Pontecagnano and Sala Consilina. This view, however, does not accord with the opinion that the lack of Greek colonies to the north of Naples shows that the Early Etruscans as early as the 8th cent. B.C. possessed some power or organization that made a Greek expansion further north into Etruria impossible (MACNAMARA 1984, 425; MOREL 1983, 128).

E. Greco believes that this explanation also applies to *Ager Picentinus* (1984, 263). But even though the archaeological evidence from the period immediately preceeding the Greek foundations in the area south of the Sele river is scarse, the Greeks did not find the area totally unpopulated when they arrived. This means either that the balance of power between Greeks and Etruscans was different north and south of the river Sele, or that the Greeks could settle in certain areas according to an agreement with the peoples of Campania, in this case the Etruscans.

At Poseidonia, 7th cent. B.C. Oinotrian geometric pottery was found at the Porta Giustizia (KILIAN 1969, 348). Other 7th cent. B.C. material was found below the first phase of the Plateia An, and close by, a fragment of an *impasto* amphora comparable to the ones from Pontecagnano and Arenosola was found, as well as other material, possibly deriving from a destroyed tomb (GRECO & THEODORESCU 1983, 72). A Pontecagnano amphora was found at S. Venera, and at the Gaudo necropolis (GRECO & THEODORESCU 1983, 73), and inside Poseidonia, Greek pottery dating to the 7th cent. B.C. (GRECO & THEODORESCU 1983, 72), underlining the interaction between the Greeks and the Etruscans. E. Greco points out the significance of the finds from Poseidonia, but he chooses to give weight to the literary evidence and supports the view that Sele was a frontier "sin da epoche molto antiche" (GRECO 1984, 264). He believes that the "affinità culturale" between the areas north and south of the Sele should not be taken as proof of the presence of the same 'ethnos' (GRECO & THEODORESCU 1983, 73).

The small finds from the sanctuary at Foce del Sele have not yet been published, but hardly any Iron Age or orientalizing material was found, and the excavators exclude the possibility of any pre-Greek activity in the sanctuary (ZANCANI MONTUORO & ZANOTTI-BIANCO 1951, 22)

C. 6 km east/north-east of Poseidonia, at Capo di Fiume (SESTIERI 1960b, 73-91; VOZA 1962b, 79-80), 6 Iron Age tombs with material which is closely connected to Pontecagnano phase Ib have also been found (VOZA 1962b, 79; D'AGOSTINO 1974a, 22).

It is therefore obvious that the Proto-Etruscans and the Etruscans did not limit themselves to the area north of the Sele, and that Sele therefore can be considered a frontier only in historical times after the foundation of Poseidonia in c. 600 B.C. The finds from Pontecagnano, Arenosola, Santa Cecilia, Poseidonia, and Capo di Fiume suggest that we should imagine a number of smaller, interconnected sites along the coast of the Sele Plain – the existence of an Iron Age I necropolis at Loc. Stucchiara c. 2,5 km south of S. Antonio could support this view (D'AGOSTINO 1965, 671 and 672 no. 5) – and in the Valle di Diana.

We still do not know what happened when the Greeks arrived in the *Ager Picentinus*, but the relationships between Etruscans and Greeks in the early period of colonization seem to have been peaceful. At Pontecagnano, Greek pottery was imported already from the late 8th cent. B.C. onwards (D'AGOSTINO 1989, 70-72), and Greek 7th cent. B.C. pottery is present also at Arenosola, e.g. a very fine Late Proto-Corinthian *oinochoe* (MARZULLO 1938), and at Poseidonia itself. Instead, the Greek colony seems to have had little influence on life at Pontecagnano. Previously, a hiatus in the archaeological finds from Pontecagnano in the period c. 550 to 400 B.C. was explained as a period of economic crisis in Pontecagnano due to the presence of Poseidonia (NAPOLI 1965, 669-670). But as more necropoleis are found at Pontecagnano (CERCHIAI 1987), the hiatus is gradually diminishing. It is, however, significant that tombs from both the 7th and advanced 6th cent. B.C. are rarely found at the same necropoleis at Pontecagnano. This points to a change in the location of the necropoleis during the first half of the 6th cent. B.C., corresponding to the proposed date for the urbanization of Pontecagnano (CERCHIAI 1987), rather than acts of hostility between Greeks and Etruscans. The Greek sanctuary of Apollo in Pontecagnano (CERCHIAI 1984), with activity from the 6th cent. B.C. on, gives the same impression.

Several sites – Pithecussai being the most important in the 8th cent. B.C. – have shown us that Greeks, Phoenicians and Etruscans could live in peaceful coexistence. In the *Ager Picentinus*, however, we find an almost unique situation. Pontecagnano, being a Villanovan site populated only from the beginning of the Iron Age, soon developed into a centre with connections to greater parts of the Italian Peninsula and Sicily, as evidenced by the finds, for instance of a Southern Etruscan hut urn from T 2500 (Pontecagnano phase Ia, D'AGOSTINO 1974b, 94-95 and pl. XXXVIII,1) and of the Sicilian *ceramica piumata* from e.g. T 580 (Pontecagnano phase Ib, D'AGOSTINO 1974b, 100-101 and fig. 21).

Situated close to Pithecussai, Pontecagnano in the 8th cent. B.C. received some of the earliest imported Greek pottery in Italy (D'AGOSTINO 1989, 70-72), and already at the beginning of the 7th cent. B.C. local workshops in the *Ager Picentinus* produced pottery in Greek style.

The Arenosola necropolis is of great importance, showing that the Etruscan culture of the 7th cent. B.C. had spread to the river Sele, and although earlier sites of the Villanovan culture are found further south, we possess no evidence of Etruscan sites there, thereby confirming the literary evidence from the 1st cent. A.D. writer Pliny.

The distance between the two 6th cent. B.C. urban centres of Pontecagnano and Poseidonia is relatively short, and the Greek sanctuary at

Foce del Sele and the Etruscan necropolis at Arenosola, overlapping in time by almost half a century, are only 5 km apart.

For the time being we can only provide hints rather than conclusions on the relations of the peoples of the *Ager Picentinus*, but further research in the area will undoubtedly provide more evidence both of the cultural interactions between Greeks and Etruscans and on its impact on Etruscan urbanization in Campania.

Helle W. Horsnæs
Ndr. Fasanvej 199, 3.th.
DK-2000 Frederiksberg


## BIBLIOGRAPHY

BAILO MODESTI, G. 1984 — Lo scavo nell'abitato antico di Pontecagnano, *AnnOrNap* 6, 215-245.

BONGHI JOVINO, M. 1986 — *Gli Etruschi di Tarquinia*. Modena.

CERCHIAI, L. 1984 — Nota preliminare sull'area sacra di Via Verdi, *AnnOrNap* 6, 247-250.

1987 — Il processo di strutturazione del politico: i Campani, *AnnOrNap* 9, 41-53.

D'AGOSTINO, B. 1965 — Nuovi apporti della documentazione archeologica nell'Agro Picentino, *StEtr* 33, 671-683.

1968 — Pontecagnano – Tombe orientalizzanti in contrada S. Antonio, *NSc* 93, 75-204.

1974a — La civiltà del ferro nell'Italia Meridionale e nella Sicilia, *Popoli e Civiltà nell'Italia Antica* 2. Roma.

1974b — Pontecagnano, *Seconda Mostra della Preistoria e della Protostoria nel Salernitano*, Salerno, 87-108.

1982 — L'ideologia funeraria nell'età del ferro in Campania: Pontecagnano. Nascita di un potere di funzione stabile, in G. Gnoli & J.-P. Vernant (eds.): *La mort, les morts dans les sociétés anciennes*, Cambridge, 203-221.

1989 — Rapporti tra l'Italia Meridionale e l'Egeo nell'VIII sec. a.C. *Atti del Secondo Congresso Internazionale Etrusco* (Firenze 1985), Vol. I, Firenze, 63-78.

*Eubei* 1978 — *Gli Eubei in Occidente* (Atti del 18 Convegno di Studi sulla Magna Grecia). Taranto.

| | |
|---|---|
| FLEMING, N.C. 1974 | Review of Schmiedt 1972, *IntJNautA* 4, 163-164. |
| GRECO, E. 1979 | Ricerche sulla 'chora' poseidonate: il "passaggio agrario" dalla fondazione della città alla fine del sec. IV a.C., *DArch* n.s. I,2, 7-26. |
| 1984 | La ricerca archeologica nell'abitato di Pontecagnano. Dibattito, *AnnOrNap* 6, 263-266. |
| GRECO, E. & THEODORESCU, D. 1983 | *Poseidonia – Pæstum, II. L'agora*. Rome. |
| HAYES, J. 1966 | Excavations at Tocra 1963-1965. The Archaic Deposits I. *BSA Suppl.* 4. |
| 1973 | Excavations at Tocra 1963-1965. The Archaic Deposits II. *BSA Suppl.* 10. |
| HENCKEN, H. 1968 | *Tarquinia, Villanovans and Early Etruscans*. Cambridge, Massachusetts. |
| HOLLOWAY, R.R. 1981 | *Italy and the Aegean 3000-700 B.C.* Louvain-la Neuve. |
| KILIAN, K. 1969 | Neue Funde zur Vorgeschichte Paestums, *RM* 76, 335-349. |
| MACNAMARA, E. 1984 | A note on the background of some Sardinian bronze typologies, and the exchange of some bronze types between Sardinia and her neighbours during the Italian Late bronze and Early Iron Age, *Opus* 3, 421-427. |
| MAGINI, G.A. 1620 | Principato Citra. *Italia*. (Reprinted in E. Mazzetti (ed.): *Cartografia Generale del Mezzogiorno e della Sicilia*, Edizioni Scientifiche Italiane 1972, pl. XXVIII). |
| MARZULLO, A. 1938 | La necropoli dell'Arenosola a destra della Foce del Sele, *Rassegna Storica Salernitana*, 2:1, 3-26. |
| MOREL, J.-P. 1983 | Greek colonization in Italy and the West, in R.R. Holloway (ed.): *Crossroads of the Mediterranean*, Louvain-la-Neuve, 123-161. |
| NAPOLI, M. 1965 | Pontecagnano: problemi topografici e storici, *StEtr* 33, 661-670. |
| PANEBIANCO, V. 1937 | Notiziario sistematico delle scoperte archeologiche nel Salernitano. *Rassegna Storica Salernitano*, 1:1, 181-189. |
| SCHMIEDT, G. 1972 | *Il livello del Mar Tirreno*. Firenze. |
| SESTIERI, P.C. 1950 | Scoperte e scavi preistorici in Italia durante 1950, Arenosola, *RivScPr* 5, 125. |
| 1960a | Necropoli dell'età del ferro a Pontecagnano, *RivScPr* 15, 207-211. |
| 1960b | Necropoli villanoviane in provincia di Salerno, *StEtr* 28, 73-107. |
| STRØM, I. et al., forthcoming | *Publication of the De Santis I necropolis at Pontecagnano.* |
| TRENDALL, A.D. 1987 | *The Red-figured Vases of Paestum*. London. |
| VOZA, G. 1962a | Arenosola – Scavi 1950, *Mostra della preistoria e della protostoria nel Salernitano*, Salerno, 89-102. |
| 1962b | Necropoli di Capodifiume, *Mostra della preistoria e della protostoria nel Salernitano*. Salerno, 79-86. |

| | |
|---|---|
| ZANCANI MON-TUORO, P. & ZANOTTI-BIANCO, U. 1951 | *Heraion alla Foce del Sele, I. Il Santuario.* Rome. |
| ZANNONI, A.R. 1808 | *Atlante Geografico del Regno di Napoli.* Napoli. |
| ZANOTTI-BIANCO, U.1940 | Le scoperte allo Heraion del Sele. *Le Vie d'Italia*, vol. 46, 892-902. |

## NOTES

1. I would like to thank Prof. Bruno d'Agostino, Istituto Universitario Orientale, Naples, who first suggested that I should study the finds from Arenosola, for his teaching and guidance during the work with my thesis. My thanks also to Dott.ssa Matilda Romito and sig. Carlo Samaritani, Museo Provinciale di Salerno, for permission to study and publish the finds, and for their helpfulness.

The manuscript for this article was finished in May 1990. Since then three important contributions related to the study of the *Ager Picentinus* have been published:

CERCHIAI, L.: Le officine etrusco-corinzie di Pontecagnano. *AnnAStorAnt.Quad.* 6, Napoli 1990.

d'AGOSTINO, B. – GASTALDI, P. (eds.): Pontecagnano II. La necropoli del Picentino 1. Le tombe della Prima Età del Ferro. *AnnAStorAnt.Quad.* 5, Napoli 1988.

GASPARRI, D.: La fotointerpretazione archeologica nella ricerca storico-topografica sui territori di Pontecagnano, Paestum e Velia, *AnnOrNap* 11, 1989, 253-265.

2. See bibliography in *EAA* suppl. 1970, "Pontecagnano"; later works are currently being published in *AnnOrNap*, Napoli.

3. See *BTCGI* III. Pisa – Roma 1984. A full publication of the material from the excavations of 1929-1931 at Arenosola is under preparation by the author.

4. This was confirmed on a visit at Santa Cecilia in June 1988 by the author together with Prof. d'Agostino and Prof. Greco, both from I.U.O., Naples.

5. There can be no doubt that the Etruscan culture developed from the Villanovan one, and it is not possible to draw a sharp distinction between the two cultures. For practical reasons, however, I use the term 'Villanovan culture' for the period c. 900 to 720 B.C. (traditionally called Villanovan I-II) and 'Etruscan culture' for the period c. 720 B.C. on (including Villanovan III/Orientalizzante Antico). As G. Bartoloni has shown (in *La Cultura Villanoviana* 1989, 92-97) it is not possible to speak of a Villanovan people. I therefore use the term 'Proto-Etruscans' to describe the people bearing the Villanovan culture.

# A RELIEF FROM CROCEAE: DIOSCURI IN ROMAN LACONIA

BIRTE POULSEN
WITH A CONTRIBUTION BY JESPER CARLSEN

The popularity of the Dioscuri is evident in Sparta during the Archaic and Classical periods, when the city was important as a political opponent of Athens. Especially from this time, accounts of the two heroes and their intervention on behalf of the Spartans are preserved. But even when Sparta lost her previous power, the old cults survived, and like other cults in Sparta, the one of the Dioscuri experienced a revival during the Roman period. In this paper we should like to discuss some aspects of the cult of the Dioscuri during this period, with special reference to the explanation of the presence of Dioscuri on a relief from the village of Croceae situated some 25 km south of Sparta.

The relief was first noticed by members of the "Expédition de Morée" in 1837, and according to E. Siegel (HENZEN 1857, 158) it had been found close to the quarries which in antiquity produced the famous *lapis Lacedaemonius* (Pliny *NH* XXXVI.55). The relief was at first built into a house, then a public fountain in Croceae, where it was much damaged from water, before it was removed and placed in the local town-hall (LE ROY 1961; HERMARY 1986, no. 63). Since 1964 the relief has again been built into a public fountain at Croceae. *Fig. 1*

The relief has the form of a small *aedicula* with gable and a base with a dedication to the Dioscuri in Latin. It is made of a greyish-blue marble, the total height being 57 cm, the width 42 cm, the part with the representation 37 cm high, and the base with the inscription 12 cm. It shows the two standing heroes naked, characterized as Dioscuri by their piloi and the two heraldic horseprotomes in the background. They are not quite en face, but slightly turned towards each other in an asymmetric pose. Both are resting on their inner leg and both hold in their left hand a spear, which was originally indicated with colour. The right hero carries a sword at his left side and pours a libation from a phiale in his right hand over two amphorae between them. Apparently *Fig. 2*

Fig. 1 Relief from Croceae (LE ROY 1961, Fig. 2).

the hero to the left carries only the spear. The condition of the relief makes a stylistic analysis difficult, but the inscription dates it to the reign of Domitian.

The representation seems at first sight to belong to a common and well-known type of dedication to the Dioscuri in Sparta and its vicinity. These dedications have their own characteristic iconography and symbols, dating from the Archaic to the Roman period (Archaic: HERMARY 1986, no. 58-59, Hellenistic: Idem, no. 34), but in spite of many similar representations, no other relief contains exactly the same elements. The horseprotomes are presumably to be understood as substitutes for the horses which accompany the Dioscuri through all

# A RELIEF FROM CROCEAE: DIOSCURI IN ROMAN LACONIA

Fig. 2 The public fountain at Croceae with the relief (photo by the authors).

periods (TOD & WACE 1906, 8, 15a, 202, 319, 490). The symbolic abbreviation, however, seems to be an invention of the Roman period, where such horseprotomes are common in connection with the freestanding sculpture used as a support for the Dioscuri[1].

Whereas the amphorae are typical attributes of the Greek Dioscuri (TOD & WACE 1906, 334, 674; HERMARY 1986, no. 34f., 59f., 62, 64, 122, 226-231), the phiale seems new in the Spartan repertory. However, the phiale is remarkably common among the representations of the Dioscuri on votive reliefs from the Spartan colony of Tarentum dating from the late 4th and the early 3th century B.C. (PIRZIO BIROLI STEFANELLI 1977, with several examples), and it occurs also in the hands of the Dioscuri on coins from Tyndaris (254-210 B.C., GABRICI 1927, 193, no. 29-34, pl. 10.2)[2].

*Fig. 3* The nearest parallel for the representation is, in fact, found among the terracotta reliefs in Tarentum, where the Dioscuri are shown in an *aedicula* with Ionian columns, and the right one is pouring a libation from the phiale in his right hand over two amphorae between them. He holds a sword and a wreath in his left hand. The Dioscuros to the left holds a sword in his left hand, while his right arm is missing. According to similar reliefs, however, he could have held a phiale in his right hand, but there are no traces of horses (PIRZIO BIROLI STEFANELLI 1977, 321f., AaII pl. LXV,1; cf. 320f., AaI pl. LXIV,2).

The explanation for the phiale in the relief at Croceae has apparently to be sought in Tarentum, and such influences from the colony on the representations in the mother city are not without precedent. A Heracles colossus of bronze made by Lysippos in Tarentum seems thus to have been the model for a representation of Heracles on Spartan coins (Strab. VI.3.1; DÖRIG 1957; GRUNAUER-VON HOERSCHELMANN 1978, 22).

During his visit to Croceae, Pausanias (III.21.4) records bronze images of the Dioscuri at the quarries which produced the green porphyry. Unfortunately he supplies no further information, and today no trace of such statues is found. Perhaps the base is identical with the one seen by E. Siegel, who mentions a quadratic base of green local stone placed at the entrance to the quarries (HENZEN 1857, 158). Due to the inscription and the description of the finding place, the relief has been related to the text of Pausanias and taken to copy the bronze group of the Croceae quarries.

*The Inscription.* (Jesper Carlsen)
CIL III 493 AND THE ADMINISTRATION OF THE QUARRY AT CROCEAE.

The fragmented Latin inscription, first recorded by the "Expédition scientifique de Morée" (BOULET 1838, 55), was published as no. 493 in *CIL* III:

DIIS CASTORI ET POLLVCI SACRVM
DOMVS AVGVSTI DISPENSATOR

Fig. 3 Votive relief, National Museum, Tarentum (Pirzio Biroli Stefanelli 1977, pl. LIV, 1).

The reading of the inscription was, however, complicated by a layer of lime from the village fountain, where both the relief and the dedication were reused, and after new observations E.S. Forster (1904, 187-188) could add a third line to the text in *CIL* III:
 DIIS CASTORI ET POLLVCI SACRV[M]
 DOMVS AVGVSTI DISPENSATOR
 DEDIT ET DEDICAVIT
This edition, being identical with *IG* V.1 no. 1569, has since been the standardtext[3], but it is now clear that also Forster's improved reading is inadequate. In line 2 some traces of lettering can be observed towards the end, and there may have been at least one more line, although the letters at the bottom of the stele are almost illegible.

In 1961 C. Le Roy, discussing the relief, also re-examined the inscription, and he suggested some valuable corrections and additions. Most important, the title *domus augusti dispensator* was changed to a name and a title, and with the reading of some part of line 4 the dedication can be dated to the reign of Domitian. In Le Roy's opinion (1961, 212-215) the inscription is to be read as follows:

DIIS CASTORI ET POLLVCI SACRVM
EVDOXVS AVGVSTI DISPENSATOR P ROM
DEDIT ET DEDICAVIT
IMP CAESARI DOMITIANO

The title *augusti dispensator*, or more commonly its abbreviated form *aug. disp*, is well attested in the early Empire, while *domus augusti dispensator* is very rare, if not unique (LIEBENAM 1903, 1193). Furthermore, Eudoxus is a well-known (slave-)name in Rome, and Le Roy's new reading is therefore to be preferred[4]. But in both cases there is no clear status indication of the *dispensator*. Normally the *dispensatores* were manumitted about the age of forty or soon after, and since he has only one name, Eudoxus must certainly still have been an Imperial slave (WEAVER 1972, 206).

Thanks to the exhaustive studies in the last decades by Boulvert, Chantraine and Weaver, the occupational titles and nomenclature in the well-established hierarchy among the Imperial slaves and freedmen of the early Empire are now very well elucidated. A *dispensator* did not belong to the domestic part of Familia Caesaris, but to the financial administration, where he was often in charge of the funds of a department (*ratio*), assisted by so-called *arcarii* or *vicarii*.

The *dispensator* was what has been called "an intermediate clerical grade" (WEAVER 1972), occupying a wide range of posts in every part of the Empire. We know, for instance, of a *dispensator ludi magni* in Rome, but also *dispensator rationis monetae* and *dispensatores a frumento* are recorded among other titles. The so-called *dispensatores hortorum* are connected with the Imperial gardens and villae, but most of the *dispensatores* found in the provinces should be related to the army or to the administration and collection of customs[5]. In any case, the appearance of an Imperial slave in the senatorial province of Achaia requires an explanation.

As indicated above, the specific functions of a *dispensator* can sometimes be gauged from indications in the title, but, unfortunately, this is not the case with Eudoxus. However, the dedication to the Dioscuri and the location of the inscription at Croceae can give some important hints. According to Strabo (VIII.5.7), a large quarry had recently been opened by private persons in the territory of Sparta[6], and Pausanias does not give any indications of the owner in his description of the quarry at Croceae. In the early Empire, quarries and mines normally belonged to the emperor, and they were exploited either under direct Imperial control or leased out to private persons. From Vipasca in Lusitania, detailed regulations and laws concerning the lease system of mines are preserved, and how this system functioned in practice can also be studied in the Norican area (ØRSTED 1985).

The lease-holders, *conductores*, must have been Roman citizens, but from Salona in Dalmatia an Imperial *aurariarum delmaruum dispensator* is mentioned (*CIL* III 1997), and another Imperial *dispensator* is found at Ampelum close to the gold mines in Dacia (*CIL* III 1301). The Imperial quarries at Smydna in Phrygia were managed by Imperial freedmen and slaves with various titles and functions, but no *dispensator* is recorded here (DUBOIS 1908, XXX-XXXIV). A *dispensator marmorum* has, however, been located at Euboea (*CIL* III 563/12289), and another is perhaps found at the Imperial quarries at Chemtou in Tunesia. If the abbreviation *disp.m.n.* in a recently published inscription should be read as *disp(ensator) m(armorum) n(umidicorum)*, as suggested by the publisher (KHANOUSSI 1988), *dispensatores* in connection with the administration of quarries are now also attested in another senatorial province, Africa Proconsularis.

Returning to *CIL* III 493, it is reasonable to think that Eudoxus administrated the exploitation of the quarry at Croceae as *dispensator*, when he made a dedication to Castor and Pollux. If so, the inscription also indicates that the quarry by the reign of Domitian was no longer owned by private citizens or leased out, but was under direct Imperial control, like other quarries in the Empire.

The period of local exploitation seems therefore to have been short, and accordingly the importance of the quarry for the relative wealth in Sparta and her territory under the Principate has been exaggerated by Kahrstedt, who argues that the quarries were in private hands (KAHRSTEDT 1954, 197). Rather, as recently pointed out also by Spawforth (CARTLEDGE & SPAWFORTH 1989, 169), agriculture and livestock provided the most important sources of private wealth, also in Roman Sparta.

## Dioscuri in Roman Sparta. The Interpretation

But what caused a *dispensator* to put up a dedication to the Dioscuri in this place during the reign of Domitian, and what function did these images at the quarries have?

There is not much evidence for a special connection between the Dioscuri and slaves, only during the Classical period in Athens, apparently, slaves working as day-labourers went to the sanctuary of the Dioscuri to wait for work (*Anecd.Bekk.* I.212.12; HEMBERG 1955, 40). As there is no obvious explanation for the dedication of Eudoxus, it will be useful to compare the different kinds of documentation for the cult of the Dioscuri during the years of Roman domination over Laconia.

During the Pre-roman period, the cult of the Dioscuri is known to have been of great importance in Sparta and the neighbouring cities. At Therapne the Dioscuri, here called Tyndarides, had their most ancient cult, and they were probably honoured originally as chthonic gods (NILSSON 1967, 408f.; WIDE 1893, 316). Later they became known as helpers, *soteres*, in critical situations at sea and on the battlefield, but at Sparta they seem especially to have been connected with the education of the ephebes (Paus. III.14.7; 20.2) and warfare (Paus. IV.27.2; Pl. *Leg.* 796B; Plut. *Mor.De mus.* 1140C; Plut. *Lyc.* 22.2). The double kingdom in Sparta was said to originate from twins, and some of the kings claimed to be descended from the Dioscuri. When one of the kings went to war, he was followed by a symbol of one of the heroes (Paus. III.1.5; Xen. *Rep.Lac.* 15.2; Hdt. V.75; CARLIER 1984, 298-304), and it is thus clear that the Dioscuri were closely connected with the Spartan aristocracy already during the Archaic period.

The symbols or attributes of the Dioscuri, stars, piloi, and amphorae sometimes entwined with snakes, appear on some of the earliest Spartan coins from c. 265 B.C. (GRUNAUER-VON HOERSCHELMANN 1978, 4-6, gr.2, pl. 1; 19-34, gr. 5-12, pl. 3-7). Only Heracles, the other son of Zeus and ancestor of royal families in Sparta, was more popular than the Dioscuri on the coins.

During the civil wars in the late Republic, Sparta first sided with Pompey at Pharsalus in 48 B.C., along with the other Greek cities. But during the turmoil following the murder of Caesar, Sparta supported the *triumviri* and later fought on Octavian's side at Actium as the only Greek city besides Mantinea. The relations between Octavian and Spar-

Fig. 4 Spartan coin with jugate heads of the Dioscuri, 48-c. 35 B.C. (GRUNAUER-VON HOERSCHELMANN 1978, pl. 9-10).

Fig. 5 Denarius, 46 B.C. (CRAWFORD 1974, pl. LIV, 19).

ta were strengthened through his marriage to Livia in 38 B.C. due to the existing clientship between Sparta and the Claudii (Suet. *Tib.* 6.2; Cass.Dio 54.7.2). Livia was also indebted to the city for the temporary asylum given her and her two year old son, Tiberius, in 40 B.C.

It cannot be all coincidence that some of the Spartan coin types during these years are more or less identical with some of the contemporary Roman coins. The obverse of a bronze coin thus shows jugate heads of the Dioscuri wearing laureate piloi with stars above their heads (GRUNAUER-VON HOERSCHELMANN 1978, 38, gr. 15, pl. 9-10). A similar motive occurs on denarii issued in 46 B.C. by the moneyer MN. CORDIUS RUFUS IIVIR (CRAWFORD 1974, no. 463.1a, pl. LIV,19), who apparently sided with Caesar, and on the coinage issued by the moneyer L. SERVIUS RUFUS in 41 B.C. (CRAWFORD 1974, no. 515.1, pl. LXII,10).

*Fig. 4*

*Fig. 5*

For his loyalty at Actium, Octavian rewarded the Spartan Eurycles with power, wealth and Roman citizenship, C. Iulius Eurycles. He was supported by several of the prominent families in Sparta, among others the priestly family, the Memmii, which for generations presided over the civic cult of the Dioscuri. This family claimed the Dioscuri as their ancestors, and Eurycles was related to them (SPAWFORTH 1985, 193f., 196). He may have been the founder and the first priest of Sparta's Imperial cult (CHRIMES 1949, 169-204; cf. SPAWFORTH 1984, 277 for arguments against this theory), as later a descendant of Eurycles, Eurycles Herklanos, an Imperial high priest during the reign of Trajan/Hadrian who claimed descent from the Dioscuri, as well as from Heracles (CARTLEDGE & SPAWFORTH 1989, 163; SPAWFORTH 1984, 277). Besides the Euryclids, only a few other families in Sparta combined descent from the Dioscuri with the priesthood of the Imperial cult (WOODWARD 1928-30, 212f., 224f.; CHRIMES 1949, 194f., 471-474).

Fig. 7 Denarius, 210 B.C. (CRAWFORD 1974, pl. 9).

Fig. 6 Spartan coin with Dioscuri on horses, 31-7 B.C. (GRUNAUER-VON HOERSCHELMANN 1978, pl. 19).

In accordance with Augustan policy, Sparta experienced a revival of many of her old cults during the reign of Eurycles (CARTLEDGE & SPAWFORTH 1989, 99). There is also new evidence for the Dioscuri, for example coins with equestrian Dioscuri on the reverse were introduced *Fig. 6* (GRUNAUER-VON HOERSCHELMANN 1978, 65f., gr. 25, pl. 19). In Republican Rome such Dioscuri, the symbol of the victorious Romans, *Fig. 7* had decorated the first issue of denarii (CRAWFORD 1974, no. 44ff., pl. 9ff.), and for about a century it was the most common reverse type. In the Spartan coinage, it was probably a reminder not only of the ancestors of Eurycles but also of the recent victory at Actium.

The evidence for the cult of the Dioscuri is not extensive for the following century, but the cult was still flourishing in many of the Greek cities during the reign of the Antonines, judging from the account of Pausanias. Although he states that only "things worthy of mention" in Sparta will be described, he includes no less than 16 sanctuaries, tombs and hero shrines, and monuments with which the Dioscuri were connected (Paus. III.12.5, 13.1, 13.6, 13.8, 14.6-7, 16.1-2, 17.2-4, 18.14, 19.7, 20.1-2).

The numismatic and epigraphic evidence supports the impression of an increased interest in the Dioscuri during the Antonine period. A type with Dioscuri on horses standing in heraldic pose appears in the Spartan coinage (GRUNAUER-VON HOERSCHELMANN 1978, 85, gr. 41, pl. 26; cf. 86, gr. 42, pl. 26; relief, HERMARY 1986, no. 18) besides the usual types. This agrees well with the increasing use of Dioscuri on medallions and coins during the Antonine period in Rome (GNECCHI 1912, II for several examples; *BMC* IV 502, no. 774f., pl. 69.11; 672, no. 1671f., pl. 89.3), and an inscription on a marble altar from Sparta seems to verify the fact that the two emperors were characterized as the new Dioscuri (*IG* V,1 447; TRUMMER 1980, 156). The Dioscuri were first used in Augustan propaganda as parallels for the heirs, the *principes iuventutis*, and the inspiration for this symbolic use of the Dioscuri may have originated from Augustus' visit to Sparta in 21 B.C.[7]

The Dioscuri were still common in the Spartan coinage during the reign of Commodus and the Severi (GRUNAUER-VON HOERSCHELMANN 1978, 87, gr. 46, pl. 27). In Rome both Geta and Caracalla were called *Castores* (*BMC* V, 196, no. 216f., pl. 32.8; *RIC* IV, 74-77, 213, no. 13, pl. 11.9 and 218, no. 38A), and in Sparta a new coin type with the Dioscuri standing with their horses in heraldic pose was introduced (GRUNAUER-VON HOERSCHELMANN 1978, 88f., gr. 49, pl. 27; gr. 54, pl. 28). The last emperors to use Dioscuri or their symbols on Spartan coinage were Gallienus and Salonina (GRUNAUER-VON HOERSCHELMANN 1978, 92f., gr. 55f., 58-60, pl. 28f.).

The cult of the Dioscuri seems to have been well organized through the whole period of Roman domination in Sparta. Due to the examinations of the epigraphic sources, we know that these hereditary priesthoods for the Dioscuri and Helena were held by wealthy families (CHRIMES 1949, 471-474). The priesthood of the cult of the Dioscuri is thus known to have been held by the Memmius family from the Augustan to at least the late Antonine period (SPAWFORTH 1985, 193-214). They also claimed the Dioscuri as their ancestors, and when the members of the Memmii are mentioned in the inscriptions, they are often characterized with the generation number after the Dioscuri, so, for example, Deximachus II as the 39th (SPAWFORTH 1985, 198f.), P. Memmius Deximachus IV as the 42nd, the latter born about A.D. 110-120 (*IG* V,1 537; SPAWFORTH 1985, 203). The Flavian, P. Memmius Deximachus III, was also connected with the training of the ephebes, a privilege confined to the Spartan aristocracy (SPAWFORTH 1985, 202; CHRIMES 1949, 111). Besides being in possession of a hereditary priesthood, a certain Pomponia Callistonice from the family of the Claudii was also in charge of the famous Dioskoureia. Together with another inscription found in Sparta, this is the only reference to a connection between the cult of the Dioscuri and the *agon* (*IG* V,1 602; *IG* V,1 559;

SPAWFORTH 1985, 239). These hereditary priesthoods are known to have still been existing during the Constantine period (SPAWFORTH 1984, 280).

A letter from Libanius to his Spartan friend Ausonius written in A.D. 365 rounds off the evidence for the cult of the Dioscuri in Sparta. The writer is concerned about the survival of the many pagan cult statues in Sparta, among these also those of the Dioscuri. The likely explanation of these and others still being extant might be that the sanctuaries were under the protection of the powerful priestly families (Lib. *Ep.* 1518; FATOUROS & KIRSCHER 1980, no. 5, 20f., 260-263; CARTLEDGE & SPAWFORTH 1989, 125).

The connection between the cult of the Dioscuri and the wealthy families thus seems to have established the basis for the cult through the centuries of Roman domination in Laconia. There is but slight evidence that the relief from Croceae and the bronze images at the quarries should be connected with one of these families in Sparta. Unfortunately we do not know the date of the statues of the Dioscuri, but the green porphyry was apparently quarried at least from the Augustan period. Apparently, C. Iulius Eurycles was credited with having furnished the great baths in Corinth with the famous Laconian porphyry (Paus. II.3.5). During his reign, there was a revival of the old cults and sanctuaries, and he was born into one of the privileged families which monopolized the highest offices for generations.

If the quarries were originally administered by one of these families which claimed descent from the Dioscuri, it would be obvious to place images of the Dioscuri there partly as a symbol of the "divine" power of the family partly in their capacity as protectors of Sparta. The quarries as private property would agree with the account of Strabo, but later the quarries seem to have been under direct Imperial control, as indicated by the inscription on the base of the relief. The representation of the Dioscuri on the relief of Eudoxus might thus be explained through the former connection between the owners of the quarries and the Dioscuri, and Eudoxus may have been inspired by the statues of the Dioscuri perhaps standing at the quarries during his lifetime.

Accademia di Danimarca
Via Omero 18
00197 Roma
Italy

# BIBLIOGRAPHY

| | |
|---|---|
| *AMuGS* | *Antike Münzen und geschnittene Steine.* |
| BLOCH, G. 1892 | Dispensator, *Dar-Sagl* II, 280-286. |
| BLOUET, A. 1838 | *Expédition scientifique de Morée* III. Paris. |
| BOULVERT, G. 1970 | *Esclaves et affranchis impériaux sous le Haut-Empire romain.* Napoli. |
| 1974 | *Domestique et fonctionnaire sous le Haut-Empire romain.* Paris. |
| CARLIER, P. 1984 | *La royauté en Grèce avant Alexandre.* Strassbourg. |
| CARTLEDGE, P. & SPAWFORTH, A. 1989 | *Hellenistic and Roman Sparta.* London. |
| CHANTRAINE, H. 1967 | *Freigelassene und Sklaven im Dienst der römischen Kaiser.* Wiesbaden. |
| CHRIMES, K.M.T. 1949 | *Ancient Sparta.* Manchester. |
| CRAWFORD, M.H. 1974 | *Roman Republican Coinage* I-III. Cambridge. |
| DÖRIG, J. 1957 | Lysipps letztes Werk, *JdI* 72, 19-43. |
| DUBOIS, Ch. 1908 | *Étude sur l'administration et l'exploitation (marbres, porphyre, granit etc.) dans le monde Romain.* Paris. |
| DWORAKOWSKA, A. 1975 | *Quarries in Ancient Greece.* Wroclaw. |
| 1983 | *Quarries in Roman Provinces.* Wroclaw. |
| FATOUROS, G. & KRISCHER, T. 1980 | *Libanios Briefe.* München. |
| FORSTER, E.S. 1904 | South-western Laconia, *BSA* 10, 158-189. |
| GABRICI, E. 1927 | *Monetazione del bronzo nella Sicilia antica.* Roma. |
| GNECCHI, F. 1912 | *I medaglioni romani* I-III. Milano. |
| GRUNAUER-VON HOERSCHELMANN, S. 1978 | Die Münzprägung der Lakedaimoner. Berlin (= *AMuGS* VII). |
| GURY, F. 1986 | Dioskouroi/Castores, *LIMC* III, 608-635. |
| HEMBERG, B. 1955 | *Anax, Anassa and Anakes.* Uppsala. |
| HENZEN, G. 1857 | *Bullettino dell'Istituto di Corrispondenza Archeologica*, 157f. |
| HERMARY, A. 1986 | Dioskouroi, *LIMC* III, 567-593. |
| HIRSCHFELD, O. 1905 | *Die kaiserlichen Verwaltungsbeamten bis auf Diocletian.* Berlin. |
| KAHRSTEDT, U. 1954 | *Das wirtschaftliche Geschick Griechenlands in der Kaiserzeit.* Bern. |
| KHANOUSSI, M. 1988 | Disp(ensator) M(armorum) N(umidicorum), *Africa* 10, 208-211. |
| LE ROY, C. 1961 | Un relief aux Dioscures à Krokeai, *BCH* 85, 206-215. |
| LIEBENAM, W. 1903 | Dispensator, *RE* V, 1189-1198. |
| *LIMC* | *Lexicon Iconographicum Mythologiae Classicae.* |
| NILSSON, M.P. 1967 | *Geschichte der griechischen Religion* I (3. ed.) München. |

| | |
|---|---|
| PICARD, Ch. 1958 | Le Dioscure à la promoté chevaline, BCH 82, 435-465. |
| PIRZIO BIROLI STEFANELLI, L. 1977 | Tabelle fittili tarantine relative al culto dei Dioscuri, *ArchCl* 29, 310-398. |
| POULSEN, B. 1991 | The Dioscuri and ruler ideology, *SOsl* 66, 115-141. |
| SPAWFORTH, A. 1984 | Notes on the Third century AD in Spartan Epigraphy, *BSA* 79, 263-288. |
| 1985 | Families at Roman Sparta and Epidaurus: Some Prosopographical Notes, *BSA* 80, 191-258. |
| THOMPSON, M. 1961 | *The New Style Silver Coinage of Athens.* New York. |
| TOD, M.N. & WACE, A.B.J. 1906 | *A Catalogue of the Spartan Museum.* Oxford. |
| TRUMMER, R. 1980 | *Die Denkmäler des Kaiserkults in der römischen Provinz Achaia.* Graz. |
| VULIC, N. 1900 | Dispensator, *Diz.Epgr.* II, 1920-1923. |
| WEAVER, P.R.C. 1972 | *Familia Caesaris.* Cambridge. |
| WIDE, S. 1893 | *Lakonische Kulte.* Leipzig. |
| WOODWARD, A.M. 1928-30 | The Theatre: Architectural Remains, *BSA* 30, 151-240. |
| ZANKER, P. 1972 | *Forum Romanum.* Tübingen. |
| ØRSTED, P. 1985 | *Roman Imperial Economy and Romanization.* Copenhagen. |

# NOTES

1. PICARD 1958 groups these monuments, but his interpretations of the horse-protomes as a symbol of the epiphany of the Dioscuri is doubtful. For other examples, HERMARY 1986, no. 51-54; GURY 1986, no. 27-33; TOD & WACE 1906, 118, 285. The Spartan relief from the 2nd century A.D. (HERMARY 1986, 50) and a coin type issued during the Antonine period (GRUNAUER-VON HOERSCHELMANN 1978, 83, 97f., gr. 39, pl. 25) both seem to reflect a statue group of the Dioscuri in Sparta itself. Horse-protomes alone occur already on the votive tablets from Tarentum dating from the late 4th century B.C. (PIRZIO BIROLI STEFANELLI 1977, 373, Ia, pl. XCIX, 2)
2. Representations of the Dioscuri with phiale are rare outside Magna Graecia. An Athenian tetradrachm and coins from Phoenician Tripolis (156/155 B.C., HERMARY 1986, 87; THOMPSON 1961, 475-492, pl. 48f.; Caligula/Claudius, HERMARY 1986, 82; *BMC* Phoenicia 208, 38 pl. 27.6 respectively) are isolated occurrences.
3. This reading is among others followed by M. Sasel Kos, *Inscriptiones Latinae in Graecia repertae. Additamenta ad CIL* III (Firenze 1979) no. 41.
4. Neither CHANTRAINE (1967, 183) nor BOULVERT (1970, 234) observed Le Roy's suggestions, but they have been welcomed by scholars of Roman Sparta (CARTLEDGE & SPAWFORTH 1989, 169).
5. For a full list of the different types of *dispensatores* with references, see BLOCH 1892 and VULIC 1900.
6. Strabo says that the quarry is "in Taygetus", but this quarry produced only marble of poor quality, and Strabo must have meant Croceae. See R. BALADIE, *Le Péloponnèse de Strabon. Étude de géographie historique.* Paris 1980. Against this: CHRIMES 1949, 73-74.
7. ZANKER 1972, 18f. The Emperor's use of the Dioscuri is discussed by POULSEN 1991.

# HELLENISTIC BLACK-GLAZE WARE FROM THE TEMPLE OF CASTOR AND POLLUX IN THE FORUM ROMANUM. THE STAMPS

KAREN SLEJ

In the following, the purpose of the stamps on black-glazed ware, starting from a series of stamped sherds from the excavations of the temple of Castor and Pollux in Rome, will be discussed. By discussing the technique, production, and distribution of the Italic black-glazed pottery it is hoped to throw light on the function of the stamps.

Black-glazed ware appears both in the Greek and in the Italic area. In Greece, especially Athens, it is well documented. The black-glazed pottery was produced from the second half of the 6th cent. to the beginning of the 1st cent. B.C. It was widely exported to Italy in the 4th and 3rd cent. B.C. and is often called *Precampana* ware in the publications. Inspired by the Greek black-glazed pottery, a local production was commenced in Italy in the 4th cent. B.C. As Morel has remarked, it is found at nearly every habitation-site and in many tombs and is therefore an important tool for the archaeologist in understanding the society of the Middle and Late Republic (MOREL 1981b, 81).

I shall briefly mention the black-glazed wares important for the following discussion:

*Attic black-glaze:* A ware produced in Athens from the 6th to the 1st cent. B.C. and exported in large amounts to the Western Mediterranean in the 4th-3rd cent. From the 5th cent., the decoration consisted of stamps, often of floral motifs, which are combined by incised wavy lines. The stamps are often seen in negative.

*"Atelier des petites estampilles"*: This production originated in Central Italy, possibly Latium, in 300-265 B.C. The characteristic shape is a simple bowl, F 2783 or 2784, and the decoration consists of simple,

often inaccurate stamps. These are arranged either with one central or 4-5 parallel stamps. There is great variation in the motifs, but the palmette or rosette are the most common. Figural motifs as well as monograms are also found.

*"Atelier des anses en oreille"*: The production of several workshops in the coastal area of Northern Etruria dating to the second half of the 3rd and especially the 2nd cent. B.C. The favorite shape is a low cup with two horizontal handles shaped as ears. The decoration consists of two kinds of stamps: the palmette and the lotus combined with concentric circles and chattering[1].

*Campana A*: A ware of reddish clay produced in Naples and perhaps Ischia. Dating from the 4th cent. to the middle of the 1st cent. B.C. and widely exported from 220 B.C. The decoration consists of a central rosette, in the oldest examples large and complex, and in the younger small and simple, or four radially placed ivy leaves surrounded by a circle of chattering.

*Campana B*: A ware made from pale clay possibly produced in Etruria in the 2nd and 1st cent. B.C. Large and widespread export. The decoration is complex and consists of 4-5 round or square radially placed stamps surrounded by concentric circles and fine chattering. In the 1st cent. there are examples of monograms.

*Arretine black-glaze:* Close to Campana B ware produced in Arezzo in the 2nd – 1st cent. B.C. and exported in large amounts. From c. 50 B.C. it develops into the Arretine terra sigillata. The decorative repertoire is close to Campana B.

## Decoration

When the Attic black-glazed pottery was decorated it was with incised, and later stamped floral motifs. Talcott surmises that the idea for the stamped decoration came from metalwork, but also stresses that the stamps on the Attic black-glazed ware begin at the same time as the stamps on amphorae. She does not, however, see a connection (TALCOTT 1935, 489-90). Others have thought that Corinth was the birthplace of this kind of decoration, for stamped and incised decoration continued in use on Corinthian coarse pottery imported to Athens well into the 5th cent. B.C. whereas the Athenian potters seem to have abandoned this kind of decoration on coarse ware in the middle of the 6th cent. B.C. (SPARKES & TALCOTT 1970, 24-25). In Athens closed as well as open vase shapes were stamped and the earliest motif was the palmette which had long been in favour on Attic black- and red-figured pottery as well as in architecture.

The Italic black-glazed wares were decorated with stamped decoration like their Attic models. It is, however, important to note that it is only a minor part of the black-glazed production that was decorated. The Italic workshops often chose a decoration which at first imitated the Attic and later acquired its own expressions.

## *The technique of stamping*

So far, no dies are known from the black-glaze ceramic workshops found in Italy, and their material is therefore uncertain. They were either made of perishable material, or excavators have not been able to interpret possible relics or traces in the excavations. No stamp dies are known from Athenian black-glaze workshops, but clay dies used in the ornamentation of Megarian bowls are known from the Athenian Agora (ROTROFF 1982, 5, no. 411-413) and from Corinth (WEINBERG 1952, pl. 135, 2851: Corinth MF 2298). Corbett has attempted, using the die from Corinth as basis, to clarify the process of stamping (CORBETT 1955, 173). To produce a stamp die, a matrix was made in clay or possibly in wood. A convex surface was required to create a palmette of equal depth showing all the petals, and it was therefore necessary to make a concave matrix; this was probably produced by an expert. The

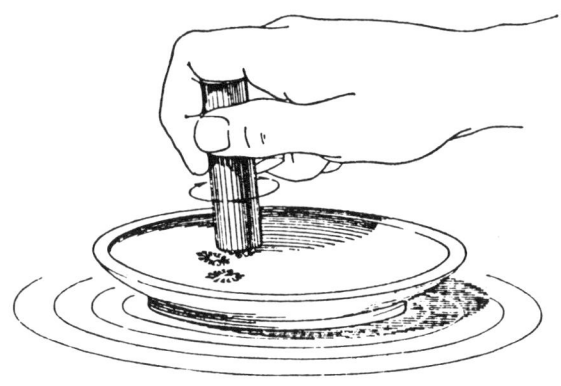

Fig. 1. The impress process
(from SPARKES & TALCOTT 1970).

work consisting of pressing clay into the matrix to produce the die could be done by anyone, and the matrix would have been used to produce a number of dies. The die was then pressed into the bottom of the vase with a rotating movement of the hand, in this manner the convex surface was rolled over the surface of the clay so that the petals became represented with equal depth (CORBETT 1955, 173).

*Fig. 1*

In the "atelier des petites estampilles", Morel believes that coins were used as dies, because some of the motifs used derive from *aes grave* (MOREL 1969, 107-110). Rotroff believes that stamps used in the production of Megarian bowl were possibly made by copying directly the relief ornaments found on metal bowls, and this possibility should also be considered for the production of dies for Italic black-glaze wares (ROTROFF 1982, 4). Also other stamped wares give ground to speculation over the material of the dies. Grace surmises that on Greek amphorae, which make their appearance in the 6th cent. B.C., some of the stamps were made from dies in a hard material, while others were made of wood, which can be seen from the blurred outlines and traces of splinters (GRACE 1935, 422, 427). For the manufacture of the Roman tile dies, Steinby thinks that wood was used, because of traces of wood splinters (STEINBY 1978, 1495). Moreover wooden dies have been found in Egypt, and Steinby feels that boxwood was suitable because of its hardness. As a rule the stamps on tiles and amphorae are larger, so wood splinters will be more easily discernable than on the small stamps on glazed pottery. Metal dies for tile-stamps have been found from Late Republican, Augustan, and Neronian times (STEINBY 1978, 1495).

It is difficult to say how long a die could be used. No investigation of this aspect has been made on the Italic black-glazed pottery, whereas two groups of Attic black-glaze from two different find complexes have been studied. Corbett has studied two large deposits from the Athenian Agora with fragments of more than 50 stamped black-glazed vases (CORBETT 1955, 172). He is able to document that the palmettes were made from four rather similar dies, which could indicate that the die had a long life and could be reproduced with the same matrix. Talcott (1935, 487), on the other hand, shows on black-glazed material from several Attic workshops that no two stamps were made by the same die. She therefore believes that the dies had a very short life especially where the palmettes are sharply outlined. In the "atelier des petites estampilles" there is a great variety of different motifs. On the material from

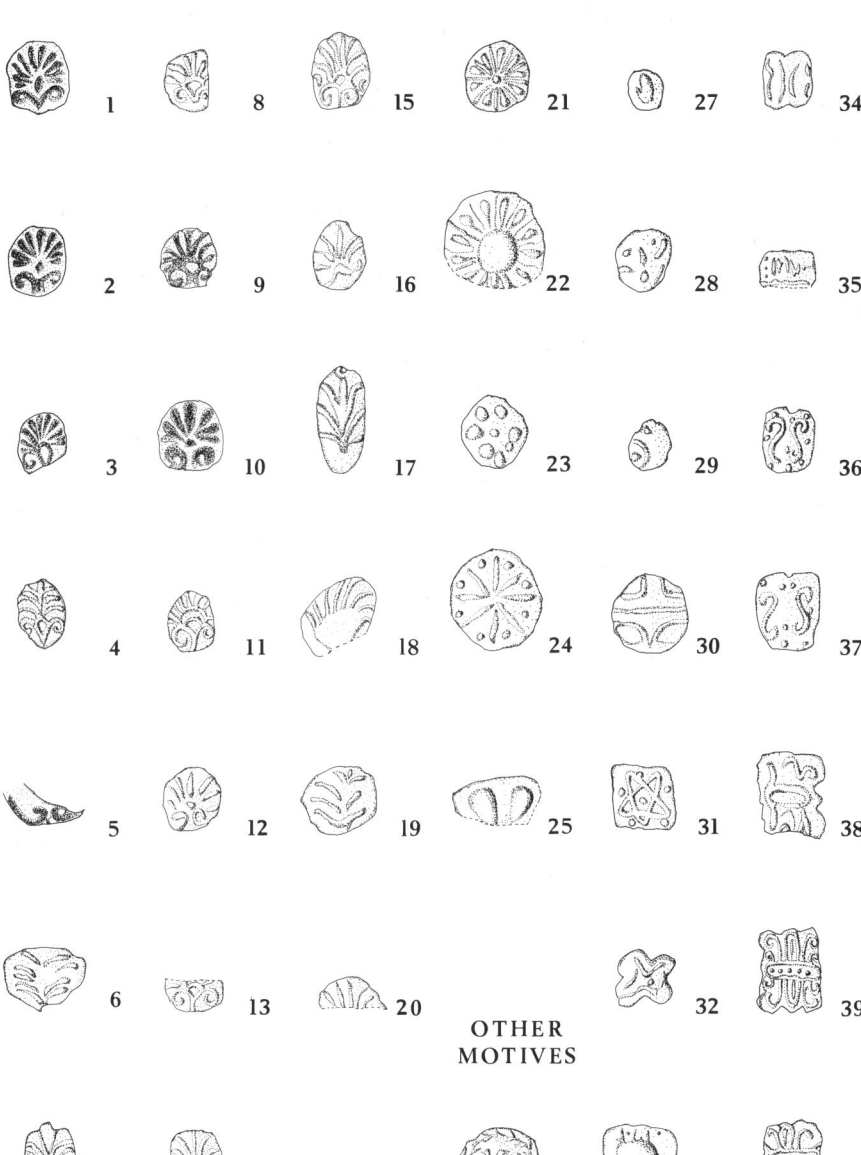

Fig. 2. The stamped motifs. Scale 1:2. (drawn by Karen Slej and Trine Neble).

Olbia in Liguria, Bats has shown that of 56 stamps, only 9 are seen two or three times (BATS 1976, 76). He does not, however, mention whether they are from the same die or only of the same motif.

## The stamped ware from the Temple of Castor and Pollux[2]

The black-glazed pottery here under discussion comes from the Scandinavian excavations of the temple of Castor and Pollux on the Forum Romanum. These excavations took place in the years 1983-87 and uncovered a large ceramic material. A large part of this pottery comes from unstratified trenches, i.e. the earth fill of the large podium, which has the date 117 B.C. as a *terminus ante quem* according to the literary sources (for the excavations as a whole see NIELSEN & ZAHLE 1986, SANDE & ZAHLE 1988, and NIELSEN 1990).

*Fig. 2* About 1000 diagnostic black-glazed sherds have been registered. Of these there are 273 bases, of which 40 bear one or more stamps in the tondo. 20 of these show different types of palmettes, 5 have rosettes, and the last 15 have either a figurative or an unidentifiable motif. The state of conservation of the material prohibits an ascription of the bases to specific forms in Morel's typology. It is only possible to give the base
*Fig. 3* type and discern whether it comes from a bowl or a patera. In fig. 3, I
*Fig. 4* show which types of bases carry the different motifs, and in fig. 4 the impress directions of the individual catalogue numbers.

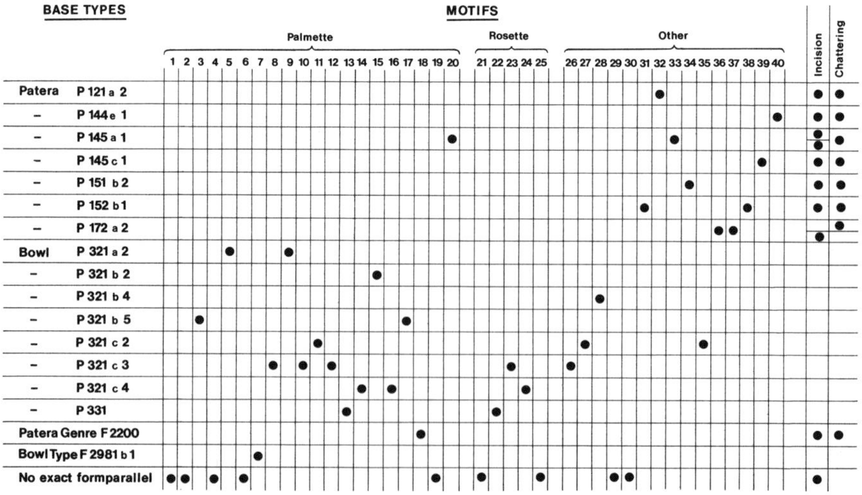

Fig. 3. The base types seen in relation to the motifs (drawing by Karen Slej and Poul Christensen).

## Impress Directions

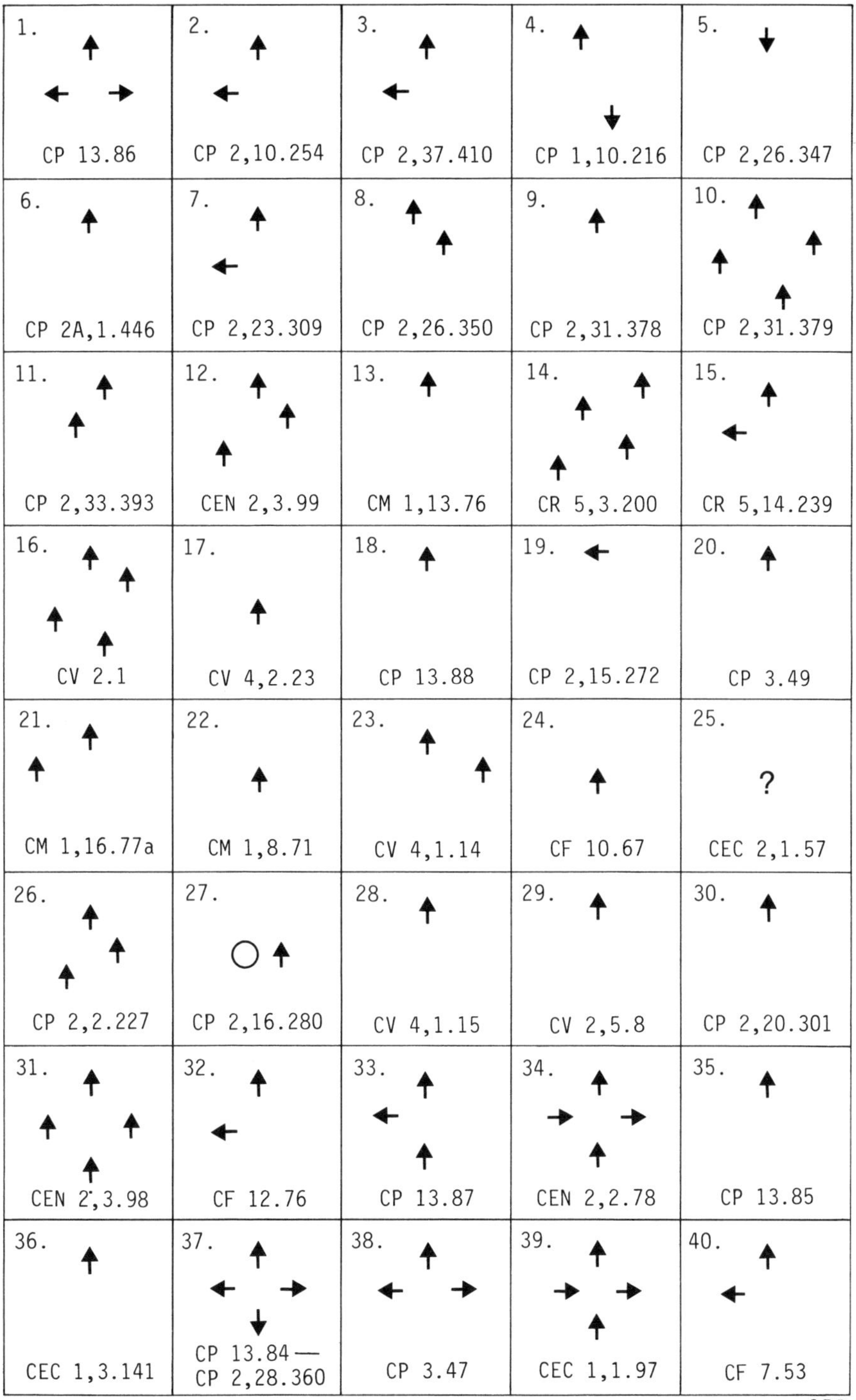

| | | | | |
|---|---|---|---|---|
| 1. ↑ ← → | 2. ↑ ← | 3. ↑ ← | 4. ↑ ↓ | 5. ↓ |
| CP 13.86 | CP 2,10.254 | CP 2,37.410 | CP 1,10.216 | CP 2,26.347 |
| 6. ↑ | 7. ↑ ← | 8. ↑ ↑ | 9. ↑ | 10. ↑ ↑ ↑ |
| CP 2A,1.446 | CP 2,23.309 | CP 2,26.350 | CP 2,31.378 | CP 2,31.379 |
| 11. ↑ ↑ | 12. ↑ ↑ ↑ | 13. ↑ | 14. ↑ ↑ ↑ | 15. ↑ ← |
| CP 2,33.393 | CEN 2,3.99 | CM 1,13.76 | CR 5,3.200 | CR 5,14.239 |
| 16. ↑ ↑ ↑ | 17. ↑ | 18. ↑ | 19. ← | 20. ↑ |
| CV 2.1 | CV 4,2.23 | CP 13.88 | CP 2,15.272 | CP 3.49 |
| 21. ↑ ↑ | 22. ↑ | 23. ↑ ↑ | 24. ↑ | 25. ? |
| CM 1,16.77a | CM 1,8.71 | CV 4,1.14 | CF 10.67 | CEC 2,1.57 |
| 26. ↑ ↑ | 27. ○ ↑ | 28. ↑ | 29. ↑ | 30. ↑ |
| CP 2,2.227 | CP 2,16.280 | CV 4,1.15 | CV 2,5.8 | CP 2,20.301 |
| 31. ↑ ↑ ↑ ↑ | 32. ↑ ← | 33. ↑ ← ↑ | 34. ↑ → → ↑ | 35. ↑ |
| CEN 2,3.98 | CF 12.76 | CP 13.87 | CEN 2,2.78 | CP 13.85 |
| 36. ↑ ← | 37. ↑ ← → ↓ | 38. ↑ ← → | 39. ↑ → ↑ | 40. ↑ ← |
| CEC 1,3.141 | CP 13.84 — CP 2,28.360 | CP 3.47 | CEC 1,1.97 | CF 7.53 |

Fig. 4. The impress directions (drawing by Karen Slej and Poul Christensen).

The stamped bases can primarily be ascribed to three classes of black-glaze: 1) Attic or imitation, or Malacena ware from the 4th and beginning of the 3rd cent. B.C., 2) Etrusco-Latial ware from the beginning of the 3rd cent., and 3) Campana B / Arretine black-glaze from the 2nd, especially the second half of the 2nd cent. B.C. The Etrusco-Latial class is problematic. In form and decoration it is close to the "atelier des petites estampilles" as defined by Morel, but in the clay and in the glaze it differs in that the glaze is fairly thin, carelessly applied, and often metallic, and the clay contains much mica and other inclusions clearly discernible to the naked eye. A provenience determined by chemical analysis could perhaps help solve this discrepancy.

When examining the parallels, one must try to distinguish whether the same die or only the same motif has been used. This is very difficult, for in most cases the publications of black-glazed ware from Italy bring the stamps only in sketches or in photographs. A search for parallels is therefore only tentative. I have chosen parallels so close to our material that I consider them to be the same stamp motifs, and only in one case is it reasonable to say that the same die has been used, see cat.no. 26. Another problem is the fact that many of the stamps are so simple in idea and execution that dies were easy to make, and the same idea could easily arise in several different workshops at the same time. Moreover I wish to stress the fact that even if parallels are found, they say nothing of the place of manufacture, only of distribution, if the stamps are regarded as workshop-marks. I shall return to this later.

The parallels known to me are found in the Etrusco-Latial material and in the Campana B wares. In the Etrusco-Latial material, the parallels come from locations already represented in Morel's distribution map for the "atelier des petites estampilles" (MOREL 1969, 95). The Roman parallels prevail with 8 examples, Olbia with 4, while Carsoli, Gabii, and Roselle have one each i.e. Rome, Liguria, Latium, and Northern Etruria. In the Campana B material, the Roman parallels again prevail with 5 examples, Bolsena with 2 and Carsoli one. This is not unusual, for it is still uncertain where in Etruria Campana B was produced, though this ware is often found in Rome.

Is it at all possible to say anything about the purpose and meaning of the stamps? To answer this question it is necessary to look at the production of the Italic black-glazed pottery.

## Production of Italic black-glazed pottery

Virtually nothing is known from the ancient written sources about the production of black-glazed pottery, or at all about ceramics, although Varro (*De l.l.* 5,50) does mention a region – *in figlinis* – Rome on the Esquiline, and kilns from here are known from the Late Republic (SCOTT RYBERG 1940, 120; PETRACCA & VIGNA 1985, 133). Ceramics played an important role in Roman daily life, but potters are not mentioned in the written sources. Bats believes that the use of pottery is closely connected with the local regional products (BATS 1987, 197). This is most likely also the case in Rome, but as yet workshops which did produce black-glaze have not been found, even though a number of products are considered to be of Roman manufacture: Heraklesschalen, Roman type D and E, and pocola-Ware (MOREL 1985a, 174). Rome in Late Republican and Early Imperial periods is often mentioned as a centre of consumption rather than of production, but it is now known that Roman workshops produced architectural terracottas which were distributed over a radius of 50 km (TORTORELLA 1981, 239). Rome was also, even during the great urbanistic developments, largely self-sufficient with bricks and tiles (STEINBY 1981, 239). I therefore believe it to be a reasonable assumption that there were in Rome a number of black-glaze ceramic workshops, not least in the light of the material from the temple of Castor and Pollux which has most parallels in Rome. None of the workshops that produced black-glaze known from Italy can give us any idea about how the production was organized, since the finds mostly consist of only waste and rings for stacking (*Napoli Antica* 1985, 378-379). Morel sees a marked difference in production before the 2nd Punic war and after (MOREL 1981b, 83). The most important differences for this discussion are:

| *Before the end of the 2nd Punic war* | *After the 2nd Punic war* |
|---|---|
| 1. Flourishing high quality production with limited diffusion | Mediocre production with limited diffusion |
| 2. No Italic wares are produced in large numbers | Some Italic wares are produced in large numbers |
| 3. The small workshops resist standardization | Standardization is prevalent everywhere |
| 4. Decoration, when found, is often complex | Decoration, when found, is very simple |

| | |
|---|---|
| 5. Monograms are found | Monograms are found very rarely; the pottery is anonymous |

The greatest difference is that before the end of the 2nd Punic war there existed a large number of small production units, while later on there was a tendency to centralize in large potteries. Even a workshop like the "atelier des petites estampilles" had a relative modest production in comparison with the Campana A ware. Morel has calculated that in a period of 150 years 9 million Campana A ware vases were exported to Gaul (MOREL 1986, 344). This figure is elicited from an estimation that 200 wine-carrying boats each year set sail for Gaul. If one out of 20 of these ships carried 6,000 black-glaze Campana A vases, as did the wreck at Grand Congloué, it would give 60,000 a year. Morel believes that this estimate is conservative, though it is only the export to Gaul which is under discussion here. Carandini distinguishes between several different types of workshops: 1) small artisans which dominate until the 3rd cent. B.C., 2) urban slaves, which are most common in the 2nd and 1st cent. B.C. and, 3) large workshops known especially from the Flavian period (CARANDINI 1981, 255-259). Morel does not believe that one can set up a chronological differentiation between groups 2 and 3, especially because the Campana A ware was produced under conditions which seem to imply large workshops (MOREL 1982b, 197-198). Possibly the pottery was produced by slaves, though there is no testimony to slave systems concerning the black-glaze ceramic production.

To get an idea about the organization of the production of the black-glaze wares and about the meaning of the stamps, it is necessary to look at other productions of pottery. Terra sigillata, which was produced as a table ware for the masses from the middle of the 1st cent. B.C., as a successor to the black-glaze wares, was in Arezzo produced in over 100 workshops according to the stamps. It is, however, not clear how many of the workshops were active at any one time (GUCCI 1985, 376). Some of the workshops had sixty employees, others only four (GUCCI 1981, 102-103). A similar workshop system may have been used in producing Campana A in Naples, though only two workshops have been identified (MOREL 1986, 342). It appears that some of the terra sigillata workshops did not cover the full process of manufacture, the same kilns were used for firing the wares of several workshops (COMFORT 1940a, 191; GUCCI 1985, 377). this phenomenon is also known in La

Graufesenque in Gaul, where the potters seem to have been freemen and not slaves as was the case in Arezzo (DELPLACE 1978, 68-69). Here the stamps serve to identify the different workshops. This, however, does not explain why all terra sigillata and all black-glaze was not stamped. In another production, bricks and tiles, it appears that only a minor part were stamped, and it might be possible that when the bricks and tiles were stacked in the kiln only the top-most were marked, in order to distinguish the work of each slave, surmising that he was paid by the piece.

## Area of distribution of black-glazed ware

Most of the Italic black-glazed ware had a very limited distribution, but the Campana A, B, and C as well as the "atelier des petites estampilles" were transported far afield. The Campana B ware seems to have been distributed over land, whereas the other wares were transported by sea. From the shipwrecks examined it is evident that the black-glazed pottery was hardly ever transported as the only cargo, but was a by-product on a ship most often carrying amphorae. The Riou and Punta Scaletta wrecks may be exceptions to the rule (MOREL 1986, 352). Further, only in a few cases, a connection between manufacturer and buyer can be seen, e.g. the Heraklesschalen, which are aimed at the cult of Hercules (MOREL 1981b, 86).

For the large productions, we must envisage an effective and established distribution net functioning on the basis of intermediaries, *negotiatores*. Sallust mentions Italic *negotiatores* in Numidia (Sallust, *Iug.*, 21,2; 26,3) to which large amounts of Campana A ware were exported in the 2nd cent. B.C., exactly the period Sallust is treating (MOREL 1981b, 93).

## The stamped motifs

On leafing through the major publications in order to find material comparable to the material from the temple of Castor and Pollux, I discovered that some motifs occured again, and again: the antithetical C's, the two-handled jar, the head of Minerva, a dolphin, a hand, and a leaf. Usually they are ascribed to the "atelier des petites estampilles". None of these motifs are found in the Castor and Pollux material, though several of them as the pentagram with dots, and the antithetical S's are easily recognizable but unparallelled (cat. nos. 31, 36, and 37).

The latter two cat. nos. 36, and 37, and cat. nos. 9, and 14 have their only parallels within this very material. Two of the motifs cat. nos. 34, and 35 look like monograms, albeit illegible. Both are dated to the 2nd cent. B.C. and belong to the Campana B class. Monograms are found in the material of the second half of the 3rd cent. B.C., but have a renaissance in the 1st cent. B.C. Though the monograms may be short for names it is impossible for us to identify the bearer of the name. Who signed his name on the pot: was it the owner of the workshop, his foreman, or a worker, and if a worker, what function did he have in the production line? (MOREL 1983, 22, and note 9 with further bibliography; MOREL 1988, 54-55).

In the "atelier des petites estampilles" there is a great variety of stamps, whereas the "atelier des anses en oreille" and the Campana A ware have very uniform and standardized motifs.

## The purpose of stamping

Above all, the stamps obviously had a decorative effect, even though it should be emphasized that only a smaller part of all black-glaze productions are decorated with stamps, and several productions, such as the "atelier des petites estampilles", carry a slovenly and indistinct stamping, where the decorative effect is very limited.

Perhaps the potter chose to stamp only selected examples, so that the customer could choose in the shop, though it is difficult to imagine such a demand in the case of long distance trade, where there are middlemen. If the stamps denote workshops their recognition will have the greatest importance near the place of origin, because it is here that the vases could be chosen from the specific workshop, while the stamps from the point of view of export have greater importance as decorative elements.

In the material from the "atelier des anses en oreille" in Bolsena two identical dies are rarely found, while the stamp motifs are similar. Balland (1969, 94) believes that this is due to production taking place, not in one workshop, but in several, where the finds give us only a limited part of the production.

In the small workshops of the 4th and 3rd cent. B.C., there seems to be no reason to use workshop-stamp, unless there were risks of confusion during production. Such a risk could arise during firing, if, for economic or practical reasons, it was found necessary to fire the production of different workshops in the same kiln. The stamps would make it possible to identify the production of the different small workshops. But also the large workshops can have found a use for a production-stamp to identify the production of individual potters. Jones (1977, 15-16) has stated, in connection with terra sigillata and Samian ware, that the stamps should often be seen as a check on the output of the single workman. In this connection I want to draw attention to the potters' accounts from La Graufesenque, grafitti on plates from c. 40-60 A.D. giving a list of names, each with a corresponding number. They are interpreted by Oxe as check marks for the supervisor at the kiln, and the names are believed to belong to the same workshops, where the production of the single workman is indicated (COMFORT 1940b, 1345-1346). The problem is that such a small part of black-glaze ware is stamped. A tempting assumption is that it is only the uppermost ware or wares in the kiln which are stamped, though an argument against this idea is that on several of the stamped specimens there are traces of the ring from the stacking in the kiln.

In conclusion: a definitive explanation of the stamping of black-glaze wares has not been given here. It will be of decisive importance to ascertain the proportion of stamped vases, and whether the stamps possibly had a different significance through the centuries. Also the creation of a *corpus* of the decorative elements, combined with an investigation of proveniences, is imperative.

# CATALOGUE
PALMETTES

1.- CP 13.86. Palmette. In negative. *Fig.* 2,1.
On a base, no form parallel, 3 of possibly 4 left radially impressed.
Attic or imitation, 4th cent. B.C.

2.- CP 2,10.254. Palmette. In negative. *Fig.* 2,2.
On a base with no form parallel, one and almost a second preserved of possibly 4, radially impressed.
Attic or imitation, 4th or beg. of 3rd cent. B.C.

3.- CP 2,37.410. Palmette. In negative. *Fig.* 2,3.
On a base, type P 321b5, one and small part of a second preserved of possibly 4, impressed radially.
Attic imitation or Etrusco-Latial, beg. of 3rd cent. B.C.

4.- CP 1,10.216. Palmette. In relief. *Fig.* 2,4.
On a base with no form parallel, one and part of a second left of possibly 4, probably radially impressed.
Resembling Malacena ware, 4th or beg. of 3rd cent. B.C.

5.- CP 2,26.347. Palmette. In negative. *Fig.* 2,5.
On a base, type P 321a2, only part of one preserved. Possibly 4 around tondo. Hastily incised circle surrounding.
Etrusco-Latial, end of 4th – beg. of 3rd cent. B.C.

6.- CP 2A,1.446. Palmette. In relief. *Fig.* 2,6.
On a base with no form parallel, one preserved of possibly 4. Surrounded by concentric circles.
Etrusco-Latial?, end of 4th – or beg. of 3rd cent. B.C.

7.- CP 2,23.309. Palmette. In relief. *Fig.* 2,7.
On a base, type F 2981b 1, one and almost a second preserved of possibly 4, radially impressed.
Etrusco-Latial, beg. of 3rd cent. B.C.
*Parallels*: Olbia – BATS 1976, 64, fig. 2:3.

8.- CP 2,26.350. Palmette. In relief. *Fig.* 2,8.
On a base, type P 321c3, one and half of another preserved of possibly 4, impressed in parallel.
Etrusco-Latial, beg. of 3rd cent. B.C.

9.- CP 2,31.378. Palmette. In negative. *Fig.* 2,9.
On a base, type P 321a2, one preserved of possibly 4.
Etrusco-Latial, beg. of 3rd cent. B.C.

10.- CP 2,31.379. Palmette. In negative. *Fig.* 2,10.
On a base, type P 321c3, 3 and most of a 4th preserved, impressed radially.
Etrusco-Latial, beg. of 3rd cent. B.C.
*Parallels*: Rome – MOREL 1965, cat. 453.
Gabii – BALLESTER 1987, 51, fig. 3:2375.

11.- CP 2,33.393. Palmette. In relief. *Fig.* 2,11.
On a base, type P 321c2, one and part of a second preserved of possibly 4, impressed in parallel.
Etrusco-Latial, beg. of 3rd cent. B.C.
*Parallels*: Olbia – BATS 1976, 64, fig. 2:4.

12.- CEN 2,3.99. Palmette. In relief. *Fig.* 2,12
On a base, type P 321c3, 3 of possibly 4 preserved, impressed in parallel.
Etrusco-Latial, beg. of 3rd cent. B.C.
*Parallels*: Carsoli – CEDERNA 1951, 209 no. 24, fig. 15.
Rome – BERNARDINI 1986, cat. of decoration no. 111.
Roselle – BOCCI 1965, 149, fig. 22:1713
Olbia – BATS 1976, 68 no 20, fig. 3:20.

13.- CM 1,13.76. Palmette. In relief. *Fig.* 2,13.
On a base, type P 331, part of one of possibly 4 preserved.
Etrusco-Latial, beg. of 3rd cent. B.C.

14.- CR 5,3.200. Palmette. In relief. *Fig.* 2,14.
On a base, type P 321c4, 4 impressed in parallel slightly off center of tondo.
Etrusco-Latial, beg. of 3rd cent. B.C.

15.- CR 5,14.239. Palmette. In relief. *Fig.* 2,15.
On a base, type P 321b2, 2 preserved of possibly 4, probably impressed radially.
Etrusco-Latial, beg. of 3rd cent. B.C.
*Parallels*: Olbia – BATS 1976, 66 no. 15, fig.3:15.

16.- CV 2.1. Palmette. In relief. *Fig.* 2,16.
On a base, type P 321c4, 3 and part of a 4th impressed in parallel slightly off center, probably two different dies.
Etrusco-Latial, beg. of 3rd cent. B.C.
*Parallels*: Rome – BERNARDINI 1986, Cat. of decoration no.105.

17.- CV 4,2.23. Palmette. In relief. *Fig.* 2,17.
On a base, type P 321b5, one impressed almost in center of tondo.
Etrusco-Latial, beg. of 3rd cent. B.C.

18.- CP 13.88. Palmette. In relief. *Fig.* 2,18.
On a base, type F 2280, one of possibly 4 left. Surrounded by chattering and incised circles.
Campanian B, 2nd cent. B.C.
*Parallels*: Bolsena – BALLAND 1969, 156, pl. 16:6.

19.- CP 2,15.272. Palmette. In relief. *Fig.* 2,19.
On a base with no form parallel, one of possibly 4 preserved. Surrounded by chattering and incised circles.
Campanian B, 2nd. cent. B.C.

20.- CP 3.49. Part of palmette. In relief. *Fig.* 2,20.
On a base, type P 145a1, only part of one of possibly 4 left. Surrounded by chattering and incised circles.
Campanian B, 2/2 of 2nd cent. B.C.

## ROSETTE

21.- CM 1,16.77a. Rosette with 9 petals and dividing ribs. In relief. *Fig.* 2,21.
On a base with no form parallel, one and part of another preserved of probably 4.
Etrusco-Latial, beg. of 3rd cent. B.C.

22.- CM 1,8.71. Rosette with 12 petals, a large central dot, and 12 dividing ribs. In relief. *Fig.* 2,22.
On a base, type P 331, one central stamp.
Etrusco-Latial, beg. of 3rd cent. B.C.

23.- CV 4,1.14. Rosette with 7 round petals around central dot. In relief. *Fig.* 2,23.
On a base, type P 321c3, one and part of a second preserved, possibly 5 or 6 around tondo. Faint incised line around stamps.
Etrusco-Latial, beg. of 3rd cent. B.C.
*Parallels*: Rome – LYNGBY & SARTORIO 1965-67, 21, fig.18:33.
Rome – GIANFROTTA 1968-69, 37 no.21, fig. 8:21, tav XXVII, 5, 4.
Rome – MOREL 1965, cat. 217.
Rome – BERNARDINI 1986, cat. of decoration no 8.

24.- CF 10.67. Rosette with 8 petals seperated by 8 points. In relief. *Fig.* 2,24.
On a base, type P 321c4, one central stamp.
Technically close to Campanian A, but form within Etrusco-Latial repertoire, 3rd cent. B.C.
*Parallels*: Rome – GIANFROTTA 1968-69, 55, fig. 9:15

25.- CEC 2,1.57. Rosette. In relief. *Fig.* 2,25.
On a base with no form parallel, part of large rosette.
As clay is gray it could be Campanian C, but more likely it is misfired or secondary fired and rosette also seen in Etrusco-Latial production, 2/2 of 3rd cent. B.C.
*Parallels:* Luni – CAVALIERI MANASSE 1973, 106 no.CM 7627, tav. 84:16.

OTHER MOTIVES

26.- CP 2,2.227. Bird-like motif framed by a wreath. In relief. *Fig.* 2,26.
On a base, type P 321c3, 2 and part of 3rd preserved of 4 in all, impressed in parallel.
Etrusco-Latial, beg. of 3rd cent. B.C.
*Parallels:* Tarquinia – CAVAGNARO VANONI 1972, 160,156 fig.8.

27.- CP 2,16.280. Motif looking like a wollen glove. In relief. *Fig.* 2,27.
On a base, type P 321c2, one of possibly 4 preserved. Faint incised circle surrounding stamps.
Etrusco-Latial, beg. of 3rd cent. B.C.

28.- CV 4,1.15. Motif consisting of irregular set lines and points. In relief. *Fig.* 2,28.
On a base, type P 321b4, one preserved of at least 4.
Etrusco-Latial, beg. of 3rd cent. B.C.

29.- CV 2,5.8. Motif composed by a crescent and a dot. In relief. *Fig.* 2,29.
On a base with no form parallel, one preserved of possibly 4 or 5. Surrounded by incised lines.
Etrusco-Latial?, 3rd cent. B.C.

30.- CP 2,20.301. Motif composed by central line and 4 halfcircles, maybe a stylized palmette. In relief. *Fig.* 2,30.
On a base with no form parallel, one of possibly 4 preserved. Faint incised concentric line around stamps.
Etrusco-Latial or Campanian B, 2nd cent. B.C.

31.- CEN 2,3.98. Pentagram with points in between. In relief. *Fig.* 2,31.
On a base, type P 152b1, 4 around tondo, impressed in parallel. Surrounded by chattering and incised lines.
Campanian B, 2/2 of 2nd cent. B.C.
*Parallels:* Carsoli – CEDERNA 1951, 210 no. 48, fig. 15.

32.- CF 12.76. Motif looking like a stylized star. In relief. *Fig.*2,32.
On a base, type P 121a2, one and small part of second preserved of probably 4. Surrounded by incised lines and chattering.
Campanian B, 2/2 or middle of 2nd cent. B.C.

33.- CP 13.87. Motif composed by a central rectangular part with a handle, with small lines and blobs attached. In relief. *Fig.* 2,33.
On a base, type P 145a1, 2 and part of 2 more preserved impressed 2 x 2 in parallel. Surrounded by concentric incised lines.
Campanian B, 2/2 of 2nd cent. B.C.
*Parallels:* Rome – GIANFROTTA 1968-69, 41 no.176, fig. 3:176

34.- CEN 2,2.78. Motif composed by irregular set lines, maybe a monogram. In relief. *Fig.* 2,34.
On a base, type P 151b2, 4 around tondo, impressed in parallel 2 x 2. Surrounded by chattering and incised lines.
Campanian B, end of 2nd cent. B.C.
*Parallels:* Rome – GIANFROTTA 1968-69, 38 no. 16, fig.3:16.

35.- CP 13.85. Motif composed by a central line and small lines set transversally hereupon, maybe a monogram. In relief. *Fig.* 2,35.
On base, type P 321c2, only part of one preserved, possibly 4.
Surrounded by concentric incised lines and chattering.
Campanian B, end of 2nd cent. B.C.

36.- CEC 1,3.141. Motif composed by contraposed S's divided by points. In relief. *Fig.* 2,36.
On a base, type P 172a2, one preserved of possibly 4. Surrounded by chattering.
Campanian B, middle of 2nd or 2/2 of 2nd cent. B.C.

37.- CP 13.84 + CP 2,28.360. Motif composed by contraposed S's divided by points. In relief. *Fig.* 2,37.
On a base, type P 172a2, composed by two fragments joined, 3 and part of 4th preserved, impressed radially. Surrounded by two deeply incised concentric lines divided by more lightly incised lines.
Campanian B, or Arretine, 2/2 of 2nd cent. B.C.

38.- CP 3.47. Motif composed by central oval with irregular lines around it, maybe a stylized palmette. In relief. *Fig.* 2,38.
On a base, type P 152b1, one entirely preserved and small fragments of two more, indicating 4 in all, impressed radially.
Campanian B, middle or 2/2 of 2nd cent. B.C.

39.- CEC 1,1.97. Motif composed by central oval with 5 points wherefrom comes 2 leaves and 4 curled lines. Possibly a stylized palmette. In relief. *Fig.* 2,39.
On a base, type P 145c1, 4 around tondo, impressed in parallel 2 x 2. Surrounded by chattering and incised lines.
Campanian B or Arretine black-glazed, end of 2nd cent. B.C.
*Parallels*: Rome – ROMANELLI 1963, 244, fig.22,b1
Bolsena – BALLAND 1969, 153, pl.16:3 and 153, inv. 66-108-18.
Rome – MOREL 1965, cat. 352 and 433.

40.- CF 7.53. Motif composed by central oval with point in middle and 2 leaves with midrib and 4 curled lines, maybe a stylized palmette. In relief. *Fig.* 2,40.
On a base, type P 144e1, 2 preserved of 4 in all, impressed radially. Surrounded by incised concentric lines and chattering.
Campanian B or Arretine black-glazed, end of 2nd cent. B.C.
*Parallels*: Sovana – PANCRAZZI 1971, 190-191, 149 fig. 107, 191 fig. 107.

Institute of Prehistoric
and Classical Archaeology,
University of Copenhagen
Vandkunsten 5
DK-1467 Copenhagen K

# BIBLIOGRAPHY

| | |
|---|---|
| BALLESTER, J.P. 1987 | El taller de las pequeñas estampillas: revisiòn y precision es a la luz de las cerámicas de barniz negro de Gabii (Latium). Los ùltimos hallazgos en el Levante y sureste español, *AEsp*, 60, 43-72. |
| BALLAND, A. 1969 | *Céramique étrusco-campanienne à vernis noir (Fouilles de l'Ecole Francaise de Rome à Bolsena (Poggio Moscini), III,1)*, *MEFRA* suppl. 6, Paris. |
| BATS, M. 1976 | La céramique à vernis noir d'Olbia en Ligurie: vases de l'atelier des petites estampilles, *RANarb*, 9, 63-80. |
| 1987 | Consommation, production et distribution de la vaisselle céramique, in: Grecs et Ibères au IVe Siècle avant Jesus-Christ. Commerce et Iconographie, *REA* 89, 3-4. |
| BERNARDINI, P. 1986 | *La ceramica a vernice nera dal Tevere, Museo Nazionale Romano. Le Ceramiche, V,1*. Roma. |
| BOCCI, P. 1965 | Catalogo della ceramica di Roselle, *StEtr* 33, 109-190. |
| CARANDINI, A. 1981 | Sviluppo e crisi delle manifatture rurali e urbane, in: *Merci*, 249-260. |
| CAVAGNARO VANONI, L. 1972 | Tarquinia, Sei tombe a camera nella necropoli dei Monterozzi in località Calvario, *NSc*, 148-194. |
| CAVALIERI MANASSE, G. 1973 | Ceramica a vernice nera, in: A. Frova (ed.), *Scavi di Luni. Relazione Preliminare delle campagne di scavo 1970-1971*, Roma, 247-277. |
| CEDERNA, A. 1951 | Carsoli (Samnium). Scoperta di un deposito votivo del III sec. a.C. (prima campagna di scavo), *NSc*, 169-224. |
| COMFORT, H. 1940a | In: T. Frank, *An Economic Survey of Ancient Rome* V. Baltimore. |
| 1940b | Terra Sigillata, *RE* suppl. VII, 1295-1352. |
| CORBETT, P.E. 1955 | Palmette stamps from an Attic black-glaze workshop, *Hesperia* 24, 172-184. |
| DELPLACE, Chr. 1978 | Les potièrs dans la société et l'économie de l'Italie et de la Gaule, *Ktema*, 3, 55-76. |
| GIANFROTTA, P.A. 1968-69 | Scavi nell'area del Teatro Argentina (1968-1969): ceramica a vernice nera ed altri materiali, *BullCom* 81, 37-72. |
| GRACE, V. 1935 | The Die used for Amphora Stamps, *Hesperia* 4, 421-429. |
| GUCCI, P. 1981 | La Ceramica italica (terra sigillata), in: *Merci*, 99-122. |
| 1985 | Terra Sigillata Italica, *EEA*, Atlante II, 365-406. |
| HAYES, J.W. 1984 | *Greek and Italian Black-Gloss Wares and Related Wares in the Royal Ontario Museum*. Toronto. |
| JONES, C. 1977 | *Arretine and Samian Pottery*. London. |
| LYNGBY, H. & SARTORIO, G. 1965-67 | Indagini archeologiche nell'area dell' antica Porta Trigemina, *BullCom* 80, 5-36. |
| MELUCCO VACCARO, A. 1970 | La ceramica etrusca a vernice nera e ceramiche ellenistiche varie, in: *Pyrgi. Scavi del santuario etrusco (1959-1967)*, *NSc suppl.* II al vol. 24. |

| | |
|---|---|
| *Merci* 1981 | A. Giardina & A. Schiavone (eds.), *Merci, mercati e scambi nel Mediterraneo* (*Società romana e produzione schiavistica*, II). Roma-Bari. |
| MOREL, J.-P. 1965 | *Céramique à vernis noir du Forum Romain et du Palatin*, MEFRA suppl. 3. Paris. |
| 1969 | L'atelier des petites estampilles, *MEFRA* 81, 59-117. |
| 1981a | *Céramique campanienne. Les formes.* Rome. |
| 1981b | La produzione della ceramica campana: aspetti economici e sociali, in: *Merci*, 81-97. |
| 1982a | Typologie, culture matérielle, histoire: l'exemple de la céramique campanienne, *RA*, 183-188. |
| 1982b | Marchandises, Marchés, Echanges dans le monde romain, *AnnAStorAnt*, IV, 193-214, (rec. of *Merci*). |
| 1983 | Les producteur de biens artisanaux en Italie à la fin de la république, in: *Les "Bourgeoisies" municipales italiennes aux IIe et Ier siècles av. J.-C.*, Centre Jean Bérard. Institut Français de Naples 7-10 décembre (1981), Paris, 21-39. |
| 1985a | La ceramica e le altre merci d'accompagno nel commercio da e per Roma in età repubblicana, in: *Misurare la terra: centuriazione e coloni nel mondo romano. Città agricoltura, materiali da Roma e dal suburbio. Mostra.* Roma. 172-179. |
| 1985b | La ceramica campana A nell'economia della Campania, in: *Napoli antica*, 372-378. |
| 1985c | La manufacture, moyen d'enrichissement dans l'Italie romaine?, in: *L'origine des richesses depensées dans la ville antique. Actes du Colloque organisé à Aix-en-Provence, 11-12 mai 1984*, présentés et réunis par Philippe Leveau. Aix-en-Provence. 87-111. |
| 1986 | Remarques sur l'art et l'artisanat de Naples antique, in: *Neapolis. Atti del 25. Convegno di studi sulla Magna Grecia.* Taranto. 305-356. |
| 1988 | Artisanat et colonisation dans l'Italie romaine aux IVe e IIIe siècles av. J.-C., *DArch* 1988, 49-63. |
| *Napoli Antica* 1985 | *Napoli Antica. Mostra.* Napoli. 1985 |
| NIELSEN, I. 1988 | The temple of Castor and Pollux on the Forum Romanum, II, *ActaArch* 59, 1-14. |
| NIELSEN, I. & ZAHLE, J. 1985 | The temple of Castor and Pollux on the Forum Romanum, I, *ActaArch* 56, 1-29. |
| PANCRAZZI, O. 1971 | Sovana. Scavi effettuati dal 1962-1964. Località Costone della Folonia, località Poggio Grezzano, *NSc*, 136-194. |
| PETRACCA, L & VIGNA, L.M. 1985 | Le fornaci di Roma e suburbio, in: *Misurare la terra: centuriazione e coloni nel mondo romano. Città agricoltura, commercio: Materiali da Roma e dal suburbio. Mostra.* Roma. 131-137. |
| ROMANELLI, P. 1963 | Lo scavo al tempio della Magna Mater sul palatino e nelle sue adiacenze, *MonAnt*, XLVI, 201-330. |

| | |
|---|---|
| ROTROFF, S.I. 1982 | Hellenistic Pottery. Athenian and Imported Moldmade Bows, *The Athenian Agora*, XXII. New Jersey. |
| SANDE, S. & ZAHLE, J. 1988 | Der Tempel der Dioskuren auf dem Forum Romanum, in: *Kaiser Augustus und die verlorene Republik*. Berlin. 213-224. |
| SCOTT RYBERG, I. 1940 | *An archaeological record of Rome from the seventh century to the second century B.C.* London-Philadelphia. |
| SPARKES, A. & TALCOTT, L. 1970 | Black and Plain Pottery of the 6th, 5th and 4th Centuries B.C., *The Athenian Agora*, XII. New Jersey. |
| STEINBY, M. 1978 | Ziegelstempel von Rom und Umgebung, *RE suppl.* XV, 1489-1531. |
| 1981 | La diffusione dell'opus doliare urbano, in: *Merci*, 237-245. |
| TALCOTT, L. 1935 | Attic Black-Glazed Stamped Ware and other Pottery from a Fifth Century Well, *Hesperia* 4, 476-523. |
| TORTORELLA, S. 1981 | Le lastre Campana, in: *Merci*, 219-225. |
| WEINBERG, G.D. 1952 | The Minor Objects, *Corinth XII*. Princeton. |

# NOTES

1. Sparkes and Talcott have drawn attention to the wrong use of the word rouletting and suggest chattering, a term used in Oriental pottery, as a more accurate term for this process (SPARKES & TALCOTT 1970, 30 and note 67). Although they retained the conventional name I have preferred to use chattering.
2. I am sincerely obliged to The Carlsberg Foundation for making the excavation and the publication work possible by generous support. Furthermore I should like to thank Trine Neble and Poul Christensen for their help in preparing for print the drawings in figs. 2, 3, and 4.

# TOWARDS A BETTER UNDERSTANDING OF THE PRODUCTION PATTERN OF ROMAN LAMPS

JOHN LUND

> "Notre connaissance des lampes ne nous permet de conclusions archéologiques qu'à l'échelle du siècle"
> REBUFFAT 1987, 90

*Introduction*
In 1919, S. Loeschcke published an authoritative study on the "Lampen aus Vindonissa", which laid the foundation for subsequent research on Roman terracotta lamps from the 1st century A.D. A host of valuable studies on Roman lamps has appeared since then, mainly museum catalogues, excavation publications and regional studies. A history of research of the subject is not called for in the present context, but the contributions by J. Deneauve (1969), E. Joly (1974), A. Leibundgut (1977), M.C. Gualandi Genito (1977 and 1986) and D.M. Bailey (1975, 1980, 1985 and 1988), to mention but a few, cannot be disregarded (for a bibliography see OZIOL 1987).

In recent years, monographs dealing with particular types, or with signed lamps, have appeared in increasing numbers (for instance PAVOLINI 1980; BONNET 1988). The historian W.V. Harris (1980) has dealt with some organizational aspects of the industry, making controversial suggestions which have provoked D.M. Bailey to a reply (BAILEY 1987). However, few will dispute the relevance of Harris's reference to M.I. Finley's call for "a more sophisticated effort to approach quantification and pattern-construction" in this field, as well as in others relating to the study of material remains as evidence for ancient trade and manufacture (HARRIS 1980, 126; FINLEY 1973, 33-34). This paper is intended as an attempt in this direction.

*Goal*
The study of Roman lamps has a potential for providing new knowledge about the organization of workshops and trade and about the

mechanics of serial production in ancient times etc. However, before a maximum of information on these topics can be extracted from the material, it is essential to clarify *when* and *where* a given lamp was manufactured. The focus here is on the first of these issues.

We are relatively well informed about the start and end dates of production of the major types of lamps in the 1st century A.D., but questions relating to the fluctuating popularity of each type have hardly been addressed: are we to assume that a new type rose to a peak of popularity overnight, or was there a gradual build-up of production figures over several decades? Did an old type become obsolete immediately after the introduction of the new one? And was the total output of the new type larger or smaller than the one it replaced?

It is the aim of this paper to examine these questions, taking lamps found in independently dated contexts as a starting point. Four test cases have been selected for treatment. They comprise six types/subtypes of lamps current in slightly different periods of time. Furthermore, two types with a relatively limited distribution (cases 1 and 2) are contrasted to two immensely popular ones (cases 3 and 4).

## Basic assumptions

The independently dated contexts in which terracotta lamps are found generally belong to four categories: 1) tombs containing datable coins, 2) settlements abandoned after a relatively short period of time, the life span of which may be determined on the basis of coins and/or historical evidence, 3) destruction horizons, including shipwrecks, dated on the basis of coin finds and/or ancient texts, 4) layers in stratigraphic excavations. It is necessary to begin by explaining the basic assumptions about these find situations made in the present paper.

Coins found in tombs naturally provide only a *terminus post quem* for the find, since an obsolete coin may have been used for the purpose (GORECKI 1975, 279-285). Such instances are documented when several coins covering a span of years are found in a single grave. However, this is not the case with the graves under consideration here. Furthermore, a time lag may be suspected if the coin in question is very worn, but such cases seem to be rare, or at any rate are rarely reported in publications. Mostly, when dealing with a specific grave containing a single coin, there is little possibility of guessing whether a time lag should be reckoned with, at least when a study of the horizontal stratigraphy and/or a seriation of the finds has not been carried out. The matter is not made easier, when we remember that the same uncertainty adheres to the lamps themselves: were they new or old when they were placed in the grave? For present purposes the date of the lamps found in tombs is taken to correspond with that of the associated coin(s).

The evidence from short-lived settlements, for instance Roman forts along the *limes*, is relatively unproblematic, although it seems clear that activity went on at some of the sites after their supposed terminal date.

Finds from destruction layers evidently have the time of the devastation as a *terminus ante quem*, but it is evident that some objects of everyday use will have been new when disaster struck, whereas others may have been in the owner's possession for several years. When dealing with finds from Pompeii and Herculaneum, it is a further complication that the precise find spots of many terracotta lamps are unknown. Consequently, only lamps known with certainty to come from the final destruction horizon are assigned a date between 70 and 79 A.D. in the following, the remaining finds being referred to the period between 50 and 79 A.D., unless an earlier date is indicated by the stratigraphy. The uncertainty concerning many finds with the provenance "Pompeii" or "Herculaneum" is underlined by the fact that some such lamps in the storerooms of the National Museum at Naples were not actually found at these places (PAVOLINI 1977, 33). The whole group of lamps in the said storerooms is therefore not included in this paper. Finds from shipwrecks constitute a specialized kind of destruction horizon, the date of which cannot be ascertained from ancient historical sources. Coins found at wreck sites give them only a *terminus post quem*. The date suggested by the excavator has been followed unless it has been challenged by others; in these cases a wider margin of date has been chosen.

Finds from layers or closed contexts in stratigraphic excavations raise other questions. Dates suggested by the excavator are not always easy to verify, and doubt may linger when a (short) range of years is suggested without support from coin finds or justification on historic grounds. Despite these uncertainties, the dates suggested by the excavator have been followed.

Finally, when a publication states that a given find or context can be dated to, for instance, "the beginning of the 2nd century A.D.", it has been assigned a date between 100 and 120 in the present paper. Likew-

# DRESSEL FORM 3

Fig. 1. Case no. 1. The chronological distribution of lamps of Dressel 1899 Form 3 (number of instances: 41).

ise: "about the middle of the 1st century A.D." is taken to indicate a date between 40 and 60 A.D.

It is fully realized that some of these assumptions are questionable and deserve a much fuller discussion (cf. FEVRIER 1980; MOREL 1981, 51-65) than is possible here, but they will have to do for the present.

*Methodology*
Finds from the independently dated contexts can rarely be referred to a specific year, but it is usually possible to specify a range of years, within which the date should be sought. A tomb containing a coin of Claudius can thus be dated between 41 and 54 A.D., and a lamp from this context may, according to one of our basic assumptions, date from any

of these years. True, we have no way of knowing which one, but it seems legitimate to divide the number of relevant finds with the number of possible years (in the present case 1 divided by 13 = 0.0769) in order to arrive at a figure expressing the "weight" of the specific find for each of the years in question. – Say that in another instance nine lamps of the same type have been found in a layer in a stratigraphical excavation dated between 37 and 90 A.D., i.e. a period of 53 years. In this case we arrive at the weighted figure (9:53 =) 0.1698 for each year, using the same method as in the first example. The corresponding figures for all dated occurrences of the type in question can easily be calculated in this way. The next step is to add the figures for each twenty-year period. Instead of twenty-year periods it is, of course, possible to total the figures by other periods, e.g. decades or even single years. However, in the present state of our knowledge it seems preferable to operate with a somewhat wide span of years in order to avoid random deviations.

The resulting total figures for each twenty-year period can be expressed graphically in the form of charts illustrating the total number of occurrences of a given type of lamp in the dated contexts.

## Case no. 1. Dressel 1899 Form 3

*Fig. 1*

DENEAUVE 1969, 105-106: Rom. III
RICCI 1973, 193-197: Forma Dressel 3
LEIBUNDGUT 1977, 16-17: 2. "Republikanische" Bildlampen mit geradem Schnauzenabschluss (II)

Lamps of this type are characterized by having a circular body, a wide and flat discus surrounded by a ridge around the edge, small, horned lugs at the side and (usually) a band handle at the rear. They have a short nozzle with splayed ends and stand on a circular base ring. The discus may be plain or carry a stylized vegetal or a figure motive, often inspired by the world of real or fabulous animals (RICCI 1973, 193-195).

Two related sub-types, which are sometimes grouped together with lamps of the type Dressel 3, are not included in the treatment:

A) Lamps with a nozzle which is basically of the canonical type but with two stylized volutes at its root (LAMBOGLIA 1950, 63-64 no. 2, 65 fig. 25 (Ventimiglia); VEGAS 1966, 71 and 100-101 nos. 15-18 pl. 1 (Neuss); RICCI 1973, 199-200: Forma Dressel 3 A).

B) Lamps which correspond to the canonical type apart from the fact that they have a triangular nozzle with volutes at its base (LOESCHCKE 1909, 209 Type 35 c fig. 17 (Haltern); HÄHNLE 1912, 49 pl. 13.7 (Haltern); ALBRECHT 1943 85-86 Type 35 c fig. 3.f (Haltern). This sub-type seems to be a cross between the type DRESSEL 1899 Form 3 and LOESCHCKE 1919 type 1 (VEGAS 1966, 71).

Occurrences in dated contexts:

### GERMANY:

*Oberaden.* A Roman fort with a life span between ca. 12 B.C. and 10/9 B.C. (SCHÖNBERGER 1969, 147): ALBRECHT 1942, 39 pl. 6.8 and 10 Typus 24. To these may be added the fragments pl. 6.2 and probably also pl. 6.13: FARKA 1977, 37 note 125; however, cf. also VEGAS 1966, 70 notes 15-16.

*Rödgen.* A Roman fort established between ca. 12 and 10 B.C. and "probably abandoned shortly after the death of Drusus in 9 B.C." (JOHNSON 1983, 232): SIMON 1961, 59 H, 66-67 no. 83 fig. 4, a nozzle fragment possibly from a lamp of the type in question.

### AUSTRIA:

*Magdalensberg.* An Early Augustan context: FARKA 1977, 189 no. 109 pl. 10. It is possible that other finds from dated contexts listed by FARKA 1977, 37 note 129 may come from lamps of the type in question, but they cannot be separated from fragments of sub-type B mentioned above.

### SWITZERLAND:

*Basle.* A pit dated between 12 and 9 B.C.: LEIBUNDGUT 1977, 16, 207 no. 11 pl. 52.

### FRANCE:

*"Épave du Titan à l'Ile du Levant".* A wreck which contained a coin struck in 89 B.C. F. Benoit dated the find to the middle of the 1st century B.C., but according to M. Ricci the cargo was contemporary with or a little later than 89 B.C. (Ricci 1973, 195); J.-P. Morel has dated the find to about 75/65 B.C. (MOREL 1981, 64 note 258): BENOIT 1958, 8-9 figs. 4-5; the two lamps are assigned a date between 89 and 50 B.C. in the present paper.

*Cavaillon.* The lower layer of pit no. 7, which contained a coin of Caius Egnatuleius dated to 101 B.C. and another coin dated to the 1st century B.C.; according to the publisher, the fill accumulated between ca. 50 B.C. and A.D. 50, especially in the 2nd half of the 1st century B.C.: DUMOULIN 1965, 27-28 nos B.1-2 fig. 33.e-f and possibly no. B.3 fig. 33.g.

### ITALY:

*Albenga.* Layer O dated between 60 and 40 B.C. (LAMBOGLIA 1970, 40): RICCI 1973, 197 note 3, two fragments.

*Luni.* 1) Sounding II, layer B, which is dated by the publisher to 40-50 A.D. However, this date is not based on coin finds, and the layer is said to contain material from the early 1st century A.D. onwards: ZACCARIA RUGGIU 1977, 297 nos CM 11832; 11832/1; 11832/2; 11837 pls. 160, 16-17 and 163, 5-6, four fragments. – 2) Sounding VI, layer F, which contained a coin of Antoninus Pius: ZACCARIA RUGGIU 1977, 297 no. CM 8000 pl. 163,7, one fragment, which may be regarded as residual.

*Rome,* the Regia. A channel with the year 36 B.C. as a terminus post quem; the find "must be dated as a whole to the last three decades of the I century B.C.": MARABINI MOEVS 1973, 52-54 nos. 1-2 pl. 96.1-2, two fragments.

*Pompeii,* Insula 5, regio VI. 1) Sounding 10, layer II, in which the finds suggested "una cronologia bassa ad epoca augusteo-tiberiana" (BONGHI JOVINO 1984, 61): ROMANAZZI 1984, 236 note 11 no. CE 1120/7. -2) Sounding 12 layer III located below the habitation layer of 79 A.D. (BONGHI JOVINO 1984, 57): ROMANAZZI 1984, 236 note 11 nos. CE 1988 and CE 1993. – 3) Sounding 12, layer VIII, which the finds indicate was "limitata nel suo termine inferiore ad epoca tiberiana" (BONGHI JOVINO 1984, 57-58): ROMANAZZI 1984, 236 note 11 no. CE 2209/8. – 4) "Vani XX-XXII", on a floor in use in 79 A.D.: ROMANAZZI 1984, 236 note 11 no. CE 951 pl. 132.3, the front part is missing. – 5) "Vani XX-XXII, scarico 3", referred to the Augustan-Tiberian period (BONGHI JOVINO 1984, 59-60): ROMANAZZI 1984, 236 note 11 no. CE 1547/1.

*Ventimiglia.* 1) Layer VI A3: RICCI 1973, 196-197 note 1, one fragment. – 2) Layer VI A2: RICCI 1973, 196-197 note 1, two fragments. – 3) Layer VI A1: RICCI 1973, 196-197 fig. 15, one fragment; the lamp is said to come from layer VI A3, but this seems to be a misprint). 4) layer V B2: RICCI 1973, 196-197 note 1, three finds. – 5) Layer V B1: RICCI 1973, 196-197 note 1, two finds. – 6) Layer V B: RICCI 1973, 196-197 note 1, one fragment. – According to N. Lamboglia, layer VI A spans the period between ca. 100 and 40 B.C., and he dated layer V to between 40 B.C. and 20 A.D. (LAMBOGLIA 1959, 240 fig. 1; MOREL 1981, 57). M. Ricci has suggested more precise dates for layer VI A3 to V B1, but the basis for this has not been published, and it seems best for the time being to adhere to the dates suggested by N. Lamboglia (RICCI 1973, 172 note 2, 197 note 1).

## ISRAEL:

*Ashdod.* Area A, layer 2, which has been "related to historical events in the second half of the first century B.C.E ... the early phase of the stratum ... can safely be dated to the period of the Herodian dynasty: DOTHAN & FREEDMAN 1967, 31-32, 62-63 no. 17 fig.11 and pl. 10.6.

## LIBYA:

*Sidi Khrebish.* 1) A "context date: 1st century A.D.": BAILEY 1985, 11 no. C 47 pl. 3. – 2) A "context date: third quarter of 1st century A.D.": BAILEY 1985, 11 no. C 48 pl. 3.

## PORTUGAL:

*Conimbriga.* "Une canalisation construite à l'époque augustéenne": ALARCAO & DA PONTE 1976, 94-95 no. 11 pl. 23, a fragmentary find; the attribution is not certain.

The chart resulting from a calculation based on these contexts indicates that the type first occurs in dated contexts in the early 1st century B.C. The number of occurrences grows gradually, culminating in the last two decades of the 1st century B.C. only to decline in the 1st century A.D.

Certain comments are called for. First of all it should be underlined that the figures are calculated on the basis of a relatively small number (41) of dated lamp finds. Furthermore, some of the examples are known only from verbal descriptions, and it is not possible to verify their attribution. It should be noted that the increase between 40 and 60 A.D. is caused by the presence of four specimens in a layer at Luni dated by the excavator to between 40 and 50. These dates were used as a basis for the calculations in accordance with one of the basic assumptions, but the layer comprised pottery and various other finds going back to at least the beginning of the 1st century A.D., and it is likely that the lamp finds should be regarded as residual finds as well.

# EAR LAMPS

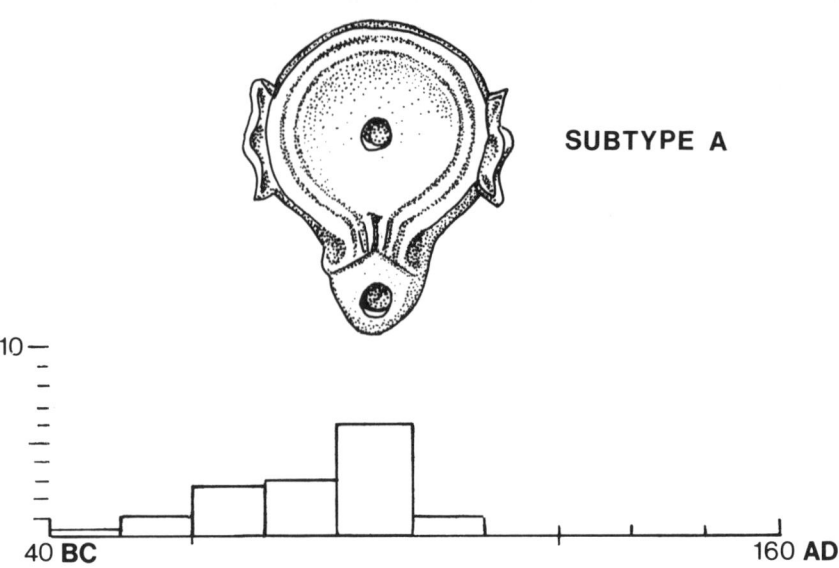

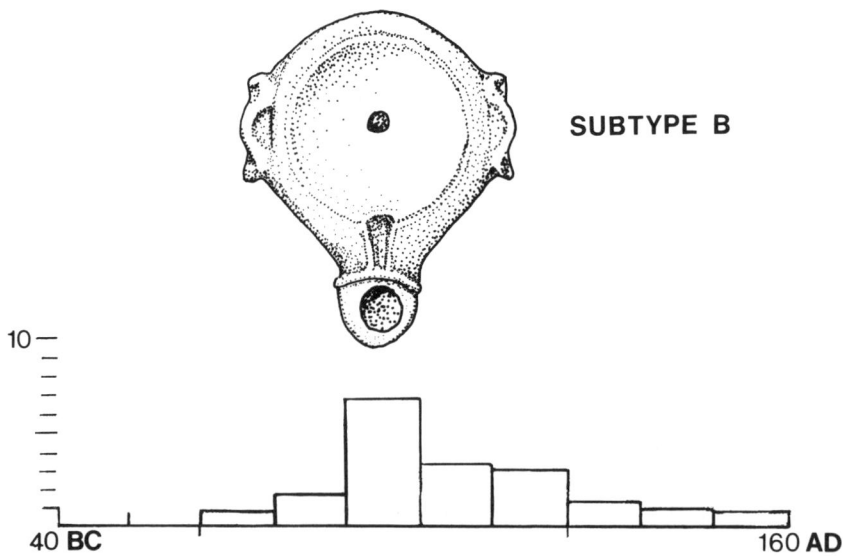

Fig. 2. Case no. 2. The chronological distribution of Ear lamps of the sub-type A (number of instances: 15) and of the sub-type B (number of specimens: 23).

The chart should, of course, not be taken as proof that lamps of the type in question actually began to be manufactured as early as the first decade of the 1st century B.C. In fact, the earliest certain occurrence seems to be the two specimens found in the so-called wreck of the Titan, which had the year 89 B.C. as a terminus post quem, and may actually date as late as 50 B.C., as suggested by F. Benoit.

*Case no. 2. Ear lamps.*                                                   *Fig. 2*
PERLZWEIG 1961, 105-106: Alpha Ear Lamps
DOMERGUE 1966, 16-17 nos. 60-68 pl. 7: Groupe III b) 1 and III b) 2
DENEAUVE 1969, 158-159: Rom. V G
LEIBUNDGUT 1977, 33-34: 6. c) Varianten zu Loeschcke Typus 5 (XVI-XVII)
BAILEY 1980, 233-236: Type G

The so-called Ear lamps are i.a. characterized by having a "circular body with a short nozzle, usually rounded, but occasionally angular at the tip. There is usually a short, narrow channel extending from the discus towards the wick-hole. Handles are found at the rear of most examples, but some lack this feature...The most distinctive characteristic of the Type is the presence, on each side of the body, of a decorative lug-handle.." (BAILEY 1980, 233). As noted by C. Domergue and A. Leibundgut, at least two sub-types exist:

A): lamps with horizontal shoulder separated from the discus by two grooves (approximately Loeschcke Sch. IV a) (cf. LEIBUNDGUT 1977, 33: XVI).

B): lamps with a slanting shoulder and a single groove separating the shoulder from the discus (Loeschcke Sch. VII b) (cf. LEIBUNDGUT 1977, 34: XVII).

Occurrences in dated contexts:

## GERMANY:
*Hofheim.* A Roman fortress dating chiefly from the reign of Claudius to the time of Vespasian (SCHÖNBERGER 1969, 152-153, 160, 165 note 157): RITTERLING 1913, 264 pl. 29.16, sub-type 2.A.
    *Trier.* Tomb 148 (St. Matthias, 1909), which contained coins of Domitian: GOETHERT-POLASCHEK 1985, 142 no. 608 pl. 67, a lamp of sub-type 2.B.

## SWITZERLAND:
*Augst.* "Tiberisch-claudischer Benützungsschicht ... zusammen mit einem As des Augustus der Lyoner Altarserie": LEIBUNDGUT 1977, 263 ad no. 631, a lamp of sub-type 2.A.

*Vindonissa.* A Roman fortress mainly dated between the Tiberian period and about 100/101 A.D.: LOESCHCKE 1919, 9, 40 and 44, 225 no. 637 pl. 17, a lamp of sub-type 2.B.

## ITALY:

*Luni.* Sounding VIII.1, layer C, dated to the end of the 2nd century A.D.: ZACCARIA RUGGIU 1977, 299 no. CM 3121/1 pl. 165,4, one fragment of a lamp of sub-type 2.B.

*Ostia,* Le Terme del Nuotatore, area so. 1) Layer V A: SALONE 1973, 397, 402, six fragments. -2) Layer IV C: SALONE 1973, 397, 402, three fragments. Layers V A-B contained finds from the time of the emperors Nero and Vespasian as well as slightly later material including a coin of Domitian which suggests that the layers should be dated about 90 A.D. (CARANDINI & PANELLA 1973, 654-655). Layer IV C yielded no certain dating evidence but is dated between layer 5 and layer 4 A-B, which is referred to the time of the emperors Trajan and Hadrian (CARANDINI & PANELLA 1973, 656). Unfortunately it is not clear to which of the two sub-types the lamps in question belong, and the evidence can therefore not be taken into account here.

*Pompeii,* Insula 5, regio VI. 1) Sounding 12, layer 8, described as fill "limitata nel suo termine inferiore ad epoca tiberiana" (BONGHI JOVINO 1984, 58): ROMANAZZI 1984, 239 and 246 no. CE 2311 + CE 2208/11 pl. 133.7, two fragments of a lamp belonging to sub-type 2.A; ROMANEZZI 1984, 239 and 246 no. CE 2209/5 pl. 134.2, one fragment belonging to sub-type 2.B; it is not known to which sub-type a third and fourth fragment belonged. – 2) Sounding 10 layer 1: ROMANAZZI 1984, 239-240 no. CE 1883/1 pl. 134.1, a fragment of sub-type 2 A. – 3) Sounding 10 layer 2, in which finds suggested "una cronologia bassa ad epoca augusteo-tiberiana" (BONGHI JOVINO 1984, 61): ROMANAZZI 1984, 239-240 no. CE 1117 and CE 1120/6 pl. 134.4, of sub-type 2 A. – 4) Sounding 10 layer 4 referred to the Tiberian period (BONGHI JOVINO 1984, 62): ROMANAZZI 1984, 239-240 no. CE 1814/4 pl. 133.8, a variant of sub-type 2 A.

*Ventimiglia.* "Vano III", layer 4, which produced a coin of Tiberius, re-struck under Nero, and further finds referred to the 1st century A.D.: LAMBOGLIA 1950, 186 no. 23, 187 fig. 109.23, a fragment presumably of sub-type 2.B.

## GREECE:

Athens, the Agora. 1) Well, D 11:1 with dumped filling of late 1st century B.C. to mid-1st century A.D.: PERLZWEIG 1961, 79 nos. 82-83 pl. 4 and p. 225, two fragments of sub-type 2.A. –2) Well, F 15:5 with use filling of first half of 1st century A.D.: PERLZWEIG 1961, 79 no. 84 pl. 4 and p. 225, a lamp of the sub-type 2.B.

## LIBYA:

*Sidi Khrebish.* 1) A context dated up to mid-3rd century A.D.: BAILEY 1985, 66 no. C 447 pl. 13, a variant of sub-type 2.A. – 2) A context dated to the second half of the 1st century A.D.: BAILEY 1985, 65 no. C 446 pl. 13, a fragment of a 2.B lamp; a more or less similar fragment was found in the Flavian Deposit 69, three came from Deposit 73 dated to the 2nd to mid-3rd centuries A.D., and a single fragment was unearthed in Deposit 76 from the first half of the 2nd century A.D. and Deposit 85 referred to the mid-3rd century A.D. respectively. Cf. BAILEY 1985, 65 ad nos. C 445-446). – 3) A context dated up to mid-3rd century A.D.: BAILEY 1985, 66 no. C 449 pl. 13, a fragment of a 2.B lamp.

## TUNISIA:

*Carthage,* the University of Michigan excavations. Deposit XVIII "early 1st century A.D., except for two late sherds": HAYES 1978, 37 no. 59 pl. 6, a fragment of a lamp of sub-type 2.A.

*Raqqada.* Tomb B 37 containing a coin dating from "l'époque de Tibère": ENNABLI 1973, 90; 117 pl. 39, a lamp of sub-type 2.B.

## ALGERIA:

*Tipasa.* Tomb 553, which contained a coin of Galba "en excellent état": LANCEL 1970, 167-168 fig. 14, a lamp of sub-type 2.B. – 2) "Tombe d'un sacrificateur", which contained a coin of Claudius and predated tomb no. 56 dated by a coin struck in 81-82 A.D. to the time of Domitian: BARADEZ 1957b, 229 no. 3 pl. 12, a lamp of sub-type 2.B with the stamp CAN *in planta pedis*.

## PORTUGAL:
*Conimbriga*. "Les niveaux flaviens et trajaniens": ALARCAO & DA PONTE 1976, 99 no. 43 pl. 25, a fragment of a lamp of sub-type 2.B.

## SPAIN:
*The Balearic Islands*. A group of objects buried in the sand, presumably part of the cargo of a wrecked ship; the find, which included a coin of Caligula struck in A.D. 40 or 41, is dated to between ca. 40 and 50 A.D. by the publisher: DOMERGUE 1966, 16-17 nos. 60-68 pl. 7, four lamps of sub-type 2.A and five lamps of sub-type 2.B, all from the workshop of Caius Clodius.

The chart shows that variant A makes its first appearance in find groups from the two final decades of the 1st century B.C. The number increases gradually reaching a peak between 40 and 60 A.D. However, the figures are calculated from an even smaller number of dated finds (15) than those of the first test case, and the peak reached between 40 and 60 A.D. is caused to a large degree by the group of lamps from the workshop of Caius Clodius found in the Balearic Islands. It seems possible that this large find has skewed the picture.

As for sub-type B, the chart calculated from a total of 23 specimens shows that it entered the scene in the first decade of the 1st century A.D. The number of dated occurrences grows gradually, reaching a peak between A.D. 40 and 60, but the type continues to be present in contexts of the second half of the 1st century A.D. and even in those of the beginning of the 2nd century A.D. After ca. A.D. 120 such lamps are found only in the dated deposits at Sidi Khrebish, where they occur up to the mid-3rd century.

## Case no. 3. Loeschcke 1919 Type IV
DENEAUVE 1969, 126-145: Rom. V A
BISI INGRASSIA 1977, 84-85: tipo VIII B-C
BAILEY 1980, 153-183: Type B
GOETHERT-POLASCHEK 1985, 97-125: Typus X b

*Fig. 3*

The characteristic features of lamps of this type are a circular body with a rounded nozzle flanked by volutes. The discus is usually decorated. Such lamps are usually handleless (BISI INGRASSIA tipo VIII B), but may have a pierced handle or a band handle (BISI INGRASSIA 1977 tipo VIII C; BAILEY 1980, 180-183: Group B (v)), and they normally stand on a low base ring.

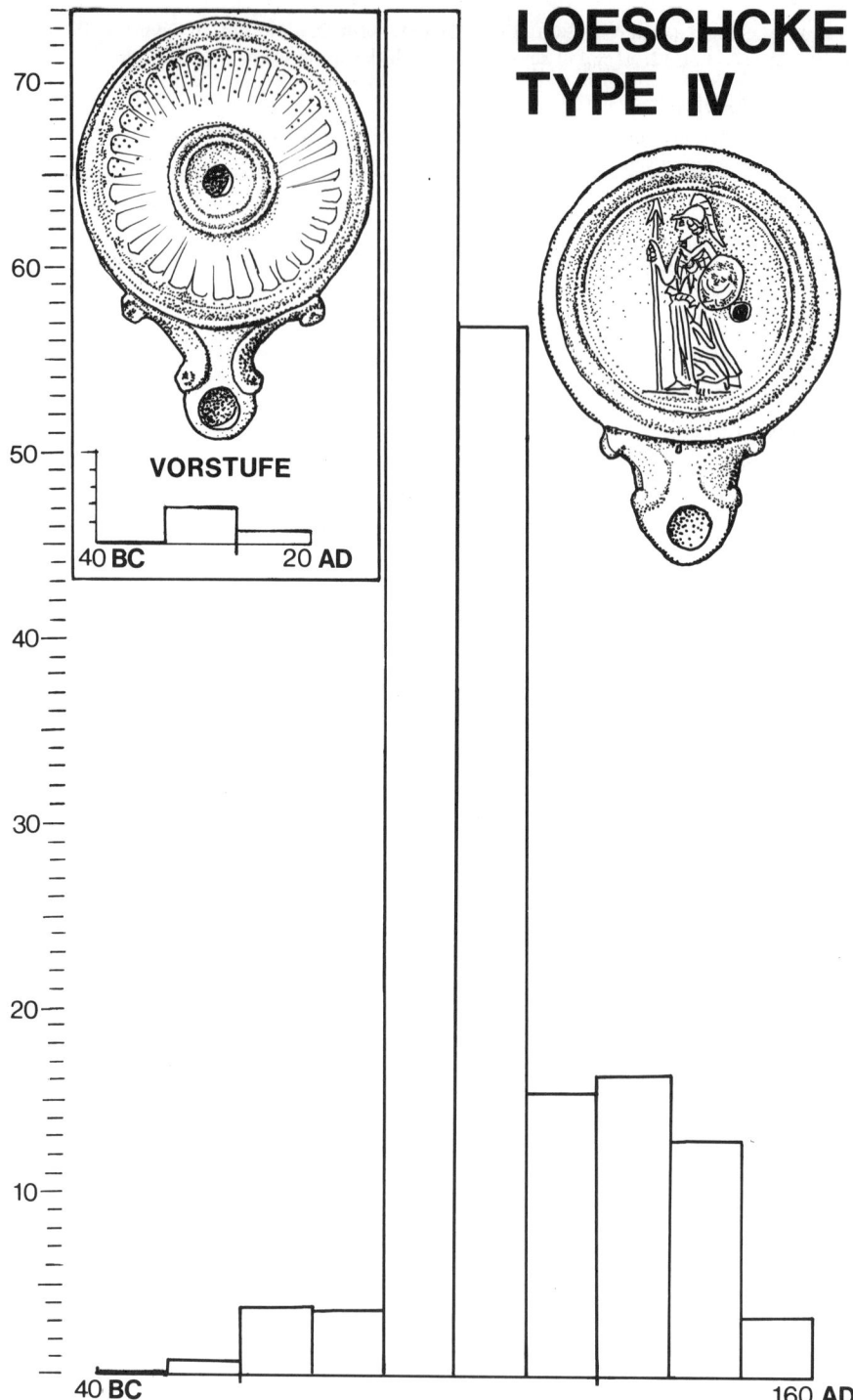

Fig. 3. Case no. 3. The overall chronological distribution of lamps of Loeschcke 1919 Type IV (number of instances: 225) and Vorstufe (number of specimens: 6).

The general development of the type was traced by S. Loeschcke, A. Leibundgut and others, who have identified a "Vorstufe" with a nozzle with a triangular contour, relatively "thin" volutes and a horizontal, rilled shoulder (LOESCHCKE 1919, 37-38 fig. 5.2-3; LEIBUNDGUT 1977, 29-30 fig. 4.1), and a "Normalform" characterized by having a broader nozzle with a less clearly defined triangular contour and a shoulder as Loeschcke Sch. 2-3 and 6-7, although Sch. 1 and 5 may also be encountered (FARKA 1977, 64 note 251; LEIBUNDGUT 1977, 29-30 fig. 4.2, for further variants see GOETHERT-POLASCHECK 1985, 98). A. Leibundgut also identified a "Spätform" with a fat nozzle surrounded by heavy volutes and a shoulder as Loeschcke Sch. 4 and 7 b (LEIBUNDGUT 1977, 30-31 fig. 4.3). However, it is not always easy to make a clear distinction between the "Normalform" and the "Spätform", and for these reasons the two have been combined in the following:

Occurrences in dated contexts:

## ENGLAND:
*Colchester.* A stratified context referred to Period VI ( 61- ca. 65 A.D.): HAWKES & HULL 1947, 201 no. 11 pl. 44, a single fragment.

## GERMANY:
*Auerberg.* A Roman settlement which judging from the coin finds began "eine Generation nach dem grossen Alpenkrieg des Jahres 15 v. Chr." and was broken off during the reign of Claudius: ULBERT 1975, 426-427 fig. 19, one specimen.

*Haltern.* A Roman fortress established about 12 to 9 B.C. and destroyed by fire in 9 A.D.: ALBRECHT 1943, 86 Typ 36 a pl. 24 b, "Vorstufe".

*Hofheim.* A Roman fortress with a life span mainly between the forties of the 1st century A.D. and the time of Vespasian (cf. SCHÖNBERGER 1969, 152-153, 160, 165 note 157): RITTERLING 1913, 266 no. 19 pl. 30.15b; 266 no. 24 pl. 30.3; 266 no. 27 pl. 29.3; 267 no. 36 pl. 29.10; 267 no. 45 pl. 29.15.

*Rheingönheim.* A Roman fortress, dated from the forties of the 1st century A.D. to about 74 A.D., although some later finds also occur: ULBERT 1969, 15-16; 57 no. 1 pl. 61, a variant without the lower pair of volutes.

*Trier.* – 1) St. Matthias, 1904, Grab 41, which contained coins of Claudius: GOETHERT-POLASCHECK 1985, 101 no. 399 pl. 59. – 2) St. Matthias, 1906, Grab 103, which contained coins of Nero: GOETHERT-POLASCHECK 1985, 103-104 no. 411 pl. 56. – 3) St. Matthias, 1908, Grab 5, which contained coins of Nero: GOETHERT-POLASCHECK 1985, 105-106 no. 422 pl. 62. – 4) St. Matthias, 1909, Grab 119, which contained coins of Nero: GOETHERT-POLASCHECK 1985, 106-107 no. 427 pl. 60. – 5) St. Matthias, 1906, Grab 108 with coins of Vespasian: GOETHERT-POLASCHECK 1985, 103 no. 409 pl. 55. – 6) St. Matthias, 1909, Grab 145 with coins of Vespasian: GOETHERT-POLASCHECK 1985, 127 no. 537 pl. 60.

## AUSTRIA:
*Laibach*, Krain: IVÁNYI 1935, 11, a lamp found with coins of Nero.

*Magdalensberg.* An Augustan context: FARKA 1977, 66 and 245 no. 635 pl. 19, Vorstufe.

*Pettau.* – 1) A tomb containing a coin of Vespasian: FISCHBACH 1896, 31 no. 262 pl. 4. -2) A tomb containing a coin of Vespasian: FISCHBACH 1896, 33 no. 294 pl. 1.

## FRANCE:

*Brumath*, Rue Jacques-Kablé and Rue Raymond-Poincaré, a destruction layer containing four coins of Vespasian and dated to 70 A.D: PÉTRY 1974, 391-392 fig. 28, seven lamps.

## ITALY:

*Herculaneum*: BISI INGRASSIA 1977, 84-85: fifteen specimens.

*Luni*. – 1) Sounding II, layer C, dated between 40 and 50 A.D.: ZACCARIA RUGGIU 1977, 298: CM 5232 pl. 163, 14. – 2) Sounding VIII.1, layer C, dated to the end of the 2nd century A.D.: ZACCARIA RUGGIU 1977, 298 no. CM 3119/1 pl. 163, 13.

*Ostia*, Le Terme del Nuotatore, area so. 1) Layer V B: SALONE 1973, 397, 402, 15 specimens. – 2) Layer V A: *loc. cit.*, 20 specimens. – 3) Layer IV C: *loc. cit.*, 8 specimens. – 4) Layers IV A-B: *loc. cit.*, 10 specimens. – 5) Layer III: *loc. cit.*, 1 specimen. – 6) Layer II: *loc. cit.*, 7 specimens. For the date of layers V A-B and IV C, see supra ad case 3. Layers IV A-B are dated to the time of the emperors Trajan and Hadrian (CARANDINI & PANELLA 1973, 656), layer III is dated to the early Severan period (CARANDINI & PANELLA 1973, 656-657) and layer II to the third or perhaps the fourth decade of the 3rd century A.D. (CARANDINI & PANELLA 1973, 657) – 7) Ambiente XVI, layer II (1 specimen) and I (2 finds): ANSELMINO 1977, 91 and 97. Layer II is dated between the late 2nd/early 3rd century A.D. and the second half of the 3rd century A.D. (PANELLA 1977, 289), and layer I contained coins, of which the latest was struck under Jovian (363-364 A.D.) (PANELLA 1977, 291).

*Pompeii*, Insula 5, regio VI. 1) Sounding 5, layer XVII: ROMANAZZI 1984, 239 no. CE 563 pl. 34, 5. – 2) Sounding 10, layer II referred to the time of Augustus and Tiberius: ROMANAZZI 1984, 239 no. CE 1165. – 3) Sounding 10, layer IV dated to the time of Tiberius: ROMANAZZI 1984, 239 no. CE 1814. – 4) Sounding 4 layer III: ROMANAZZI 1984, 239 no. CE 1965.

*Rome*. A drain below the Basilica Julia closed between 12 B.C. and 12 A.D.: MARABINI MOEVS 1973, 52 note 59.

## YUGOSLAVIA:

*Buccari*, Croatia. Found with a coin of Hadrian: LOESCHCKE 1919, 38 note 72.

## GREECE:

*Athens*, the Agora. 1) Well, D 12:1 in use filling 1) first half of 1st century: PERLZWEIG 1961, 76 no. 50 pl. 3, 225. – 2) Well, R 13:1 with "dumped filling of late 1st century B.C.": PERLZWEIG 1961, 76-77 no. 52 pl. 3, 228, "Vorstufe?". – 3) Well, S 21:3 with "accumulated use fillings of the first half of the 1st to the first half of the 3rd century.., lowest level": PERLZWEIG 1961, 78 no. 72 pl. 3, 228. – 4) Well, B 20:1 with "use filling of second half of 1st to middle of 2nd century": PERLZWEIG 1961, 81 no. 99 pl. 4, 224. – 5) Well, F11:1 with "dumped filling of 1st and early 2nd centuries": PERLZWEIG 1961, 81 no. 102 pl. 4, 225. – 6) Cistern, D 4:1 with "dumped fillings of 1st and early 2nd centuries": PERLZWEIG 1961, 81 no. 104 pl. 4, 224-225.

## LIBYA:

*Sidi Khrebish*. – 1) A context date "mainly Hellenistic, perhaps early 1st century B.C.": BAILEY 1985, 32 no. C 179 pl. 9, "Vorstufe". – 2) A "context date: third quarter of 1st century A.D.": BAILEY 1985, 34 ad no. C 190 bis; 35-36 no. C 207 pl. 10; 33 ad no. C 189, a total of four fragments. -3) A "context date: Flavian": BAILEY 1985, 32 no. C 180 pl. 9, "Vorstufe"; 37 no. C 218 pl. 10 and 33 ad no. C 189. – 4) A "context date: second half of 1st century A.D.": BAILEY 1985, 32 no. C 182 pl. 9; 35 no. C 206 fig. 5. – 5) A "context date: 1st century A.D.": BAILEY 1985, 34-35 no. C 196 pl. 10; 35 no. C 201 pl. 10; 36 no. C 217 pl. 10. and 37 no. C 220 pl. 10. – 6) A "context date: 1st century A.D. ... with one 7th century fine-ware sherd (intrusive?)": BAILEY 1985, 34 no. C 195 pl. 10. – 7) A context date: early 2nd century A.D.: BAILEY 1985, 33 ad no. C 189, three fragments. – 8) A "context date: first half of 2nd century A.D.": BAILEY 1985, 33 no. C 186 pl. 9. – 9) A context date of "mid-3rd century A.D.": BAILEY 1985, 32 no. C 178 pl. 9, "Vorstufe"; 37 ad no. C 220. – 10) A "context date: 2nd to mid-3rd centuries A.D.": BAILEY 1985, 32 no. C 181 pl. 9; 35 no. C 203 fig. 5; 36 no. C 208 fig. 5; 36 no. C 209 fig. 5; 36 no. C 210 fig. 5;

36 no. C 211 fig. 5; 36 no. C 216 pl. 10; 33 ad no. C 189, a total of eighteen fragments. – 11) An early 3rd century A.D. context: BAILEY 1985, 33 ad no. C 189. – 12) A "context date: up to mid-3rd century A.D.": BAILEY 1985, 33 no. C 187 fig. 4.; 33 no. C 189 pl. 9; 35 no. C 199 fig. 4; 36 no. C 213 fig. 5 and 37 no. C 219 pl. 10. – 13) A "context date: mainly mid-3rd century A.D.": BAILEY 1985, 33 no. C 188 pl. 9. – 14) A mid-3rd century A.D.? context: BAILEY 1985, 33 ad no. C 189. – 15) A "context date: 3rd century A.D. or later": BAILEY 1985, 35 no. C 202 pl. 10.- 16) A "context date: 4th century A.D.": BAILEY 1985, 33-34 no. C 190 and 34 no. C 194 pl. 10. – 17) A "context date: late 4th century A.D.": BAILEY 1985, 35 no. C 198 pl. 10. – 18) A "context date: 5th century A.D.": BAILEY 1985, 34 no. C 190 bis. – 19) A mid-6th century A.D. context: BAILEY 1985, 33 ad no. C 189-20) A "context date: 7th century A.D.": BAILEY 1985, 34 no. C 192 pl. 10 and no. C 193 pl. 10 and 35 no. C 197.

## TUNISIA:

*Raqqada.* Tomb C 1, which contained a coin from the 1st century A.D.: ENNABLI 1973, 88.

## ALGERIA:

*Tipasa.* "Tombe d'un sacrificateur", which contained a coin of Claudius and predated tomb no. 56 with a coin of Domitian struck in 81-82 A.D.: BARADEZ 1957b, 227-233 nos. 1 (with no trace of use), 2, 9, 11, 12 and 13 pl. 12, i.e. two whole lamps and fragments of four more.

## SPAIN:

*Ampurias.* Layer IIB, dated between 100 and 130 A.D.: ALMAGRO & LAMBOGLIA 1959, 12-13 fig. 14.4.

*The Balearic Islands.* A group of objects buried in the sand, presumably part of the cargo of a wrecked ship; the find, which included a coin of Caligula struck in A.D. 40 or 41, is dated to between ca. 40 and 50 A.D. by the publisher: DOMERGUE 1966, 14-16, 22-30 nos 4-52 pls. 1-7, 48 specimens.

The chart is based on a larger number of dated finds (a total of 225 specimens) than the previous test cases, and the resulting picture may therefore be more reliable. An attempt has therefore been made to break the figures down according to geographical region.

The "Vorstufe" (6 dated finds) is more or less restricted to the Augustan period – as previously assumed by its usual prefix: "Augusteische Vorstufe".

Lamps of the "Normalform" seem to begin to appear in Italy before the first decade of the 1st century A.D. This could support the conventional view that the type originated here. At any rate, the developed type is present in most of the areas in contexts of the first four decades of the 1st century A.D. Then the number of occurrences grows steeply, reaching a peak between A.D. 40 and 60; the figures decline somewhat between A.D. 60 and 80, but the number of instances remains high in absolute terms in the following decades.

It should be stressed that the peak between A.D. 40 and 60 is caused by a single large find (from the Balearic islands). If we look at the evidence from Italy alone, the highest number of occurrences is attained

*Fig. 4a*

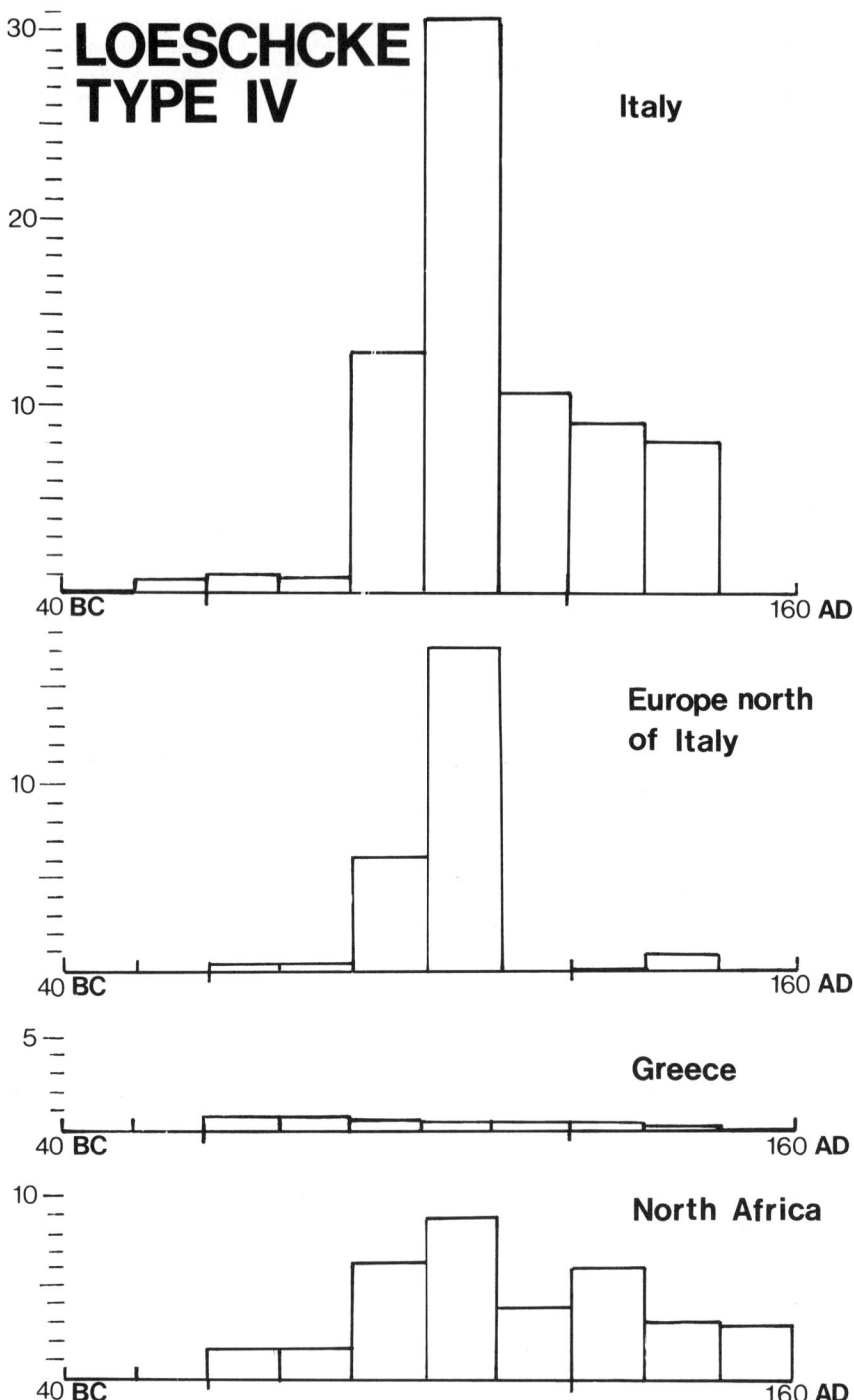

Fig. 4a. Case no. 3. The chronological distribution of lamps of Loeschcke 1919 Type IV in Italy, Europe north of the Alps, Greece and North Africa.

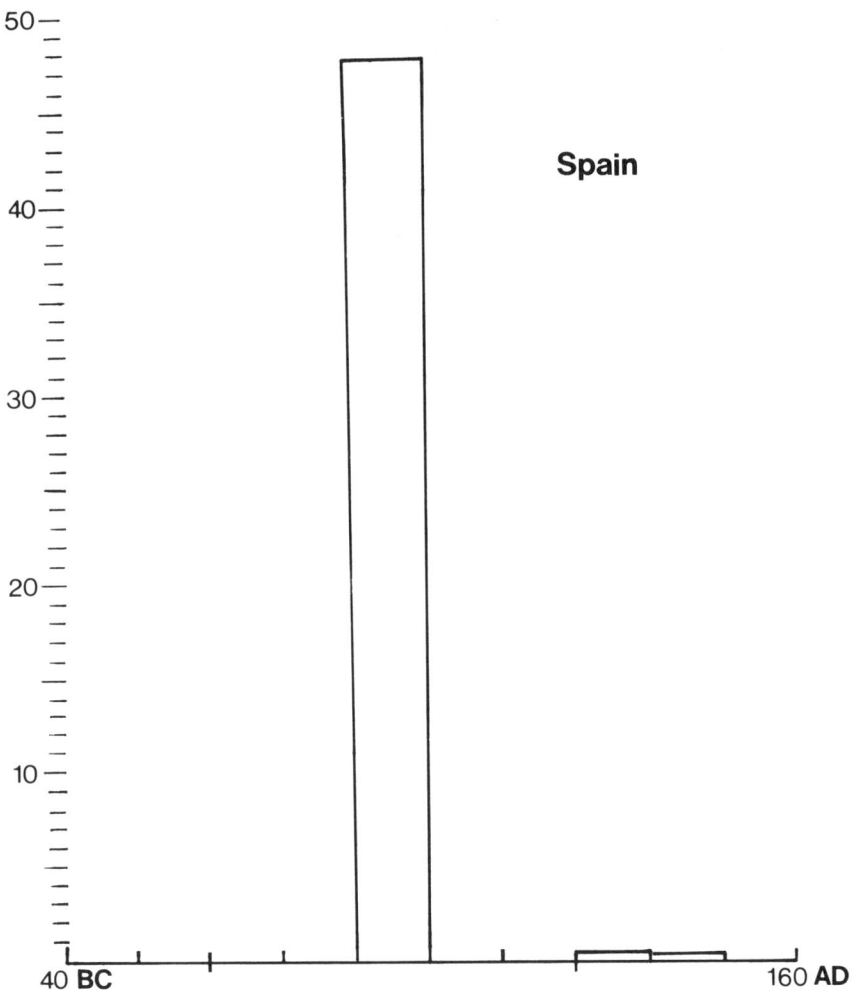

Fig. 4b. Case no. 3. The chronological distribution of lamps of Loeschcke 1919 Type IV in Spain.

between A.D. 60 and 80, and the same holds true for Europe to the north of the Italian peninsula, and even in North Africa. The corresponding chart for Greece is less clear, possibly because it is based on fewer occurrences. It is difficult to say if the inclusion of the large number of occurrences in the find from the Balearic Islands has distorted the overall picture, but as we shall see later, there is some evidence that this may not be the case.

*Fig. 4b*

The number of finds decreases after A.D. 100 and declines sharply after A.D. 140. Occurrences after then should probably be regarded as

285

# LOESCHCKE TYPE V

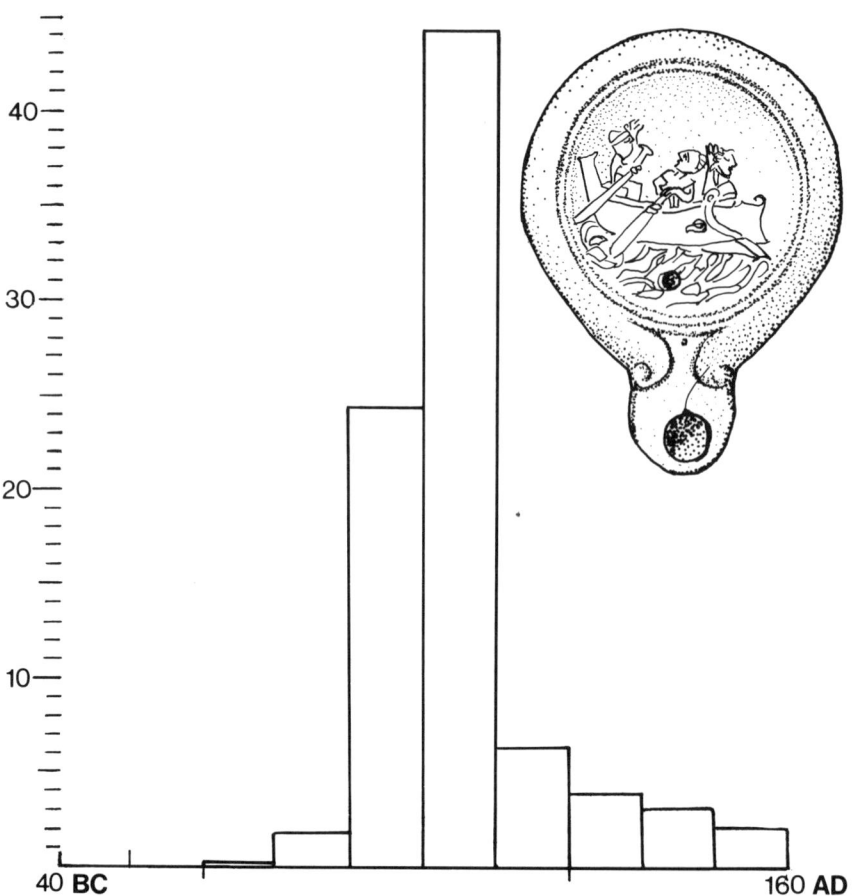

Fig. 5. Case no. 4. The overall chronological distribution of lamps of Loeschcke 1919 Type V (number of specimens: 107).

residual, but it may be noted that the number of finds after this date continues only to be high among the finds from North Africa, especially Sidi Khrebish. This may indicate that the type had a longer life span here than elsewhere, but it is also possible that the reason is simply that this site has been carefully excavated, with more attention to the dated contexts than normally seen.

## Case no. 4. Loeschcke Type V
Fig. 5

DENEAUVE 1969, 149-157: Rom. V D
BISI INGRASSIA 1977, 87: tipo VIII G
LEIBUNDGUT 1977, 32: 6 Lampen mit Schultervoluten und runder Schnauze (XIV-XVII)
BAILEY 1980, 184-198: Type C
GOETHERT-POLASCHEK 1985, 136-141: Typus XI

Lamps of Loeschcke's type V are characterized by having a rounded nozzle with volutes growing from the sloping shoulders, which are sometimes decorated with ovules or other ornaments. They are normally provided with a pierced handle and have a raised base – occasionally a base ring. The shoulder form is usually Loeschcke's Sch. VIIa or VIIIa and VIIIb (FARKA 1977, 68; BAILEY 1985, 62). A. Leibundgut distinguished between a "Normalform", which often has an ovulo as a shoulder decoration and a plain discus, and a "Spätform", with "eine gedrungene Kontur, breite Voluten und stärker gerundete, plumpere Schnauze" (LEIBUNDGUT 1977, 32-33), but these are grouped together in the following.

Occurrences in dated contexts:

### GERMANY:
*Hofheim.* A Roman fort dated mainly between the forties of the 1st century A.D. and the time of Vespasian. (SCHÖNBERGER 1969, 152-153, 160, 165 note 157): RITTERLING 1913, 267 no. 41 pl. 29.1.

*Rottweil.* A Roman fort founded in the Flavian period: LOESCHCKE 1919, 43 note 85.

*Okarben.* A Roman fort believed to have been established in the Flavian period and abandoned under Trajan or Hadrian; however a few coins of even later date have also been found here (cf. SCHÖNBERGER 1969-1970, 155 and 165; WOLFF 1902, 16): WOLFF 1902, 36 no. B III Lampen 1 pl. 5.3, found in the "weiteren Umgebung von Okarben".

*Trier.* – 1) St. Matthias 1907, Grab 161 containing coins of Claudius: GOETHERT-POLASCHECK 1985, 138-139 no. 591 pl. 66. – 2) St. Matthias 1906, Grab 17 containing a coin of Domitian: GOETHERT-POLASCHECK 1985, 137 no. 584 pl. 67.

### FRANCE:
*Brumath*, Rue Jacques-Kablé and Rue Raymond-Poincaré. A destruction layer containing four coins of Vespasian and dated to 70 A.D: PÉTRY 1974, 391-392 fig. 28, three lamps.

### ITALY:
*Herculaneum*, "nuovi scavi": BISI INGRASSIA 1977, 87, 32 specimens.

*Luni.* – 1) Sounding V, layer D, dated to the third quarter of the 3rd century A.D.: ZACCARIA RUGGIU 1977, 298 nos. CM 7048, 7162, 7167, 7274 pls 163, 15-16; 164, 1 – 2) Sounding V, layer E, dated to the last quarter of the 4th century A.D.: ZACCARIA RUGGIU 1977, 298 nos. CM 7304 and 8124 pls. 164, 2-3.

*Ostia*, Le Terme del Nuotatore, area so. 1) Layer V A: SALONE 1973, 397, 402, two specimens. – 2) Layers IV A-B: *loc. cit.*, three specimens. – 3) Layer II: *loc. cit.*, 2 finds. For the date of these layers see supra ad case 3.

*Pompeii*, Insula 5, regio VI. – 1) "Sul pavimento del 79 d.C.": ROMANAZZI 1984, 238 nos. CE 301 pl. 131.9 and CE 309/4. – 2) "Pavimento dell'abitazione ellenistica A del vano XV: ROMANAZZI 1984, 238 no. CE 826 pl. 132.8.- 3) Sounding 4, layer III: ROMANAZZI 1984, 238 no. CE 1714/2 pl. 133.1. – 4) Sounding 12, layer VIII: ROMANAZZI 1984, 238 nos. CE 2208/1 pl. 133.2, no. CE 2208/7 and CE 2209/9 pl. 133.4. For all of these finds L. Romanazzi concludes that "i dati dello scavo parrebbero indicare una cronologia entro il primo quarto del secolo o poco oltre." They are consequently referred to the period between 25 A.D. and 79 A.D. in the present publication – *Pompeii*. A lamp workshop at the porta di Nocera: CERULLI IRELLI 1977, 59-60, tipo D, nine lamps and three matrices for lamps.

## GREECE:

*Athens*, the Agora. 1) Well, N 20:5 with "use filling of second half of 1st to early 2nd century": PERLZWEIG 1961, 82 no. 115 pl. 5, 227. – 2) Well, C 12:1 "use filling of mid-2nd into 3rd century": PERLZWEIG 1961, 82 no. 117 pl. 5, 224.

*Corinth*. 1) A manhole to a drain at the west end of the Agora containing "several coins, most of them from the time of Domitian": BRONEER 1930, 82 ad no. 467 pl. 10. – 2) A well, which also contained "a coin of Agrippina the Younger": BRONEER 1930, 82 ad no. 459 pl. 10. – 3) In fill in the "Roman Cellar Building" containing coins, of which the latest (with the exception of a coin from the 13th century A.D.) was struck under Nero: SLANE 1986, 300 no. 145 pl. 69.

## LIBYA:

*Sidi Khrebish*. 1) A context date of the third quarter of the 1st century A.D.: BAILEY 1985, 63 no. C 433 pl. 12. – 2) A context dating from the Flavian period: BAILEY 1985, 63 no. C 432 bis fig. 7. – 3) A 1st century context: BAILEY 1985, 63 no. C 434 pl. 12. – 4) A deposit dated to the 2nd to mid-3rd centuries A.D.: BAILEY 1985, 63 ad no. C 434 and 63 ad no. C 435 and 65 no. C 444 pl. 13, a total of fourteen fragments. – 5) A context dated to the mid-3rd century A.D.: BAILEY 1985, 63 no. C 432 fig. 7 and 63 ad no. C 435. – 6) A deposit dated to the 7th century A.D. or later: BAILEY 1985, 63 ad no. C 434.

## ALGERIA:

*Tipasa*. 1) Funerary deposit Z 1: LANCEL 1967, 60-61 pl. 3, a coin of Hadrian was found lying on the lamp in question, which had the signature MADI(EC?). – 2) Tomb 310, which contained a coin of Vespasian: LANCEL 1970, 168-169 fig. 15. – 3) Tomb no. B. 56 containing a coin of Domitian struck in A.D. 81- 82: BARADEZ 1956a, 197 and BARADEZ 1957b, 225.

## SPAIN:

*The Balearic Islands*. A group of objects buried in the sand, presumably part of the cargo of a wrecked ship; the find, which included a coin of Caligula struck in A.D. 40 or 41, is dated to between ca. 40 and 50 A.D. by the publisher: DOMERGUE 1966, 16-17 nos. 53-59 pls. 2. 4 and 10.

Fig. 6

The chart, which is based on 107 finds of such lamps, illustrates that the type begins to appear in dated contexts of the third and fourth decades of the 1st century A.D. We see a sharp increase in occurrences between 40 and 60 A.D., and the figures reach a peak between 60 and 80 A.D.

When the figures are broken down according to the same geographical regions as in the former example, we can see that the finds from Italy and those from Europe north of the Italian peninsula and Greece resemble each other to a considerable degree. Disregarding later intrusive

# TOWARDS A BETTER UNDERSTANDING OF THE PRODUCTION PATTERN

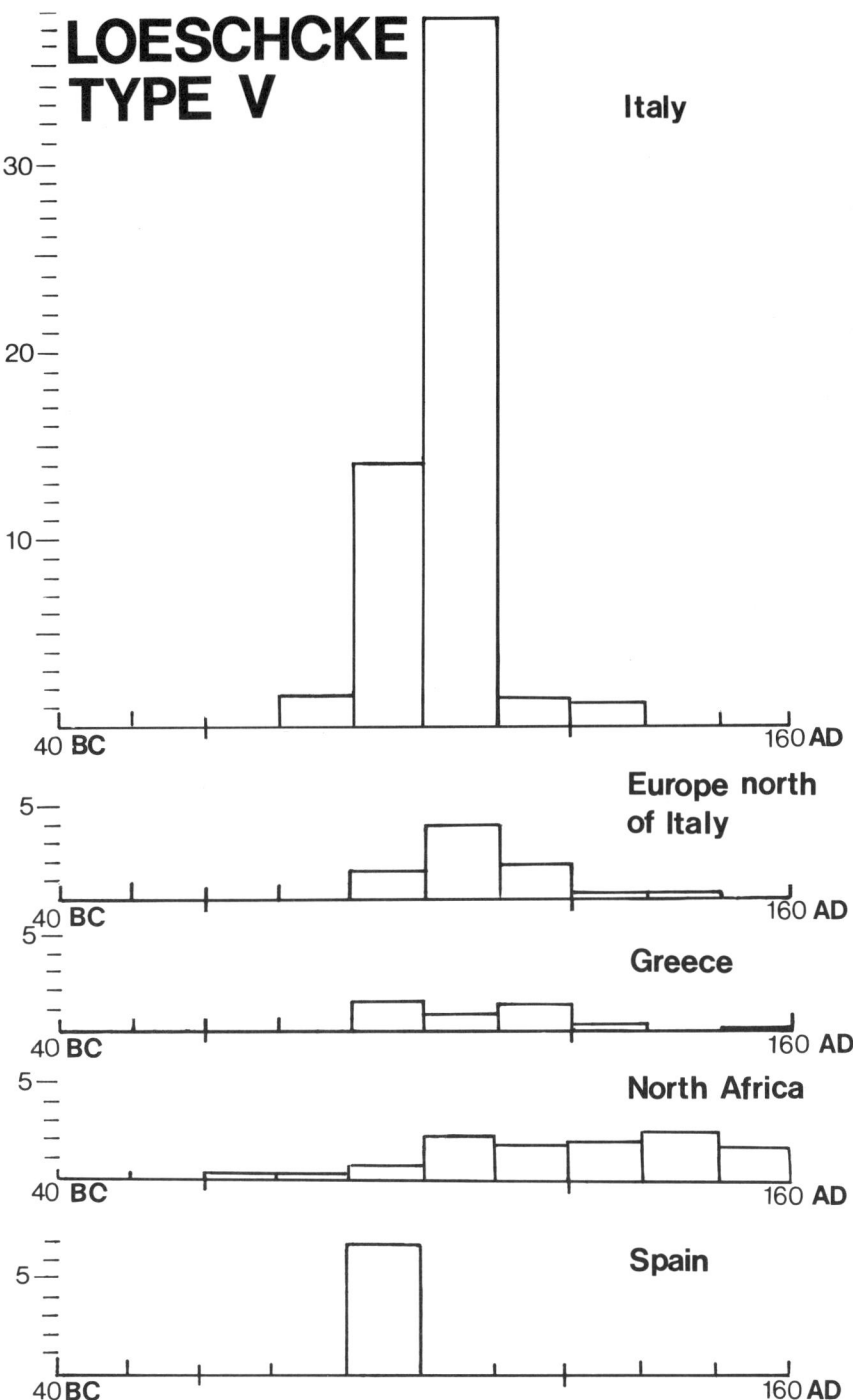

Fig. 6. Case no. 4. The chronological distribution of lamps of Loeschcke 1919 Type V in Italy, Europe north of the Alps, Greece, North Africa and Spain.

finds lamps of the type in question cease about A.D. 120 in Italy, about A.D. 140 in Europe and A.D. 180 in Greece. However, the chart depicting the situation in North Africa differs from these in showing an unbroken number of occurrences through the 2nd and most of the 3rd century A.D. It will be remembered that a similar situation existed with regard to test case 3, and the previously mentioned possible explanations also apply in this case.

*Conclusions*
It is interesting that the charts for all four test cases correspond more or less to a normal distribution pattern. This holds true for the charts based on a relatively small number of occurrences and those based on a large number of dated finds. This confirms the impression that some reliance can be placed on the results.

It seems reasonable to suggest that the rise and decline of the numbers reflects the production pattern of the involved types of lamps, although this is difficult to prove. Anyway, the following remarks are based on the assumption that this is the case.

Generally speaking, it is easier to determine the approximate starting date for the production of a given type than its end date, which is somewhat obscured by the relatively large number of residual finds, which may occur in much later contexts. The large number of finds in late contexts at Sidi Khrebish cannot be satisfactorily explained at the present stage. It will, perhaps, prove more satisfactory in the future to calculate numbers for each of the four independently dated find-situations mentioned at the outset, since the findings from one context-type could be then be used as a check on those of the others.

A comparison between the total number of independently dated lamps of the two cases 3 (=231 specimens) and 4 (=107 examples) may be revealing in another way. It suggests that the total output of lamps of the former type (Loeschcke IV) was substantially larger than that of the latter (Loeschcke V) – expressed in percentages: 68% vs. 32%. This is hardly surprising, since the corresponding figures for the lamps in the British Museum, for instance, are 75% vs. 25% (BAILEY 1980, 153-183 and 184-199), and for the "Lampes de Carthage" published by J. Deneauve 70% vs. 30% (1969, 126-145 and 149-157). The figures are so close to each other that a coincidence seems unlikely, and it may be concluded from this observation that the total production figure for lamps of Loeschcke's type IV (case 3) was approximately three times higher than that of his type V (case 4).

It was noted supra, that the peak of popularity for Loeschcke's type IV (case 3) between A.D. 40 and 60 was largely the result of a single large find. This should be kept in mind when a comparison is made between the charts showing the totalled figures for this type and those of his type V (case 4). If we accept the findings at face value, this means that the former reached a peak of popularity slightly earlier than the latter. Interestingly, this accords well with an observation made by G. Cerulli Irelli that Loeschcke type V, "si può considerare dominante tra i prodotti in uso a Pompei" (CERULLI IRELLI 1977, 59). However, caution should be applied, since the figures on which the charts are calculated to some extent rely on the finds published by Cerulli Irelli herself, and there is thus a danger of circular reasoning. Furthermore, the charts indicate that lamps of Loeschcke's type IV were actually better represented in actual numbers from A.D. 60 to A.D. 80 than lamps of his type V, although the former type was in decline relatively speaking.

The methodology applied here may not in itself facilitate assigning an exact date to a specific lamp found in an undated context, and in that respect the statement by Rebuffat quoted at the outset still holds true. However, when similar charts depicting the production patterns of the other major types are produced and combined with our knowledge of the workshops involved in the production (derived from signed lamps), it will, hopefully, prove possible to gain a better overall understanding of production trends and perhaps even of market mechanisms.

The results presented in this paper lay no claim to providing a final solution to the complex problems under consideration. Some of the basic assumptions can be challenged, and new finds of lamps in dated contexts will necessitate revisions of the charts. However, with each new find in a dated context, the picture, which is admittedly blurred now, will come more and more into focus.

The Danish National Museum
Frederiksholms Kanal 12
DK-1220 Copenhagen K

The drawings were made by Jette Eeg.

# BIBLIOGRAPHY

| | |
|---|---|
| ALARCÃO, A. MOUTINHO & DA PONTE, S. 1976 | Les Lampes in: J. Alarcão & R. Etienne et al., *Fouilles de Conimbriga* VI. Paris, 93-114. |
| ALBRECHT, Chr. (ed.) 1942 | *Das römerlager in Oberaden und das Uferkastell in Beckinghausen an der Lippe.* Dortmund. |
| 1943 | Ausgrabungen bei Haltern. Die Fundstücke der Jahre 1912-13 und 1925-32 (mit Ausnahme der Terra Sigillata und der Münz-Funde), in: A. Stieren (ed.), *Die Funde von Haltern seit 1925* (Bodenaltertümer Westfalens VI 1943), 80-120. |
| ALMAGRO, M. & LAMBOGLIA, N. 1959 | La estratigrafia del decumano A de Ampurias, *Ampurias* 21 1959, 1-28. |
| ANSELMINO, L. 1977 | Lucerne, in: Carandini & Panella (eds.) 1977, 86-100. |
| BAILEY, D.M. 1975 | *A Catalogue of the Lamps in the British Museum, 1, Greek, Hellenistic, and Early Roman Pottery Lamps.* London. |
| 1980 | *A Catalogue of the Lamps in the British Museum, 2, Roman Lamps Made in Italy.* London. |
| 1985 | *Excavations at Sidi Khrebish Benghazi (Berenice), Volume III Part 2, The Lamps* (Supplements to LibyaAnt 5). Tripoli. |
| 1987 | The Roman Terracotta Lamp Industry, Another View about Exports, in: Oziol & Rebuffat et al. 1987, 59-63. |
| 1988 | *A Catalogue of the Lamps in the British Museum, 3, Roman Provincial Lamps.* London. |
| BARADEZ, J. 1957a | Nouvelles fouilles à Tipasa: Dans une nécropole païenne, *Libyca* 5 1957, 159-220. |
| 1957b | Nouvelles fouilles à Tipasa, Survivances du culte de Baal et Tanit au 1er siècle de l'ère chrétienne, 1re Partie, Tombe d'un sacrificateur, *Libyca* 5 1957, 221-275. |
| 1968 | Les nécropoles de Tipasa: Tombes du cimitière occidental côtier, *AntAfr* 2 1968, 77-93. |
| BENOIT, F. 1958 | Nouvelles Épaves de Provence, *Gallia* 16 1958, 5-39. |
| BISI INGRASSIA, A.M. 1977 | Le lucerne fittili dei nuovi scave di Ercolano, in: Aavv, *L'instrumentum domesticum di Ercolano e Pompei nella prima età imperiale.* Roma, 73-104. |
| BONNET, J. 1988 | *Lampes céramiques signées, Définition critique d'ateliers du Haut Empire* (Documents d'Archéologie Française 13). Paris. |
| BONGHI JOVINO, M. (ed.) 1984 | *Ricerche a Pompei, l'insula 5 della Regio VI dalle origini al 79 d.C. I (campagne di scavo 1976-1979)* (Bibliotheca Archaeologica 5). Roma. |
| BRONEER, O. 1930 | *Corinth IV*, Part II, Terracotta Lamps. Cambridge, Massachusetts. |
| CARANDINI, A. & PANELLA, C. 1973. | Datazione degli strati e delle fasi edilizie del saggio nell'Area SO, in: Carandini & Panella (eds.) 1973, 654-657. |
| 1973 | *Ostia* III (Seminario di archeologia e storia dell'arte greca e romana del l'Università di Roma, Studi miscellanei 21). Roma. |
| 1977 (eds.) | *Ostia* IV (Seminario di archeologia e storia dell'arte greca e romana dell'università di Roma, Studi miscellanei 23). Roma. |

# TOWARDS A BETTER UNDERSTANDING OF THE PRODUCTION PATTERN

CERULLI IRELLLI, G., 1977 — Una officina di lucerne fittili a Pompei, in: Aavv, *L'instrumentum domesticum di Ercolano e Pompei nella prima età imperiale*, Roma, 53-72.

DENEAUVE, J. 1969 — *Lampes de Carthage*. Paris.

DOMERGUE, C 1966 — Un envoi de lampes du potier Caius Clodius, *Mélanges de la casa de Velazquez* 2 1966, 5-40.

DOTHAN, M. & FREEDMAN, D.N. 1967 — Ashdod I, The First Season of Excavations 1962, *'Atiqot* 7.

DUMOULIN, A. 1965 — Les puits et fosses de la colline Saint-Jacques à Cavaillon (Vaucluse), *Gallia* 23 1965, 1-85.

ENNABLI, A. 1973 — Lampes en terre cuite, in: *La nécropole romaine de Raqqada* (Collection notes et documents, vol. VIII). Tunis, 83-143.

FARKA, C. 1977 — *Die römischen Lampen vom Magdalensberg*. Klagenfurt.

FEVRIER, P.-A. 1980 — A propos de la ceramique de la Mediterranee occidentale, in: P. Lévêque J.-P. Morel (eds.) *Céramiques héllenistiques et romaines* (Centre de Recherches d'Histoire Ancienne 36). Paris, 159-199.

FINLEY, M.I. 1973 — *The Ancient Economy*. London.

FISCHBACH, O. 1896 — Römische Lampen aus Poetovio, *Mittheilungen des historischen Vereines für Steiermark* 44, 3-64.

GOETHERT-POLASCHEK, K. 1985 — *Katalog der römischen Lampen des Rheinischen Landesmuseums Trier*. Mainz am Rhein.

GORECKI, J. 1975 — Studien zur Sitte der Münzbeigabe in römerzeitlichen Körpergräbern zwischen Rhein, Mosel und Somme, *Bericht der Römisch-Germanischen Kommision* 56, 179-467.

GUALANDI GENITO, M.C., 1977 — *Lucerne fittili delle collezioni del Museo Civico archeologico di Bologna*. Bologna.

1986 — *Le lucerne antiche del Trentino*. Trento.

HÄHNLE, K. 1912 — Ausgrabungen bei Haltern. Die keramischen Funde der Jahre 1908-1910, *Mitteilungen der Altertums-Kommission für Westfalen* 6, 33-66.

HARRIS, W. V. 1980 — Roman Terracotta Lamps: the Organization of an Industry, *JRS* 70, 126-145.

HAYES, J. W. 1978 — Pottery Report-1976 in: J. H. Humphrey (ed.), *Excavations at Carthage 1976 conducted by the University of Michigan*, Vol. IV. Ann Arbor, 23-98.

HAWKES, C.F.C. & HULL, M. R. 1947 — *Camulodunum, First Report on the Excavations at Colchester 1930-1939*. London.

IVÁNYI, D. 1935 — *Die Pannonischen Lampen, Eine typologisch-chronologische Übersicht*. Budapest.

JOHNSON, A. 1983 — *Roman Forts*. New York.

JOLY, E. 1974 — *Lucerne del Museo di Sabratha* (Monografie di archeologia libica 11). Roma.

LAMBOGLIA, N. 1950 — *Gli scavi di Albintimilium e la cronologia della ceramica romana, parte prima, Campagne di scavo 1938-1940*. Bordighera.

| | |
|---|---|
| 1959 | Prime osservazioni sugli strati preromani di Albium Intemelium, *RivStlig* 25, 239-247. |
| 1970 | La topografia e stratigrafia di Albingaunum dopo gli scavi 1955-1956, *RivStLig* 36, 23-62. |
| LANCEL, S. 1967 | Tipasitana I: fouilles dans la nécropole occidentale de Tipasa, *BAAlger* 1 1962-1965, 41-74. |
| 1970 | Tipasitana IV : La nécropole romaine occidentale de la porte de Césarée. – Rapport préliminaire, *BAAlger* 4, 149-266. |
| LEIBUNDGUT, A. 1977 | *Die Römischen Lampen in der Schweiz.* Bern. |
| LOESCHCKE, S. 1909 | *Keramische Funde in Haltern, Mitteilungen der Altertums-Kommission für Westfalen* 5. |
| 1919 | *Lampen aus Vindonissa, Ein Beitrag zur Geschichte von Vindonissa und des antiken Beleuchtungswesen.* Zürich. |
| MARABINI MOEVS, M.T. 1973 | *The Roman Thin Walled Pottery from Cosa (1948-1954), MAAR* 32. |
| MOREL, J.-P. 1981 | *Céramique campanienne: Les formes* (Bibliothèque des écoles françaises d'Athènes et de Rome fasc. 144). Roma. |
| OZIOL, Th. 1987 | *Bibliographie générale,* in: Oziol & Rebuffat et al. 1987, 97-125. |
| OZIOL, Th. & REBUFFAT, R., et al. 1987 | *Les lampes de terre cuite en Méditerranée des origines à Justinien.* Lyon. |
| PANELLA, C. 1977 | Datazione degli strati, in: CARANDINI & PANELLA (eds.) 1977, 286-292. |
| PAVOLINI, C. 1977 | Le lucerne fittili romane del museo Nazionale di Napoli, in: Aavv, *L'instrumentum domesticum di Ercolano e Pompei nella prima età imperiale.* Roma, 33-51. |
| 1980 | Una produzione italica di lucerne: le Vogelkopflampen ad ansa trasversale, *Bullettino della Commissione Archeologica Comunale di Roma* 85, (1976-1977) 45-134. |
| PERLZWEIG, J. 1961 | *The Athenian Agora VII, Lamps of the Roman Period.* Princeton, New Jersey |
| PÉTRY, F. 1974 | Circonscription d'Alsace, *Gallia* 32, 367-400 |
| REBUFFAT, R. 1987 | Lampes Romaines à Gholaia (Bu Njem, Libye), in: Oziol & Rebuffat et al. 1987, 83-90. |
| RICCI, M. 1973 | Per una cronologia delle lucerne tardo-repubbliche, *RivStLig* 39, 168-234. |
| RITTERLING, E. 1913 | *Das frührömische Lager bei Hofheim im Taunus* (Annalen des Vereins für Nassauische Altertumskunde und Geschichtsforschung 40). Wiesbaden. |
| ROMANAZZI, L. 1984 | Lucerne in: BONGHI JOVINO (ed.) 1984, 234-249. |
| SALONE, C. 1973 | Lucerne, in: CARANDINI & C. PANELLA (eds.) 1973, 395-404. |
| SCHÖNBERGER, H. 1969 | The Roman Frontier in Germany: an Archaeological Survey, *JRS* 59 1969, 144-197. |
| SIMON, H.-G. 1961 | Die Funde aus dem Bereich des Lagers in Rödgen, *Saalburg Jahrbuch* 19, 59-88. |

| | |
|---|---|
| SLANE, K. W. 1986 | Two Deposits from the Early Roman Cellar Building, Corinth, *Hesperia* 55, 271-318. |
| ULBERT, G. 1969 | *Das frühromische Kastell Rheingönheim, Die Funde aus den Jahren 1912 und 1913* (Limesforschungen 9). Berlin. |
| 1975 | Der Auerberg, Vorbericht über die Ausgrabungen von 1968-1974, in: *Ausgrabungen in Deutschland gefördert von der deutschen Forschungsgemeinschaft 1950-1975* I. Vorgeschichte, Römerzeit), Mainz, 409-433. |
| VEGAS, M. 1966 | Die Römischen Lampen von Neuss, in: *Limesforschungen 7, Novaesium II.* Berlin, 63-127. |
| WOLFF, G. 1902 | *Das Kastell Okarben* (Der Obergermanisch-Raetische Limes des Roemerreiches Lieferung XVI, Band II, B, Nr. 25a). Heidelberg. |
| ZACCARIA RUGGIU, A. 1977 | Lucerne, in: A. Frova (ed.), *Scavi di Luni, II. Relazione delle campagne di scavo 1972-1974.* Roma, 290-304. |

# ROMA: ASPETTI DELLA FORTIFICAZIONE FLUVIALE*

LOTTE EMILIE HERTZ

Nei primi due secoli d.C. l'Impero Romano era così forte che i provvedimenti per la difesa furono necessari esclusivamente lungo le frontiere. Le città all'interno dell'Impero non ne avevano bisogno: le mura costruite in questo periodo sono il prodotto di un orgoglio municipale (v. per es. Fano e Sepino; PIETRANGELI 1957, 462). Infatti con la *Pax Romana* il clima generale era tranquillo.

Con Marco Aurelio iniziano i segni di quella che sarà poi la crisi del III secolo: pestilenze, invasioni dei "barbari", ribellioni nelle province da parte dei generali. Più grave ancora era stato il periodo di crisi seguito alla morte di Commodo, quando si giunse a mettere all'incanto la carica stessa dell'Imperatore.

Giunto al potere Settimio Severo restaurò l'unità nell' Impero e rafforzò i confini e iniziò una radicale riorganizzazione dell'apparato statale, a cui diede esplicitamente il carattere di autocrazia militare.

La fine violenta della monarchia, cioè l'uccisione di Alessandro Severo nel 235, aprí bruscamente un vuoto di potere, dato che non esisteva la classe senatoria capace di garantire la continuità delle istituzioni; in questo vuoto si inseriva adesso la forza di un esercito in cui era prevalente l'elemento barbarico. Questo vuoto del potere centrale favorisce gli insuccessi: alla crisi militare si accompagna la crisi economica, politica e morale che mina alla base la compagine dello stato. La crisi demografica si rifletteva anche sulla situazione dell'esercito e sulla sempre più grave difficoltà di reclutamento. Sono sempre più numerosi i barbari, accolti come ospiti nei territori dell'Impero, che entravano a fare parte delle legioni. La dissersione in massa dalle campagne e l'affluenza verso i centri urbani da parte dei piccoli proprietari, incalzati dal progressivo estendersi del latifondo, determina un costante peggioramento della situazione economica. Dal campo dominante della agricoltura la crisi economica si estende a tutti i settori. Ne è conseguenza una grave crisi monetaria ed un accentuarsi di un'economia

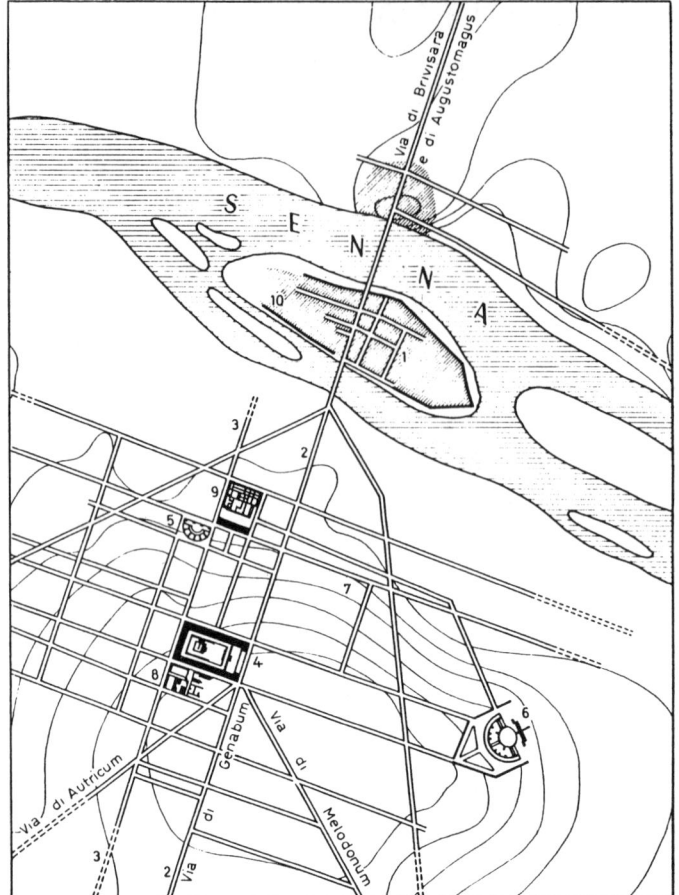

Fig. 1. Pianta di Parigi. Si vedono le mura tardoantiche su Ile de la Cité (da *EAA* 5, p. 953).

chiusa, che tende all'autosufficienza della grandi proprietà terrieri. Moti di origine sociale, sommosse militari, secessioni di province minacciano frequentemente l'unità stessa dell'Impero. Tutte le forze sociali si esprimono nominando i propri Imperatori, che si alternano in brevi e caotici regni. Ai confini gli attacchi delle popolazioni barbariche si intensificano e si fanno sempre più minacciosi: le incursioni si spingono sino all'Italia settentrionale.

In questo periodo cominciano a fiorire le costruzioni di fortificazioni urbane. Si costruiscono mura difensive in quasi settanta città nella Gallia, circa quaranta in Spagna e probabilmente settanta in Italia

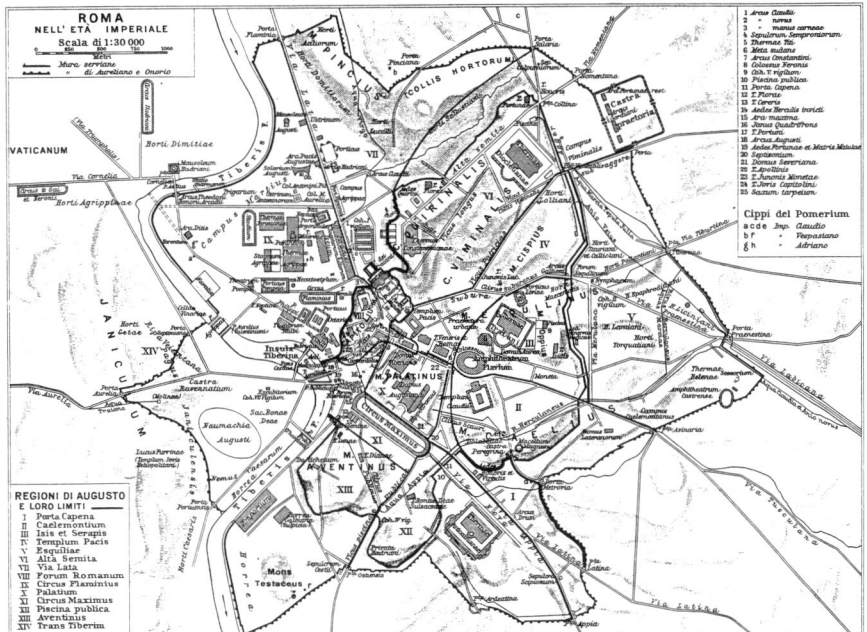

Fig. 2. Pianta diRoma. Il corso delle mura aureliane è disegnato in rosso (da *Atlanti Storiche de Agostini* p. 22).

(JOHNSON 1983, 10). Queste mura hanno quasi tutte delle caratteristiche in comune, come per es. l'inglobamento di edifici preesistenti. Roma è un ottimo esempio in quanto le mura aureliane hanno inglobato l'Anfiteatro Castrense, i Castra Praetoria, la Piramide di Caio Cestio, gli acquedotti ecc. (RICHMOND 1930, 15-26). Altre caratteristiche tipiche sono: la riutilizzazione dei materiali provenienti da edifici demoliti, le moltissime torri per l'impiego di una numerosa artiglieria e poi, da non dimenticare, la pianta quadrangolare e i lati rettilinei, anche se questo tipo di pianta viene sconsigliato da Vitruvio (I, 5,2). Vale in particolare per le città fondate presso fiumi, la regola di costruire la cinta muraria intorno al centro amministrativo. Qui pongo come esempio Parigi dove solamente Ile de la Cité è stata fortificata, anche se l'area *Fig. 1* urbana era molto più vasta.

Roma e Verona divergono da questa norma in quanto le mura tar- *Fig. 2-3* doantiche di queste due città sono costruite su ambedue le sponde dei fiumi Tevere e Adige (RICHMOND 1930; 1935).

A Roma è stato incorporato nelle mura di Aureliano anche il *Mons*

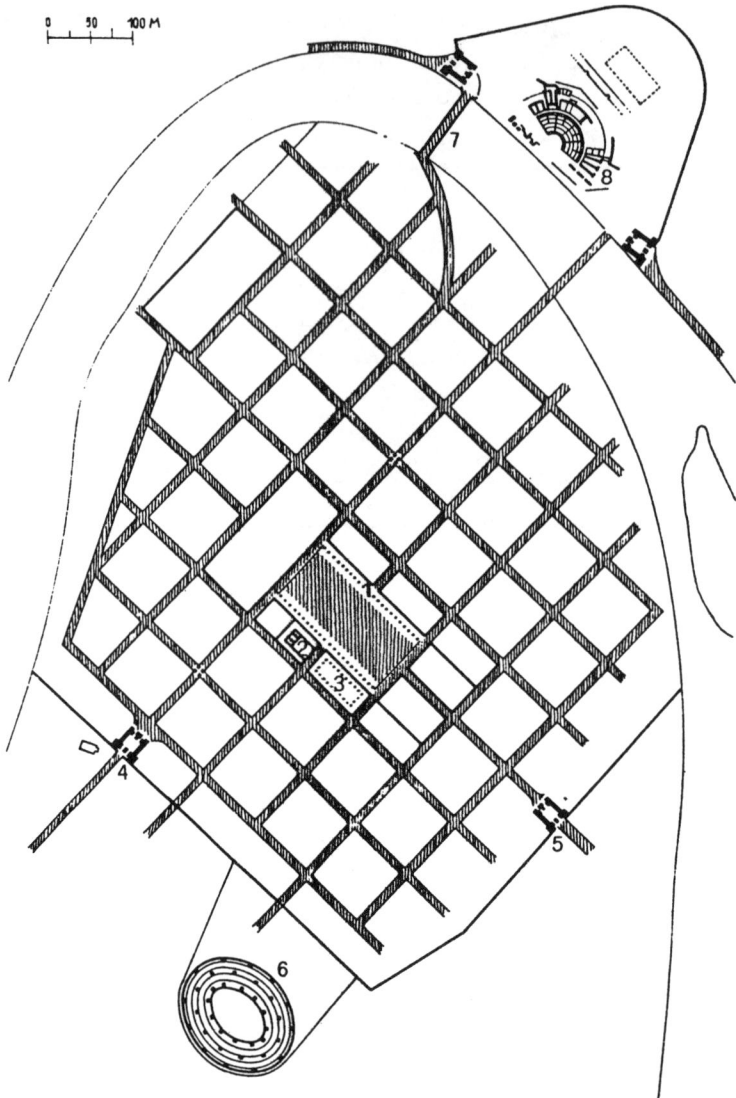

Fig. 3. Pianta di Verona. In nero il corso delle mura gallieniche (da *Guide archeologiche Laterza: Emilia Venezia*, p.162).

*Janiculum*. Ma perchè era necessario integrare il fiume e il Gianicolo nel progetto difensivo?

Pare che questo colle sia stato sempre di vitale importanza per la città dal punto di vista militare: era una ottima base di osservazione e perciò non doveva essere occupato dal nemico. Livio (I, 33,6) scrive che Anco Marzio "incluse alla città il Gianicolo, perchè il nemico non ne facesse la sua *arx* nel caso di un attacco contro Roma. Non soltanto fu fortificato con mura, ma fu anche congiunto al resto della città mediante il Ponte Sublicio per facilitare le comunicazioni fra le due sponde".

Anche se non si conoscono resti nel terreno, Säflund (1932, 188-190) congettura che il Gianicolo fosse munito con mura, non soltanto con una fortezza isolata, ma con mura vere e proprie. Lui deroga, comunque, al fatto che queste mura siano state costruite da Anco Marzio, e sarebbero invece del 87 a.C.. Un altro punto importante, per Säflund, è l'avvenimento del 43 a.C. quando il senato decide di custodire sul Gianicolo l'erario che generalmente era conservato nell'*arx* capitolina. Questo fatto, ovviamente, indica che il Gianicolo era incluso entro le mura urbane, perchè sarebbe stato pericoloso affidare l'erario a una custodia isolata.

Nel III secolo d.C. il problema non è più l'erario ma probabilmente i mulini sulle pendici del Gianicolo dei quali ci parla Procopio (*B.G.* I, 19): "Ora dirò in qual modo i Romani costruirono il muro da ambo le parti del fiume. Il luogo, là dove la cinta sorge sulla corrente del fiume è piano e di assai facile accesso. Di fronte a questo luogo, aldilà del Tevere, si trova un gran colle dove da tempo antico furono costruiti tutti i mulini della città poichè una gran massa d'acqua portata dall'acquedotto alla cima di quel colle cade di là con grande impeto lungo il declivio. Perciò i Romani antichi pensarono di circondare di muro il colle e la ripa del fiume da quella parte affinché i nemici non potessero danneggiare i mulini e passato il fiume facilmente far danno al muro della città. Avendo dunque gettato un ponte sul fiume pensarono di unire insieme il muro e costruite molte case nella regione opposta fecero sì che il Tevere corresse in mezzo alla città".

La datazione di questi mulini è sempre stata un punto di discordia. Wikander (1979, 13-36) afferma che si può dedurre un *terminus post quem* dal trattato di Frontinus, *De aquae ductu urbis Romae*, scritto nel 97/98 d.C., perchè non vi è menzionato alcun mulino ad acqua. Dall'altra parte, continua Wikander, sappiamo anche che i mulini sul Gianicolo sono di grande importanza nel 398 perchè sono citati in un editto di Onorio e Arcadio (*Cod. Theod.*, XIV, 15,4). I mulini, allora, sono stati costruiti dentro quest'arco di tempo. E ancora, Procopio (*B.G.* I, 19,9) scrive espressamente che le mura aureliane sul lato destro del Tevere furono costruite proprio per difendere i mulini. Perciò Wikander sostiene che questi mulini gianicolensi sono stati costruiti durante la fine del III secolo o un secolo più tardi.

Un'altra teoria sulla datazione dei mulini viene data da Coarelli (1987, 429-456). Lui si oppone alla datazione data da Wikander. Secondo Corelli, il testo di Procopio allude all'esistenza dei mulini anteriormente alla costruzione delle mura. Questo perchè la costruzione del Ponte di Probo sarebbe un miglioramento di un sistema già da qualche tempo esistente. Anche Wikander, però, spiega il Ponte di Probo in funzione dei collegamenti tra mulini e emporio. Questo afferma sempre la costruzione dei mulini nel corso del III secolo. Eppure Coarelli vuole dare una datazione più precisa. In uno studio su un mulino ad acqua nelle Terme di Caracalla, Schiøler & Wikander (1983, 47-64) affermano che questo mulino è stato realizzato da Severo Alessandro. Per Coarelli questa affermazione dimostra che anche le installazioni dei mulini sul Gianicolo sono dovute a Severo Alessandro: una preoccupazione politica del governo centrale circa la distribuzione farina e pane.

Accettando la datazione proposta da Coarelli, le mura aureliane in Trastevere sarebbero state costruite non soltanto per difendere i mulini, ma anche per avere il controllo di ambedue le sponde perchè gli assalitori non potessero tagliare i rifornimenti soprattutto idrici. Infatti non appena i vulnerabillissimi acquedotti della città verranno tagliati, la popolazione si ridurrà a vivere nell' ansa nord-ovest del fiume col conseguente abbandono delle zone alte (QUERCIOLI 1982, 124).

La difesa del Tevere costituisce ora un altro problema perchè i nemici scendendo da nord secondo la corrente del fiume, potevano facilmente entrare in Roma.

Confrontando Roma con Verona che ha una situazione geografica simile, vediamo che le mura gallieniche del 265 ca. scavalcono l'Adige su due ponti tra loro poco distanti per raggiungere e circondare il Colle S. Pietro. Questo colle è stato incluso nel sistema difensivo perchè sarebbe rischioso abbandonarlo a eventuali attaccanti e anche per controllare meglio il traffico fluviale (MARCHINI 1978, 82). Importante è anche il teatro che appunto si trova addossato al Colle S. Pietro. È ben nota la ricorrente di fare partecipare il teatro ad una sequenza monumentale dominante: a Verona il teatro aperto sull'altra sponda dell'Adige lungo le pendici della collina di S. Pietro chiude la prospettiva assiale del *decumanus* che costeggia lo spiazzo del *Capitolium* (GROS & TORELLI 1988, 222).

Ritornando a Roma vediamo che il *braccio settentrionale* delle mura aureliane in Trastevere scavalcava il fiume su dei piloni (COZZA 1986, 104, fig. 3) trovati poco a monto di Ponte Sisto. Questi piloni sono stati visti sin dal 1880 e come il primo Borsari li attribuì al Ponte di Agrippa. Il Ponte di Argrippa, invece, è stato riconosciuto nell'attuale ponte Sisto ricostruito nel 1475 da Sisto IV appunto sui resti di un ponte più antico (LE GALL 1953, 210; COZZA 1986, 104) che era detto sia *pons Agrippae, Antonini, Aurelii, e Valentiniani*.

Cozza (1986, 104-107) propone di riferire i soprannominati piloni al ponte descritto da procopio (*B.G.* I, 19), dove Le Gall (1953, 210-211) li vuole fare partecipare a un sistema difensivo (... *ils ont pu servir à soutenir un dispositif destiné à empêcher des barques ennemies de pénétrer à l'interieur de la ville.*). È molto difficile individuare la natura di questi piloni perchè l'unica fonte che ne parla è Procopio e egli non scrive mai il nome del ponte. Sembra anche quasi improbabile immaginare due ponti costruiti con una distanza di solo 150 metri l'uno dall'altro.

Questi piloni appartengono senza dubbio a un tipo di ponte sul quale correva il muro o meglio era il muro che scavalcava il fiume su questi piloni. Ovviamente è stato lasciato dello spazio aperto tra il fiume e il muro perchè potessero passare le navi mercantili. Ecco perchè assomiglia un ponte. Su questo tipo di ponte passava probabilmente il cammino di ronda ed era fortificato come il resto delle mura con feritoie e merli oppure come il ponte di Pondel (il quale consta di due viadotti a diverso livello: quello superiore scoperto e quello inferiore coperto), sebbene di età augustea e con una funzione diversa da quella difensiva. In tempo di guerra, per chiudere il passaggio lasciato aperto nel muro per fare passare le barche, furono usate delle catene di ferro o una rete di ferro che furono attaccate ai piloni o alle mura. Procopio (*B.G.* I, 19,25) scrive che Belisario "attaccò al ponte lunghe catene di ferro che arrivarono da una parte all'altra del fiume (ἀλύσεις μακρὰς σιδηρᾶς πρὸ τῆς γεφύρας ἤρτησεν, ἐξικνουμένας ἐς Τίβεριν ὅλον). Tutti gli oggetti che furono portate con la corrente si fermarono davanti a queste catene ... Belisario fece questo non tanto per i mulini, ma perchè pensò che il nemico potesse venire oltre il ponte proprio in questo punto con

Fig. 4. Du Perac 1577 (FRUTAZ, *Le Piante di Roma*).

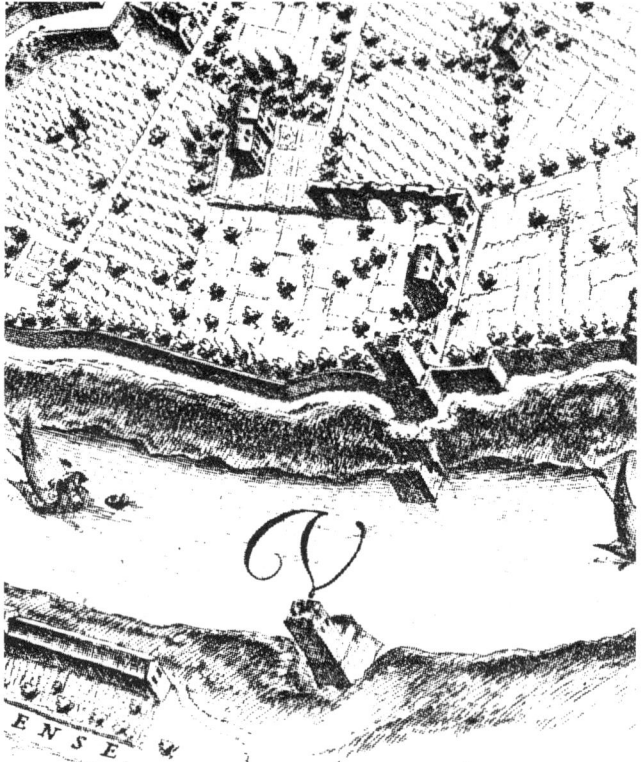

Fig. 5. Falda 1676 (FRUTAZ, *Le Piante di Roma*).

molte barche e entrare in Roma ...". Il cosiddetto ponte nominato dallo storiografo greco deve essere questi piloni sui quali passava il muro, perché se fosse stato il ponte di Agrippa che si trova 150 metri più a valle, il nemico avrebbe potuto farsi portare dalla corrente del fiume, entrare in città e assediarla.

Ora si pone il problema del *braccio meridionale* delle mura aureliane in Trastevere, perchè anche qui ci doveva essere un tipo di fortificazione sul fiume, anche se non ce ne resta quasi nessuna testimonianza. In questa zona le mura aureliane, provenienti da porta Ostiensis, passano a sud del Monte Testaccio; arrivate alla riva fluviale giravano di 90 gradi lungo il fiume, racchiudendo in questo modo i principali sistemi orreari, fino quasi allo estremo ovest della *Porticus Aemilia*; una grande torre vi fungeva da termine, e sulla riva opposta una gemella, dalla quale il corso delle mura continuava su per il Gianicolo (RODRIQUEZ ALMEIDA 1984, 109). Cozza (1989, 138-143) ha proposto un ponte tra queste due torri terminali che appunto stavano all'altezza della porta Portuensis, illustrate nelle piante di Du Perac dal 1577 e di Falda dal 1676. *Fig. 4-5* Questo ponte ipotetico avrebbe funzionato come una chiusura del fiume – altrimenti il nemico avrebbe potuto entrare in città da questa parte.

Nel 1984 la Sopraintendenza Archeologica di Roma ha fatto un rilevamento sonografico del fiume. Proprio nella zona che ci interessa è stato registrato un edificio rettangolare con i due lati lunghi trasversali al Tevere e dodici cumuli di pietrame, sparsi in successione al centro *Fig. 6* dell'alveo. Cozza (1989, 139-140) congettura nell'edificio rettangolare una torre e nei cumuli di pietrame il materiale trascinato dalla corrente dopo l'avvenuto crollo di un ponte.

Con la sopraffatta analisi del *braccio settentrionale* e il suo scavalcamento del fiume, vorrei proporre una simile sistemazione per il *braccio meridionale*, cioè dei piloni sui quali possano scavalcare le mura.

Se passiamo al IX secolo Papa Leone IV (847-855), per il pericolo dei Saraceni, restaura le mura e le porte di Roma. Rialza anche quindici torri, delle quali particolarmente importanti sono le due costruite presso la porta Portuensis, presso la riva del Tevere. La torre sul fiume fu fortificata non solo con pietre ma anche con ferro (*ipsam igitur turrem non solum lapidibus verum etiam ferro munire curavit*) per cui in caso di un attacco nemico nessuna nave avrebbe potuto passare. Questo passo del *Liber Pontificalis* (ed. Duchesne II, 115) è stato interpretato da Nibby (1821, 264-266) come se tra le due torri ci fosse una catena di sbarramento. Questa ipotesi è stata ripresa da Mocchegiani

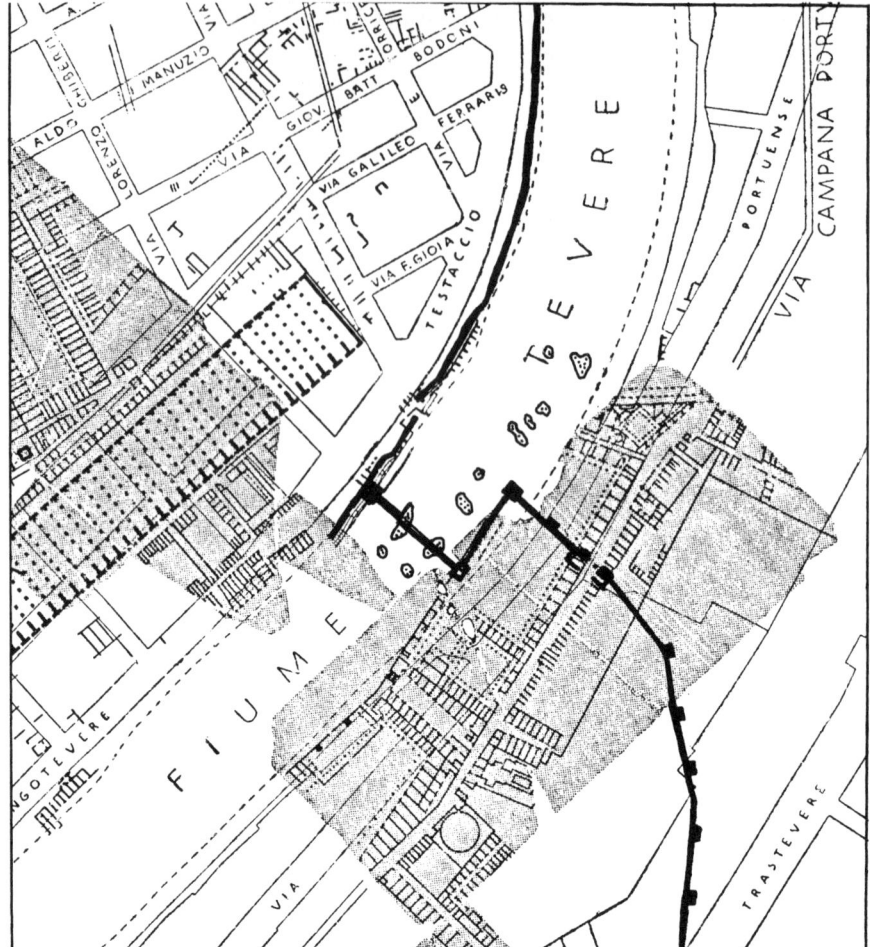

Fig. 6. Schema della topografia antica (GATTI 1960). Resti sommersi del rilevamento sonografico 1984 (puntini); ricostruzione del tracciato delle mura (nero). (Da COZZA, *BullCom* 92, 1987-1988, p. 142.

Carpano (1985, 51), mentre Cozza (1989, 143) deroga a questa teoria. Per lui si tratta di una torre rinforzata con grosse pietre tenute insieme con grappe di ferro (anche se si accetta la variante E: *ferreis m.c. catenis*).

Lanciani (1902-12, IV, 84-85) scrive che Gregorio XIII nel 1575 restaurò le difese del porto di ripa erette da Leone IV *"propter saracenorum periculum"* e consistenti in due torri "una di là e l'altra di quà da Tevere, che si riguardano assieme, nelle quali erano già certi anelloni di ferro per attraversare il fiume con grosse catene ... Nel 1628 alla riva del Tevere in una vigna vicina a Porta Portese fu trovato un grandissimo marmo con uno di essi anelloni assai rugginosi attaccato ...".

Il sistema fortificatorio che legava il *braccio meridionale* delle mura aureliane in Trastevere alla riva opposta era, come si è già visto, scomparso al tempo di Leone IV. Egli restaura quindici torri e dopo sbarra il Tevere con catene di ferro. Una totale ricostruzione del sistema difensivo del Tevere sarebbe stato un compito troppo impegnativo, e perciò il Papa si accontentava di sbarrare il Tevere soltanto con catene di ferro.

Se il crollo della difesa fluviale si era verificato già all'epoca della guerra greco-gotica è difficile giudicare perché non abbiamo nessuna fonte che ci dà una notizia al riguardo. Io vorrei ipotizzare che ciò fosse avvenuto tra il 553 e il 847, perchè sappiamo che i Goti non sono entrati in Roma durante la guerra greco-gotica, e se il Tevere fosse stato aperto in questo punto, i Goti sarebbero facilmente entrati in Roma. Anche il fatto, che Procopio non nomina questo punto della città come debole, significa, che qui non c'erano dei problemi di difendere la città. L'ipotizzare la scomparsa del sistema fortificatorio entro le due date soprammenzionate pare probabile anche perchè Roma viene abbandonata durante questi secoli.

Il calo demografico del V-VI secolo, dovuto a vari fattori (invasioni, epidemie, perdita del ruolo politico e amministrativo di Roma, in quanto non più capitale dell'Impero, ecc.), produce, dapprima, un diradamento dell'abitato, con la sopravvivenza di nuclei sparsi all'interno dell'area racchiusa delle mura aureliane, ma, già dall'alto medioevo, non tarda a determinare l'abbandono della zona collinosa e la concentrazione della popolazione lungo la sponda del fiume. Fra i motivi che producono questo spostamento risulta di non poca rilevanza, dopo l'interruzione della rete di acquedotti della Roma antica, la facilità di rifornimento idrico, che avviene ora attingendo acqua direttamente dal fiume o dai pozzi, attraverso i quali più facilmente si raggiunge la falda idrica nell'area di fondovalle. L'abitato viene così a restringersi nella zona pianeggiante, prevalentemente – come per il passato – lungo la riva sinistra del Tevere, in corrispondenza dell'Isola Tiberina, a nord e ovest del Teatro di Marcello. La riva destra, invece, vede sopravvivere, anche se in dimensioni ridotte, l'antico agglomenrato del Trastevere, ed assiste alla nascita di quella che può definirsi l'unica effettiva crescita urbana

Fig. 7. Porto Pisano, bassorilievo genovese che celebra la vittoria di Corrado Doria nel 1290. Da sinistra a destra: torri del Fanale, Sorise e di San Vito; catena di chiusura dele canale del porto e fondaco-fortezza. (Genova, Museo di Sant' Agostino). (Da *Città portuali del Mediterraneo*, fig. 137).

della città mediovale: la *Civitas Leoniana* intorno alla basilica di S. Pietro (MOTTA 1986, 120). Il risultato di questi cambiamenti è una città topograficamente frazionata, che seppure lentamente, sostituisce la difesa globale con un concetto di difesa locale e personale. Per questi motivi le mura aureliane e in particolare i sistemi fortificatori del Tevere non sono state mantenute con cura durante i primi secoli dell'alto medioevo.

Credo che il silenzio che troviamo nelle fonti antiche sulla fortificazione fluviale e in particolare della fortificazione del Tevere (abbiamo soltanto la testimonianza di Procopio), deriva dal fatto che non era una consuetudine costruire le mura difensive su ambedue le sponde di un fiume. Abbiamo, come già visto, solamente Roma e Verona, e queste due città avevano appunto dei problemi particolari descritti innanzi.

L'uso di catene di ferro o reti di ferro per sbarrare un fiume in caso di un attacco nemico era sicuramente un sistema di difesa ovvio nell'Impero Romano. Enrico Guidoni (1989, 215) parlando delle città-porto fluviali nomina le difese approntate da Leone IV contro le incursioni saracene, consistenti appunto in un completo sbarramento del fiume mediante catene tese tra due torri: un espediente, questo, adottato comunemente per sbarrare sia l'accesso ai porti marittimi sia la navigazione fluviale. Fu usato nel Porto di Pisa, il quale, però, fu preso dai Genovesi nel 1362. Sebbene questo tipo di difesa non si sia visto del

*Fig. 7*

tutto sicuro, fu usato per esempio nella fortezza settecentesca di Sveaborg in Finlandia; senza dubbio è stato impiegato anche in altri luoghi fino a questo periodo e magari anche più tardi.

Institute of Prehistoric
and Classical Archaeology
University of Copenhagen
DK-1467 Copenhagen K

## NOTA

\* Questo articolo è un approfondimento di una parte della mia tesi di laurea, discussa all'Università di Perugia e pubblicata da Lucos Cozza in *BullCom* 92, 1988. Riguardava il braccio meridionale delle mura aureliane in Trastevere: dal Tevere alla porta Portuensis e da questa alla porta Aurelia-S. Pancrazio. In questo luogo vorrei cercare di mettere fuoco sul problema della fortificazione fluviale in particolare a Roma.

## BIBLIOGRAFIA

| | |
|---|---|
| ADAM, J. P. 1982 | *L'architecture militaire grecque*. Paris. |
| BALIL, A. 1960 | La defensa de Hispania en el Bajo Imperio, *Zephyrus*, 11, 179-197. |
| CASSANELLI, L., DELFINI, G. & FONTI, D. 1974 | *Le Mura di Roma*. Roma. |
| CASTAGNOLI, F. 1952 | Documenti di scavi eseguiti in Roma negli anni 1860-70, *BullCom* 73, 123-187. |
| 1958 | *Topografia e urbanistica di Roma*. Roma. |
| COARELLI, F. 1987 | La situazione edilizia di Roma sotto Severo Alessandro, *Urbs, espace urbaine et histoire*. Actes du colloque international, Rome, 1986). |
| COZZA, L. 1986 | Mura Aureliane 1. Trastevere, il braccio settentrionale da Tevere a Porta Aurelia-S. Pancrazio, *BullCom* 91, 103-130. |
| 1988 | Mura Aureliane 2. Trastevere, il braccio meridionale da Tevere a Porta Aurelia-S. Pancrazio, *BullCom* 92, 137-174. |
| COZZO, G. 1970 | *Ingegneria romana*. Roma. |
| FRUTAZ, A. P. 1962 | *Le piante di Roma*. Roma. |
| GROS, P. & TORELLI, M. 1988 | *Storia della urbanistica*. Bari. |
| GUIDONI, E. 1989 | La città-porto fluviale in Italia, *Città portuali del Mediterraneo* (Atti Convegno Internazionale di Genova, 1985) Genova. |
| HOMO, L. 1967 | *Essai sur le Règne de l'Empereur Aurelian* (270-275). Roma. |
| JOHNSON, S. 1983 | *Late Roman Fortifications*. London |

KRAUTHEIMER, R. 1980   *Rome: Profile of a City 312-1308.* New Jersey.

LANCIANI, R. 1902-1912   *Storia degli scavi di Roma e notizie intorno le collezioni romane di antichità.* Roma.

1980   *The Destruction of Ancient Rome.* New York.

LAWRENCE, A. W. 1979   *Greek Aims in Fortification.* Oxford.

LE GALL, J. 1953   *Le Tibre dans l'Antiquitè.* Paris.

LUGLI, G. 1938   *I monumenti antichi di Roma e suburbio III.* Roma.
1970   *Itinerari di Roma antica.* Milano.

MARCHINI, G. P. 1978   Verona romana e paleocristiana, *Ritratto di Verona,* a cura di Lionello Luppi. Verona.

MARSDEN, E. W. 1969   *Greek and Roman Artillery.* Oxford.

MOCCHEGIANI CARPANO, 1985   Siti archeologici 3-7, *BollNum,* 50-54.

MOTTA, R. 1986   *Tevere, un'antica via per il mediterraneo. Catalogo di mostra.* Roma.

NIBBY, A. 1821   *Le mura di Roma.* Roma.

PIETRANGELI, C. 1957   Osservazioni sulle mura delle città umbre, *Atti del V convegno dell'architettura* (1948). Firenze.

QUERCIOLI, M. 1982   *Le mura e le porte di Roma.* Roma.

RICHMOND, I. A. 1930   *The City Wall of Imperial Rome.* Oxford.

RICHMOND, I. A. & HOLFORD, W. G. 1935   Roman Verona: The Archaeology of Its Townplan, *BSR,* XIII, 69-76.

RODRIQUEZ ALMEIDA, E.1984   *Il monte Testaccio.* Roma.

ROSTOVTZEFF, M. 1926   *The Social and Economic History of the Roman Empire.* Oxford.

SÄFLUND, G. 1932   *Le mura di Roma repubblicana.* Uppsala.

SCHIØLER, T. & WIKANDER, Ö. 1983   A Roman Water-mill in the Bath of Caracalla, *OpRom,* XIV, 47-64.

WARD-PERKINS, J. B. 1974   *Cities of Ancient Greece and Italy.* New York.

WIKANDER, Ö. 1979   Water-mills in ancient Rome, *OpRom,* XII, 13-36.

WINTER, F. E. 1971   *Greek Fortifications.* Toronto.

# A GROUP OF 15TH/16TH CENTURY JUGS FROM WESTERN CRETE*

MARGRETE HAHN

*Introduction*
The six glazed jugs published and discussed in this paper have over a number of years found their way to the store rooms of the Archaeological Museum of Khania, Crete. They are all stray finds from villages near Khania, and have been brought to the museum by their finders. Information about exact find spots and context is scarce, and the intrinsic value of each jug perhaps not great. Nevertheless, the study of Postbyzantine pottery from Greece is still in the initial phase, and consequently any contribution to this field should be considered of interest.

From the Kastelli of Khania, the Greek-Swedish Excavations (GSE) have since 1969 unearthed a large amount of Postbyzantine pottery, partly from stratified layers and sealed deposits, which establishes a chronological frame. This material is, however, mostly very fragmentary, as a result of the heavy bombing of the town in 1941, whereas the jugs published in this article are rather well preserved. They provide us with entire profiles which may help in visualizing from which shapes some of the small fragments from the GSE may derive (HAHN 1989; HAHN**).

*General Background*
After the catastrophe of the 4th Crusade, Crete fell in 1204 to Bonifacius of Montferrat, who soon sold the island to Venice. At this time, Venetian merchants already had trading posts in Crete, but so had the Genoese, and during the following years the Venetians were in constant conflict with the Genoese, who were determined not to give up their advantageous commercial strongholds without a struggle. Khania, which according to some Venetian sources was founded or refounded in the area of ancient Kydonia in 1252 by a group of immigrants from Venice, was on more than one occasion conquered by the Genoese, but in 1294 the Venetian Doge succeded in suppressing the

last Genoese rebellion in the area (XANTHOUDIDOU 1939, 23, 43, 60). Khania remained under Venetian control until 1649, when the town, as the first in Crete, succumbed to Turkish supremacy.

Pottery finds that can be related to the periods immediately before 1204 are scarce in Western Crete, and this applies to some extent also to the rest of the island, but they suffice to show that Crete took part in the general interchange of ceramics in the Eastern Mediterranean.

During the centuries of Venetian occupation, Crete saw an increasing amount of imports from the main pottery centres of Italy, not only of Maiolica but also of lead-glazed wares, especially *sgraffito* wares. Maiolica is an earthenware covered with tin glaze which provides the body with an opaque, smooth surface as a background suitable for further decoration. This technique had its origin some time in the 9th cent. in the Near East, whence it spread through the Islamic world to Italy and Spain. The medieval Italian Maiolica types are referred to as Protomaiolica and Archaic Maiolica, while the term Maiolica is normally used for the tin-glazed wares of the Renaissance. The *sgraffito* technique consists in covering the unfired body with a slip of another colour, normally white, and then incising the decorative motif through this slip. The thus decorated pottery is then glazed. Byzantine sgraffito pottery had its highlights in Greece and the Levant between the 11th and the 13th cent., in the later part of this period commonly with added green and brown enhancement of the decoration. Whether introduced by Levantine potters or through other channels, sgraffito wares were produced also in Italy, mainly Northern Italy, possibly from as early as the 13th cent. (BLAKE 1986; GELICHI 1986). The Italian sgraffito production reached its apogee in the 15th/16th cent. and had through commerce, especially with the Venetian-dominated areas in the Mediterranean, influence on the local pottery production there. Thus there were local Cretan potteries which produced wares more or less influenced by the imported ones, and a Khania workshop has been located very near the GSE excavations (HAHN 1989, 229 and fig.10; HAHN \*\*), where it was in use at least from the 15th/16th cent. and into the Turkish period. The clay used by the Khania workshop ranges in colour from red to brown and contains white, red and dark brown to blackish inclusions and varying amounts of sparkling mica.

In the Byzantine period in Greece, jugs were not very numerous among glazed pottery and almost totally absent from the sgraffito

# A GROUP OF 15TH/16TH CENTURY JUGS FROM WESTERN CRETE

Figs. 1-6. Drawings by Margrete Hahn. Scale 1:3.

wares. When they do appear, they exhibit a great variety of shapes and sizes (MORGAN 1942, 97). In the Post-Byzantine period jugs become more popular, perhaps under inspiration from Italy, where glazed jugs were much in demand, but where the shapes were not very varied. The most common Italian jug is the trefoil-mouthed, which in very broad terms tends to develop from a lengthy oval shape in Protomaiolica and Archaic Maiolica, into a more globular type in the 15th/16th cent. (FERRARI 1960, 106). Handles are either broad strap-handles or have an oval to spherical section, and they often end on the belly in a "tail", a feature which first appeared in the middle of the 14th cent. (NEPOTI 1986, 413).

A group of Italian jugs has a moulded ring at the transition from neck to belly. In some cases the moulding is not very pronounced, but is instead stressed, in a few cases replaced, by incised horizontal lines. These Italian neck-ring jugs seem to appear some time in the 14th cent. (NEPOTI 1986, 415), but when they carry a sgraffito decoration they are normally later and continue into the beginning of the 17th cent. (PRINGLE 1977, 117 No. 51; RACKHAM 1940 No 84 pl. 14, No 507 pl. 79; REGGI 1971 Nos. 251 and 361). The neck-ring shape is, however, seen as a plain-glazed ware at Corinth (MORGAN 1942, 62-63 and fig. 46) already in the 13th cent. and continues there into the Turkish period. Morgan points out that neither the fabric nor the skill to create

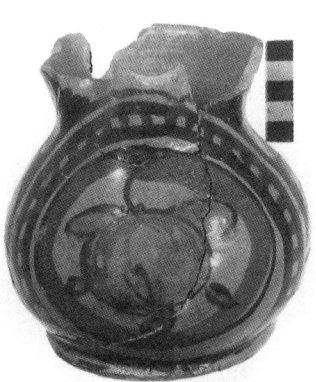

Pl. 1. Maiolica jug with apple decoration. Cat. No. 1. (Photo Erik Hallager).

Pl. 2. Sgraffito jug found in the harbour of Khania. (Photo Margrete Hahn).

this very strict form existed at Corinth. The same may be said of Khania, where the neck-ring jugs nevertheless were imitated by the local potters (GSE, HAHN 1989b, 229, and Nos. 2-5 below), but the origin of this type of jug remains to be found. The shape suggests a metal prototype, perhaps from islamic areas.

## The six Jugs

The group presented in this paper is composed of one Maiolica jug and five sgraffito jugs, four of which are neck-ring jugs.

The small Maiolica jug, No. 1, which is an import, is characteristic of Italian jugs from the middle and second half of the 15th cent., and may have been manufactured at Faenza (SIVIERO 1975, 96).

### 1. Maiolica jug. Khania No. 6233. Fig. 1. Pl. 1.

| | |
|---|---|
| Provenience: | Grave in the church of the Metamorphosis, Vamos 4/2 1940. |
| Preservation: | Reconstructed from several fragments. Part of mouth missing. |
| Shape: | Globular jug with disc base, short neck and trefoil mouth. Vertical strap-handle from under rim to mid-belly where it ends in a "tail". H. 13.6 cm; D. base 10.8 cm |
| Clay: | Hard yellowish-brown |
| Slip: | None |
| Glaze: | Greyish-blue tin glaze inside and outside |
| Decoration: | Front medallion framed by "ladder" design in blue and dark blue. In the centre an apple in orange, lemon and green. |
| Origin: | Faenza? mid-15th cent. |

The remaining jugs Nos. 2-6 are sgraffito jugs and show influence from the Byzantine tradition as well as from the North Italian sgraffito production.

The placing of the decoration in vertical panels is a trait which is very common on Italian sgraffito jugs. A central panel, or medallion, is often accentuated, as seen on the sgraffito jug of very likely Venetian manufacture, which was found some years ago in the harbour of Khania (Pl. 2) (HAHN 1988). Such central panels seem to have been inspired from the Maiolica, cf. the jug No. 1. Especially in the later Italian sgraffito wares, the decoration often degenerates into panels filled with carelessly incised spirals or wavy lines. (SIVIERO 1975, 72).

Of definitely local manufacture are Nos. 2-3, with their distinctive Khania fabric. The incised sgraffito triangles with cross-hatching of No. 2 might suggest an earlier date, but are met with also in a 16th cent. bowl from Este (SIVIERO 1975, 79), and this, together with the shape of

Pl. 3. Sgraffito neck-ring jug. Cat. No. 2. (Photo Erik Hallager).

Pl. 4. Sgraffito neck-ring jug with oak leaves. Cat. No. 4. (Photo Erik Hallager).

the jug, makes it more likely that the jug belongs in the 15th/16th cent. and thus to the established working period of the Khania potters.

*2. Sgraffito neck-ring jug. Khania No. 6243. Fig. 2. Pl. 3*

| | |
|---|---|
| Provenience: | Unknown |
| Preservation: | Rim and part of neck missing, otherwise completely preserved. Front side much worn. Incrustations from the sea on both sides. |
| Shape: | Globular jug with disc base. Moulded ring at transition from neck to belly. Neck sloping slightly inwards. Vertical handle, oval in section, from under rim and ending in "tail" on shoulder. H. 13.7 cm; D. base 10.4 cm |
| Clay: | Hard red clay with grey core and red, brown and white inclusions and a little mica. |
| Slip: | Thick creamy white to pinkish inside neck and outside almost down to base. |
| Glaze: | Inside light green to yellowish lead glaze. Outside green covering glaze. |
| Decoration: | Incised panels on belly. Cross-hatched lozenges in the panels enhanced with alternating green and yellow. Under base, red circular mark probably caused by the mouth of another vase during the stacking in the kiln. |

No. 3 is very worn, but the decoration of the belly falls within the same category as Nos. 4-6 below. Furthermore, there are traces of enhancement of the decoration with bluish colour, a trait which to my knowledge is not seen in sgraffito wares until the 15th cent., when it appears occasionally, especially in the Venetian area (ZURLI & IANUCCI 1982, 108; *Aquileia* 1977, figs. 181, 205, 206). On the neck of the jug there are faint traces of division into panels.

## 3. Sgraffito neck-ring jug. Khania No. 6232. Fig. 3

| | |
|---|---|
| Provenience: | Kandanos, West Crete. |
| Preservation: | Almost all of rim, part of neck and most of handle, except attachment on belly, missing. Otherwise completely preserved. |
| Shape: | Oval jug with disc base. Moulded ring on shoulder. Straight short neck and trefoil mouth. Vertical handle, oval in section, attached high up on the belly and ending in "tail". H. 16.7 cm; D. base 10.1 cm |
| Clay: | Hard red-brown clay with red, brown and white inclusions and some mica. |
| Slip: | White inside neck and outside almost down to base. |
| Glaze: | Very worn. Outside traces of pearly green lead glaze, patches of yellow, black and blue. |
| Decoration: | Almost obliterated. On neck, faint traces of vertical incised panels, and on belly, of curves and loops. |

The small neck-ring jug No. 4 has a short trumpet-shaped neck and a plain rim. The jug carries a double slip, which is not unusual, but is often seen, also among the local Khania ware, to cover a gritty body and give a better contrast between the upper white slip and the lines incised down to the dark slip. The fabric of the jug is not local, but seems to come close to the following No. 5. The motif of stylized oak leaves is common in the repertoire of Italian Maiolica of the 15th/16th cent. (HAHN 1989 fig. 8, 232 n. 12). The yellow-brown glaze and the sparse addition of green giving a nearly monochrome appearance is suggestive of a monochrome *sgraffito* ware, which appeared in the 15th cent. in Northwest Italy. This ware became more plentiful in the 16th cent. and spread all over Italy and beyond (BLAKE 1986). In spite of the easily recognizable Italian oak-leaf motif, the neat little jug may, however, also go together with No. 5, which comes close to some Thessalian sgraffito wares of the so-called Aniconic Style from the 15th-16th cent. (GOURGIOTIS 1984).

## 4. Sgraffito neck-ring jug. Khania No. 6245. Fig. 4. Pl. 4

| | |
|---|---|
| Provenience: | Ag. Marina (?). On the north coast, west of Khania. |
| Preservation: | Completely preserved except for part of rim and handle. Base chipped. |
| Shape: | Small globular jug with low spreading base. Moulded ring at transition from neck to shoulder, and another ring around the neck in the zone of the upper handle-attachment. Trumpet-shaped neck and plain round mouth. Vertical handle, oval in section, from under rim to mid-belly where it ends in a "tail". H. 13.5 cm; D. base 9.0 cm |
| Clay: | Red, hard and gritty. |
| Slip: | Double slip. First brown slip all over, then creamy white inside neck and outside almost down to base. |

Pl. 5. Sgraffito neck-ring jug with round mouth. Cat. No. 5. (Photo Erik Hallager).    Pl. 6. Sgraffito neck-ring jug with trefoil mouth. Cat. No. 6. (Photo Erik Hallager).

| | |
|---|---|
| Glaze: | Yellowish-brown lead glaze on both sides. |
| Decoration: | Incised horizontal bands under rim. On neck, horizontal zone with double medallions each containing an oak leaf. On belly, a horizontal zone with double arcs each containing an oak leaf. Sparsely added green and darker yellowish-brown. |

## 5. *Sgraffito neck-ring jug. Khania No. 6234. Fig. 5. Pl. 5*

| | |
|---|---|
| Provenience: | Ag. Marina. On the north coast, west of Khania. |
| Preservation: | Completely preserved but for part of rim and neck. |
| Shape: | Globular jug with low spreading base, high cylindrical neck and everted rim. Low moulded ring at transition from neck to shoulder. Vertical handle, oval in section, ending in a "tail" on mid-belly. H. 18.8. cm; D. base 8.7 cm |
| Clay: | Dark red, hard and gritty. |
| Slip: | Brown on both sides. |
| Glaze: | Inside yellow lead glaze. Outside brown glaze to mid-belly. |
| Decoration: | Incised horizontal bands under rim, on both sides of neck-ring and on mid-belly. In the neck zone, sgraffito loops and rosettes. On belly, loops and double arcs with rosettes. Touched up with a little green. |

The last jug, No. 6, may be of local Khania manufacture, although the fabric is much coarser than normal for this ware. The disc base seems to have been made apart and then slapped onto the jug. Some effort has, however, been made in shaping the handle and with the inner glaze of the jug. The general appearance of the vase, with the sketchy incised spirals and rosettes, tends to place it within the same chronological frame as the rest of the group.

## 6. Sgraffito jug. Khania No. 6231. Fig. 6. Pl. 6

| | |
|---|---|
| Provenience: | Thymia, Keroneia, near Malaxa, south of Khania. |
| Preservation: | Almost completely preserved. Part of rim and neck missing. Much worn. |
| Shape: | Globular jug with disc base and trefoil mouth. Vertical round handle from under rim to mid-belly, where it ends in a "tail". H. 19.7 cm; D. base 9.7 cm |
| Clay: | Red-brown, hard and gritty. |
| Slip: | Thick, pinkish inside neck and half way down outside. |
| Glaze: | Inside opaque white tin (?) glaze. Outside, partly glazed with yellow lead-glaze. |
| Decoration: | Worn, but part of horizontal incised lines and sgraffito loops and spirals touched up with green and brown. |

## *Conclusion*

The six jugs are, as mentioned above, all the results of chance finds, and can thus be dated only from parallels in fabric, shape and decoration. The Maiolica jug is a very obvious example of import from 15th cent. Italy. Fragments of similar jugs have been found in the GSE excavation in contexts dating from the end of the 15th to the beginning of the 16th cent. and all are imported wares (HAHN 1989, 232). The local Khania production is represented by the two neck-ring jugs Nos. 2-3, but it seems very likely that also No. 6 is local, in which case it testifies to the manufacture at Khania of other closed shapes than neck-ring jugs. The GSE excavations have, however, not yielded any local sgraffito fragments which with certainty can be attributed to other closed shapes than neck-ring jugs. More numerous are the fragments of local sgraffito bowls which in quality of fabric and technique conform with the jugs Nos. 2-3 and 6, and in the same way are in keeping with the sgraffito products of the 15th and 16th cent. such as they are developed in Northern Italy and in Greek workshops continuing the Byzantine tradition (HAHN 1989, 232, fig. 10). The remaining two jugs Nos. 4-5 are not of Khania manufacture. From the GSE excavations there are several sgraffito sherds which derive from jugs and bowls of the same fabric, and the type may have been imported from Thessaly, although another Cretan workshop cannot be ruled out. A future clay analysis may solve this problem.

Degnegyden 25
DK-5690 Tommerup

\* I am grateful to mrs. Stavroula Markoulaki, Department of Prehistorical and Classical Archaeology, Khania and to mr. Michalis Andrianakis, Department od Byzantine Archaeology, Khania for permission to publish these jugs.

## BIBLIOGRAPHY

| | |
|---|---|
| Aquileia 1977 | L.Bertacchi a.o., *Catalogo: Ceramiche dal XIV al XIX secolo dagli scavi archeologici di Aquileia*. Padova. |
| BLAKE, H. 1986 | The medieval incised slipped pottery of north-west Italy, *La ceramica medievale nel mediterraneo occidentale*, 317-352 (Siena/Faenza 1984). Firenze. |
| FERRARI, V. 1960 | *La ceramica graffita ferrarese nei secoli XV-XVI*. Ferrara. |
| GELICHI, S. 1986 | La ceramica ingubbiata medievale nell'Italia nord-orientale. *La ceramica medievale nel mediterraneo occidentale*, 409-418 (Siena/Faenza 1984). Firenze. |
| GOURGIOTIS 1984 | Γ.Κ.Γουργιώτης, Όψιμη βυζαντινή κεραμεική, Ρυθμός sgraffiti, *Αρχαιολογία* 12, 68-71. |
| HAHN, 1988 | Παράσταση αμαρτωλής γυναίκας σε κανάτα της αναγέννησης, *Κρητική "Εστία*, περίοδος Δ, Τόμος 2, Χανία, 88-101. |
| 1989 | Byzantine and Postbyzantine Pottery from the Greek-Swedish Excavations at Khania, Crete. *Recherches sur la céramique byzantine*, édité par V. Deroche et J.-M. Spieser, *BCH* supplément XVIII, 227-232. |
| \*\* | M. Hahn, *OpAth* forthcoming. |
| MORGAN 1942 | C. H. Morgan, *Corinth XI. The Byzantine Pottery*. Cambridge Mass. |
| NEPOTI, S. 1986 | La maiolica aracaica nella Valle Padana. *La ceramica medievale nel mediterraneo occidentale*, 409-418. (Siena/Faenza 1984). Firenze. |
| PRINGLE, D. 1977 | La ceramica dell'area sud del convento di S. Silvestro a Genova. *AMediev* 4, 100-160. |
| RACKHAM, B. 1940 | *Catalogue of Italian Maiolica I-II. Victoria and Albert Museum. Department of Ceramics*. London. |
| REGGI, G.L. 1971 | *La ceramica graffita in Emilia-Romagna del secolo XIV al secolo XIX*. Modena. |
| SIVIERO, G.B. 1975 | *Ceramica dal XIII al XVII secolo da collezioni pubbliche e private in Este. Catalogo del Museo Atestino*. Este. |
| XANTHOUDIDOU 1939 | Σ. Χανθουδίδου, *"Η Ενετοκρατία εν Κρήτη, καί οι κατα τών ενετών αγώνες τών Κρήτων*. Athen. |
| ZURLI & IANNUCCI 1982 | *Ceramiche dalle collezioni del Museo Nazionale di Ravenna*. Catalogo a cura di Francesco Zurli e Anna Maria Iannucci. Bologna. |

# LACONIAN POTTERY IN THE NATIONAL MUSEUM, COPENHAGEN

## BODIL BUNDGAARD RASMUSSEN

Among the many Greek vases in the National Museum which were brought to Denmark in the last century by King Christian VIII and which cover almost all periods and all types of Greek pottery one variety was conspicuously absent, namely Laconian pottery. The decoration of a Siana cup, Chr VIII 958, has strong affinities with Laconian, and was published as such (*CVA Copenhagen* 3 pl.100, 1a-b), but it is now considered East Greek (WALTER-KARYDI 1973, 141 no. 8). Since the days of Christian VIII the vase collection has grown considerably, but the first fairly well preserved Laconian pot did not enter the collection until 1978, when a Laconian cup from the 6th century B.C. was acquired, thanks to a generous grant from the Ny Carlsberg Foundation, Cat. no. 14. In 1989 a second Laconian vase, a small lakaina also from the 6th century B.C., was acquired as a donation by the Robert and Erna Nielsen Foundation, Cat. no. 15. Prior to these acquisitions, the collection counted only fragments of Laconian pottery, altogether thirteen sherds. Nine sherds, Cat. nos. 1-5 and 8-11, come from the excavations at the Apollon sanctuary at Amyklaia and the Artemis Orthia sanctuary in Sparta undertaken by the British School in Athens. They were received in 1958 in exchange for seven sherds from the Danish excavations in Rhodes. Four sherds, Cat. nos. 6, 7, 12 and 13, are stray finds from Sparta donated to the collection by the finders.

*Fig. 3*
*Fig. 4*
*Fig. 1a*
*Fig. 2a*

The sherd collection comprises Protogeometric, Geometric and Laconian I, II, and III sherds. These will be discussed and catalogued below together with the two more complete vessels.

*Fig. 1a-b*

The two sherds Cat. nos. 1 and 2 are part of a find comprising several hundred body sherds of Protogeometric pottery from the Apollon sanctuary at Amyklai, a few miles south of Sparta, the main find-spot of Protogeometric in Laconia. The material from the excavations was dispersed to several places, the museum in Sparta, the British School of Archaeology in Athens, the American School of Classical Studies in

Fig. 1a. Cat.nos. 1-7.

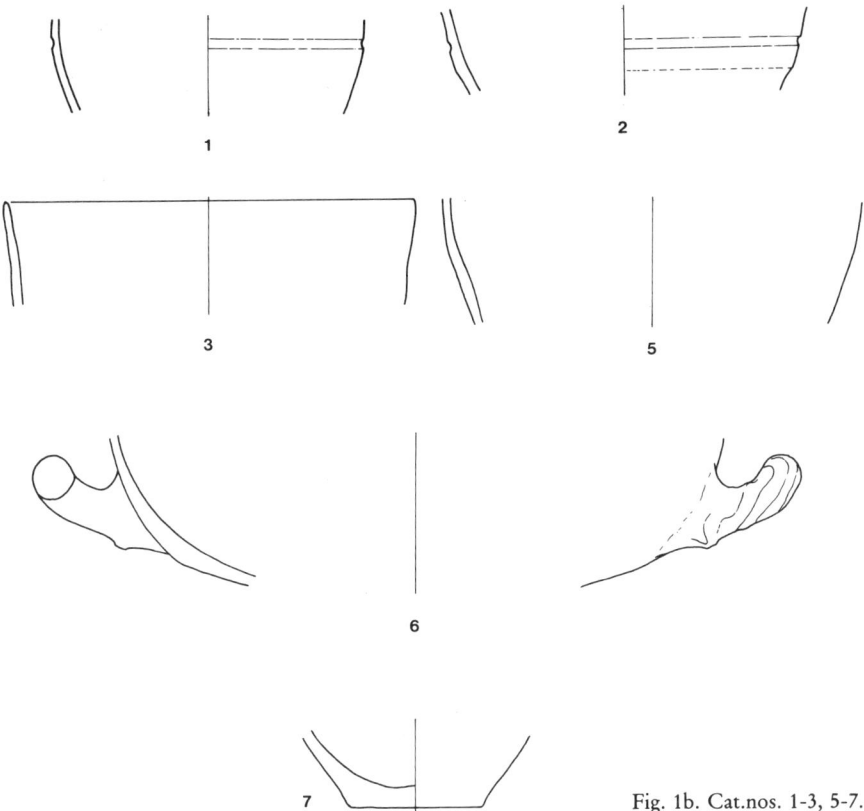

Fig. 1b. Cat.nos. 1-3, 5-7.

Athens, the Ashmolean Museum in Oxford, and the Museum of Classical Archaeology in Cambridge. Like Copenhagen, also Mainz and Heidelberg own a few sherds. The Protogeometric material from Amyklai consists of a mass of small fragments and very few complete pots. It was for a long time thought to be of no value as E.A. Lane put it: "...nor do I think the mass of characterless fragments would yield much to the most patient investigator" (LANE 1933-34, 101). Now, however, the patient work of W.D.E. Coulson has proved differently (COULSON 1985, 29-84). By studying approximately 1300 sherds Coulson has been able to extract more precise information about shapes and decorative schemes. Coldstream mentions only two Protogeometric Laconian shapes, but Coulson has identified eight different types of vessels, open ones being the more common. As our fragments are body sherds, it is difficult to determine what type of vessel they belong to,

323

Fig. 2a. Cat.nos. 8-13.

but they seem to be from flaring skyphoi, Coulson type G (COULSON 1985, 46). On flaring skyphoi, a horizontal groove is often used to mark off the decorative zone from the monochrome lower body. Close parallels to our sherds are, not surprisingly, found among sherds from Amyklai now in Cambridge (*CVA Cambridge* 1, pl. 3, 94 and 91).

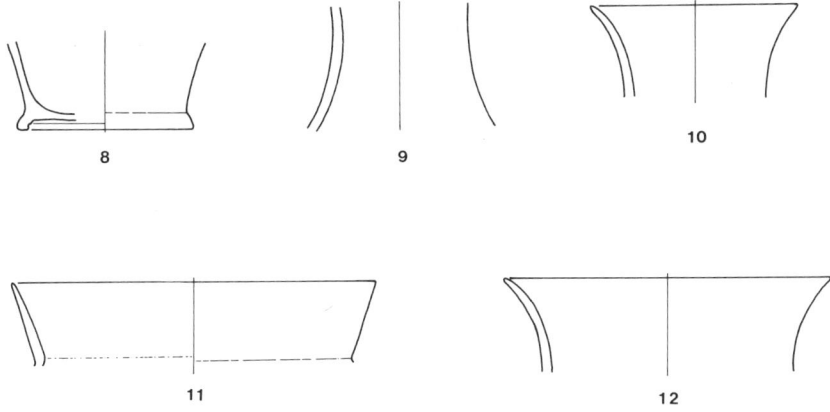

Fig. 2b. Cat.nos. 8-12.

The five sherds Cat. nos. 3-7 belong to the Geometric period. The Geometric pottery appears around 750 B.C.in Laconia. It seems that the isolation of Laconia in the Dark Age was at last broken towards the middle of the 8th century, and influence from the Argive Geometric is noticeable in the decoration of the pottery (COLDSTREAM 1968, 214). The finds of the Geometric period are mainly from Sparta and from Amyklai, and mostly fragments, with only a few whole pots or whole profiles. The shapes comprise cups, stemmed bowls, small bowls, jugs, and for the first time the typical Laconian shape, the lakaina. The clay is coarser and softer than in Protogeometric, the paint is duller, and a white slip is introduced. The Geometric period comes to an end around 650 B.C. (BOARDMAN 1968, 4), the pottery showing some Subgeometric elements around this time. I. Margreiter in her recent work (1988) on early Laconian pottery introduces the terms "vorarchaisch" and "frűharchaisch" for the 6th century, thus avoiding the traditional battle about dates.

The four sherds Cat. nos. 8-11 show the characteristic decorative schemes of Laconian I and II, the squat rays and the rows of dots and squares, as do their counterparts in Cambridge (*CVA Cambridge* 1, pls. 3, 28, 29 and 30). The two stray finds Cat. nos. 12-13 belong to Laconian III in which plant-like motives become dominant in analogy with Middle-Corinthian, from which the Laconian painters draw heavily. The tiny sherd Cat. no. 13 with the rosette decoration concludes this little survey of the Laconian sherd material at the National Museum.

*Fig. 2a-b*

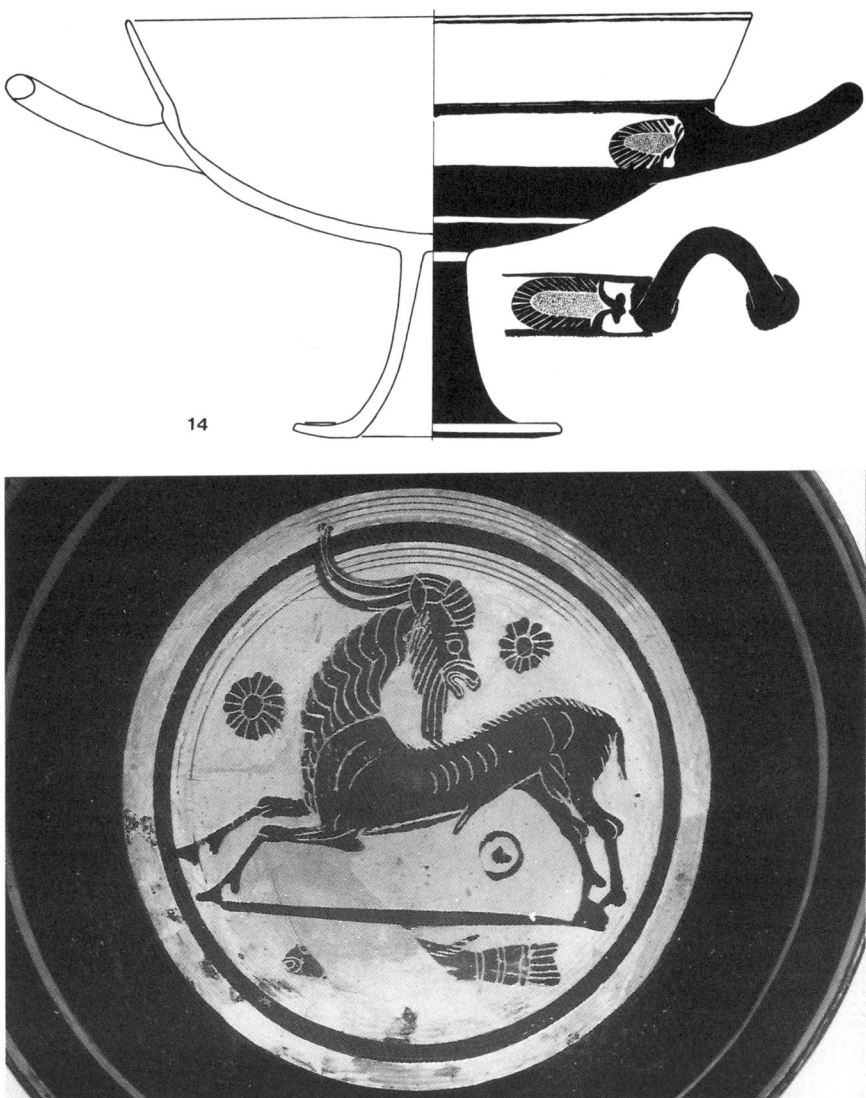

Fig. 3. Cat.no. 14.

The small collection of sherds may not seem impressive at first glance, but it covers very well the different periods from Protogeometric to Late Archaic in regard to shapes as well as decorative elements and constitutes a small but instructive compendium of Laconian pottery to which the cup and the recently acquired lakaina lend additional substance.

*Fig. 3* The shape of the cup Cat. no. 14 is very similar to the Attic Little Master cup, the lip-cup. E.A. Lane has identified a small group of cups of this shape: "with a slightly convex lip passing imperceptibly into the bowl; the stem is high and the foot sharp at the edge. The handle-zone and a small ring just above the junction with stem are reserved; also bands inside at the top and bottom of the lip" (LANE 1933-34, 150-51). The type is equivalent to Stibbe's "Formgruppe IX" mainly used by the Rider Painter (STIBBE 1972,37). The covering of the exterior in black glaze is not a common feature in Laconian, but is often seen on East Greek cups as on inv.nr. Chr.VIII 958 mentioned above. Laconian parallels are found in a cup in Munich, 381 (*CVA, Munich* 6, pl. 290,1) and in another in Tarent (PELAGATTI 1955-56, 23, fig. 18u).

The decoration is done in a rather imprecise and slipshod manner. The black lines at the lip are of an uneven thickness and the palmettes are hasty, crude work. The same applies to the drawing of the goat in the tondo, which has also been done in a quick and careless manner. The palmettes at the handles, irregularly drawn with purple hearts and one crossbar at the stem, are closest to the type used by the Rider Painter, Stibbe's type 9 (STIBBE 1972, 159). The very same type is seen on a cup in Kiel B 515, (*CVA Kiel* 1, 1988, pl.5 1-3), attributed to the Rider Painter and on the above mentioned cup in Munich, 381. Palmettes with two crossbars are seen on three cups in the group put together by Lane of this particular shape: London BM 3; Metropolitan Museum 14.30.26; Würzburg 166, (LANE 1933-34,151) and on a cup in Leipzig without no. (STIBBE 1972, 159).

The decoration of the tondo with only one figure is not very common in Laconian, and using the wild goat as a motive is even rarer. Only two other known cups depict wild goats: one is a cup in Taranto from the excavations of Contrada Vaccarella (PELAGATTI 1933-34,32) and the other a Droop-cup in Munich (*CVA Munich* 6, 35 pl. 292), both attributed to the Hunt Painter, the latter being an imitation of the former. The drawing and incision of our wild goat do not reach the same elegant quality as the Taranto cup, but are rather crude.

Shape, ornament and figure drawing all point away from the Hunt Painter as the master of our cup and towards a painter of a lesser quality, the Rider Painter, who is by Stibbe called a "Nachahmer" (STIBBE 1972, 151), since he fitted his style to that of the greater artists as they came along, the Boread Painter, the Naukratis Painter, the

Arkesilas Painter and after the middle of the 6th century the Hunt Painter. And it is as such we must regard our cup: as a work by the Rider Painter while he was leaning heavily on the Hunt Painter after the middle of the 6th century. It fits into Stibbe's group D of the Rider Painter, 550-540 B.C. (STIBBE 1972, 168-172). A fragment by the Rider Painter in the Louvre, E 666 (STIBBE no. 304, pl. 107,4 and ROLLEY 1959, 280, no. 7), depicts Herakles and a bull. The bull turns its head back towards the left like our jumping goat. The incision on the neck, indicating how the skin wrinkles when the head is turned, bears a marked resemblance to the incision in our goat. A dinos in the Louvre, E 662, also showing Herakles and a bull (STIBBE 1972 no. 313, pl.110.4) show the same drawing at the muzzle marking it off with an extra line around the open mouth (STIBBE 1972, 171), "Kringel um Maul", another point in favour of the Rider Painter.

The fragmentary lakaina Cat. no. 15 reached the museum in a much restored and overpainted condition, but after restoration it now stands without the modern fillings and has regained some of its original lustre. *Fig. 4*

This particular type of drinking cup was first called a lakaina by J.P. Droop (DROOP 1907-8, 58), who borrowed the term lakaina from Athenaios (XI,484). Athenaios describes a drinking vessel called "lakaina" either because it was made of Laconian clay or because it was often used in Laconia. Since Droop applied the term to this particular type of vase, the name has been almost universally accepted. Only E.Kirsten has attempted to apply it to another type of drinking vessel (KIRSTEN 1957). Kirsten argued that the passage in Athenaios rather indicates a large deep drinking bowl and he suggested that the cup we all call a Droop cup should be renamed "lakaina". The little cup Droop called a lakaina Kirsten wanted to call a "kothon". The "kothon" is mentioned by Athenaios (XI,483b) and by Plutarch (*Lyk*,9) as a Spartan pot good for "clearing the water". Kirsten pointed out that the form of the "lakaina", in Droop's terminology, will serve such a purpose and therefore should be named "kothon". He went on to compare the shape to the shape of the harbour in Carthage, which is also called "kothon". This attempt to change the terminology has however had no succes and the name "lakaina" has stuck to the form as mentioned above. I. Scheibler has convincingly argued against Kirsten's use of the term "kothon" and has put forward another candidate for the name, the simple mug (SCHEIBLER 1968, 389-397, fig.1). She has drawn attention to another

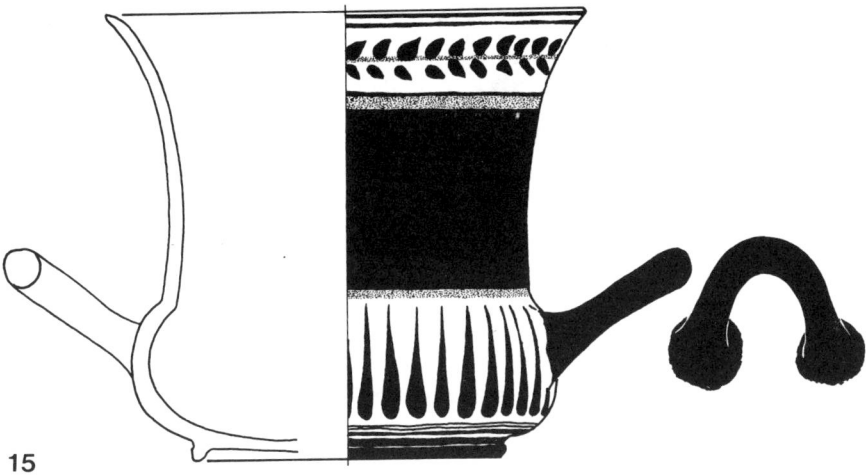

Fig. 4. Cat.no. 15.

passage in Athenaios (XI, 66), where he speaks of the Laconian kothon as belonging to a soldier's kit. The lakaina, in Droop terms, is much too fragile to be even considered military equipment and the little solid mug seems much more appropriate. So as already done above, we shall follow common practice and use the name "lakaina" for our new acquisition.

The lakaina was peculiar to Laconian pottery almost from its first appearance in the Geometric period (COLDSTREAM 1968, 215, pl.46m and MARGREITER 1988, Taf. 43). A number of fragments and more or less complete examples have come to light in the excavations at the sanctuary of Artemis Orthia in Sparta. Only twenty pieces of the type without figure decoration, complete or fragmentary, have hitherto been found outside Laconia. We have one from Samos, one from Perachora, five from Tocra, two from Carthage, and nine from Italy. (Of these nine, one is in the museum of Tarento, five in the museum of Syracuse, two in the museum of Tarquinia, and one is in the Antikensammlung in Basel). The museums in Leipzig and Leningrad each own one piece, but there is no information of the provenance. To these twenty pieces we can now add the one in Copenhagen as probably found outside Laconia.

The Geometric lakainas (MARGREITER 1988, 497-505, 508 pl. 43) were small pots with a straight wall and a lip that leans slightly outwards. They appear plumper than the type with the thin flaring wall that emerged in the last quarter of the 7th century B.C. and became the canonic type (MARGREITHER 1988, 663 pl. 57).

Two pieces from Sparta (MARGREITER 1988, 664 Taf.58 and 667 "früharchaisch") show on the lip the characteristic decoration of Laconian II consisting of a row of squares between lines and flanked by rows of dots. The squares are more widely spaced on the lakaina in Basel (*CVA Basel* 1,pl.22,4), which is close to Margreiter 664. The lakaina in Leningrad (WALDHAUER 1923, 24, 2-9) is of the same type and decoration, as is another one from Tocra (BOARDMAN & HAYES 1966, 89, pl. 67), which J.Hayes dated to about 590-70, the period of Laconian II, in accordance with material from grave groups in Taranto, where grave 182 yielded a similar lakaina together with Middle-Corinthian vases of the first quarter of the 6th century B.C. (PELAGATTI 1955-56, 22, fig.16).

The two lakainas in the Bardo museum in Tunis both have a leaf band on the lip (DUGAS 1928, 55-56). Although it is different from the one on our lakaina, these two pots are the closest parallels. They were placed in the early sixth century by Lane (1933-34, 180), but their shape, or at least that of the one illustrated by Dugas, seems to me to be later. It has a high, slim body, not as well proportioned as ours. Also the decoration is of a more hasty and imprecise character, all characteristics of Laconian IV. Our lakaina may be placed before the two Bardo pieces, in Laconian III or in the beginning of Laconian IV in the second half of the 6th century B.C.

## CATALOGUE

Cat. no. 1. Body sherd of light red clay (2.5YR 6/6) with a light reddish brown core containing lime particles (2.5YR 6/4). Unslipped, decorated in black paint with a metallic sheen (7.5YR 2/0). The decoration on the exterior consists of cross-hatching in metopal panels. To the left a patch of black paint as around a handle. At the lower left edge, black coating. Under this decoration is a black horizontal groove and an undecorated band. On the interior, black coating. H. 3.0 cm. W.2.5 cm. From Amyklai. Protogeometric period. Inv. no. 13879a.

Cat. no. 2. Body sherd, clay and paint as Cat. no. 1. Decorated on the exterior with cross-hatched triangle in metopal panel with hatching. Below the decorative zone, a groove in black paint and an undecorated band. The lower part is black. On the interior, black coating. H. 3.0 cm. W. 2.7 cm. From Amyklai. Protogeometric period. Inv. no. 13879b.

Cat. no. 3. Rim fragment of soft light red clay (2.5YR 6/8) with a very pale brown slip (10YR 8/3) and decoration in dark brown paint (7.5YR 3/2) and red paint. Due to the softness of the clay, most of the decoration and the slip has worn away. What is left is three horizontal lines in red paint along the rim, below these a band of vertical zig-zags in dark brown paint and below the zigzags traces of two horizontal red lines. Along the rim on the interior traces of three red lines on a band of white slip. The lower part covered in brown paint. H. 3.5 cm. W. 4.2 cm. From the Artemis Orthia sanctuary at Sparta. Geometric period. Inv. no. 13880a. The sherd is probably from a deep skyphos, as the almost straight profile indicates. An identical decoration is seen on a sherd from Eurotas (MARGREITER 1988, pl. 30, 359).

Cat. no. 4. Body fragment, clay and paint as Cat. no. 3. On the exterior a metopal decoration below a horizontal line. Counting from the left, it consists of a thick wavy vertical line, four straight vertical lines and traces of three lines of a half circle. On the interior, black coating. H.2.1 cm. W. 2,6 cm. From the Artemis Orthia sanctuary at Sparta. Geometric period. Inv. no. 13880b.

Cat. no. 5. Body fragment, clay and paint as Cat. no. 3-4. On the exterior a decoration of four horizontal zig-zag lines above three horizontal straight lines. Below these part of three vertical lines. On the interior at the upper part a narrow band of white and a narrow band of red paint. The rest has black coating. H. 4.4 cm. W. 2.8 cm. From the Artemis Orthia sanctuary at Sparta. Geometric period. Inv. no. 13880c. Fig.5. This sherd finds parallels in sherds from the Heroon and Arthemis Orthia (MARGREITER 1988, pl. 22, 250 and pl.34, 398).

Cat. no. 6. Rim fragment consisting of two sherds joined together of a reddish yellow clay (7.5YR 8/6) decorated in dark reddish brown paint (5YR 3/3), with part of a twisted handle. The handle is brown. In the handle zone vertical lines. Below the handle three horizontal lines, a row of dots and two horizontal lines are seen. On the interior, traces of reddish brown paint on the upper part. H. 3.8 cm. W. 7.5 cm. Stray find from Sparta. Geometric period. Inv. no. 13975. The drawing shows that the sherd belongs to a large shallow bowl with a diameter of 20 cm.

Cat. no. 7. Bottom fragment with part of convex wall. Very pale brown clay (10YR 8/3) with traces of decoration in brown paint. The sherd is so worn that it is almost impossible to make out what the decoration was like. The interior is undecorated. H. 2.5 cm. Diam. of foot 4.3 cm. Stray find from Sparta. Geometric period. Inv. no. 13976. This sherd is from a skyphos or a bowl with a convex wall.

Cat. no. 8. Bottom and side fragment of a skyphos. Brownish yellow clay (10YR 6/6), fired hard and with a white slip (10YR 8/2). Decoration in black glaze (5Y 2.5/1) and dark red (10R 3/6). Around the low ring-foot, rays in black glaze. Below the rays a black line and in the groove between body and flaring foot, a red band. At the outer rim of the foot a black band. On interior black coating. H. 3,0 cm, W 4,8 cm. From Artemis Orthia. Inv. no. 13881a. Laconian I or "früharchaisch". Belongs to the common type of skyphos with a straight lower wall and an outcurving lip (MARGREITER 1988, nos. 672-681, "Steilrandskyphos" pl. 59).

Cat. no. 9. Body fragment. Clay and paint as Cat. no. 8. The decoration consists of horizontal lines in black and red paint of varying width and two or more lines of dots. On the interior, black coating. H. 4.3 cm. W. 3.7 cm. From Artemis Orthia. Inv. no. 13881b. The decoration of the sherd, the alternating bands and lines finds a close parallel in the almost complete lakaina in the museum in Sparta, labelled by Margreiter "vorarchaisch" (MARGREITER, 1989, no. 500) and by Coldstream Late Geometric (COLDSTREAM 1977, fig. 52c). The sherd may be from a small lakaina of this early type or from a slender onehandled cup (Margreiter pl. 63, no. 714).

Cat. no. 10. Rim fragment of a lakaina. Clay and paint as Cat. no. 8-9. On the exterior the decoration on the rim shows a row of small black squares widely spaced between horizontal lines and rows of dots, bordered by a red band. Below this decoration, the sherd is covered in black paint. On the interior, black coating. H. 3.3 cm. W. 2.8 cm. From Arthemis Orthia. Inv. no. 13881c. An exact parallel to the decoration is seen on a lakaina in Basel (*CVA Basel* 1, Pl. 22, 4), Laconian I.

Cat. no. 11. Rim fragment of a skyphos of the same shape as Cat. no. 8. Clay and paint as Cat. no.

8-10. On the exterior, on the rim, a band of black squares with red centres between two lines, flanked by rows of dots. The lower part of the sherd is black. On the interior, black coating. H. 3.1 cm. W. 3.0 cm. From Artemis Orthia. Laconian I-II. Inv. no. 13881d.

Cat. no. 12. Fragment of a flaring rim. The clay is reddish brown (5YR 5/4), the slip is white (10YR 8/2) and the decoration is done in black (5YR 2.5/1) and dusky red (10YR 3/3). On the exterior, is a black band at the rim and below this, traces of leaf ornaments or an unrecognizable figure in black-figure on the white slip. On the interior of the flaring rim, a row of tongues separated by vertical lines in red paint on a white slip between black horizontal lines. Below the decorative zone, black coating. H. 3.3 cm. W. 5.0 cm. Stray find from Sparta. Laconian III. Inv. no. 13977. The sherd belongs to a lakaina identical to our newly acquired one only slightly larger.

Cat. no. 13. Fragment of reddish brown clay with mica. The slip covering one side is white and the decoration is in black and purple paint: part of a rosette surrounded by two concentric circles. The other side of the sherd is covered in black paint. 2.7 cm x 1.5 cm. Stray find from Sparta, (given to Kinch on Rhodes in 1908 by A.B.L.Wace). Laconian III. Inv. no. 12362. The sherd is straight and may belong to a lid. A similar decoration is seen on a sherd from a flat-based cup found in Tocra (Tocra I,87,pl.64,948), but our sherd could not belong to such a cup, for the side painted carelessly in black was clearly not meant to be seen.

Cat. no. 14. Small cup on a tall conical foot. The clay is reddish yellow (7.5YR 7/6). The cup is unslipped and decorated in black glaze (10YR 2/1) and dusky red (7.5YR 3/4) in black-figure technique. The base and stem are black. Under the base and inside the stem, a black band. The lower part of the bowl is decorated in two broad bands of black glaze reaching to the handles. A reserved band marks the junction of the foot and the bowl and another separates the black bands. At the handles are incised palmettes with added red in the centres. The handles are black. A black line of uneven thickness marks the lip just above the handles and another runs along the rim. The inside has the reverse scheme of decoration: reserved lines at the top and bottom of the lip mark off the black glazed zones. The tondo is surrounded by two zones each consisting of three thin lines in diluted black glaze separated by a red and a black band. In the tondo a wild goat is jumping towards the right on a black line, its head turned back towards the left. The goat is drawn in Black Figure technique with a lot of details incised. The tail is painted in purple. To the right and left of the head a rosette. Underneath the body of the goat a ring-rosette. Below the jumping line a fish is swimming towards the right. The middle part of the fish is missing. The cup is restored from several fragments. H. 12.5 cm. Diam. of cup 18.5 cm. Diam. at handles 26.0 cm.Inv. no. 15210. We have no information of where the cup was found. At the time of aqcuisition and at its first brief publication the cup was attributed to the Hunt Painter *(ArbejdsmarkKøb* 1979, 173).

Cat. no. 15. Lakaina of a reddish brown clay, (2.5YR 5/4). The thin wall of the cup is high and flaring, the foot a low ring foot. The lip and the bowl are covered in a white slip on the outside and decorated in black glaze and purple paint. Below the rim are two black lines and a myrtle wreath with black leaves on a purple branch. The rest of the wall is covered in black glaze ( 2. 5YR 2/0) with a lustrous sheen. A purple band over the black separates the rim zone from the black wall, and another purple band marks the junction of wall and bowl. On the bowl are thin black rays standing on two black lines. The handles are black, and the ring-foot is black both outside and inside. The bottom is slipped. Most of the bottom is missing, making it impossible to tell wether it was decorated or not. The inside is covered in black paint. On one side a large fragment reaching from the lip into the bottom is missing. Two fragments at the rim and part of one handle are also missing. The vase has been assembled from several fragments. H. 9.5 cm. Diam. at the lip 10,4 cm, diam. incl.handles 15.0 cm. We have no information of the provenance of the vase. Inv. no. 15536.

Bodil Bundgaard Rasmussen
Dept. of Near Eastern and Classical Antiquities
The National Museum
Frederiksholms Kanal 12
DK-1220 Copenhagen K

# BIBLIOGRAPHY

| | |
|---|---|
| BOARDMAN, J. 1963 | Arthemis Orthia and Chronology, *BSA* 58, 1-7. |
| BOARDMAN, J. & HAYES, J. 1966 | *Excavations at Tocra 1963-1965. The Archaic Deposits* I. London. |
| CARTLEDGE, P. 1979 | *Sparta and Lakonia. A Regional History 1300-362 B.C.* London. |
| COLDSTREAM, J.N. 1968 | *Greek Geometric Pottery. A Survey of Ten Local Styles and Their Chronology*. London. |
| 1977 | *Geometric Greece*. London. |
| COULSON, W.D.E. 1985 | The Dark Age Pottery of Sparta, *BSA* 80, 25-84. |
| DAWKINS, R.M. 1929 | The Sanctuary of Artemis Orthia at Sparta. *JHS Supp*.5. London |
| DROOP, J.P. 1929 | The Laconian Pottery in the Sanctuary of Arthemis Orthia at Sparta. *JHS SUPPL.* 5, 52-116. |
| DUGAS, CH. 1928 | Les Vases Lacono-Cyrénéens, *RA* 27, 50-66. |
| KIRSTEN, E. 1957 | Kothon in Sparta und Karthago, in: K. Schauenburg Hersg., *Charites. Studien zur Altertumswissenschaft*. Bonn, 110-118. |
| LANE, E.A. 1933-34 | Lakonian Vasepainting, *BSA* 34, 99-189. |
| MARGREITER, I. 1988 | *Frühe lakonische Keramik von geometrischer bis zu archaischer Zeit. Schriften aus dem Athenaion der klassischen archäologie Salzburg* 5. Waldsassen-Bayern. |
| PELAGATTI, P., 1955-56 | La Ceramica del Museo di Taranto, *ASAtene* 33-34, 7-44. |
| *Perugia* 1986 | La Ceramica Laconica, Atti del Seminario, Perugia 23-24 Febbraio, (1981) (*Archaeologia Perusina* 3). Roma. |
| ROLLEY, C. 1959 | Le Peintre des Cavaliers, *BCH* LXXXIII, 275-284. |
| SCHEIBLER, I. 1964 | Exaleiptra, *JdI* 79, 72-108. |
| 1968 | Kothon – Exaleiptron. Addenda, *AA*, 389-397. |
| SHEFTON, B. 1954 | Three Laconian Vase-Painters, *BSA* 49, 299-310. |
| STIBBE, C. L. 1972 | *Lakonische Vasenmaler des 6.Jhdts. v. Chr.* Amsterdam |
| WALDHAUER, O. 1923-24 | Zur Lakonischen Keramik, *JdI* 38-39, 28-37. |

# A NEW BUCCHERO KANTHAROS WITH INCISED FRIEZE FOUND AT VULCI

## HELLE SALSKOV ROBERTS

Although bucchero has long been regarded as the Etruscan contribution to pottery *par excellence* many questions still remain unanswered as to use, date, place of production, export within Etruria itself, to the rest of Italy and abroad, relationship to other kinds of pottery and to ivory and metal objects, especially those with a similar function.

Much useful work dealing with some of these problems has been published within the last generation (VILLARD 1962, DE JULIIS 1968, RAMAGE 1970, VERSÁR 1973, GRAN AYMERICH 1973, BONAMICI 1974, RASMUSSEN 1979, 1985, SALSKOV ROBERTS 1988, BRIJDER 1988), but as also pointed out by these authors, there have been many obstacles to the progress of research, some of which still remain.

One of the greatest is the limited number of known find-spots and lack of information about the burial contexts, partly due to the negligence of early excavators and tomb robbers, but also partly due to the difficulty in ascertaining which objects belong to which specific deposition in the large Etruscan family tombs, most of which are found in a damaged condition that defies even the most careful modern excavation techniques.

Another difficulty has been that many burials, at least the early ones, seem to be characterized either by grave goods consisting of bucchero and the related impasto or by contents of Greek or "Italo-Greek" pottery, obviously hindering cross-reference between the wares and leading to the assumption of either a chronological, sociological or ethnical difference in the use of these products.

A special difficulty stems from the very uniqueness of bucchero, creating a psychological barrier against seeing affinities between *e.g.* the technically – and aesthetically – superior light-coloured ware with polychrome decoration and the simpler dark ware of local Italic tradition.

Not all, however, were stopped by this barrier. Ll. Brown, studying his lion motif, extended his research to objects of ivory, metal, stone

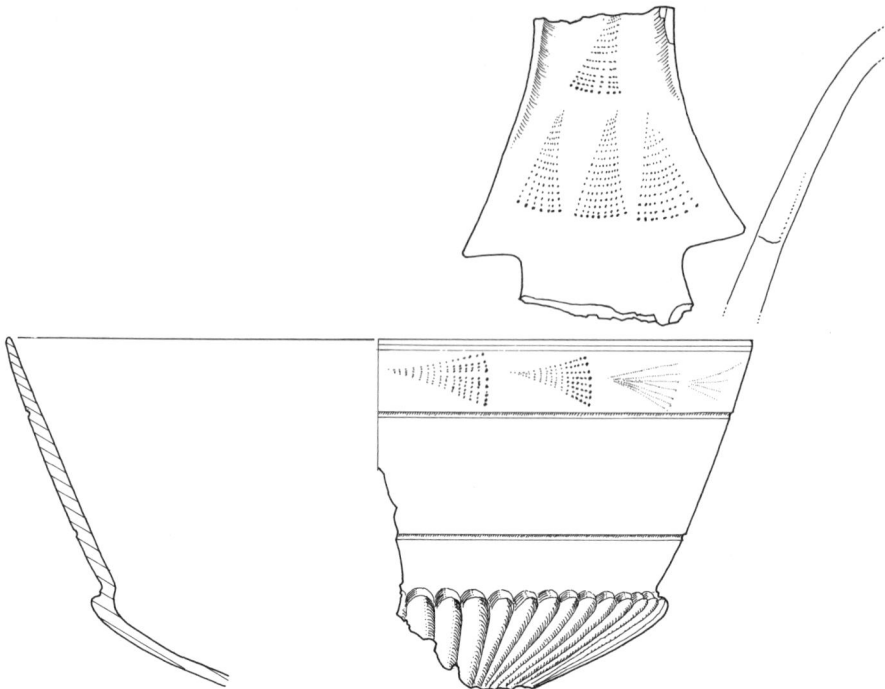

Fig. 1-1d. Bucchero kantharos fragments. Private collection, Copenhagen. Drawing Grete Karl Sørensen. Photo HSR.

and pottery of various kinds, including bucchero (BROWN 1960) and, earlier, Magi recognized the motif of the Corinthian padded dancer on the bucchero olla in the Vatican from Montalto di Castro (BEAZLEY & MAGI 1939, 115), but, for some reason or other, the implications of these observations were not generally acknowledged, until some archaeologists recently gave new attention to such affinities, which has brought considerable progress to the study of bucchero (CRISTOFANI 1969, 61 ff., BONAMICI 1974, 10 f.).

Any new example of incised bucchero with a known find-spot has, however, the possibility of adding valuable information to our still modest pool of knowledge, which is why I seize the opportunity of publishing three large fragments of a bucchero kantharos with incised decoration which was found at Vulci during the excavations conducted by the Società Hercle in 1962.

*Fig. 1-2*

# A NEW BUCCHERO KANTHAROS WITH INCISED FRIEZE FOUND AT VULCI

Fig. 2. Drawing Grete Karl Sørensen.

>Bibl.: *Materiali di Antichità* 1964, no. 750 sporadico N. 3.
>Smaller fragment of bowl: 10,2 cm×16 cm.
>Larger fragment of bowl: 13,4 cm×20 cm.
>H. of bowl to carination: 8,9 cm.
>Original diam. of bowl: ab. 28 cm.
>H. of handle fragment: 10 cm.
>Width at broadest point of handle: 9,1 cm.

The bucchero ware is dark grey to black and contains some mica and chalk particles. The core is blackish all through, with only a slightly lighter colour at the greatest thickness. The surface is burnished, but on a third of the large fragment and on the entire small fragment of the bowl the surface is matt and greyish, most likely due to having been in wet conditions. The handle fragment is black and lustrous on both sides. In some of the incisions there are traces of red filling. Possibly also some white inlay.

Under the rim are two thin wet-incised lines and at the side of the bowl two deeper and broader wet-incised furrows framing an incised frieze. Under the two thin lines a row of impressed closed horizontal fans, the outer dots of which are considerably bigger and deeper than the others. The underside of the bowl is fluted.

The handle has a rhomboid shape with a narrower lower part. The sides are slightly turned upwards. On one side is a row of three impressed vertical fans at the broadest point and one fan at the narrower part over these.

The incised frieze on the smaller fragment of the bowl has a stag with two-branched antlers proceeding toward the right. Above, a many-petalled rosette. In front walks a male sphinx with outspread wings. Under this a volute and in front a bird with thin body, long neck and large feet. Then follows a double-bodied panther with dotted necks. The eyes have rather large white dots for pupils, likely to be inlays. Over the body to the left a hanging palmette ornament. The larger fragment has a walking ram with a palmette above and preceded by a goat and a lion devouring a human male which is confronted by another lion, with tongue hanging out. Under this a sprouting volute and over its back a hanging palmette.Behind it follows a griffin with an owl perched on its back. Between its legs and after it grow volutes. Then follows a panther, through whose head and body the break occurs. The *ductus* of the incised lines is steady.

## Shape

The height and shape of the foot remain unknown and so does the exact angle and height of the handles, but the following kantharoi may be called to attention as for the original shape of the Vulci kantharos:

*Fig. 3*

  *b* Villa Giulia 56.116, from Monte Oliviero, Prima Porta, Veio.
  *c* Berlin F 1541
  *d* Berlin 3224
  *e* Louvre C 562
  *f* Tomb of the Bearded Sphinx no. 22, Vulci
  *g* Agora P 23.454
  *h* Perachora nos. 4119, 4120, 4122, 4126
  *i* Napoli 80426

The first example from Veio is included in Rasmussen's type 3 d, of which he particularly notices the majestic proportions with a diameter of 20-30 cms (RASMUSSEN 1979, 103-104, pl. 31, fig. 165). The Vulci fragments come from a bowl with a diameter of c. 28 cms.

*Figs. 3 c, d, e* and *i* have no known context, whereas *Fig. 3 f* comes from the Tomb of the Bearded Sphinx, Vulci, the contents of which cover the range 630-580 B.C. (*Nuovi Tesori* 1970, 34), the Agora

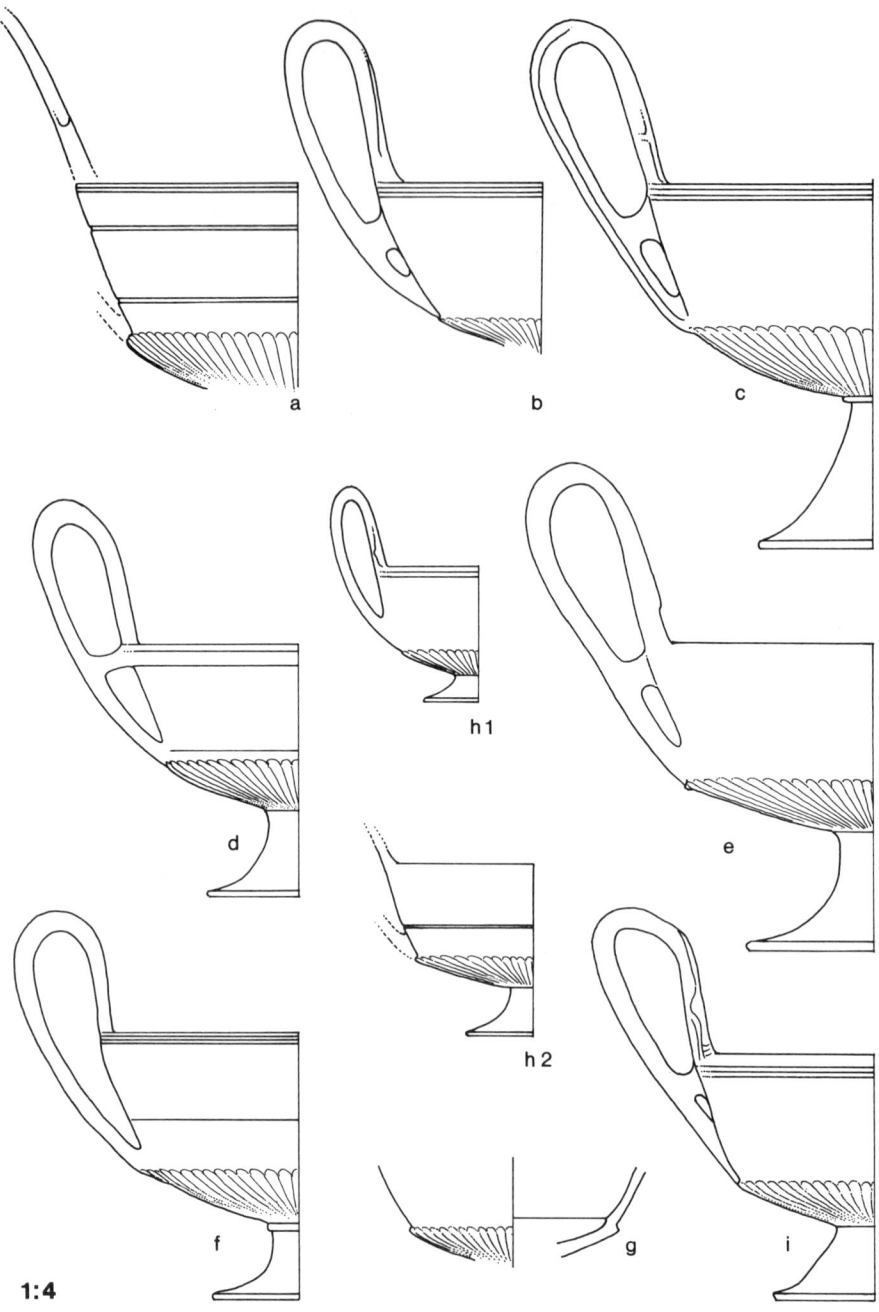

Fig. 3b-i. Profiles of kantharoi. Drawing Poul Christensen.

# A NEW BUCCHERO KANTHAROS WITH INCISED FRIEZE FOUND AT VULCI

Fig. 4. Bicorporate panther on bucchero amphora. Louvre C 567.

kantharos *Fig. 3 g* comes from a late 7th Century B.C. context (DUNBABIN 1962, 386 n. 1) and the Perachora fragments, belonging to more than twenty pieces, were found with EC material (DUNBABIN 1962, 385-386 with n. 1).

This kantharos type thus seems to be made from the last quarter of the 7th Century B.C. but is likely to have continued in use into the first quarter of the 6th Century, as shown by the MC context from Old Smyrna and perhaps even as late as the second quarter of the 6th Century on the evidence of material from Spain and Sicily (DUNBABIN 1962, 386 n. 3, RASMUSSEN 1979, 104).

*The incised decoration:*

*Bicorporate panther*
The most distinctive motif of the incised frieze is that of the bicorporate panther, which is not at all common on incised bucchero, but does occur on:

Bucchero
1. "Nikosthenic" amphora, Louvre C 567. POTTIER 1897-1922, pl. 26.   *Fig. 4*
2. "Nikosthenic" amphora, Barcelona Mus. Arq. without no. GRAN AYMERICH 1973, 290-291, fig. 30.   *Fig. 5*
3. Kalyx, Napoli 80.405. DE JULIIS 1968, pls. 16,3-4; 19,2.
4. Band handle amphora, Cerveteri Magazzino, from the Banditaccia necropolis. VERZÁR 1973, 48, fig. 7.

Furthermore, it is used on à-jour bucchero handles, *e.g.* on the amphora Villa Giulia A 208, MINGAZZINI 1930, pls. VII, 3; IV, 8.

In polychrome vase-painting there are more examples:

Fig. 5. "Nikosthenic" bucchero amphora. Barcelona Museo Arqueologico, without no. Photo HSR.

Fig. 6. Etrusco-Corinthian alabastron from the necropolis of Ferento. After *Cat. Stockholm*.

## Polychrome

1. Fondazione Lerici, Cerveteri t. 154 n. 21. *ArchCl*, 13, 1961, pl. II.
2. Villa Giulia 64.226, t. della Panatenaica di Vulci n. 28. FALCONI AMORELLI, 1968, 45.
3. Villa Giulia 82.524, Veio, Monte Michele t. G no. 2. CRISTOFANI 1969, pl. XXIII.
4. Alabastron, Coll. Rossi Danielli, from the necropolis of Ferento. *Cat. Stockholm* 1972-73 no. 169, pl. XXIIa.   *Fig. 6*
5. Alabastron, Louvre E 460. POTTIER 1897-1922, pl. 41.
6. Globular aryballos, Vatican 146. ALBIZZATI 1925-39, pl. 13.
7. Alabastron, Utrecht Univ. Coll. 246. *Studi Banti* 1965, pl. II, b-c.
8. Globular aryballos, Louvre E 414. SZILÁGYI 1972, 23 no. 18.
9. Olpe, Tarquinia RC 9173. SZILÁGYI 1972, pl. VI a.
10. Globular aryballos, Florence Arch. Mus. 78.069, from Pozzuolo. SZILÁGYI 1986, pl.3,1.
11. Globular aryballos, Siena Mus. Etr. without no. ex Coll. Casuccini, fromChiusi. SZILÁGYI 1986, 15.
12. Alabastron, Genf Mus. d'art et d'histoire I, 182, from Italy. SZILÁGYI 1986, 15.
13. Alabastron, Florence Arch. Mus. 9679, from Cortona. NEPPI MODONA 1925, pl. 12,8.
14. Oinochoe, USA Market, SZILÁGYI 1989, pl. IV.
15. Pontic amphora, British Museum B 57. HANNESTAD 1974, no. 11, pl. 8.
16. Pontic amphora, Orvieto 2665 (43), from Orvieto. HANNESTAD 1974, no. 31, pls. 22-23.
17. Pontic amphora, New York MMA 55.7. BANTI 1965, pl. 67.
18. Pontic amphora, Vatican 231, from Vulci. BEAZLEY 1947, pl. 1,1-2.
19. Alabastron, no. 1521 from Perachora. DUNBABIN 1962, pl. 60.   *Fig. 7*

## Stone

1. Lastrone, Tarquinia Mus. Naz., from Tarquinia. BANTI 1965, pl. 40.

## Bronze

1. Situla, Mus. Naz. Atestino 3582 (3015), Este Boldù-Dolfin I, FREY 1969, folding pl. 2, no. 36.

## Ivory

1. Plaque with low relief carving, from Castelbellino (Picenum), *MonAnt* 35-36, pl. XXVI g.

None of the three first bucchero examples with a bicorporate panther has a known provenance. No. 4 in the Cerveteri Magazzino may be from t. 99 of the Banditaccia necropolis. The bicorporate creature is lying down, with front paws intertwined, and on the whole represents a concept not very close to the Vulci fragment.

For the Louvre amphora C 567 a tentative attribution to a Veientine centre has been suggested (BONAMICI 1974, 133). The kalyx Napoli 80.405 could be identical to the object on a drawing published by Micali in 1844, which would mean a Veientine provenance, also thought to be likely from stylistic reasons by DE JULIIS 1968, 36 and BONAMICI 1974, 154-155.

Fig. 7. Bicorporate panther on alabastron ascribed to the Sphinx Painter. Perachora no. 1521, after *Perachora* II.

The popularity of the motif in polychrome vase-painting does, however, point in another direction. The Lerici *anforone* from Cerveteri has convincingly been attributed to the Painter of the Bearded Sphinxes (ill: COLONNA 1961, pl. II), active at Vulci in the last decades of the 7th Century (ZEVI 1969. COLONNA in *Nuovi Tesori* 1970, 36).

A later use of the motif is found in the *anforone* no. 28 from the Tomb of the Panathenian amphora, Vulci, ascribed to the Group af Vatican 127, now generally accepted as having been produced at Vulci during the second quarter of the 6th Century (BROWN 1960, 56-57. CRISTOFANI & ZEVI 1965, 28-31; FALCONI AMORELLI 1968, 45).

The oinochoe no. 14 is ascribed by Szilágyi to the Burrell Painter working at Vulci around the middle of the century.

Even later, from the third quarter of the 6th Century, the bicorporate panther is used on the neck of Pontic amphorae, *e.g.* nos. 15-18 in the above list, by the Paris Painter (HANNESTAD 1974, 27-28).

From the necropolis of Ferento comes an Etrusco-Corinthian alabastron by the Tree Painter active in the first quarter of the 6th Century B.C. (AMYX 1965. MORANDI 1972, 77), to whom also an alabastron in Utrecht is ascribed.

The bicorporate panther is, in fact, a favourite motif of the Grasmere Group, represented by no. 9, the olpe Tarquinia RC 9173 from the first quarter of the 6th Century (SZILÁGYI 1972, 55-60). The group is considered by Szilágyi to be localized at Tarquinia as a kind of provincial variety of the Vulcian olpai.

The inspiration for this Oriental motif is likely to have come to Etruria via the Greek intermediary, although it is rare in Corinthian vase-painting. In fact, Dunbabin has no parallel to offer for the EC alabastron 1521 found at Perachora, ascribed to an intermediate stage of the Sphinx Painter, *i.e.* 615-605 B.C.

Other bicorporate animals do, however, appear occasionally in Greek vase-painting, *e.g..* a double sitting sphinx on the Chigi jug (FRIIS-JOHANSEN 1923, pl. XL, 1c) and a panther-bird on a EC olpe from Kameiros, British Museum 1352 (ARIAS 1962, pl. VII).

The Oriental prototype can be traced, for example, to the gold amphora from Luristan in the Kevorkian Collection (CULICAN 1965, pl. 26), with a prominent plastic head or to the plaque from Ziwiye in the Metropolitan Museum (*BMetrMus* 13, 1954-55, 216), where the winged panthers are resting their front paws on a small palmette tree, which explains the position of the Perachora example and the design on the Barcelona amphora. A presumably older Oriental type is represented in the Weil Collection in Paris (SLOMANN 1967, fig. 96).

Apart from this feature the Oriental examples cannot be said to be very close to either the Corinthian or the Etrusco-Corinthian variations.

The Vulci kantharos shows the same type of panther head and general position as the Louvre amphora C 567, but is different in various details of stylization. The Vulci piece is, in fact, closer to the Corinthian design than any of the other examples mentioned, whereas the panther head of the Tarquinia olpe of the Grasmere Group is fairly close to that of the Barcelona bucchero amphora.

*Fig. 8*

The panther head of the Vulci kantharos is of the same type as the one sculptured on the nenfro slabs in Tarquinia, whether provided with one or two bodies (BANTI 1965, pl. 40). Cf. also the panther sculpture (HUS 1977, pl. 14c).

The proportions and the long tails doubling back on the relief are, however, more like the Louvre amphora C 567.

The Tarquinia *lastroni* are usally thought to be from about the middle or the third quarter of the 6th Century (RIIS 1941, 66, 160 no. 4; JANNOT 1976, 98 no. 3), but Colonna, whose publication is expected

Fig. 8. Detail of bucchero fragment from Vulci. Photo HSR.

shortly, has indicated an earlier date in that century (*Mostra Torino* 1967, 101 n. 310). The intimate relationship with the Pontic amphorae is, however, recognized (HANNESTAD 1974, 27-28) and the monograph of that author places the production of these vases in the third quarter of the 6th Century.

Recently, Bruni claims to have found evidence showing that the *lastroni* with simple geometric decoration have started in the second quarter of the 7th Century B.C. He does, however, place the slabs decorated with figure reliefs in the first half of the 6th Centure B.C. (BRUNI 1986, 18-19; 112).

The bronze example from Este, being derived from an Etruscan prototype, does not provide any important clue as to the date of these, although the situla art is definitely interesting in showing how various decorative motifs may work out in bronze (On the date of the situlae, see FREY 1969, 57; 81-82).

Fig. 9. Detail of bucchero fragment from Vulci. Photo HSR.

## *Sphinx (Human profile)*

The profile of the walking winged sphinx next to the bicorporate panther shows a very low forehead and continues into a rather large nose, small pouting mouth and a very prominent chin, which I think derives from a beard.

*Fig. 9*

## Bucchero

1. Kantharos, Berlin 3224 (two examples).
2. Kantharos n. 22, tomb of the Bearded Sphinx, Vulci. BONAMICI 1974, no.46, pl. XXXIII,b (but hardly visible).
3. Kantharos handle, Musées Royaux, *CVA* Belgique 3, pl. 14a-b. (Head of centaur).
4. Oinochoe, Louvre C 559, BONAMICI no. 73, pl. XXXIVa-b. (Two examples).
5. Olla, whereabouts unknown, Campanari 1839, pl. 1. BONAMICI 1974, no. 28, pl. XIV.
6. Kalyx, Florence Arch. Mus. 81.517, from Veio. Monte Michele. t. Dno. 14. CRISTOFANI 1969, 65, fig. 27. (Two ex.).

*Fig. 10*
*Fig. 11*
*Fig. 12*

## Polychrome impasto

1. Krater, Cerveteri, t. Regolini-Galassi, no. 326, PARETI 1947, pl. XLVI.

Fig. 10 a-c. Bucchero kantharos. Berlin 3224. Museum photo.

# A NEW BUCCHERO KANTHAROS WITH INCISED FRIEZE FOUND AT VULCI

Fig. 11. Bucchero kantharos from tomb of the Bearded Sphinx, Vulci.

Fig. 12. Bucchero kantharos handle. Museaux Royaux Bruxelles.

Fig. 13. Olpe ascribed to the Painter of the Bearded Sphinxes. Munich 243. Museum photo.

### Polychrome Fine Ware

*Fig. 13*
1. Olpe, Munich. SZILÁGYI 1977, pl. XVa.
2. Olpe, Copenhagen 8339, from Orvieto. *CVA* 2, pl. 96,2.
3. Oinochoe, Vatican 72, ALBIZZATI, pl. 5.
4. Oinochoe, Vatican 86, ALBIZZATI, pl. 8.
5. Black-ground aryballos, Oslo, private Coll., SEEBERG 1973, pl. 18.

### Bronze

1. Plaque, Villa Giulia 13.201, from Palestrina t. Barberini no. 83. CURTIS 1925, pl. 34.
*Fig. 14* 2. Amphora, Florence Arch. Mus. 73.087. JOHANSEN 1971, pl. XL, g-h.

The bucchero kantharos Berlin 3224 has already been mentioned as being of a shape similar to the Vulci kantharos. Although the profiles of the sphinxes are rather similar a number of other details are different and that precludes any thought of the same artist being responsible.

Fig. 14 a-b. Details from bronze amphora from Orvieto. After Johansen.

Fig. 14 c. Details from bronze amphora from Orvieto. After Johansen.

One sphinx is wingless, which is rare (SEEBERG 1973, 101) and the other has one wing, different to those on the Vulci kantharos.

No. 2 on the kantharos from the Tomb of the Bearded Sphinx, Vulci, cannot be seen properly on the published photograph, but the wing and the details of the hind quarters are different.

The profile of the centaur on the Brussels handle no. 3 is also in a different style, although it has some common proportions.

Neither the two specimens of walking sphinxes on the Louvre oinochoe C 559 nor the sitting sphinx on the Campanari olla show any close affinity with the Vulci fragment.

The two bearded sphinxes on the Monte Michele kalyx are also quite different in profiles, general proportions, wings and internal incisions, although the shape of the bowl and the row of fans under the rim are features shared with the Vulci kantharos.

In contrast, the sphinxes of the Bearded Sphinx Painter show a concept of the wings that makes a transposition to the sphinx of the Vulci kantharos fully understandable, *e.g.* no. 1., Munich 242, SZSILÁGYI 1977, pl. XV a.

The Oslo aryballos no. 5 links up with the Campanari bucchero olla no. 5, but not directly with the Vulci kantharos.

In bronze, the plaque from the Barberini tomb has a male sphinx with outspread wings, of a structure not unlike those on the Vulci incision. The Barberini sphinx head is, however, closer to that of the Campanari bucchero olla no. 5.

But particularly close are the male profiles of the Orvieto repoussé amphora (JOHANSEN 1971, pl. XL g-h). The peculiar human figures on this amphora surely derive from the Corinthian padded dancers, as do their counterparts on the bucchero olletta from Montalto di Castro, now in the Vatican (BEAZLEY & MAGI 1939, 114-115; BONAMICI 1974, 171). These strange apparitions became known to the Etruscan artists through imports of Corinthian pottery from the EC period onwards.

Apart from the human profiles also the predelection for dotting parts of bodies, *e.g.* the necks of felines, is also common to the Orvieto bronze and the Vulci bucchero. This way of distinguishing the neck area can furthermore be found on the British Museum stamnoid olla inv. 1927, 1-10,1 (*CVA* BM 7, IV Ba, 12 fig. 4, pl. 13, no. 5).

Another characteristic detail of the sphinx on the Vulci fragment is the drawing of the front legs with small pouches at the joints which is repeated on the front legs of most of the other animals. None of the other incised animals reviewed here has that kind of leg, but the bicorporate panther on the Corinthian alabastron ascribed to the Sphinx Painter has a stylization of the front legs that could well develop into the Etruscan incision. An even closer model may be seen on other fragmented alabastra ascribed to the Sphinx Painter, DUNBABIN 1962, nos. 1510-1511, 141, pl. 59).

This feature is adopted by Etrusco-Corinthian painters like the Feoli Painter, *e.g.* Würzburg 768 from Vulci, and the Grosseto Painter (*ArchCl* 20, 1968, pl. V, 2; pl. XIII).

An earlier example of pouches on legs of lions can be seen on a loomweight decorated by the Head-in-air Painter from about the middle of the 7th Century B.C. The two confronted lions, of a facial type different to that of the Vulci kantharos, are each resting one front paw on a hook or volute growing from the ground.

*Lion devouring human body*
The popular Etruscan motif of a lion with a half-consumed human

body, usually just a leg, dangling from its mouth, is also represented on the bucchero kantharos from the Tomb of the Bearded Sphinx, Vulci.

The type of head with several folds on the upper lip is close to the lion heads on the new Vulci kantharos fragments. This type ultimately derives from the Assyrian lion through North Syria in the Late Hittite period (HUS 1961, 203). The type is clearly seen on several slabs from the Palace of Ashurbapal, Nineveh (BARNETT *APR*, pls. 89; 95).

Another man-eating lion on incised bucchero is found on the kylix from Narce (BONAMICI 1974 no. 37, 185 fig. 14).

An example of the head type, but without any human victim, is seen on the bucchero kantharos fragments from Tarquinia, now in the Tarquinia Museum (BROWN 1960, 60-61, pl. XXI, c). Cf also the kantharos fragment from Monte Oliviero, Veio (BONAMICI 1974, pl. XXI, b). But this type is far from the only one to catch on in bucchero incision (BROWN 1960).

A Greek version of the TR period can be seen on a fragment from Perachora (DUNBABIN 1962, no. 2286, pl. 91), ascribed to "near the Palermo Painter".

In Etrusco-Corinthian vase-painting it becomes standard in the Grasmere Group already mentioned (SZILÁGYI 1972, 57 fig. 7 b).

In bronze, the lion with one human leg remaining is represented on the Orvieto amphora (JOHANSEN 1971, pl. XXXIX, b), on the Ny Carlsberg repoussé H 81 a, K 68 and on the belt plaque H 81 a, M 73 (JOHANSEN 1971, pls. XVIII; XX).

In ivory, the lion with one leg dangling can be found on the pyxis in the Louvre MND 409 from Chiusi (BROWN 1960, pl. XIV, a. 2).

The rarer version with two human legs is found on the bucchero oinochoe Louvre C 559 already referred to (BONAMICI 1974, no. 73, pl. XXXIV, b) and on a "Nicosthenic" bucchero amphora in the Villa Giulia, no. 50.364 (BONAMICI no. 89, pl. XLII, b).

## *Griffin*

The griffin on the Vulci kantharos has an open beak and two curls of hair, one of which is likely to be derived from a cheek pouch. Again, the Louvre ivory pyxis has a related griffin, and so has the Barberini ivory arm no. 24 with two confronted griffins in the upper register. These examples, however, only have one curl.

In one of the ostrich eggs from Vulci one of the two confronted griffins clearly shows the cheek pouch and one curl (*IIAA* 1986, 402 fig. 1).

In bucchero there are not many close parallels to be found. For the design with one curl curving around the cheek and one further back one can, however, quote the kantharos in the Museum of the Conservators in Rome, inv. 384 (BONAMICI 1974 no. 90, pl. XLIV, b).

In silver, a griffin with an open beak and two curls is found on the situla fragments no. 151 from the Regolini-Galassi Tomb (PARETI 1947, pl. XV).

## Goat

The types seen on the Vulci kantharos do not find very close parallels in incised bucchero. On the other hand, the head and strongly ringed horn on the Dutuit bronze fragment is rather similar (BROWN 1960, pl. XXII, c).

It is also the type chosen by the Painter of the Bearded Sphinxes (SZILÁGYI 1977, XVII, a, b).

The most distinctive feature is, however, the vertical stylization on the necks, which does not occur on other bucchero incisions. These lines can be found on the Tarquinia *lastroni*, e.g. on the stag of the *fig. 15*. An indication of such lines being more appropriate to carving than to incision may be taken from the Barberini ivory arm no. 24, where they are used on the neck area of both a stag and, more prominently, of a lion looking back.

*Fig. 15*

*Fig. 16*

A somewhat similar system of vertical lines, although interrupted by a transversal dotted band, is found on the Ny Carlsberg bronze fragment H 81a G 37 (JOHANSEN 1971, pl. XII).

Common to goats, lions and bicorporate panthers are two nearly straight lines across the bellies. A parallel to this can be found on the nenfro stele from Vulci, now in the Florence Archaeological Museum. Cf also *lastrone* no. 7 in the Tarquinia Museum (*MonAnt* 36, 1937, 199 fig. 40).

*Fig. 17*

## Volutes

The volutes growing from the ground are – at any rate in the thinner version described as hooks – very common in PC vase-painting, but are not frequent in bucchero incisions. One example is the large kantharos

Fig. 15. Nenfro relief from Tarquinia. Florence Archaeological Museum. Photo HSR.

Fig. 16. Ivory arm no. 24 from The Barberini Tomb. Photo HSR.

Fig. 17. Detail of stele from Vulci. Florence Archaeological Museum. Photo HSR.

from Monte Oliviero, Veio, now in the Villa Giulia no. 56.117 (JOHANSEN 1971, pl. LV, b).

It is also seen in polychrome vase-painting on a dark-ground olla-amphora, British Museum 1929, 6-10, 2.

In relief work it is found on the Tarquinia *lastrone* no. 12 in Tarquinia (*MonAnt* 36, 1937, 201 fig. 41 (double volutes) and on the Pania ivory pyxis (good details visible on *ARID* 17-18, 1989, 48-49, figs. 9-10 (single and double)).

The other filling ornaments of palmette-type on the Vulci bucchero frieze are not easily parallelled.

## Owl

The owl perched on the back of the griffin is also rare in bucchero, the only relevant example being on the kylix from Narce already referred to (BONAMICI 1974, no. 37, 185 fig. 14).

## Conclusion

### Date

The analysis of the motifs has brought forward the name of the Early Corinthian Sphinx Painter as having provided the prototype of the bicorporate panther and some features of detail. Until now there have not been many examples demonstrating this essential phase in the formation of Etruscan art as clearly as that.

In terms of absolute chronology this means the last fifteen years of the 7th Century B.C. for the transmission of this particular motif.

On several occasions reference has been made to the Painter of the Bearded Sphinxes, which fits well with such a chronological frame.

The Orvieto bronze amphora also has the EC period as its background, but is most likely itself form the 6th Century.

The parallels to various groups of Etrusco-Corinthian vase-painting point to the first quarter of the 6th Century B.C.

### Location

The new fragments have, unlike much incised bucchero material, a known provenance.

Classical archaeologists, trained to a large extent on the study of Greek pottery, should – more than anyone – be on guard against accepting find-spots as an indication of place of production without other supporting evidence.

But in this case the find-spot coincides with the place of activity of the Painter of the Bearded Sphinxes, the Group of Vatican 127 and the Burrell Painter. Other relevant groups like the Grasmere Group are thought to belong to the Vulcian provincial sphere Tarquinia, where also the sculpture has provided interesting parallels. Vulci itself has produced the stele referred to for certain details.

These indications all point to Vulci as the likely place of production for the kantharos found there, and, consequently, for a bucchero production concurrent with the polychrome vase output.

As a matter of fact, it would be strange if this was not the case, considering the rich activity of Vulci in other fields at the time in question. Bucchero is a type of pottery not requiring high temperatures or sophisticated technical installations – a theme I hope to deal with some other time – and, as a consequence, there is no reason why a production should not start wherever there was a demand for the product.

## Connections between Vulci and other centres in Etruria and beyond.

In the stylistic analysis of the motifs the importance of the Orvieto bronze amphora has been evident. A Chiusine origin for this piece has tentatively been suggested by Camporeale (CAMPOREALE, 1974, 117-118).

Many parallels have been drawn to the ivory pyxides from Chiusi, and some to an ostrich egg from the Isis Tomb, Vulci, pointing to a lively interchange between Vulci and Inland Etruria. On this route the bicorporate panther has turned up in the necropolis of Ferento.

Some affinity with pieces found at Veio has also been noted. Veio has sometimes been suggested as the centre issuing some bucchero pieces incised with the bicorporate panther (DE JULIIS 1968, 36; BONAMICI 1974, 154-155), obviously based on a certain similarity between the products of Southern Etruria, where attention has been focused until lately, and the more Central Etruscan sphere, where the importance of Vulci now stands out more and more.

Recently Szilágyi has given an excellent survey of the relationship between the major Etruscan centres, based mainly on a study of the Etrusco-Corinthian pottery, but also with a view to the relevance of impasto and bucchero products, pointing out the dominant influence of Cerveteri in the last half of the 7th Century, with Veio and Vulci in the second place. From Vulci a line radiates toward Inland Etruria, especially the Volsinian area.

In the suborientalizing period between 580 and 550 B.C. Vulci assumes the leading position as far the Etrusco-Corinthian pottery is concerned (SZILÁGYI 1989, 634-635).

The same tendency seems to manifest itself also in other objects of other materials as *e.g.* bucchero, bronze, ivory and – possibly somewhat later – stone, as the study of the motif of the bicorporate has shown.

The Archaic road system in Etruria is not known at present, but the existence of a road connecting Veio with Chiusi and Orvieto along the Tiber valley has been suggested (CIOTTI 1974, 151-155), which would explain certain affinities between finds from Veio and the Vulci region.

Pursuing the motif of the bicorporate panther the attention is directed beyond Etruria itself to Este in the Po valley and to Castelbellino in the region of Picenum, just a few more examples underlining the vitality and far-reaching connections of Vulci in the 6th Century.

University of Copenhagen
Institute of Classical Philology
Njalsgade 94
DK-2300 Copenhagen S


Note:

As always, one is drawing heavily on the work of a great number of scholars. For the particular problems of incised bucchero I have benefited greatly from discussions with Richard De Puma, Tom Rasmussen, Annette Rathje, Brian Shefton, J. Szilágyi and Axel Seeberg.

I am indebted to Mr. Poul Christensen for the drawings of the profiles and to Miss Grete Karl Sørensen for the drawings of the Vulci fragments.

## BIBLIOGRAPHY

| | |
|---|---|
| ALBIZZATI, C. | *Vasi dipinti del Vaticano*, Vatican City, without year. |
| AMYX, D. A. 1965 | Some Etrusco-Corinthian Vase-Painters, *Studi Banti*, 1-14. |
| ARIAS, P. E. 1962 | *A History of Greek Vase Painting*. London. |
| BANTI, L. 1965 | *Die Welt der Etrusker*. Stuttgart. |
| BARNETT, *APR* | R. D. Barnett, *Assyrian Palace Reliefs*. London without year. |
| BEAZLEY, J. D. & MAGI, F. 1939 | *La Raccolta B. Guglielmi nel Museo Gregoriano Etrusco*. I, Vatican City. |
| BRUNI, S. 1986 | *I lastroni a scala*. Materiali del Museo Archeologico Nazionale di Tarquinia 9. Rome. |
| BEAZLEY, J. D. 1947 | *Etruscan Vase Painting*. Oxford. |
| BONAMICI, M. 1974 | *I buccheri con figurazioni graffite*. Florence. |
| BRIJDER, H. A. G. 1988 | The Shapes of Etruscan Bronze Kantharoi from the Seventh Cen- |

tury B.C. and the Earliest Attic Black-Figure Kantharoi, *BaBesch* 63, 103-114.

| | |
|---|---|
| BROWN, Ll. 1960 | *The Etruscan Lion*. Oxford. |
| CAMPOREALE, G. 1974 | Irradiazione della cultura Chiusina arcaica, *Etruria Interna*, 99-130. |
| Cat. Stockholm 1972-73 | *Gli Etruschi. Nuove ricerche e scoperte*. Mostra 6 nov. 1972-28 gen. 1973. Viterbo 1972. |
| CIOTTI, U. 1974 | Orvieto, Perugia e l'Umbria anche come mediatrice di scambi con l'Adriatico, *Etruria Interna*, 151-155. |
| COLONNA, G. 1961 | La ceramica etrusco-corinzia e la problematica storica dell'orientalizzante recente in Etruria, *ArchCl* 13, 9-25. |
| CRISTOFANI M. & ZEVI, F. 1965 | La tomba Campana di Veio. Il corredo, *ArchCl* 17, 1-35, 284-285. |
| CRISTOFANI, M. 1969 | *Le tombe da Monte Michele nel Museo Archeologico di Firenze*. Florence. |
| CULICAN, W. 1965 | *The Medes and Persians*. London. |
| CURTIS, C. D. 1925 | The Barberini Tomb, *MAAR* 5, 9-50. |
| DE JULIIS, E. M. 1968 | Buccheri figurati del Museo Archeologico Nazionale di Napoli, *ArchCl* 20, 24-57. |
| DUNBABIN, T. J. 1962 | *Perachora. The Sanctuaries of Hera Akraia and Limenia*. II, Oxford. |
| Etruria Interna 1974 | *Aspetti e problemi dell'Etruria Interna. Atti dell'VIII Convegno Nazionale di Studi Etruschi ed Italici*, Orvieto, 27-30 giugno 1972. Florence. |
| FALCONI AMORELLI, M. T. 1968 | *La tomba della Panatenaica di Vulci*. Quaderni di Villa Giulia Numero 3. Rome. |
| FREY, O.-H. 1969 | *Die Entstehung der Situlenkunst*. Berlin. |
| FRIIS JOHANSEN, K. 1923 | *Les vases sicyoniens*. Copenhagen. |
| GRAN AYMERICH, J. M. J. 1973 | Un conjunto de vasos de buchero inciso, *TrabPrHist* 30, 217-300. |
| HANNESTAD, L. 1974 | *The Paris Painter*. Copenhagen. |
| HUS, A. 1961 | *Recherches sur la statuaire en pierre étrusque archaïque*. Paris. |
| 1977 | La statuaire en pierre archaïque de Vulci, *Civiltà arcaica di Vulci. Atti del X Convegno di Studi Etruschi e Italici*, 1975. Florence. |
| *IIAA* 1986 | J. Swaddling (ed.), *Italian Iron Age Artifacts in the British Museum. Papers of the Sixth British Museum Classical Colloquium*, London. |
| JANNOT, J.-R. 1976 | Deux nouveaux reliefs "tarquiniens", *AK* 19, 94-100. |
| JOHANSEN, FL. 1971 | *Reliefs en bronze d'Etrurie*. Copenhagen. |
| LERICI, C. M. 1959 | *Prospezioni archeologiche a Tarquinia*. Without place. |
| Materiali di Antichità 1964 | *Materiali di Antichità Varia II. Scavi di Vulci*. |

| | |
|---|---|
| MINGAZZINI, P. 1930 | *Vasi della Collezione Castellani.* Roma. |
| MORANDI, A. 1972 | *La Collezione Rossi Danielli. Gli Etruschi. Nuove ricerche e scoperte,* 71-77, Viterbo. |
| *Mostra Torino* 1967 | *Civiltà degli Etruschi,* Mostra a Torino, giugno-luglio 1967. Turin. |
| NEPPI MODONA, A. 1925 | *Cortona etrusca e romana nella storia e nell'arte,* Florence. |
| *Nuovi Tesori* 1970 | *Nuovi Tesori dell'Antica Tuscia.* Viterbo. |
| PARETI, L. 1947 | *La tomba Regolini-Galassi del Museo Gregoriano Etrusco.* Vatican City. |
| POTTIER, E. 1897-1922 | *Vases antiques du Louvre,* I-II. Paris. |
| RAMAGE, N. HIRSCHLAND 1970 | Studies in Early Etruscan Bucchero, *BSR* 38, 1-61. |
| RASMUSSEN, TOM B. 1979 | *Bucchero Pottery From Southern Etruria.* Cambridge. |
| 1985 | Etruscan Shapes in Attic Pottery, *AK* 28, 33-39. |
| RIIS, P. J. 1941 | *Tyrrhenica,* Copenhagen. |
| SALSKOV ROBERTS, H. 1988 | Some Observations on Etruscan Bowls With Supports in the Shape of Caryatids or Adorned by Reliefs, *ActaHyp,* 1, 69-80. |
| SEEBERG, A. 1973 | Tomba Campana, Corinth, Veii, *HambBeitrA* 3, 65-118. |
| SKYDSGAARD, J. E. 1974 | Transhumance in Ancient Italy, *ARID* 7, 7-35. |
| SLOMANN, V. 1967 | *Bicorporates.* I-II. Copenhagen. |
| *Studi Banti* 1965 | *Studi in onore di Luisa Banti.* Rome. |
| SZILÁGYI, J. 1972 | Le fabbriche di ceramica etrusco-corinzia a Tarquinia, *StEtr* 40, 19-71. |
| 1977 | Considerazioni sulla ceramica etrusco-corinzia di Vulci: Risultati e problemi, *La civiltà arcaica di Vulci e la sua espansione, Atti del X Convegno di Studi etruschi e italici,* 29 maggio – 2 giugno 1975, 49-63. Florence. |
| 1986 | Der Pozzuolo-Maler, *Festschrift K. Schauenburg,* 15-19, Mainz a/R. |
| 1989 | *La pittura etrusca figurata dall'etrusco-geometrico all'etrusco-corinzio. Atti del Secondo Congresso Internazionale etrusco,* Firenze 26 Maggio – 2 Giugno 1985, vol. II. Rome. |
| VERZÁR, M 1973 | Eine Gruppe etruskischer Bandhenkelamphoren, *AK* 16, 45-56. |
| VILLARD, F. 1962 | Les canthares de bucchero et la chronologie du commerce étrusque d'exportation. *Coll. Latomus* 58, *Hommage à Albert Grenier,* 3, 1625-1635. |

# A DATED PALMYRENE BUST IN THE DANISH NATIONAL MUSEUM

GUNHILD PLOUG
WITH A CONTRIBUTION BY F. O. HVIDBERG-HANSEN

In 1962 The Department of Near Eastern and Classical Antiquities purchased a male Palmyrene bust from Mr. John Sarkis, art dealer in Beirut (*ArbejdsmarkKøb* 1966, 160). No information about the original context of the bust was available, a shortcoming shared by numerous busts from Palmyra, the metropolis in the Syrian desert. According to the inscription on the present bust (*Appendix*), it once served as funerary monument for the Palmyrene Zabd'atê, who died in the year A.D. 160.

In Palmyra, burials took place outside the habitation quarters e.g. in the Valley of the Tombs west of the city, where to this day a number of tower tombs are conspicuous. By A.D. 160, however, this type of tomb had not been built for some twenty years, so the bust of Zabd'atê more likely stems from the subterranean, galleried type, the hypogeum, or from the more luxurious type, the so-called funerary temple, a ground-level tomb (SCHMIDT-COLINET 1989). The Palmyrene busts functioned as sealing plaques, closing off the burial compartments of the loculi, the tall slots in the walls of the tomb. Generally, each loculus comprised five such compartments produced with a number of inset, horizontal shelves carrying the corpses, in many cases identified by the inscription occurring on the sealing plaque in association with the bust, the "image", of the deceased. The year of death too may appear in these inscriptions, though rather rarely. Including the bust of Zabd'atê, the number of dated busts so far amounts to no more than 58 (PLOUG 1992, Introduction), as opposed to more than a thousand undated, though not anonymous busts. When H. Ingholt (1928) made the dated busts the nucleus of his epochal work, the 48 were already known. In the light of the considerable increase since 1928 in the number of undated busts yielded by excavations in particular, the increase over the last some sixty years of just ten dated items seems to suggest that the

majority of the dated busts may now be known to us. 57 of the 58 dated busts are evenly dispersed over the period A.D. 99 – A.D. 253. These dated pieces are of course fundamental in explaining the different aspects of the development in the stylistics of the funerary art of Palmyra. Seven of the dated busts belong to the Ny Carlsberg Glyptotek, as well as a dated banquet relief (PLOUG 1992, Nos. 1-8); including the bust of Zabd'atê, Copenhagen now commands a significant portion of the

Fig. 1-2. Palmyrene bust, The Danish National Museum, I.N. 14489. (Museum photo).

dated material constituting the basis of the study of the succession of the undated busts. In the present review and in the catalogue (*op.cit.*) the assignments of undated busts to periods of twenty years (A.D. 150-70, A.D. 170-90 etc) referred to are based on the results of such a study by the present writer; a publication is forthcoming.

The following description is in accordance with those presented in the said catalogue. It consequently leaves out the particulars included in the groupings by M. A. R. Colledge (1976, Appendices I-II); references to these groupings are added here and in the catalogue as a heading to the descriptive text.

*Fig. 1-2*   *Zabd'atê.* I. N. 14489. H. 0.676 m. W. 0.575 m.Th. 0.23 m. Gr.depth of relief 0.145 m. Hard yellowish limestone. Severe damage to left side and upper right corner of slab. Slight damage to right eyebrow, below right eye, to right cheek, both sides of nose, helix of right ear, right shoulder, lower side of left hand, little fingers and to the drapery. One crack from middle of left lower eyelid, across cheek to lobe of left ear, another from left wrist, below left hand to middle of stomach. Upper half of background worked with claws, lower half with the punch. Flesh and drapery chiseled and rasped; marks of chisel left on neck and on drapery below hands.
*Colledge*: Group II/Qa – himation: 9, tunic: B.
*Position of bust*: Frontal. *Proportions*: Hands over-large. Left upper arm too short, left forearm optically foreshortened. *Forehead*: Smooth. *Eyes*: Oblong, right one almond-shaped, left one diamond-shaped. Upper lid broad, distinctly elongated, moderately domed. Lower lid not very thick-lidded, distinctly elongated, highly curved. Iris and pupil indicated by small concentric circles, with that of iris cut at top and bottom by the lids. *Eyebrows*: Almost straight. Distinctly undercut. *Cheeks*: Smooth. *Nose*: Underside left flat. Short, highly curved nostril line. *Mouth*: Smooth, very full lips. Pronounced Cupid's bow, rounded. Corners indicated by distinct, triangular cutting. *Beard*: Starting midway down ears; small area below mouth left free; unbroken, curved beard-line. On cheeks, three tiers of vertical striations, with incised line separating the tiers; on chin vertical, unbroken, wavy striations. Moustache cohering with beard; centrally parted tier of oblique striations, leaving small area above lip free. *Ears*: Vaguely shaped as a question mark. Broad, flat helix, distinctly off-set from narrow antihelix; small, very pronounced concha; large, circular tragus. *Hair*: Dressed in long, unbroken wavy locks with lower ends on right half of crown pointing left, those on left half pointing right, the parting occurring just left of nose. Almost horizontal hairline. *Neck*: Smooth. *Hands*: All fingers of right hand outstretched; thumb in front of diagonal folds. Index and little fingers of left hand outstretched. *Tunic*: V-neck. *Rings*: Two on left hand, one at centre of index finger, one at base of little finger; circular bezel and "stone". *Schedula*: Trapezoidal stick, thin. *Wreath*: Left of effigy. Laurel. Emblem at centre; circular, central depression, numerous radial lines inside. *Drapery*: Pendant from wreath; plain centre within ridged folds arranged in three concentric semicircles. Tassel at bottom. *Fold pattern*: Arrangements of: pointed folds – in the himation over right arm as two slightly oblique folds, the smaller one with midrib, the taller enclosing smaller one with midgroove; lanceolate folds – in the himation over left arm as an open-topped, oblique fold with midrib; stepped folds – in the himation in vertical and oblique falls over left arm and in radial falls over chest and stomach, in the tunic in broken semicircles over the chest; ridged folds – in the himation in vertical and diagonal bunches.

In accordance with Near Eastern tradition, the depth of the relief of Zabd'atê's bust is moderate. The slightness of the protrusion of the body is emphasized by the broad shoulders and the modelling of the arms confined to that of the forearms resting against the chest. His shoulders are hardly raised from the background, a phenomenon met with also on the bust of Tomalekê (PARLASCA 1985, pl. 151 A.D. 123) and on certain others (PLOUG 1992, Nos. 12,22-26 A.D. 120-40, 30 A.D. 135-50). The inner contours of the upper arms are entirely concealed by the drapery, as has been common practice regarding right arms since the earliest representations (TANABE 1986, pl. 45 A.D. 32). As to the left arm, the distinction between arm and chest is obvious on a great many busts from the first half of the second century A.D.; around A.D. 130, however, an attenuation of this feature began to appear on certain busts, for instance on the bust dated A.D. 133/4 (PLOUG 1992, No. 5). This trend, expressive of influence from Western styles, is particularly pronounced on busts possibly dating around A.D.150 (*op.-cit*. No. 18) and in the following decade as instanced by two busts dated A.D. 154/5 and A.D. 155 (INGHOLT 1928, pl. 3.2-3). On Zabd'atê's bust, this development appears as complete. The foreshortening of his left arm is likewise a result of a process starting on certain busts of the first half of the century. Reductions of the natural forms were never alien to the Palmyrene artists, and that of the left arm occurred already on busts from the early second century A.D. (INGHOLT 1928, pl. 10.2,4 A.D. 113/4, A.D. 123); the exaggerated foreshortening, however, was not introduced until late in A.D. 135-50 (PLOUG 1992, Nos. 16,30), presumably in an attempt to create a further illusion of depth, a principle common to the art of the West. Western influence obviously underlies a female bust (*op.cit.* No. 6 A.D. 149) whose forearms appear in high relief with the wrists released from the background; the left forearm is optically forshortened but the upper arm is anatomically too short. However, we are left with an impression of a three-quarters view. Some male busts of A.D. 150-70 (INGHOLT 1928, pl. 2.3 A.D. 155, *PS* 161 = *CIS* 4575, *PS* 200 = *CIS* 4275, *PS* 249 = *CIS* 4324, TANABE 1986, pl. 291) display this angle too, but none of them include high relief or a release of the arm. Instead they achieve the said effect through an optical foreshortening of the arm upper as well as of the lower. On the bust of Zabd'atê, only the forearm is optically foreshortened. The upper arm again is too short, thus appearing as frontal. The hand is likewise frontal. On certain later second-century busts, the optical foreshortening of the left forearm has reached its climax, it is simply totally hidden behind the hand (PLOUG 1992, No. 49). The relief art of Palmyra is in the main two-dimensional. However, purported by a twist of their neck, the heads of some busts sculpted after A.D. 150 appear to be placed at an angle to the background (on the third dimension in general COLLEDGE 1976, 129-130). According to the above, the left arm of many busts postdating A.D. 150 is likewise a member presenting an illusion of depth.

Zabd'atê wears the Greek style of dress, a short-sleeved tunic almost entirely covered by the himation wrapping the figure. In Palmyrene art, this attire, since the earliest representations, has been the customary dress for priests (TANABE 1986, pls. 45 A.D. 32, 170 around A.D. 100, 417 A.D. 135-50, 189, 396 A.D. 190-210, 309 A.D. 230-50) and civilians; only rarely does it appear as attire for gods (*op.cit.* pl. 120 1st cent. A.D.). In addition to the said attire, the priests of the second and the third century A.D. also favoured the Parthian style of dress, while civilians stuck to the former wear. As to the arrangement of Zabd'atê's himation, it differs from the standard arrangement (COLLEDGE 1976, Appendix I: 1; e.g. PLOUG 1992, No. 47) in displaying the diagonal bunch of folds passing under the vertical folds that fall from his left shoulder. The latter arrangement appears only rarely on busts of the first half of the second century A.D. (TANABE 1986, pl. 311 around A.D. 140), more frequently on those of the second half of the century (*PS* 175 = *CIS* 4299, TANABE 1986, pl. 296 A.D. 150-70, *PS* 212 = *CIS* 4272, *PS* 214 = *CIS* 4334, *PS* 231 = *CIS* 4499, INGHOLT 1930, pl. 41.2 A.D. 170-90, INGHOLT Ar. No. 822 = *CIS* 4608 around A.D. 190, TANABE 1986, pl. 286 A.D. 190-210).

Zabd'atê displays a Western hairstyle, but differing from the Neronian "coma in gradus formata" (PLOUG 1992, No. 5), the customary coiffure on male busts of the first half of the second century A.D. The Neronian fashion continued in the second half of the century, though less prevalently (TANABE 1986, pls. 295, 301 A.D. 150-70, INGHOLT 1928, pl. 5.1 A.D. 181, GAWLIKOWSKI 1987, No. 13 A.D. 192, COLLEDGE 1976 fig. 80 around A.D. 190). Apart from the surviving Neronian model, the Western fashions influencing the hairstyle of the Palmyrene busts after the middle of the second century A.D. were the Hadrianic and Antonine coiffures. The long, unbroken wavy locks of Zabd'atê certainly reflect the general trend of the Hadrianic mode to wave tufts, though the lock-ends on Zabd'atê do not appear as "flexo ad pectinem capillo" (INGHOLT 1928, 109, POULSEN 1974, 17). The latter fashion did occur in Palmyra in A.D. 150-70 (*PS* 184, *PS* 195, TANABE 1986, pl. 291), however, it was particularly popular there in A.D. 170-90 (*PS* 179= *CIS* 4432, *PS* 212 = *CIS* 4272, *PS* 214 = *CIS* 4334, *PS* 228 = *CIS* 4273). So far, there exists no counterpart to the hairstyle of Zabd'atê, yet the coiffures of two busts seem related (*PS* 199 = *CIS* 4563, INGHOLT *Ar. No.* 813 A.D. 150-70); none of them, however, has a central parting, which on Zabd'atê is peculiar in exhibiting opposed lock-ends. This trait, on the other hand, appears on a bust displaying an extraordinary version of the "coma in gradus formata" coiffure (PLOUG 1992, No. 3 around A.D. 150). The introduction in Palmyra of new Western hairstyles was associated with that of the beard, which since its adoption by Hadrian had become fashionable in the Roman world. With the exception of just a few busts (INGHOLT *Ar. Nos.* 797 = *CIS* 4595, 1092 = *CIS* 4529, TANABE 1986, pl. 321 A.D. 135-50), the Palmyrene busts from the first half of the second century A.D. are beardless, in accordance with the previous Western manner. Shortly after the mid-century, however, several busts (e.g. *PS* 190 = *CIS* 4602, TANABE 1986, pls. 306, 319, PLOUG 1992, No. 47), including two dated instances (INGHOLT 1928, pl. 3.2 A.D. 154/5, 4.1 A.D. 157) suddenly sport a beard. The full beard of Zabd'atê, obviously of Roman shape, is rendered with parallel striations, perhaps depicting a close-cut beard; the same rendering is displayed by a bust in the Ny Carlsberg Glyptotek (PLOUG 1992, No. 47), but is otherwise rare in Palmyra. Similar striations appear on Parthian sculptures, but only on those which are now regarded as Late Parthian (MATHIESEN 1989). Thus by the mid-century the said formula may just possibly have existed in Parthia. If so, that region was very likely the source of the Palmyrene occurrences (COLLEDGE 1976, 142 note 525).

Zabd'atê and the contemporaneous bust depicting the priest Taimarṣŭ (INGHOLT 1928, pl. 4.2 A.D. 161) both exhibit a broad, almost square face. The former differs from the latter in displaying very heavy jaws, though. Still, both heads relate to shapes occurring around A.D.150 (GAWLIKOWSKI 1987, No. 7, PLOUG 1992, No. 30) and likewise have successors in the second half of the century (TANABE 1986, pls. 308 A.D. 177/8, 316 A.D. 150-70). In this period, heavy jaws also became a characteristic of many other faces, taller and often slimmer than that of Zabd'atê (*PS* 249 = *CIS* 4324, *PS* 254 =*CIS* 4403, PARLASCA 1985, pl. 149.2, TANABE 1986, pl. 317 A.D. 150-70, *PS* 179 = *CIS*

4432, INGHOLT *Ar. No.* 320A A.D. 170-90, TANABE 1986, pls. 289, 290 around A.D. 190). The eyes of Zabd'atê appear to be slightly differently shaped. The almond-shaped right eye is of a shape met with on busts from about A.D. 150 (PLOUG 1992, No. 30), likewise on those of A.D. 150-70 (TANABE 1986, pl. 292) and A.D. 170-90 (*PS* 251 = *CIS* 4288; *PS* 214 = *CIS* 4334 is late in the period). The left eye is different, and more diamond-shaped, perhaps an incidental shortcoming on the part of the sculptor. When compared with the eyes prior to A.D. 150, those of Zabd'atê are shorter and narrower. These traits were characteristics fashionable for the eyes on Roman sculptures after the time of Hadrian, thus also the likely source for the small eyes on many Palmyrene busts postdating A.D. 150. Drilled pupils were another Roman trait to be met with on many Palmyrene busts, the earliest ones dated shortly after A.D. 150 (INGHOLT 1928, pls. 13.1 A.D. 151, 3.3 A.D. 155). The adoption of this trait, however, was not complete, as instanced by the bust of Zabd'atê and other busts of A.D. 150-70; these all exhibit a pupil rendered as an engraved circle, the customary rendering on busts of the first half of the second century A.D. The undercut eyebrows of Zabd'atê show no indication of plastically rendered hairs, as was common practice otherwise on contemporaneous Roman sculptures. The mouth of Zabd'atê, with its full lips, has an exact counterpart in that of a female bust (PARLASCA 1985, pl. 149.2 A.D. 150-70) and is closely related to that of a male bust (PLOUG 1992, No. 47 A.D. 150-70). All dated busts belonging to the period A.D. 150-70 (INGHOLT 1928, pls. 3.2-3, 4.1-2, 13, TANABE 1986, pl. 370 A.D. 168/9), and likewise many undated ones (e.g. TANABE 1986, pls. 291, 294, 317), display similar full lips, those busts of A.D. 150-70 exhibiting the archaistic touch, (INGHOLT 1928, pl. 4.4 A.D. 176, TANABE 1986, pls. 295, 296, 301), however, mouths with thin lips, imitating a type displayed by two busts dated A.D. 141 and A.D. 146 (INGHOLT 1928, pls. 2.3, 11.4). The ears of Zabd'atê project sidewards, as was the norm on most busts of the first half of the second century A.D. The priestly bust dated A.D. 161 (INGHOLT 1928, pl. 4.2) and other items of A.D. 150-70 (*PS* 163 = *CIS* 4545, *PS* 175 = *CIS* 4299, *PS* 253 = *CIS* 4497, *PS* 254 = *CIS* 4403, TANABE 1986, pl. 291), excepting those exhibiting the archaistic touch, display, however, less projecting ears, a trait also met with just before the middle of the century (PLOUG 1992, No. 6 A.D. 149). The (unequally sized) ears of Zabd'atê and the priestly bust share the same shape and likewise some details, for instance the small, very pronouced concha, just possibly occurring on one more bust (*PS* 254 = *CIS* 4403), otherwise unequalled so far on busts of A.D. 150-70. The prominent tragus displayed by Zabd'atê, but not by the priest, is on the other hand a detail met with frequently on busts of this period (INGHOLT 1928, pl. 3.3 A.D. 155, *PS* 65 = *CIS* 4537, *PS* 180, *PS* 200 = *CIS* 4275, *PS* 233, *PS* 249 = *CIS* 4324, TANABE 1986, pls. 317, 319).

Generally the jewellery of Palmyrene men is confined to finger-rings. Most busts of the first half of the second century display one at the base of the left hand's little finger. Zabd'atê, however, wears an additional one at the centre of his index finger, likewise Wahbâ A.D. 154/5 (INGHOLT 1934, pl. 10.2) and a few other busts of A.D. 150-70 (*PS* 175 = *CIS* 4299, *PS* 180, TANABE 1986 pl. 300). The type of ring depicted was the Roman one with circular or oval bezel (PLOUG 1992, No. 5). The most common attribute of male Palmyrene busts, the schedula, a "book-roll" which presumably symbolizes the deed to the grave (COLLEDGE 1976, 154) appears on Zabd'atê as trapezoidal, one of the traditional shapes confined to no particular period. Zabd'atê is bare-headed. However, his headgear, a laurel wreath, is seen beside him with a device pendant from it. A tassel at bottom suggests a textile, an assumption confirmed by the presence on another bust of an elaborately arranged drapery below a wreath (*PS* 196 = *CIS* 4420 around A.D. 190). Associated with the wreath, the drapery occurs in other versions too: two rather simple ones (INGHOLT *Ar. Nos.* 1386 around A.D. 150, 839 A.D. 190-210) more closely related to that of Zabd'atê than is the elaborate version, and a version almost transformed into an "Ionic capital" (PARLASCA 1985 pl. 146.3, ASAA'D 1987, fig. 2 A.D. 230-50). The said elaborate version is associated too with a modius (GAWLIKOWSKI 1987, No. 9 A.D. 190-210), while a drapery combined with another modius (COLLEDGE 1976, fig. 79 A.D. 210-30) is arranged slightly differently. Whether the drapery is associated with wreaths (*PS* 301 = *CIS* 4504 A.D. 230-50) or modii (*PS* 286 = *CIS* 4337 A.D. 230-50) seen beside the effigy, the symbolism of it is certainly of funerary character. In Palmyrene art, the wreath did not appear as a male headdress until after the middle of the second century A.D. (INGHOLT 1928, pl. 2.2 A.D. 154/5, PLOUG 1992, No. 48) and its sudden adoption is yet another sign of the strong Roman influence shortly after the middle of the century. Besides being a mark of distinction, the exact meaning in Palmyra of the wearing of the wreath is not clear, although it must have had a religious aspect (COLLEDGE 1976, 140).

The fold pattern of Zabd'atê is distinguished by the presence of pointed folds, a Palmyrene fold shape never applied to the busts of the first half of the second century A.D. (PLOUG 1992, Introduction). As instanced by the bust of 'Atê'aqab (INGHOLT 1928, pl. 4.1 A.D. 157), the pointed folds were created shortly after the middle of the century. Those of 'Atê'aqab are small and form an inconspicuous detail in the totality of the folds; such an appearance indicates that the inspiration behind the pointed folds was Western. As to the pointed folds on Zabd'atê's bust, this relationship is not obvious. The entire fold pattern of his bust is expressive of the Palmyrene love of linearity, and when enlarged, the appearance of this new fold shape easily met the oriental sense for long, unbroken lines. The drapery over the right arm offered the best opportunity for exhibiting the enlarged version and other busts certainly displayed the same arangement as that of Zabd'atê (*PS* 180, PLOUG 1992, No. 47 A.D. 150-70, *PS* 212 = *CIS* 4272 A.D. 170-90), while others, particularly so in A.D. 170-90 (*PS* 214 = *CIS* 4334, *PS* 223, *PS* 231 = *CIS* 4499), exhibited just one pointed fold. The lanceolate fold shape on Zabd'atê's bust is presented by only one open-topped fold appearing over his left arm. This fold shape was created around A.D. 100 (PLOUG 1992, Introduction) and was popular throughout the first half of the second century; it occurs too on busts of the next fifty years, but without its earlier, ornamental significance. The stepped folds displayed over chest, stomach and left arm belong among the earliest Palmyrene fold shapes and presumably have an Achaemenian ancestry (*loc.cit.*). This fold shape was the prevailing one on most first-century sculptures (e.g. TANABE 1986, pls. 55, 89, 120, 144), likewise on many busts of the first half of the second century A.D. (PLOUG 1992, No. 10).

Zabd'atê's year of death, A.D. 160, falls within a period when Roman influences on Palmyra are known to have been considerable, among these also artistic inspirations. Our bust bears witness to these, as instanced by the coiffure, the moderately sized eyes, the foreshortening of the lower left arm and even the pointed folds. Despite the Western traits, the technique and style must be said in all other respects to be truly traditional, though without an actual archaistic touch. A similar case is the bust in the Ny Carlsberg Glyptotek (PLOUG 1992, No. 47) which in addition to certain details likewise shares the type of material with our bust; perhaps the two busts originated in the same workshop.

Department of Antiquities
Ny Carlsberg Glyptotek
Dantes Plads 7
DK-1556 Copenhagen V


## BIBLIOGRAPHY AND ABBREVIATIONS

| | |
|---|---|
| *ArbejdsmarkKøb* | *Nationalmuseets arbejdsmark*. København. |
| *ARID* | *Analecta Romana Instituti Danici*. |
| ASAA'D, K. 1987 | Das Museum von Palmyra, *LinzForsch* 16, 258-267. |
| *AHS* | *Archaeologie et Histoire de la Syrie*. |
| *AIUON* | *Annali Istituto Universitatis Orientale Napoli*. |
| CALLIERI, F. 1986 | Rilievi funerari palmireni nella collezione Zeri, *AIUON* 8, 223-248. |
| *CIS* | *Corpus Inscriptionum Semiticarum*. Paris. Pars sequnda, tomes tertius. Fasc. 2 (1947) tabulae (1954). |
| COLLEDGE, M. A. R. 1976 | *The Art of Palmyra*. London. |
| *DaM* | *Damazener Mitteilungen*. |
| GAWLIKOWSKI, M. 1987 | Die Skulpturen von Palmyra, *LinzForsch* 16, 283-339. |
| INGHOLT, H. 1928 | *Studier over Palmyrensk Skulptur*. København. |
| 1934 | Palmyrene Sculptures in Beirut, *Berytus* 1, 32-43. |
| INGHOLT, Ar. No. | Referring to unpublished items in the archive of H. Ingholt, now in Ny Carlsberg Glyptotek. The publication of the archive by G. Ploug is forthcoming. |
| *LinzForsch* | *Linzer archaeologische Forschungen*. |
| MAKOWSKY, K. C. 1983 | Recherches sur la tombeau de A'ailami et Zebida, *DaM* 1, 175-187. |
| 1985 | La sculpture funéraire palmyrenienne et sa fonction dans l'architecture sépulchrale, *StPal* 8, 69-117. |
| MATHIESEN, H.E. 1989 | Stylistic Trends in Late Parthian Sculpture. A Survey, *ARID* 17-18, 117-126. |
| *MemAOM* | *Memoirs of the Ancient Orient Museum*. |
| PARLASCA, K. 1985 | Das Verhältnis der palmyrenischen Grabplastik zur römischen Porträtkunst, *RM* 92, 343-356. |
| PLOUG, G. 1992 | *The Palmyrene Sculptures. Ny Carlsberg Glyptotek*. Copenhagen. |
| *PS* | Referring to the PS-numbers by Ingholt 1928. |

POULSEN, V. 1974  Les portraits romains II. Copenhague.
RM  Römische Mitteilungen.
SCHMIDT-COLINET, A. 1989  L'architecture funéraire de Palmyre, *AHS* II, 447-456.
StPal  Studia Palmyrenskie.
TANABE, K. 1986  Sculptures of Palmyra, *MemAOM* I.

# APPENDIX

# F.O. HVIDBERG-HANSEN

## The Inscription on the Palmyrene Bust

*Transliteration:*

ZBD'TH
BR BR''
ZBD'TH
YWM 27
BṬBT
ŠNT 400
71
ḤBL

*Translation:*

Zabd'atê
son of Bar'â
Zabd'atê
Day twenty-seven
in January
Year 471 (= 160 A.D.)
Alas!

*Commentary:*

*l.* : *Zabd'atê*, a well-known Palmyrene masculine personal name meaning "Gift of 'Atê", cf. STARK 1971, 18; 46; for the vocalization of the name from Greek Palmyrene inscriptions, cf. LIDZBARSKI 1898, 265. 'Atê is a divine name, either of a god or a goddess; if a goddess, most likely the Canaanite-Phoenician 'Anat, see discussion in FÉVRIER 1931, 127-34; HVIDBERG-HANSEN 1979, I, 94 with notes 196-197 (vol. II, 124-26), and TEIXIDOR 1979, 72-73.

*l.* 2: BR is the common Aramaic word meaning "son". BR' is a *hypocoristicon* to BR'TH, "Son af 'Atê", cf. STARK, 1971, 12; 78-79.

*l.* 4: YWM the general semitic word meaning "day".

*l.* 5: BTBT consists of the preposition B, "in, on", and the name of the month Ṭebet, i.e. January; this name originates from the Babylonian-Assyrian Calendars, cf. HUNGER, 1976, 300-03 (Ṭebêtu); KOEHLER & BAUMGARTNER 1974, 353-54; the name occurs in Book of Esther 2, 16 and on Nabatean inscriptions, cf.: CANTINEAU 1930, vol. II, 101 *CIS II*, 198, 2; 212, 9 etc. and in Palmyrene inscriptions cf. CHABOT, Répert. d. Épigr. sém. I, no. 156; 391; *ibid.* II no. 719; 1046A and 1080 and the bilingual *CIS* II, 4203; to the Palmyrene calendar cf. CLERMONT-GANNEAU, 1897 § 5, 55-76.

*l.* 6: ŠNT feminine noun in singular, in genitive annexion to the numerals in l.6 and l.7.

*l.* 7: HBL an interjection, often used in Palmyrene funerary inscriptions cf. CANTINEAU 1935, 140.

Finn O. Hvidberg-Hansen.
Institute of Semitic Philology,
University of Aarhus.

# BIBLIOGRAPHY

| | |
|---|---|
| CANTINEAU, J. 1930 | *Le Nabatéen* I-II. Paris. |
| 1935 | *Gramm. du palmyrénien épigraphique.* Le Caire. |
| CHABOT, J.-B. 1900-05 | *Répert. d. Épigr. sém.* I. Paris. |
| 1907-14 | *Répert. d. Épigr. sém.* II. Paris. |
| CIS II = | *Corpus Inscriptionum Semiticarum, Pars secunda.* Paris 1926-47. |

| | |
|---|---|
| CLERMONT-GANNEAU, Ch. 1897 | *Étud. d'archéol. orient.* II. Paris. |
| FÉVRIER, J. G. 1931 | *La rel. des Palmyréniens.* Paris. |
| HUNGER, H. 1976 | *Reallex. der Assyriologie u. vorderasiat. Archäologie*, Bd. 5. Leipzig. |
| HVIDBERG-HANSEN, F. O. 1979 | *La déesse TNT. Vol. I-II.* Copenhague. |
| KOEHLER, L. & BAUMGARTNER, W. 1974 | *Hebr. u. Aram. Lex. zum Alten Testament.* Leiden. |
| LIDZBARSKI, M. 1898 | *Handb. d. Nordsemit. Epigraphik.* Weimar. |
| STARK, J. K. 1971 | *Personal Names in Palmyr. Inscriptions.* Oxford. |
| TEIXIDOR, J. 1979 | *The Pantheon of Palmyra.* Leiden. |

# A DORYPHOROS IN DISGUISE

METTE MOLTESEN
WITH AN ADDENDUM BY RUTH TSCHÄPE

In the year 1900 the Ny Carlsberg Glyptotek purchased two Roman marble statues from the art dealer Simonetti in Rome. The one, cat. no. 113, is a replica of Polykleitos' Discophoros, but the support in the guise of a sea-monster could identify it as a Poseidon (POULSEN 1951, 101). The other, cat. no. 158, is the Polykleitan Doryphoros transformed into a Pan, characterized by the Pan-flute hanging on the tree-trunk support and the *nebris* worn as a cloak (POULSEN 1951, 124). The head and arms were restored.

*Fig. 1a-d*

The two more than life-sized Polykleitan statues had just been published by Paul Arndt in *EA* nos. 1167 and 68, when they stood in the garden of the Villa Martinori quondam Poniatowski (*EA* text, 48), and were purchased by Carl Jacobsen only after some hesitation. In November they were inventoried in the Glyptotek, and the Discophoros has since been exhibited in a prominent place in the galleries (ZANKER 1974, 4 pl. 1.6; FLEISCHER 1980, 9 who interprets him as Perseus, KREIKENBOM 1990, 145 I 7).

*Fig. 2*

Not so the Pan, Dionysos or satyr, as he was then named. For ages he has led a shadow life in the store-rooms, but in the autumn of 1990 travelled to Frankfurt to be displayed in the large Polykleitos exhibition (*Polyklet*, 627 cat.no. 157, KREIKENBOM 1990, 167 III 16).

Here is his story as it could be told in three chapters. In the first, we see the statue as a Roman copy of one of the most celebrated statues of Antiquity, the Doryphoros by Polykleitos – supposed to be the work on which he based his treatise on the Canon (ZANKER 1974, 11 taf. 6.6).[1] It appears that we have in fact a very good, rather faithful, copy of the statue dated to the late Hadrianic-early Antonine period i.e. the middle of the second cent. AD (*BrBr* text to 439, MUTHMANN 1951, 42), a period when the Polykleitan athletic types had a renaissance, albeit in a somewhat softened edition. The quality of workmanship seems, however, to be comparable to the Pourtalès torso from the

*Fig. 3a-d*

Palatine, now in Berlin, considered to be of Augustan date (v. STEUBEN 1973, 55, *Polyklet*, ca. no. 43, KREIKENBOM 1990, 165 III 9).

The second chapter would be about the Roman statue of Pan, characterized, as stated above, by the *nebris*, a goatskin stretched over the

Fig.1 a-d. Doryphoros/Pan, Ny Carlsberg Glyptotek cat. no. 158 with restored head and arms of c. 1550 for the placement in the Villa Giulia.

chest and tied over the right shoulder, with the legs of the animal hanging down to his buttocks, the *syrinx* hanging on the tree-trunk and further by a *pedum* or *lagobolon* which he carried over his left shoulder,

Fig.2 Doryphoros/Pan in the Villa Antinori quondam Poniatowski (EA 1168).

as can be seen from *puntelli* on the front, as well as on the back of the shoulder. This could suggest a satyr as seen in the "Einschenkende Satyr" in the Museo delle Terme (MUTHMANN 1951, 73 taf. 13 fig.29, *Le Sculture* I.5, 137 no.59). A close parallel is seen in the handsome statue with a similar *nebris* found in the Villa Adriana and now in the Museo delle Terme (*Le Sculture* I.1 70-72 no.58), which is named Dionysos/Bacchus (*LIMC* III.1 543, no. 5; III.2 pl.428 no.5). But the combination of *nebris*, *syrinx*, and *pedum* and his more mature age suggest a human Pan as he was depicted for example in Roman wall-paintings and mosaics (*EAA* V, 920-22). A statue of Pan, perhaps surrounded by nymphs, would fit well in a garden or nymphaeum setting, but unfortunately we know nothing of its provenance (HÜBNER 1912, 109 for the possible sources for the Villa Giulia statuary).

The third chapter, in this case the more interesting, is the story of the statue in more recent times (PRAY BOBER 1986,107-8 no.71). The first representation we have of it is in the Roman sketchbooks of Marten van Heemskerck I.29,v (*JdI* 1891,142 and *EAA* III.1126), who during his Roman sojourn in 1532-38 made drawings of the antique sculptures in the Casa Santacroce near Piazza Giudea (the present P. Santa Maria del Pianto). Aldovrandi (ALDOVRANDI 1558, 236, the material collected in the year 1550) comments on the same scene : "Vi si vede Pane idio di pastori ignudo, fuori che si avolge sopra una pelle di animale: sta poggiato in un tronco, nel quale è attaccato una zampogna di otto canne". In this representation we clearly recognize our statue without restorations, resting on a plinth profiled in a double torus, characteristic of the second cent. AD. Another version of the statue without restorations is seen in an engraving by the Bolognese painter Bartolomeo Passarotti, who worked in Rome c. 1551-65 (PRAY-BOBER 1986, no. 71a). Here we cannot see the plinth, and the neck is so vague that we cannot be sure if there was a head, but the arms are definitely missing.

*Fig. 4*

The next time we meet the Pan-statue is in 1585 in the engravings by Vaccaria and Cavallieri, who probably worked from the same original. Here he has been restored with a new head, youthful with longish wisps of hair, turned to the right, the "Spielbeinseite", as was also the original head, and with two new arms, the left bent forward with a soft and effeminate hand, and the right holding something that seems to grow from the tree-trunk (CAVALLIERI 1585 taf. 62 recorded before

*Fig. 5*

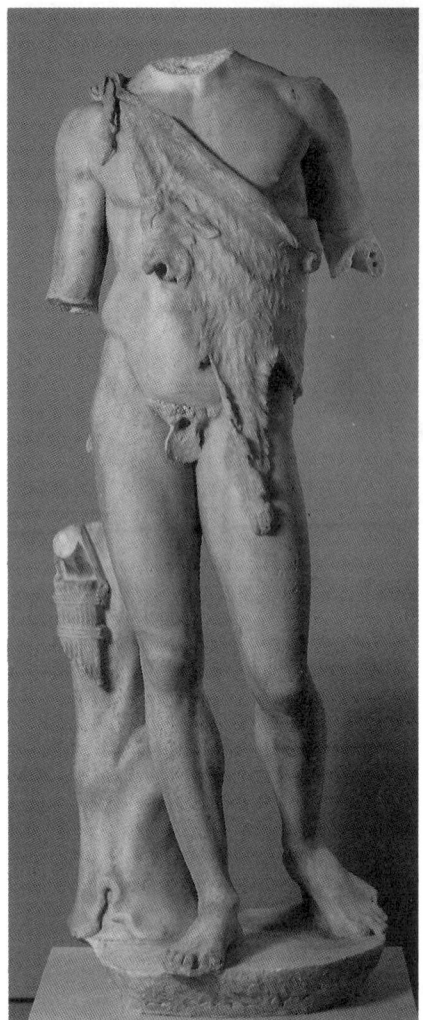 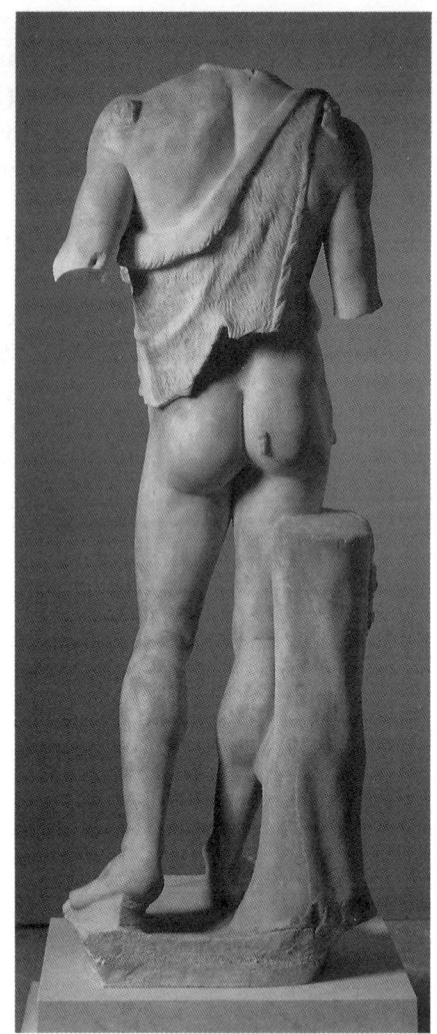

1578, Vaccaria 1585 ). Apparently he was a popular motif, for also Girolamo da Carpi has a small sketch of the statue in its restored state (Canedy 1976, 66-67 R 132). This may not surprise us, when we realize where the statue was placed. Cavallieri gives the caption : "Pastoris signum marmoreum Romae in villa Iul. III Pont.Max.", so our statue was placed in one of the most famous buildings in Rome of the 16th cent., the Villa Giulia.[2]

Julius III del Monte held the pontificate from 1550-55. In this short

 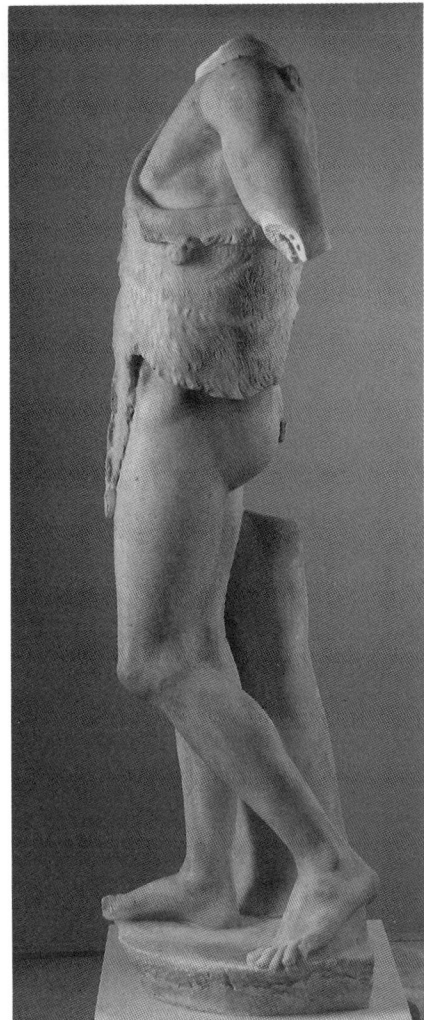

Fig.3 a-d. Doryphoros/Pan, Ny Carlsberg Glyptotek cat.no. 158, without restorations 1989.

time he commissioned many artists, painters, sculptors, and architects who would become the first in their field in the following fifty years.

His major building programme was the lavish villa outside the Porta Flaminia, later known as the Villa Giulia. This was a very complicated building, "an elaborate palimpsest, a series of superimposed projects, each one partially carried out and then in part replaced by later schemes", says Coolidge writing on the building programme of the villa (COOLIDGE 1943, 179) in which it is nearly impossible to distinguish

385

Fig.4 Doryphoros/Pan in the Casa Santa Croce by Marten van Heemskerck 1532-38.

the parts played by the many collaborators: Vignola, Vasari, Ammanati, even Michelangelo and all their followers (FALK 1971).

The beautiful *casino* which now houses the Etruscan Museum was richly adorned with paintings and sculpture, and in the courtyards and nymphaeum were many antique sculptures, of which only a very few still remain: the two reclining water-gods, Tiber and Arno, and some busts (FALK 1971, 170 lists the sculptures in 1555).

As was the custom in the Renaissance, the building was elaborately decorated with sculptures ancient and "modern", and probably mixtures of the two. Lanciani relates that the Pope did not buy sculpture in advance, but as building activities progressed (LANCIANI 1902-12, 20), so if we knew where our Pan statue was placed, we would be able to pin-point when it was acquired.

Unfortunately, none of the sections and drawings of the villa show us the statue in position. In its restored state it measures 2.01 m., and the only niches for decoration in the villa that could house a statue of that size are the five niches on either side of the Main Courtyard (COOLIDGE 1943, fig.6).

*Fig. 6*

According to the building accounts, the work on the main courtyard

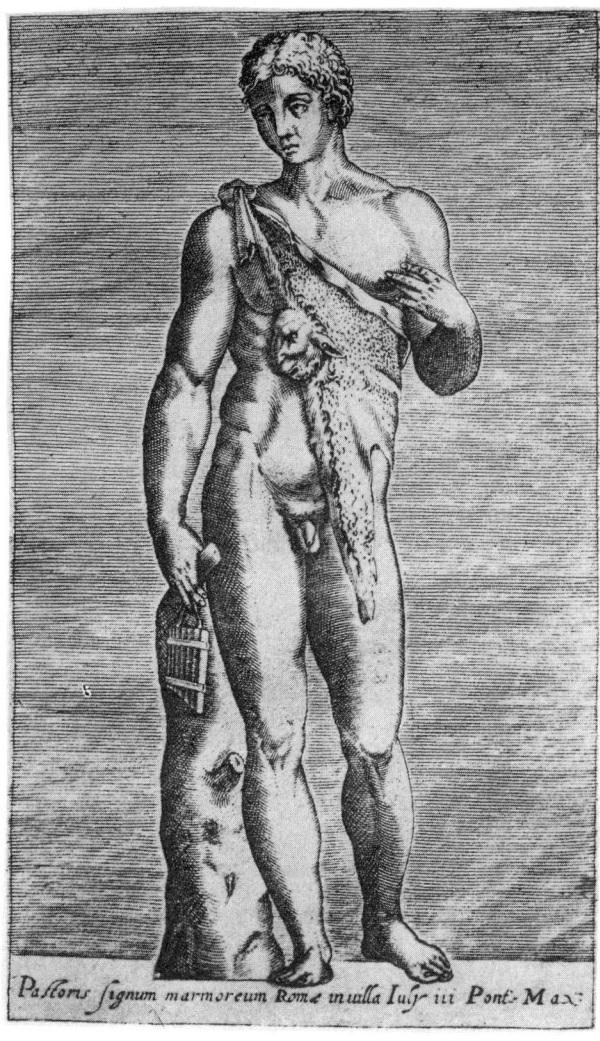

Fig.5 Doryphoros/Pan in the Villa Giulia in an etching by Cavallieri 1585.

was not initiated until September 1554, and the architect as well as chief sculptor was Bartolomeo Ammanati, who worked on the project till May 1555. This gives as close a date for the acquisition – and probably for the restoration – as anyone could wish for.

Bartolomeo Ammanati (1511-92) was born and bred in Florence (POPE HENNESY 1970, 372-73). In his youth he worked in Padua, where his patron was the law-professor Marco Mantova Benavides, an ardent collector of art, ancient and contemporary (CANDIDA 1967, 15-22), for

Fig.6 Section of the right side of the Main Courtyard of the Villa Giulia (COOLIDGE Fig.6.)

*Fig. 7*  whom he created the statues of Jupiter and Apollo flanking the door of his house. In the Apollo, we see a very clear classical influence: the stance is a mirror image of our Pan, and the head is an edition of the Apollo Belvedere. In the courtyard, he placed a colossus of Hercules, which according to Benavides was the first of its size since antiquity.[3] The last work for Benavides was his tomb in the Chiesa degli Erimitani in Padua (KINNEY 1976, 114-166).

In 1548, Ammanati moved to Rome, with letters of introduction from Benavides to the cardinals of the city, in which he compares Ammanati's work to the ancient masters Polykleitos and Phidias (DAVIS 1976, 484). Here Julius III commissioned him with the del Monte monuments in S.Pietro in Montorio, and with the nymphaeum in the Villa Giulia, named after him the Fontana dell'Ammanati. This in fact made him the chief sculptor in the Pope's service (KINNEY 1976, 199). While working in Rome, he kept up his relationship with his former patron Benavides by correspondence. A letter written by Ammanati to Benavides, dated May 2, 1555, is a very complete description of the Villa Giulia and its glories (Pesaro, Bibl.Oliv. 378 pag. 91, FALK 1971, 171-73).

After describing the *casino* he proceeds through the main courtyard, adorned with seven niches on either side, in each of which there was an antique statue. In the middle of the right side was a group of Mars and Venus, to the right of them Hercules resting on his club and: "seguita l'altra nicchia, nella quale è dentro il dio Pan con le sue zampogne ed una pelle in mano, del resto tutto ignudo", and in the next one a statue of Lavinia, daughter of King Latinus. In the three niches on the left were Venus and Cupido, Silvanus, and another female statue at the end. Apart from the fact that our Pan wears the skin over his shoulders and

Fig.7 Bartolomeo Ammanati, Apollo in the Palazzo Benavides in Padua.

does not hold it in his hand, I think we must accept that this is our statue.

Now it would be interesting to know whether Ammanati himself could have had a hand in the restoration of our statue. In a letter from 1560 he states that he has worked 34 months on the Villa and has only been paid now and then and that although he had many collaborators working from his designs, he himself made sculptures in marble as well as in stucco and stone (FALK 1971, 112-14 for their names). Pianetti, the foreman of the *scarpellini*, elaborates on this theme "... et lui encora lavorava de sia mano et al marmo et alle figure di peperino..." (BIAGI 1923, 65).

Although no mention is made of it by his biographers Vasari and Borghini, it seems certain that Ammanati has restored antique sculpture. A Venus in the Casa Vasari in Arezzo is a stucco trial piece for the restoration of an antique Venus in the Uffizi (IN 155, KENTNER 1963, 79-92), which he later used again for his bronze Venus, cast in 1559, now in the Museo del Prado. A further influence is seen in his later works for example the Terra for the fountain in the Palazzo Vecchio, and later in a more manneristic version in the statue of Ops, created for the *studiolo* of Francesco I.

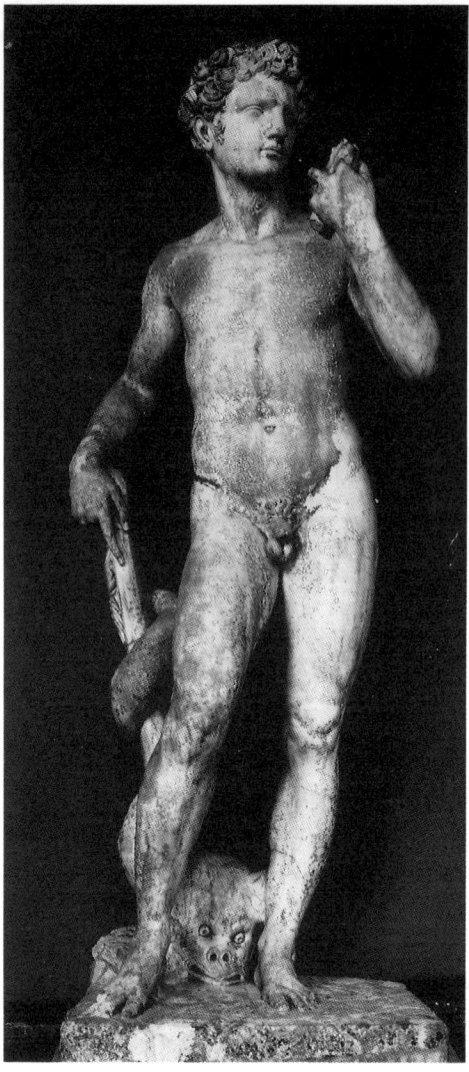

Fig.8 Bartolomeo Ammanati, Prudenza. Museo Nazionale del Bargello, Florence (Photo Alinari 46267).

It is worth considering whether the restoration of the Pan, by the master himself or one of his collaborators, influenced his later style.

Of the later works from Ammanati's hand, we must choose the naked male statues. The grandest is the huge Neptun in the fountain still standing in the Piazza della Signoria. Here we find the erect holding of the neck, the long wispy hair at the back and the illogical rendering of the rest of the hair. Further, we have the soft, effeminate wrists and tapering fingers. Another figure is the Prudenza from the un-

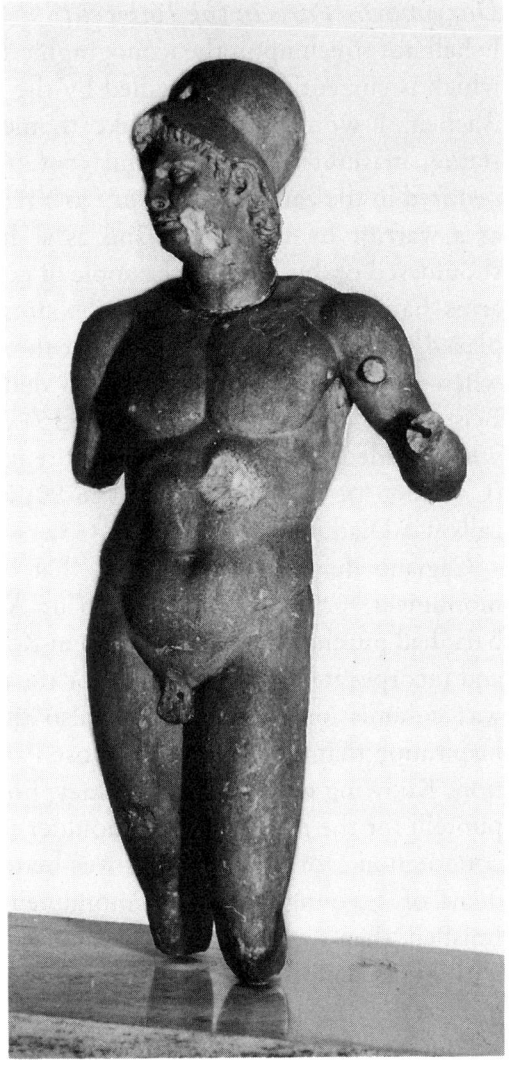

Fig.9 Doryphoros/Paris, Museo del Duomo, Milan. (Photo courtesy of Archivio-Fototeca della veneranda Fabbrica del Duomo di Milano).

finished fountain for the Sala Grande in the Palazzo Vecchio, now in the Museo Nazionale del Bargello (HEIKAMP 1978, 127). This statue, *Fig. 8* though classical in stance, does not follow the Doryphoros' contraposto and is much weaker in its proportions, truly a Renaissance piece, but arms and hands and the way they hold the attributes are very similar. The Prudenza holds an anchor around which a dolphin winds its tail, and is thus identified with Apollo Delphinios, and is thought by contemporary writers to allude to Augustus and to Cosimo I.

## Doryphoros/Paris in the 16th cent

I shall not touch upon the iconographic programme of the Villa Giulia, which is currently being studied by the art-historian Ruth Tschäpe of Aachen. I would, however, like to mention a close parallel to the statue, inasmuch as it is a 2nd cent. AD copy of the Doryphoros restored in the early 16th century as a representation of Paris, qualified as a warrior by the helmet and as a shepherd prince by the *pedum* shouldered on his left and the apple of contention in his right hand (the arms have been dismantled in the present setting). This statue was placed on the pinnacle no. XLIV of the cathedral in Milan until 1886, when it was moved to the Museo dell'Opera del Duomo (Inv.203, BOSSAGLIA & CINOTTI 1978, 25 no. 154 pl. 165).[4] Originally, the statue was intended for the tomb of the French *condottiere* Gaston de Foix (CAGIANO DE AZEVEDO 1958, 186-90; SETTIS 1986, 482, erroneously calls it a Diadumenos; *Polyklet*, 463).

*Fig. 9*

Cagiano de Azevedo surmises that one of the two artists of this monument, Cristoforo Lombardo or Agostino Busti, called Il Bambaia, had purchased a Roman torso in Rome in 1514 and had restored it and incorporated it in the design for the monument for which Bambaia was commissioned in 1515. He also thinks that it was pure artistic inspiration that caused them to chose Paris as the motif for the restoration. Knowing our own torso it may, however, have been traces of the puntelli for the *pedum* on the shoulder that suggested a shepherd. The connotation Doryphoros/Paris was better suited to the funeral monument of a young warrior, a monument which, however, was never finished, than to the roof of the cathedral where it was placed together with other sculptures from the same project in 1518.

That the Renaissance restorer knew that it was a Doryphoros is seen by the fact that in the restoration combining the antique torso and the "modern" head a cameo mounted in gold representing the Doryhoros was found. With his restoration, the artist made his own interpretation of this statue, not an anonymous spear-bearer but a prince, a Trojan soldier, a shepherd and a connoisseur of beauty, and as such he restored the torso identifying the ancient hero Paris with the young French *condottiere*.

The Paris as well as our Pan are examples of the artistic restorations of the Renaissance "Il frammento, da arido documento, diventa elemento vitale per stabilire quella continuità ideale dalla antichità agli uomini del rinascimento che per questi più che idea fissa era fede" (CAGIANO DE AZEVEDO 1948). This was before Winckelmann, when the artist gave way to the archaeologist as restorer, where a sculpture ceased to be a work of art and became a document to be interpreted, explained and completed.

It is then up to the art-historian to see whether the Doryphoros/Pan can be given an iconographic explanation in this setting. An interesting point is the theory that the Villa Giulia had been intended for use as a theatre and that the design of the main courtyard may have been based on stage sets (COOLIDGE 1943, 215). It is noteworthy that Ammanati started his Roman career by creating stage sets for the theatre.

## After Villa Giulia

The fourth chapter is the "Nachleben" of the statue. In March 1555, Pope Julius III died, and after having continued work on the nymphaeum in the Villa Giulia for two months, Ammanati left for Florence without having received his pay. Here he was introduced by Vasari to the Medici family and continued his work as a sculptor, initially on the sculpture for the remodelling of the Palazzo Vecchio with a fountain, in which, as we have seen were, the Terra and the Prudenza were incorporated. Later he concentrated on buildings and became one of the leading mannerist architects in Florence. He enlarged the Palazzo Pitti and built the Palazzo Giugni and later the Palazzo della Signoria in Lucca and the Collegio Romano in Rome. In his later years, he became very religious and repented his former life. In a letter to the Accademia del Disegno (1582), he recounts how he regrets that he has made so many nude statues, and in 1588 when the fountain figures were placed in the Palazzo Pitti, he asks that their nakedness be hidden. In 1590, a goldsmith was paid for a gilded fig-leaf for one of the statues (HEIKAMP 1978, 143 ).

Julius' brother, Balduino del Monte, had been given the Villa Giulia by deed before the death of Julius, but he died in the following year and his natural son Fabiano inherited him. Fabiano could not pay his debts, and because the buildings had been paid for from public funds, the Villa was confiscated by the Camera Apostolica. In 1561, Cosimo I took over the palace in the Campo Marzio, which had also been restored by Ammanati, hence called the Palazzo Firenze. The Villa Giulia, however, fell into decay, the fountains of the Aqua Vergine became silent,

Fig. 10 a-d Doryphoros/Pan, Ny Carlsberg Glyptotek cat.no. 158. The head created for the placing of the statue in the Villa Giulia ca. 1550.

and the villa was looted of its antiques. Some were brought to Florence when the villa was turned over to the Medici, and others were brought to the Vatican. This goes for a series of Greek inscribed herms (HÜLSEN 1901, 126-30, LANCIANI 1902-12, 31). Here they were incorporated in the Cortile del Belvedere. On 12.8 1564, 164 transports of sculptures and inscriptions had passed from the Villa to the Vatican (LANCIANI 1902-12, 29) and it is surmised that there were originally c. 300 sculptures in the villa. In a catalogue from 1706, there are only 12 sculptures and 17 inscriptions left in the Villa Giulia. The Medici Pope Pius IV restored the Villa and used it for distinguished guests, the last being Queen Christina of Sweden (LANCIANI 1902-12, 27).

The next mention we have of our statue is in Clarac (CLARAC 1841, pl. 126 H, no. 1791 B), where it is grouped among the shepherds. The information given is that he is in Greek marble, and measures 9 palmi and 6 on. and is placed in the Palazzo Altemps (*Roma Capitale*, 162 no. 25) where he was joined by the Discophoros/Poseidon (CLARAC 1841, pl. 802 E, no. 2007 B) restored as Hercules. It may be, however, that their original placing was not the Palazzo Altemps on the Piazza S.Apollinaire but rather the Villa Altemps situated on the Via Flaminia. The reason is that in Matz-Duhn (1881) both statues are placed in the gardens of the Villa Martinori quondam Poniatowski. The 16th cent. Villa Sinibaldi was bought by the Polish prince Stanislaus Poniatowski in 1800. The *casino*, rebuilt by Valadier in 1804 is situated on the Via di Villa Giulia (Viale del Arco Oscuro) and is the immediate neighbour of the Villa Giulia (BUSIRI VICI 1971, 274 figs. 96, 107-8). At the time of writing, the casino of the Villa Poniatowski is being restored and will, in due time, be used as an annex to the *Villa Giulia*.

In 1870 part of the property was sold to a signor Pietro Martinori. Here we find the Pan-statue and the Discophoros mounted with the Scopaic Hercules head, Ny Carlsberg Glyptotek cat.no. 255, and here in the garden they were photographed in rather a decrepit state for the *EA* in 1899. In Reinach (1904, 36,2), our Pan had passed from the Collezione Martinori to the art-dealer Simonetti from whom Carl Jacobsen had already bought it some years earlier. And here the ring closes.

*Fig. 10a-d*

I hope to have demonstrated that the Roman statue of Pan built over the torso of the Doryphoros was restored, and used by Bartolomeo Ammanati for the decoration of the main courtyard in the Villa Giulia in 1554, following the artistic principles of the Renaissance, and that it thereafter led a rather quiet life, being moved about in the gardens of the adjacent villas.

When the Roman private collections were dispersed in the late 19th cent., it came onto the art-market and ended up together with its faithful companion in the Glyptotek. Ten years ago, we would probably have removed the restorations to reveal the "true" Roman work of art. Now we feel more reluctant and have constructed fastenings for the head and arms, so that they can be taken off or left on at will. I hope this is to the satisfaction of art-historians, for this is truly a work of art of the mid-16th cent. and one of the very few remaining statues from the embellishment of the splendid Villa Giulia.

Mette Moltesen
Ny Carlsberg Glyptotek
Dantes Plads 7
DK-1556 Copenhagen V

## NOTES

1. For the Canon, see v.STEUBEN 1973, and TOBIN 1975.
2. I am greatly indepted to Ms. Ruth Tschäpe of Aachen, who has written an unpublished dissertation on the sculptural programme of the Villa Giulia, and has given me expert advice. I am pleased to be able to bring her opinion on the iconographic pattern of the placing of the Pan as an addendum to my article.
3. In his book: *Enchiridion rerum singularium additis etiam in studiosorum gratiam scholiis*, Venezia 1551, l X, 238 and l XII, 365, he says of the colossus: "Et forte non ab re erit exemplum Polycletii Sicyonii adducere, cuius statua cum omnium esset absolutissima, canon idest regula appalata est, unde omnes artifices omnia artis lineamenta sumebant, ut hac tempestate Bartholomei Ammanati Florentini colossus, altitudine pedum 20 lapideus, quem primus sculpere post antiquos in aedibus nostris, et mirabili quidem artificio, ausus est, aetatis suae (quod maxime mirum videtur) anno 33, ita ut cum antiquis facile contendat."
4. The measurements are given as 115 x 53 x 29 cms. i.e.rather a small copy. The statue has been severely overworked especially the rendering of the pelvis is strangely effeminate.